NO PLATFORM

This book is the first to outline the history of the tactic of 'no platforming' at British universities since the 1970s, looking at more than four decades of student protest against racist and fascist figures on campus.

The tactic of 'no platforming' has been used at British universities and colleges since the National Union of Students adopted the policy in the mid-1970s. The author traces the origins of the tactic from the militant anti-fascism of the 1930s–1940s and looks at how it has developed since the 1970s, being applied to various targets over the last 40 years, including sexists, homophobes, right-wing politicians and Islamic fundamentalists. This book provides a historical intervention in the current debates over the alleged free speech 'crisis' perceived to be plaguing universities in Britain, as well as North America and Australasia.

No Platform: A History of Anti-Fascism, Universities and the Limits of Free Speech is for academics and students, as well as the general reader, interested in modern British history, politics and higher education. Readers interested in contemporary debates over freedom of speech and academic freedom will also have much to discover in this book.

Evan Smith is a research fellow in history at the College of Humanities, Arts and Social Sciences at Flinders University in South Australia. He has published widely on the history of political extremism, social movements, national security and borders in Britain, Australia and South Africa. He is the author of *British Communism and the Politics of Race* (2018) and co-editor (with Jon Piccini and Matthew Worley) of *The Far Left in Australia since 1945* (Routledge, 2018).

ROUTLEDGE STUDIES IN FASCISM AND THE FAR RIGHT

Series editors Nigel Copsey, Teesside University, UK and Graham Macklin, Center for Research on Extremism (C-REX), University of Oslo, Norway.

This new book series focuses upon fascist, far right and right-wing politics primarily within a historical context but also drawing on insights from other disciplinary perspectives. Its scope also includes radical-right populism, cultural manifestations of the far right and points of convergence and exchange with the mainstream and traditional right.

Titles include:

A Fascist Decade of War
1935–1945 in International Perspective
Edited by Marco Maria Aterrano and Karine Varley

No Platform
A History of Anti-Fascism, Universities and the Limits of Free Speech
Evan Smith

Reflections on the Extreme Right in Western Europe, 1990–2008
Christopher T. Husbands

American Antifa
The Tactics, Culture, and Practice of Militant Antifascism
Stanislav Vysotsky

Hitler Redux
The Incredible History of Hitler's So-Called Table Talks
Mikael Nilsson

Researching the Far Right
Theory, Method and Practice
Edited by Stephen D. Ashe, Joel Busher, Graham Macklin and Aaron Winter

For more information about this series, please visit: https://www.routledge.com/Routledge-Studies-in-Fascism-and-the-Far-Right/book-series/FFR

NO PLATFORM

A History of Anti-Fascism, Universities and the Limits of Free Speech

Evan Smith

Routledge
Taylor & Francis Group
LONDON AND NEW YORK

First published 2020
by Routledge
2 Park Square, Milton Park, Abingdon, Oxon OX14 4RN

and by Routledge
52 Vanderbilt Avenue, New York, NY 10017

Routledge is an imprint of the Taylor & Francis Group, an informa business

British Library Cataloguing-in-Publication Data
A catalogue record for this book is available from the British Library

Library of Congress Cataloging-in-Publication Data
Names: Smith, Evan, 1981- author.
Title: No platform : a history of anti-fascism, universities and the limits of free speech / Evan Smith.
Description: Abingdon, Oxon ; New York, NY : Routledge, 2020. |
Series: Fascism and the far right | Includes bibliographical references and index.
Identifiers: LCCN 2019058304 | ISBN 9781138591677 (hardback) |
ISBN 9781138591684 (paperback) | ISBN 9780429455131 (ebook)
Subjects: LCSH: Academic freedom--Great Britain. | Freedom of speech--Great Britain. | College students--Political activity--Great Britain. |
Student movements--Great Britain. | Anti-fascist movements--Great Britain. |
Education, Higher--Political aspects--Great Britain.
Classification: LCC LC72.5.G7 S65 2020 | DDC 371.1/04--dc23
LC record available at https://lccn.loc.gov/2019058304

ISBN: 978-1-138-59167-7 (hbk)
ISBN: 978-1-138-59168-4 (pbk)
ISBN: 978-0-429-45513-1 (ebk)

Typeset in Bembo
by Taylor & Francis Books

MIX
Paper from responsible sources
FSC™ C013985

Printed in the United Kingdom
by Henry Ling Limited

CONTENTS

ACKNOWLEDGEMENTS

This book started as a series of blogposts outlining the original 'no platform' policy of the National Union of Students as the controversy surrounding Germaine Greer at Cardiff University broke. As the debate over 'no platform' has intensified in Britain and elsewhere in the English-speaking world, these blogposts transformed into a book length project. Over the last half decade, the growth of the far right has made this book, unfortunately, timelier than when I started writing about this topic. The purpose of this book, therefore, is to be a historical intervention in the debate over 'no platform' and help us understand why the tactic has been used by students, as well as other activists, since the 1970s.

I am grateful to Craig Fowlie, Becky McPhee and Jessica Holmes from Routledge, as well as Nigel Copsey and Graham Macklin from the Fascism and the Far Right series, who all had confidence in this book and encouraged me from the first day to explore this history.

Writing a book on British history while living in Australia is difficult and this has meant I have depended on numerous people, archives and libraries to obtain the necessary primary source material. The research for and the writing of this book has also been completed while in various states of precarious and fixed-term employment, which has only been overcome with the support from the people listed below. I thank them all greatly for their help.

I would like to thank Mike Day from the NUS Archives, Anna Towlson from Archives and Special Collections at LSE, Daniel Jones from the Searchlight Archives at the University of Northampton, Jenny Childs from the Cadbury Research Library at the University of Birmingham, Helen Ward and Simon Dixon from Special Collections at the University of Leicester, Helen Burton from Special Collections at Keele University, Katrina Legg, Emily Hewitt and Susan Thomas from the Richard Burton Archives at Swansea University, Nigel Cochrane from Library Services at the University of Essex, Robert Winckworth from the College

Archive at University College London, Angela Mandrioli from Special Collections at the University of Exeter, Julie Parry from Special Collections at the University of Bradford, Angela Heard-Shaw at the Hull History Centre, Kylie Jarrett from Special Collections at Flinders University, Anabel Farrell from the Conservative Party Archives and Angie Goodgame at the Bodleian Libraries (University of Oxford), Elizabeth Morrison from the Modern Records Centre at the University of Warwick, Lisa Tallis and Mark Barrett from Special Collections at Cardiff University, Justine Mann from the University of East Anglia Archives, Karen Anderson from Special Collections at the University of Bristol, Karl Magee from the University of Stirling Archives, Erich Kesse from the Archives and Special Collections at SOAS, James Peters from the University Archives Centre at the University of Manchester, Jade Leonard and Lesley Ruthven from the Special Collections and Archives at Goldsmiths, Lara Nelson and Emily Rawlings from the Archives and Special Collections at the University of Southampton, and Elspeth Healey and Kathy Lafferty from the Spencer Research Library at the University of Kansas.

As well as these very helpful archivists and librarians, my thanks to all the colleagues and comrades who have helped me to source research materials. The project could not have been completed without help from Christian Høgsbjerg, Dave Rich, Joel Barnes, Daniel Edmonds, Rob Marsden, Keith Sinclair, Gavin Brown, Lizzie Seal, Jodi Burkett, Liam Liburd, Tim Schmalz, James Heartfield, David Gottlieb, Daryl Leeworthy, Julie Kimber, Brett Holman, Maurice Casey, Kerrie McGovern, Benjamin Bland, Kyle Harvey, Michael Bueckert, Naomi Lloyd-Jones, Phil Malcolm, Matthew Bailey, Max Kaiser, Mark Hobbs, Sebastian Dobson and Mael Sobrany.

I also appreciate the conversations that I have had with a number of people on the topics covered in this book (in person or on social media), including Laura Butterworth, Lauren Pikó, Lucy Robinson, Jon Piccini, Andy Fleming, David Lockwood, Aaron Winter, André Brett, Dion Georgiou, Bodie Ashton, Jimmy Yan, Phil Burton-Cartledge, David Convery, Geoff Collier, Paul Flewers, Dan Frost, Nicki Jameson, Kevin Ovenden, Chris Williams, Sebastian Budgen, Satnam Virdee, Stephen Ashe, Alana Lentin, Mark Bray, Shane Burley, Anandi Ramamurthy, Alex Ettling, Vashti Jane Fox, Andrew Coates, Jeff Sparrow, Jason Wilson, Paul Jackson, Jayne Persian, Mike Waite-Woods, Kurt Sengul, Jordan McSwiney and Tim Martin. I am sorry if I have missed anyone out!

The manuscript has been read in whole or in part by David Renton, Alasdair Hynd, Matthew Worley, Ian Birchall, Kate Davison, Aurelien Mondon, David Gottlieb, Gavan Titley, Romain Fathi, Benjamin Jones and Elizabeth Humphrys. I thank them for their insightful feedback. All errors in the final version are mine.

I would also like to thank my colleagues at Flinders University – Andrekos Varnava, Matthew Fitzpatrick, Marinella Marmo, Rob Manwaring, Prudence Flowers, Catherine Kevin, Peter Monteath, Melanie Oppenheimer, Erin Sebo, Narmon Tulsi and Elizabeth Weeks – for their support over the years.

I thank my parents, Robert and Helen, and my parents-in-law, Peter and Felicity, for their continued support as I persist with my research endeavours. Most of all, I thank my family, Zenna, Remy and Honor. I couldn't have done it without them.

1

'NO PLATFORM' IN HISTORICAL AND CONTEMPORARY CONTEXT

In October 2018, the short-lived UK Universities Minister Sam Gyimah wrote about the alleged 'culture of censorship creeping into society', particularly in the context of universities and colleges.[1] He argued that this was a new phenomenon, exacerbated by social media, and proclaimed:

> a cultural shift is taking place, and diversity of thought is becoming harder to find as societal views become highly polarised between the left and the right. A culture of censorship has gradually been creeping in, and a monoculture is now emerging where some views are 'in' and others are clearly 'out'.[2]

For Gyimah, 'the rise of no-platforming, safe spaces, trigger warnings and protest' was to blame for cultural shift, with him claiming that these practices were 'all too easy [being] appropriated as tools to deny a voice to those who hold opinions that go against the sanctioned view'.[3] This was, in his eyes, 'catastrophic for democratic debate and puts at risk the fundamental right to be heard that many have fought and died for'.[4]

Gyimah suggested that these protest tactics threatened civility on campus and did not allow 'all sides' of a debate to be heard 'without fear of harassment or intimidation'.[5] However the Universities Minister did not seem to acknowledge that those who were being 'no platformed', such as fascists, racists, sexists, homophobes and transphobes, were often the ones who were threatening civility and creating a culture of harassment and intimidation at universities.

While suggesting that debate had lost its civility, Gyimah also declared that '[g]oing to university is meant to be an assault on the senses' and that they should be spaces with 'dissenting voices and challenging opinions'.[6] This is a sentiment that has been shared by many commentators and politicians in recent years – that higher education needed to expose students to ideas that they might find offensive and that attempts to avoid this demonstrated that students of today were overtly sensitive.

Popularised in the UK discourse by a contributor to *Spiked Online*, Claire Fox, the term 'snowflake' has been used to negatively describe these supposedly naïve and politically correct students who are unable to engage with 'challenging' ideas. In her 2016 book, *I Find That Offensive*, Fox suggests that a mixture of identity politics and risk aversion embraced by today's students threatens the 'liberal values of tolerance and resilience', supposedly menacing the prospect of free speech on campus.[7] On the other side of the Atlantic, Greg Lukianoff and Jonathan Haidt have argued that students in the United States have come to see themselves as 'fragile' and unwilling to engage with provocative and controversial ideas.[8]

This is a concept that has been readily accepted by many in the mainstream media and the political sphere, from the centre left to hard right, in Britain, as well as across the Western world. For example, in 2015, Nick Cohen in *The Guardian* wrote: 'Rather than being free institutions where the young could expand their minds, British universities were becoming "theological colleges" where secular priests enforced prohibitions.'[9]

Meanwhile, former UKIP leader and now leader of the Brexit Party, Nigel Farage, has recently stated while speaking in the United States that left-wing students were a threat to democracy, proclaiming:

> I mean frankly the real fascism these days, the real intolerance isn't Matteo Salvini or Donald Trump, it's those on the left who wish to shout down the other side and indeed on campuses like this, across America and across the whole of the UK, attempt to no platform speakers who've got ideas they don't like. That's the real modern fascism, the attempt to close down free speech.[10]

For those supposedly concerned about free speech at universities, students are at the same time both fragile, risk averse 'snowflakes' and heavy-handed McCarthy-like warriors. Students are to be both pitied and feared.

Nigel Farage's speech to an American audience about the topic shows that this panic about censorious students has gone global. In an era of a resurgent far right, conservatives and libertarians in the United States, Canada, Australia and New Zealand have expressed alarm about the end of freedom of speech on university campuses. At a moment when students have seemingly become more vocal about rejecting all forms of hate speech (including racism, misogyny, homophobia and transphobia), the concept of free speech has been weaponised by the right in its various guises as a smokescreen to air offensiveness and to promulgate far right ideas about race, sexuality and gender. As Will Davies has written:

> the very notion of 'free speech' has become a trap. Neo-fascist or alt-right movements now use it to attack alleged 'political correctness', using the principle of free expression to push hateful and threatening messages towards minority groups … Whereas intellectual freedom was once advanced in Europe as the right to publish texts that were critical of the establishment, it has now become tied up with spurious arguments surrounding the 'right to offend'.[11]

Far right figures, such as co-founder of the English Defence League, Tommy Robinson (real name Stephen Yaxley Lennon), or alt-right personality Milo Yiannopoulos, have thus portrayed themselves as the defenders of free speech against the politically correct elites. These figures have been further enabled by the free speech absolutism celebrated by a series of right-wing and right libertarian commentators and politicians. This has become a lucrative industry, generating a number of books, countless media articles and dozens of television and radio appearances for those who promote the idea of a free speech 'crisis'.

At the centre of this moral panic about the free speech 'crisis' at British universities is the concept of 'no platform'. 'No platform' is, at its core, a policy instituted by the National Union of Students (NUS) that has allowed student unions to withhold resources, such union-run spaces and funds, from fascist and racist organisations and speakers, as well as disinvite these speakers if invited by certain student groups, or encourage protest activities that attempt to prevent these people from speaking on campus, such as pickets. Extending from this policy, some have used the principle of 'no platform' to argue for the disruption of fascist and racists from speaking at universities or from having a physical presence on campus. These forms of disruption, discouraged by the NUS and individual student unions, can take the form of heckling, throwing various things or the physical occupation of the contested space. This has often led to disagreements between student activists over the official use of the 'no platform' policy and the more spontaneous student activities that have sought to directly challenge fascists and racists who have come onto campus. There has also been heated debate over the limits of the 'no platform' policy, as some have pushed for it to be extended to other forms of oppression and that sexists, homophobes and transphobes should also be 'no platformed'. At various points in time, some have also argued that Zionists or Islamic fundamentalists should be subject to the 'no platform' policy. Despite a short revoking of the policy in the late 1970s, the policy of 'no platform' has remained in place for over 45 years.

In the current climate, 'no platforming' is seen as the primary tactic used by the student left to purportedly undermine free speech, alongside the creation of 'safe spaces' and the use of 'trigger warnings'. The denial of a platform for those deemed to be espousing hateful or harmful speech, a tactic widely known as 'no platform' in Britain since the mid-1970s, has been viewed as a modern scourge that has mutated away from its anti-fascist origins to become a blunt tool used by the bureaucratic student unions to shut down controversial ideas. Tom Slater, one of *Spiked Online*'s key contributors, wrote in *The Spectator* in 2016: 'Where once SUs reserved censorship for fascists, now radical feminists, secularists and anti-Islamists – from Germaine Greer to Maryam Namazie and Julie Bindel – are seen as beyond the pale, liable to compromise the "mental safety" of students.'[12]

The moral panic about students has shifted, from a concern about students being violent subversives to students being intolerant zealots – and 'no platform' is seen as central to how students quash dissent. This is a reflection of a shift in perceptions of the power of the student movement over the last four decades, which has been in decline since the days of Thatcherism. Although the collective force of students occasionally rears its head (such as during the 2010–11 protests against tuition fees),[13] the student movement nowadays is no longer seen as the subversive threat that it once supposedly was. But universities are still seen as sites of resistance to the status quo and where political correctness and wokeness reign. A recent Policy Exchange report by Thomas Simpson and controversial academic Eric Kaufmann claimed that 'Britain's universities are being stifled by a culture on conformity' and that 'academic freedom is being significantly infringed' by a combination of student activists and partisan academics.[14]

The purpose of this book is to challenge the narrative of a newly emergent student movement that has repurposed 'no platform' for spurious politically correct agendas. The book explores the shifts in 'no platform' as a tactic, as well as the reaction to it. Although formally introduced by the NUS in 1974 as a reaction to the rise of the National Front (NF) in Britain, 'no platform' had its antecedents in the anti-fascist battles of the 1930s and 1940s, and the student movement of the late 1960s and early 1970s. Since then, it has been continually re-evaluated. While its primary focus has been on fascists and racists, it has been used against a number of different targets of student protest. Sometimes this has been controversial, such as its use in the 1970s against pro-Israel student groups, against anti-abortionists in the 1980s or against Islamic fundamentalists in the 1990s. Even in the twenty-first century, it remains a living and reflexive tactic, which students themselves determine, debate and continue to argue over. Overall the tactic of 'no platform' has generally been employed to prevent explicitly racist, sexist, homophobic or transphobic speakers from having a platform to broadcast their views in a university environment. Proponents argue that to allow these hateful views to be promoted on campus would contribute to a harmful environment for certain groups, such as ethnic minorities, women and LGBTQ+ people. Furthermore, allowing these views to be promoted would help to normalise discrimination, harassment and violence against these groups of people. The logic behind this position is that speakers that advocate these kinds of views and argue for the denial of rights of certain groups of people should not have the opportunity to publicly speak, recruit and organise on campus. This is the fundamental point of 'no platform'.

A brief history of 'no platform'

The NUS policy of 'no platform' came in the mid-1970s as a tactic to prevent the spread of fascist and racist ideas on campus at a time when the National Front looked to be making headway in the British political landscape. On the back of the 1973 oil crisis and the controversy over the Conservative government's acceptance of Ugandan Asian refugees in 1972–73, the NF were making inroads as a right-wing political vehicle, primarily for disaffected Tories. Over the previous few years, the NF had fostered an intimidating presence at British universities, breaking up several left-wing meetings and harassing student protestors, as well as forming the National Front Students' Association in 1973.

The phrase 'no platform' had first been used by the International Marxist Group (a Trotskyist group that had grown with the student radicalism of the late 1960s) two years earlier.[15] The idea of 'no platform' was based on a long-standing anti-fascist tactic of denying fascists the physical space to organise, meet and recruit. The left-wing students who proposed the tactic were particularly inspired by the militant anti-fascism movement against Oswald Mosley in the 1930s and 1940s, often led by the Communist Party and various Jewish activists.

Since the late 1960s, there had been impromptu protests at various universities against right-wing speakers, such as Enoch Powell, and by 1973 these had grown increasingly confrontational. In May 1973, the racist psychologist Hans Eysenck was assaulted by Maoists at the London School of Economics, which caused panic amongst the press, politicians and some within the universities. The 'no platform' policy, although driven by the far left of the student movement, was essentially a bureaucratic measure that formalised the ad hoc protests that had occurred over the last half decade.

At the NUS conference in April 1974, the resolution that student unions deny a platform to 'openly racist or fascist organisations or societies' and prevent them having a presence on campus 'by whatever means necessary' was passed.[16] The resolution was part of a wider resolution dealing with the discrimination faced by overseas students in Britain. Promoted by the student left representatives from the International Marxist Group (IMG) and the International Socialists (IS), it was also supported by the Broad Left faction within the NUS (which was an alliance of the Communist Party and left Labour students).

The policy was controversial from the start, with several student unions declaring that they would not enforce the policy at their universities. It was hotly debated at a special NUS conference in June, just a few months later. However the special conference was held on the same weekend in London as a major NF event at Red Lion Square. There was a large counter-demonstration that was attended by many of the students who were also attending the NUS conference. The confrontation between elements of the crowd and the police outside Conway Hall that day led to a number of injuries and the death of one protestor, Kevin Gately, a student from the University of Warwick. The 'no platform' policy was being debated as word filtered back from Red Lion Square about the actions of the police. The news of this possibly contributed to the NUS representatives voting to maintain the policy.

The policy has remained in place from this time (except for a brief period between December 1977 and April 1978), but has been persistently contested from sections of the NUS and the wider student body in Britain. For example, in 1977, the application of the 'no platform' policy to pro-Israel student groups caused considerable controversy, with the NUS leadership censuring the student unions that did this and implementing a temporary suspension of the overall policy.

In the early 1980s, several student unions expanded the 'no platform' policy to apply it not just to fascists and racists, but also sexists (including some pro-life speakers) and homophobes. This happened at a time when the left (including the student left) was re-evaluating the relationship between traditional class-based politics and the new social movements that had emerged in the 1960s and 1970s, increasingly referred to in the 1980s as 'identity politics'.[17] Anti-racism in the form of anti-fascism was taken seriously by the left and the student movement, leading to the enforcement of the 'no platform' policy against explicit fascists and racists. However, issues of sexism and homophobia were still sidelined by many on the left. The call for the 'no platforming' of sexists and homophobes was part of a broader push for the recognition of the politics of identity by the student left in the 1980s.

Meanwhile some of those who promoted the tactic of 'no platform' in the student movement in the 1970s, and within the anti-fascist movement more generally, disagreed with the expansion of the 'no platform' policy. They argued that 'no platform' was created with the original purpose of opposing the threat of organised fascism on campus, such as that presented by the National Front. They felt that sexists and homophobes, while offensive, did not present the same kind of threat as the fascists that the policy was originally developed to combat.

That said, the notion of 'no platform' for sexists and homophobes needs to be seen in a wider context of the student unions attempting to address the sexual and homophobic harassment and violence experienced by students, both on and off campus. Like the 'no platform' for fascists and racists line taken by the NUS, the policy of 'no platform' for sexists and homophobes was not just an action to be taken against certain types of speech, but saw these forms of speech as precursors to acts of violence which required a pre-emptive response.

From the early days of the policy, there were concerns that student unions would 'no platform' Conservative MPs, and individual student unions indeed attempted to do this, ignoring the guidance of the NUS that Conservative Party speakers were not to be subject to the policy. In 1978, Sir Keith Joseph was 'no platformed' at the LSE and two years later, the Immigration Minister Timothy Raison was also 'no platformed' at the same institution. The Raison incident partly contributed to the LSE student union reversing its 'no platform' policy.

Between 1985 and 1987, the issue of protests against visits from hard right MPs to university campuses came to a head with several MPs being confronted by protestors, sometimes leading to violence.[18] The hardline Federation of Conservative Students (FCS), alongside Conservative Associations at various universities, invited controversial speakers, with many suggesting that this was being done for notoriety and provoke reactions from the rest of the student body.

In March 1985, Home Secretary Leon Brittan visited the University of Manchester, where a large crowd of students clashed with the police. In early 1986, pro-South Africa Tory MP John Carlisle attempted to speak at several universities, which resulted in him being assaulted at Bradford University and denied a platform at Leeds Polytechnic, Oxford University and the University of East Anglia. Later in the same year, Enoch Powell was disrupted by protestors at Cardiff and Bristol universities. At some of these protests, the policy of 'no platform' was evoked, but at others it was not. A number of the protests and disruptions were conducted despite the efforts of the student unions to dissuade more militant students and protestors from taking action. At the national level, the NUS 'no platform' policy made a distinction between fascists (who were to be 'no platformed') and hard right politicians (who were to be allowed to speak) but was often ignored by more militant protestors from the left. The various disruptions, such as at Bradford and Bristol, showed that disruptive protests happened outside the bounds of the politics of the student union.

These protests led to the Thatcher government attempting to curb the use of 'no platform' by student unions through the Education (No. 2) Act 1986, demonstrating that calls for government intervention to 'protect' free speech on campus are nothing new. This legislated that universities and colleges needed to ensure free speech or risk forfeiting government support. However it did not seem to stretch to student unions, which were separate legal entities (although operating on university grounds). Within a few years of the 1986 Act coming into effect, some Tories were still complaining about the supposed lack of free speech on campus. University administrations also used compliance with the Public Order Act 1986 to dissuade certain speakers from visiting, citing public safety concerns. This was challenged in court by Conservative students at the University of Liverpool in late 1988 and early 1989, who sought to invite diplomats from the South African Embassy to speak. The resulting court ruling found that there were some limits to public disorder concerns with regards to allowing controversial speakers on campus, and university administrations could not use the threat of public disorder arbitrarily to dismiss their responsibilities under the 1986 Act; but since this time, universities have generally erred on the side of caution.

In the 1990s, the renewed threat of the British National Party (BNP), as well as the growth of the Islamic fundamentalist group Hizb ut-Tahrir on university campuses, saw the issue of 'no platform' gain prominence again. While anti-fascists were increasingly concerned about the electoral breakthrough of the BNP in 1993, the NUS leadership seemed to focus on the Islamic group and sought to limit Hizb ut-Tahrir's presence. The NUS was not able to 'no platform' the group entirely in the 1990s (it would eventually do so in 2004), but a significant number of individual student unions banned Hizb ut-Tahrir at this time.

Despite faltering in the mid-1990s after its earlier rise, the BNP, now under the leadership of Nick Griffin, became a significant threat in the 2000s as it gained a number of seats in local elections. These electoral successes and Griffin's attempts to clean up the image of the BNP saw him invited to speak at several universities throughout the decade, including Oxford, Cambridge and St Andrews. A strong student resistance to this ensured that Griffin had to cancel most of these speaking engagements, although he was able to speak at the Oxford Union in late 2007, continuing a tradition of the Oxford Union inviting fascist and racist speakers since the days of Oswald Mosley.

At the same time, there was a resumed resistance to 'no platform' by some students under the guise of absolute free speech, which particularly chimed with certain commentators in the media. In 2001, the Free Speech Society at Leeds University invited Nick Griffin to speak, as two of the society's leading members were also members of the BNP at the time (demonstrating how free speech absolutism could be exploited by the far right). In 2007, students at the University of East Anglia pushed for the student union to hold a referendum over the policy of 'no platform', with the campaign led by a student involved in the Academics for Academic Freedom group, which was linked to the free speech absolutists at *Spiked Online*. *Spiked* had emerged from a network of writers who were centred around the magazine *Living Marxism*, which had been the journal of the Revolutionary Communist Party (RCP) in the 1990s before the organisation folded. Beginning in the mid-1980s, the RCP and its successors strongly opposed 'no platform' and promoted absolute free speech, including for fascists and explicit racists. In the 2000s, *Spiked* supported pushes by student groups to counter the 'no platform' policies held by student unions and the NUS, seeing 'no platforming' as a greater threat on campus than fascists speaking. In the recent controversies over 'no platform' and free speech at British universities, the people associated with *Spiked* have been highly influential in the media landscape in calling for an end to 'no platform'. This leads to the present moment, when the moral panic against 'no platform' has been heightened.

'No platform' and shifting attitudes towards hate speech

The history of 'no platform' and its expansion over the last four decades corresponds with shifting attitudes towards explicit forms of racial hatred in Britain, now commonly referred to under the banner of 'hate speech'. First codified under the Race Relations Act in the 1960s, there had been debate over legislating against hateful speech going back to the inter-war period. In the 1930s and 1940s, prosecution of anti-Semitic publications fell largely under the charge of 'seditious libel', but as Kenneth Lasson and Iain Channing show, 'the authorities refused to prosecute anti-Semitic or racist libel unless it could be proved that it had provoked disorder' and there were few cases when proponents of explicit anti-Semitic propaganda were brought before the courts.[19] The Public Order Act, which had been introduced in 1936 after the 'Battle of Cable Street', had the power to prosecute people for using 'threatening, abusive or insulting words or behaviour with intent to provoke a breach of the peace or whereby a breach of the peace is likely', but it was not used to prosecute expressions of racial hatred until the early 1960s.[20] After a disorderly public meeting in Trafalgar Square in July 1962, the leaders of the National Socialist Movement (NSM), Colin Jordan and John Tyndall, were 'summoned under the Public Order Act to appear at Bow Street [Magistrates Court]' as a result of their anti-Semitic speeches.[21]

As will be discussed in Chapter 2, since the end of the Second World War, anti-fascists had been trying to have anti-Semitic speech and the dissemination of anti-Semitic propaganda made a criminal offence. With the arrival of many migrants from the colonies in the late 1940s and throughout the 1950s, a number of these anti-fascist activists also pushed for other expressions of race hatred and racial discrimination to be penalised by law, led by Fenner Brockway, a Labour MP and founder of the Movement for Colonial Freedom. Before racial discrimination laws became part of the Labour Party manifesto in 1964, those who campaigned with Brockway proposed that any new legislation tackling racial discrimination would have to include actions against incitement to racial hatred, rather than amending the Public Order Act. The Public Order Act, argued many anti-fascist and anti-racist activists from this period, could be used against *all* political activities, especially of the left, while a separate piece of legislation could be used only against racists and fascists.[22]

In 1965, the Wilson government introduced the Race Relations Act, which legislated against a number of forms of racial discrimination in public. Section 6 of the Act made it an offence 'with intent to stir up hatred against any section of the public … distinguished by colour, race or ethnic or national origins'.[23] Jordan and other anti-Semites were amongst the first prosecuted under the new legislation (although with differing degrees of success), but controversially the Act was also used to prosecute several black power figures in Britain, which undermined many progressives' faith in the new laws.[24] A problem with the original wording of Section 6 was the need to show 'intent to stir up hatred' and after the overturn of a case involving a member of the Jordan's NSM, this became a sticking point for the Attorney General in pursuing further cases.[25] In his inquiry after the death of an anti-fascist protestor at Red Lion Square in 1974 (discussed in Chapter 4), Lord Scarman described Section 6 of the Act as 'merely an embarrassment to the police', with the 'proof of intent' restricting its usefulness.[26]

Gavin Schaffer has shown that the question of intent also played a factor in the failed prosecution of the Racial Preservation Society (RPS) in 1968, which published pseudo-academic scientific racism.[27] The acquittal of members of the RPS was, Schaffer suggests, 'rooted in the jury's belief that the views of the Society were not intended to provoke hatred' and that: '[t]he lack of violence in the rhetoric of the Society, the absence of over anti-Semitism, and the more sober tone, enabled the RPS to walk the tightrope of the new race relations legislation …'[28]

This led to 'a new safe passage for those who wished to represent racist views in British society' and as Schaffer and Simon Peplow show, this explains why politicians such as Enoch Powell and Duncan Sandys escaped prosecution for their anti-immigration outbursts in the late 1960s, as the language they used was more measured, rather than less racist.[29]

After this, section 6 of the Race Relations Act was not heavily used until it was amended in 1976 to remove the need to show intent, but throughout the late 1970s and 1980s, it was predominantly members of fascist organisations, such as the National Front and the British National Party, who were prosecuted under the Act. Hard right politicians, such as those examined in Chapter 6, escaped the attention of the law, even though a number indulged in anti-immigrant and pro-apartheid rhetoric. The precedent of the first years of the policy left a lasting legacy, which 'legitimised a space for racist utterances with certain formal and tonal qualities'.[30]

It was into this space that the debate about the tactic of 'no platform' erupted. An argument was repeatedly made that 'no platforming' was unnecessary because speakers who indulged in racist language could be prosecuted under the Race Relations Act and that this should be threshold – all 'lawful' speech should be allowed because the extremes were already policed by this legislation. An example came in the House of Commons in 1986 as the Conservatives looked to introduce a bill to 'protect' free speech at British universities. Fred Silvester, a backbencher who proposed an original version of the bill, argued:

> The House determines the limits of free speech and the limits of tolerance. If a person makes a speech which is contrary to the Race Relations Act or any other law there is a remedy through the courts. If a person speaks in that manner at a university or anywhere else outside the House he will be arraigned before a court, and rightly so. If we find that the boundaries are inadequate it is for the House to change them. It is not up to a bunch of students, who are irresponsible to the law, to decide which person is suitable to have the right to speak at a university.[31]

This argument overlooked the fact that prosecutions for violations of the Race Relations Act or the Public Order Act could only come after the person had spoken, contributing to the potential risks of allowing that person to speak, which the tactic of 'no platform' was to guard against. Furthermore, the likelihood of a speaker being prosecuted for incitement of racial hatred was very low, particularly if speakers did belong to an explicitly fascist organisation.

At the present moment, there are a number of pieces of legislation which facilitate the prosecution of various forms of hate speech, and in general, extreme forms of racism (and to a lesser extent, misogyny and homophobia) are now seen as beyond the pale. Critics of 'no platform' often point to the legal considerations that need to be taken into account by speakers, and argue that all other 'lawful' speech should be allowed, even though what is considered lawful and unlawful is a matter of interpretation.

So while racism in the abstract is seen as bad, this has led to what Gavan Titley has described as 'the debatability of racism': 'In the contemporary political context, to speak publicly about racism is to be immediately integrated into an intensive process of delineation, deflection and denial, a contest over who gets to *define* racism, when "everyone" gets to speak about it.'[32]

Like the discussion of the Race Relations Act in the 1960s, discussion about what is racism becomes about intent, and this has led to the notion that just asking questions about certain topics, such as immigration, integration, crime and terrorism, need to be framed as 'not racism' in order to protect free speech.[33] As Alana Lentin has written, '[t]he prevalent view among white people, reflected by a large part of the media, is that we live at a time when purportedly commonsense views about race dare not be spoken', hence calls for more freedom of speech to allow these topics to be debated.[34] The university, often referred to as the hub of the 'market place of ideas', becomes a central location for hosting these debates. But as Titley argues (and this book shows) 'the production of "free speech events" [such as university debates] has become a generative mode of capturing public and media space for racist agitation',[35] as well as other forms of misogyny, homophobia and transphobia. 'No platform' has been one of the tools used by students to counter attempts to use the university campus as the site for this agitation.

'No platform', safe spaces and trigger warnings

The focus of this book is the history of the tactic and policy of 'no platform', which emerged out of the anti-fascist movement of the 1970s. Today, 'no platform' is often discussed in tandem with the notion of 'safe spaces' and 'trigger warnings', both of which have a different origin. But for those who oppose these measures, they are often grouped together to portray an overly censorious environment at universities and colleges.

Malcolm Harris has traced the development of the concept of 'safe spaces' from the feminist and gay rights activist circles of the 1960s and 1970s in the United States to the college campus,[36] pointing to the scholarship of Moira Kenney and Christina B. Hanhardt on this subject. Harris described the concept of the 'safe space' as a place 'where people could find practical resistance to political and social repression'.[37] In her book *Mapping Gay LA*, Kenny described it as the following:

> in the context of the women's movement, the notion of safe space implies a certain license to speak and act freely, form collective strength, and generate strategies for resistance … [T]he women's movement sought to create a radically different sort of place, one where the energy and collective effort to create place were the defining features. Safe space, in the women's movement, was a means rather than an end and not only a physical space but also a space created by the coming together of women searching for community.[38]

Hanhardt has shown that 'safe spaces' first emerged as refuges from homophobic violence and emphasised collective safety, particularly against state violence and persecution by the police in the United States.[39] By the turn of the twenty-first century, the idea of the 'safe space' had transferred from the feminist and LGBTQ+ environments to the college campus.

The term also transferred across the Atlantic in the 2000s. That is not to say that the concept of autonomous, separate and/or inclusive spaces were alien to Britain prior to this. Scholars have shown that since the 1960s, gays and lesbians, as well as feminists, had been organising autonomous spaces for both activist and living purposes.[40] The term began to be used in student union circles in the mid-2000s as LGBT rights became a more prominent concern for student unions.[41] Chris Waugh shows that 'safe spaces' have been used since then as attempts 'to create counterpublics for marginalised groups' and thus serve two purposes: 'firstly, they provide spaces for groups to recuperate, reconvene, and create new strategies and vocabularies for resistance. Secondly, the presence of these counterpublics makes visible collective and individual traumas which disrupt neoliberal narratives of self-resilience'.[42]

Similar to the term 'safe spaces', 'trigger warnings' first emerged in North America. Francesca Laguardia, Venezia Michalsen and Holly Rider-Milkovich have written that '[t]he term "trigger" is rooted in the field of mental health, with the diagnosis of post-traumatic stress disorder', but the term became more broadly used in the early 2010s in the feminist blogosphere.[43] Clare Forstie explained that these warnings were 'initially intended to provide readers with a warning that material may prompt traumatic responses specifically from sexual assault survivors'.[44] In 2013, the term started to be used in North American universities 'to allow students to make decisions about whether to avoid potentially traumatic material in the classroom'.[45] Within a few years, British newspapers were reporting that the concept had spread to UK universities, with *The Independent* stating that a 'growing number' of universities were taking up the practice, including Edinburgh, LSE, Goldsmiths, Stirling and Central Lancashire.[46] Tony Pollard, an archaeologist of war graves at the University of Glasgow, defended the use of trigger or content warnings in his teaching, writing:

> Some of the material I refer to in my classes is disturbing, with images of the dead appearing regularly. Some of it is material that disturbed me when I first encountered it, and it might well disturb my students. Students are a diverse group, and some of them might have suffered domestic abuse, violent attack or trauma in war – and in some of my classes I know that they have. In these cases, such exposure might trigger flash backs or aggravate recently suppressed trauma. It is only common sense to provide these individuals, and those who just can't stomach images of dead bodies in shallow graves, with the option to walk out of the classroom.[47]

Despite these reasonable arguments for using 'trigger warnings' while teaching, they have formed part of a Holy Trinity of campus censorship in the eyes of many commentators, alongside 'no platform' and 'safe spaces'. While both 'safe spaces' and 'trigger warnings' are more recent concepts, 'no platform' has a much longer history and that history is the focus of this book.

Academic freedom, racism and the 'intellectual dark web'

Debates about free speech at universities and 'no platform' often overlap with discussions of academic freedom. Since the 1970s, there have been student campaigns against academics in Britain involved in controversial research topics, such as eugenics, racial science and racialised psychology, as well as those academics who have used their platform to pronounce racist, sexist and homophobic ideas. This has involved disruptions of speeches by visiting academics, such as those against Hans Eysenck and Samuel P. Huntington in 1973 (discussed in Chapter 3), as well as later campaigns for certain academics to be censured in some way. In the 1980s, students led campaigns against Andrew Brons, a leading member of the National Front, at Harrogate College, and Professor John Vincent at the University of Bristol, alleging that he had written racist and sexist columns for *The Sun* (both of these cases are discussed in Chapters 5 and 6 respectively). Also in the 1980s was the campaign against Robert Gayre at the University of Glasgow, one of the founders of the racial science journal, *Mankind Quarterly*, who had the Gayre Chair in Scottish Literature removed by the university after protests by anti-racists.[48] Students at the University of Ulster also campaigned against *Mankind Quarterly*'s deputy editor Richard Lynn in the early 1980s.[49] In the 1990s, students and the Anti-Nazi League (ANL) protested against psychologist Chris Brand at the University of Edinburgh for his promotion of the links between IQ and race (with Brand's right to free speech being defended by the Revolutionary Communist Party in its final days).[50] In the early-to-mid-2000s, Frank Ellis, a Russian studies scholar at the University of Leeds, was the target of a campaign for his associations with the American far right.[51]

At times, these campaigns against were framed as part of the broader 'no platform' movement, such as the campaigns against Brons and Vincent, but other times, the campaigns against these academics were more informed by the longer campaign against racism in psychology and the sciences. This campaign began around the same time as the student movement developed the 'no platform' policy in the early 1970s, with students and academics, as well as other anti-racist campaigners, being involved in both. In 1974, a group of left-wing educators and psychologists formed the Campaign on Racism, IQ and the Class Society to 'expose the "scientific" racialism behind the theories propoganded [sic] by Professors Eysenck, [Arthur] Jensen and [William] Shockley', producing pamphlets and running education sessions to combat academic racism and its use in the education system.[52] The inaugural meeting of the campaign at the Polytechnic of Central London in March 1974 was disrupted by figures from the National Front, leading to a discussion amongst attendees over whether the gate-crashers should have been allowed to speak (a month before the NUS' 'no platform' policy was adopted).[53]

The relaunching of the anti-fascist magazine, *Searchlight*, in 1975 became the vehicle for the anti-fascist movement to campaign against racialised science and psychology, identifying the academics in Britain (as well as overseas) who continued to espouse racial theories from their university positions. In 1979, Michael Billig, who had recently produced a psychological study of National Front members,[54] published a pamphlet with *Searchlight* titled *Psychology, Racism and Fascism*, which outlined how racialised psychology, science and anthropology was being promoted by academics in Britain, North America and Europe, coinciding with the rise of fascism in the 1970s.[55] Billig stated in his conclusion:

> It has not been too difficult to demonstrate that journals like *The Mankind Quarterly*, *Nouvelle Ecole* and *Neue Anthropologie* are perpetuating, to a greater or lesser extent, the traditions of [Hans] Günther and Nazi race-science. What is more, this tradition, rejuvenated by the boost of modern research into race and IQ, is now attempting to return to academic circles from the obscurities of fascist organisations like the Northern League.[56]

The work by Billig and *Searchlight* was highly influential on Britain's anti-fascist and anti-racist movements and campaigns to highlight the 'scientific' racism that was still perpetuated by some academics. In the pre-internet age of the 1980s and

1990s, *Searchlight* performed an important function in disseminating information about the work of academics, such as Robert Gayre, Richard Lynn and Chris Brand, and assisting anti-racist campaigns against them.

After the Race Relations (Amendment) Act 2000 required all public institutions, including universities and colleges, to take action to promote racial equality, the issue of racism being promulgated by academics drew attention to several cases of (allegedly) racist statements being made by lecturers at various universities, including computing lecturer Geoffrey Sampson at Sussex, English lecturer Tom Paulin at Oxford, and the previously mentioned Frank Ellis at Leeds.[57] Unlike those academics who espoused ideas about racialised science and psychology, like Eysenck, Gayre or Lynn, it was acknowledged that in most cases in the early 2000s, the academics' comments were made 'in a personal capacity about subjects outside their academic field', but the issue was raised of how lecturers could make such statements and continue their employment when universities had clear anti-discrimination policies.[58] While the Association of University Teachers (one of the predecessors of the current University College Union) was ambivalent about how university staff should be dealt with, particularly as academic freedom was a cornerstone of AUT's programme, the NUS suggested that it could be seen as a continuation of their 'no platform' policy. In 2002, the President of the NUS, Owain James, argued:

> If a lecturer has made racist comments and the university keeps them on the payroll they are in effect giving that lecturer a platform. The campus environment must remain a safe and tolerant one where no student feels threatened in any way. That clearly cannot be the case if a racist lecturer is allowed to remain in post.[59]

However, while student unions could enforce (or attempt to enforce) the policy of 'no platform' over events held by student groups on campus, including the invitation of speakers by students, its policy did not extend to the classroom. The rhetoric of 'no platform' was sometimes employed in campaigns against academics, but these campaigns should be seen as quite separate from the primary focus of the 'no platform' policies at British universities.

In the last decade, the myth of a free speech 'crisis' at British universities has drawn together the debate over 'no platforming' and academic freedom once again. Angela Saini has outlined how scientific racism has had a resurgence in recent years, using the veil of intellectual inquiry and academic freedom to disseminate racist views to far right audiences. This has been assisted, Saini argues, by the internet and social media, which gave scientific racists 'simpler ways to access and grow their networks'.[60] She quotes Keith Hurt, an anti-racist researcher in the United States, as stating, 'Scientific racism has come out of the shadows, at least partly because wider society has made room for it.'[61] 'Race realism', one of the by-words used by those who endorse racialised science and psychology in the twenty-first century, has found a receptive audience amongst the broader rise of the global far right.

This work in racialised science and psychology has intersected with other academics and public figures who promote anti-feminism, homophobia, transphobia, racial populism and the defence of 'Western civilisation' (including the British Empire). This has been described loosely as the 'intellectual dark web'[62] and brings together a number of people (many self-identifying as conservatives, libertarians or 'classical liberals') from Britain, North America and Australasia to rebel against supposed 'political correctness' and the 'cultural left'.[63] Aurelien Mondon and Aaron Winter have described them as a 'growing cohort of reactionary academics, pundits and pseudo-intellectuals', who:

> position themselves against what they claim to be a politically correct, left-wing, social-justice establishment that promotes feminism, LGBTQ+ rights, anti-racism, multi-culturalism, identity politics and cultural relativism, and often see themselves as defenders of the enlightenment, universalism, rationality, equality of opportunity (as opposed to outcome) and the achievements and worth of western civilisation.[64]

On both sides of the Atlantic (as well as in Australasia), these figures have generated a following by presenting themselves as standing up to the 'politically correct' elites in academia and the mainstream media. However, when they have been challenged, particularly by students and scholars on campus, they have strongly objected to this, seeing it as an attack on their academic freedom. For example, when anti-feminist and anti-trans Canadian psychologist Jordan Peterson had a visiting fellowship at Cambridge University rescinded in March 2019 after considerable student and staff objections,[65] he suggested that the Faculty of Divinity had succumbed to 'the diversity-inclusivity-equity mob' and that the Faculty's actions proved that they 'don't give a damn about the perilous decline of Christianity'.[66] Noah Carl, an academic who had previously argued that debate about 'race, genes and IQ' was being stifled,[67] was dismissed from Cambridge University in May 2019 after a special investigation panel found that Carl 'had put a body of work into the public domain that did not comply with established criteria for research ethics and integrity' and 'in the course of pursuing this problematic work, [he] had collaborated with a number of individuals who were known to hold extremist views'.[68] Writing in the *Daily Mail*, Carl called the campaign against his appointment as 'just the latest incident of what has become known as "academic mobbing" – where tens or hundreds of scholars join forces to condemn their colleagues'.[69] These scholars were, Carl suggested, 'part of a broader trend in which individuals who express dissident viewpoints are hectored, pilloried, shouted down, prevented from speaking, and sometimes even hounded out of their jobs'.[70] Echoing Sam Gyimah's earlier outlined sentiments, Carl stated that 'universities are meant to be places where we can explore controversial ideas, challenge received wisdom, and debate conflicting perspectives' and further proclaimed: 'Those of us who believe in free speech and open inquiry, regardless of our political leanings, need to take back control from the illiberal activists and re-establish universities as places where the search for truth takes centre stage.'[71]

In December 2018, two academics, Matthew Goodwin and Eric Kaufmann, organised a debate in London – with *Spiked*'s Claire Fox, *Times* columnist David Aaronovitch and former head of the Commission of Racial Equality Trevor Phillips – on the topic of 'Is Rising Ethnic Diversity a Threat to the West?'. The event was co-sponsored by Fox's Academy of Ideas, a thinktank which is closely aligned with those at *Spiked*. Goodwin had recently published a book with Roger Eatwell titled *National Populism*, which argued that the centre left had to 'appreciate how people feel' about immigration and 'ethnic change', suggesting that tighter borders and reform of the 'type' of migrants allowed to arrive was needed.[72] Kaufmann had a forthcoming book called *Whiteshift* that went further than Goodwin and Eatwell. Denigrating 'the cultural Left' for their support for multiculturalism, Kaufmann has argued for 'ethno-traditional nationhood', with 'slower immigration to permit enough immigrants to voluntary assimilate into the ethnic majority, maintain the white ethno-tradition'.[73] Mondon and Winter charge that both books 'pushed a similar narrative entrenching the idea of reactionary democracy in pseudo-scientific language' that 'the rise of the far right is a democratic rebellion emerging within the left-behind and it is only natural that "white natives" feel threatened by change'.[74] These authors, Mondon and Winter argue, 'participate in the legitimisation of the ideas core to the far right and therefore play a key part in potentially increasing its reach'.[75]

Concerned about the increased normalisation of far right ideas, over 200 scholars wrote an open letter criticising the event organised by Goodwin and Kaufmann, which declared:

> As academics and activists, we do not need to be convinced as to the importance of public debate. However, this debate was framed within the terms of white supremacist discourse. Far from being courageous or representative of the views of a 'silent majority', this is a reactionary, opportunistic and intentionally provocative approach, with no concern for the public implications and effect of this framing. By presupposing an ethnically homogenous 'west' in which ethnic diversity, immigration and multiculturalism are a 'problem' to be fixed, it automatically targets communities already suffering from discrimination as part of the 'problem'.[76]

Despite a slight change in the title of the debate after these complaints, the event went ahead. But Goodwin and Kaufmann were disgruntled with the critical response they had received, writing a lengthy justification of their event for the alt right website, *Quillette*. Acknowledging that 'we were not formally asked to cancel the debate', there was pressure on some participants to withdraw, with Goodwin and Kaufmann describing the criticisms of their event as 'a smear campaign', 'relying on trolling, reputational damage and peer pressure to police virtue'.[77] The two lamented that 'some of our most vociferous opponents' included 'those who teach our young adults in universities' and expressed, 'We only hope this brand of anti-intellectualism does not penetrate more widely within the academy, both in Britain and elsewhere.'[78]

In his book *Whiteshift*, Kaufmann continued to rail against the 'growing assertiveness of left-modernists on campus' in North America and Britain, seeing this as 'a synergy between a vocal minority of radical students and a group of activist administrators and faculty' that has led to 'a new wave of left-wing campus activism', further enabled by 'silent liberals'.[79] Kaufmann saw this 'problem' as 'primarily coming from the left' and called on academics to 'decry ... the no-platforming of right-wing speakers'.[80] When Kaufmann was invited to speak at Bristol University in April 2019, around 30 students walked out, while others questioned why Kaufmann had been asked to present at the university.[81] On twitter, Kaufmann complained that a 'small, vocal minority' had the potential to 'no platform' his event and while acknowledging that they did not actually shut down the event, he asked whether there should penalties 'in order to deter such actions in the future'.[82]

Alongside these other alt-right talking points being promoted by academics, there has also been a revival of pro-empire rhetoric by scholars, described by Priyamvada Gopal as a 'retrograde strain of making the so-called case for colonialism'.[83] In Britain, this has often been a defence of the British Empire, but in the wider Anglosphere, this has often been expanded out to a defence of Western civilisation (for example, the ongoing controversy with the Ramsay Centre for Western Civilisation at Australian universities).[84] This can be seen as part of the backlash to the 'Rhodes Must Fall' campaign, which started with students at the University of Cape Town in South Africa and spread to universities in the global North (primarily in Britain and North America).[85] The University of Oxford has been both one of the epicentres of this campaign and the reaction against it, with Nigel Biggar's 'Ethics and Empire' project. Biggar, a theology professor, wrote a piece for *Standpoint* magazine in 2016 which claimed that the 'Rhodes Must Fall' campaign was 'built on a misunderstanding of the past and a manipulation of the truth'[86] and his 'Ethics and Empire' project, launched in 2017, has proposed that there were ethical elements of the British Empire, such as ending the slave trade, giving black Africans the vote in the Cape Colony and the Second World War, that could be weighed against the mass killings and deaths overseen by the British.[87] Since then, Richard Drayton has written, Biggar's work has 'become a touchstone for right-wing political commentary', presenting the professor as 'one of a majority whose rightwards views have been drowned out by a noisy bullying liberal but illiberal minority, a majority which at last will speak'.[88]

An open letter by more than 50 academics from Oxford condemned Biggar's project and his media interventions in defence of empire, declaring that Biggar's public pronouncements 'reinforce a pervasive sense that contemporary inequalities in access to and experience at our university are underpinned by a complacent, even celebratory, attitude towards its imperial past' and therefore be rejected and disengaged with.[89] Biggar was quoted in the *Daily Mail* as describing the open letter as 'collective online bullying', but the actions by these academics would 'not close the discussion down'[90] (even though the project held invitation-only events that critics were likely not invited to attend). In *The Times*, Biggar complained that 'informal peer pressure is limiting intellectual debate at [Oxford] university and claimed that 'junior academics feared they could not challenge orthodox views [on] empire',[91] despite more than 15 junior or early career academics signing the open letter to *The Conversation*. Trevor Phillips described Biggar as 'incredibly courageous' and decried the alleged 'Stalinist imposition of one reading of history' on the legacy of the British Empire, suggesting that this would lead to the 'suppression of free speech'.[92]

The critical campaigns against Nigel Biggar and Noah Carl, as well as against Jordan Peterson and Eric Kaufmann, have been used by conservatives, right libertarians and 'classical liberals' to suggest that, in the words of Toby Young, it was 'impossible to deny that free speech is under threat in Britain's universities'.[93] For these free speech warriors, the 'no platforming' conducted by students against racist, sexist, homophobic and transphobic speakers and the campaigns against certain academics are seen as two prongs of the same attack – an offensive of the 'woke' and the left against those who don't conform to political correctness and the 'groupthink' of modern academia. In the contemporary discourse, the two are often combined,[94] although, like the relationship between 'no platform', 'safe spaces' and 'trigger warnings', they are quite distinct phenomena with converging and diverging histories. This book attempts to outline the history of 'no platforming' at British universities, mentioning critical moments where academic freedom becomes an issue, but the topic of the limits of academic freedom and campaigns against certain scholars over the last 50 years is worthy of another study all by itself.

Media platforms and deplatforming

Another debate that happens in the orbit of 'no platforming' is around the mainstream media (particularly television and radio) providing a platform for the far right and other figures that air racist, sexist, homophobic and transphobic views. Since the 1930s, the British press and the British Broadcasting Corporation have portrayed explicit fascist groups in a negative light, but have, at times, allowed fascists and racists (not to mention misogynists, homophobes and transphobes) a platform. Janet Dack has shown that while some British newspapers gave some positive coverage to Mosley's British Union of Fascists in the 1930s, after the violence at Olympia in 1934, the newspapers and the BBC were, broadly speaking, 'opposed to Mosley' and the BUF and 'clearly anti-fascist'.[95] In the immediate aftermath of the events of Olympia in June 1934, Mosley was 'given the opportunity to defend the actions of the BUF' on the BBC, but Dack shows that 'following the debates on the violence at Olympia in Parliament and in the press', Mosley became *person non grata* at the Corporation.[96] Robert Skidelsky suggests that this was due to pressure brought on the BBC by the government at the time.[97] Mosley would not appear on the BBC (this time on television) until 1968, when he appeared on *Panorama* – he had also been interviewed by David Frost on ITV the previous year.[98]

While the BBC denied Mosley a platform, it did give airtime to other fascists at different points throughout the post-war era. In 1959, the BBC show *Panorama* interviewed the White Defence League's Colin Jordan.[99] John Tyndall and Martin Webster were both interviewed in the 1970s at the height of the National Front's activities, interviews which were condemned by the National Union of Journalists (NUJ).[100] Furthermore, both the BBC and ITV aired electoral broadcasts for the NF at the 1974 and 1979 elections.

Barry Troyna wrote in *Patterns of Prejudice* in 1980:

> while NF politics are generally denounced in news and editorial coverage of the party there is less agreement about how the news media can most effectively convey to their audience opposition to the Front and, as a corollary how to discourage electoral support.[101]

This concern led to campaigns by the NUJ, as well as the Anti-Nazi League and the London-based Campaign Against Racism in the Media (CARM), for greater media scrutiny of the NF and for the media, especially the television stations, to deny a platform to the NF in the late 1970s. CARM, an offshoot of the All London Anti-Racist, Anti-Fascist Co-Ordinating Committee, called for journalists 'to adopt a hostile line when reporting statements and activities of fascists and racists', as well as for journalists 'to boycott letters/phone-ins from National Front/ National party candidates and supporters'.[102] The NUJ produced a pamphlet titled *Black and Front*, which produced a number of guidelines for journalists reporting on the NF, which suggested: 'DON'T report racist parties on an even keel with Tories, Labour and Liberals. Even if they get some electoral support the fascists will only flourish if journalists fail to expose their racist, anti-democratic views'.[103]

The NUJ argued that journalists could not ignore the NF, but told journalists, 'you can go in for exposés and investigative reporting instead of re-telling what they say in press handouts or at news conferences'.[104] Barry Troyna and Nigel Copsey both note that there was a backlash by some in the media against these campaigns, with some insisting that 'the National Front, as a legally formed political party, could not be denied a broadcast simply because the ANL disapproved of its policies'.[105]

In the mid-1990s when the British National Party started to get national attention after its 'Rights for Whites' campaign in the East End of London and its subsequent win in the Tower Hamlets council by-elections, both television and the newspapers gave BNP members a platform. For example, the BNP's Deputy Leader Richard Edmonds appeared twice on the BBC in January 1993, to which *Searchlight* complained that Edmonds was given 'screen time to pretend the BNP is a normal political party, without challenge'.[106] As a result of this renewed media interest, the members of the reformed Anti-Nazi League founded Media Workers Against the Nazis, which followed the principle laid out in the 1970s that the media should not give fascists and racists platforms to present their ideology. An example of the campaigning of this group came in April 1994 when a BNP press officer had a letter published in *The Independent* newspaper, which led to journalist Paul Foot and several colleagues (including Seamus Milne) writing to the paper on behalf of Media Workers Against the Nazis, asking why the paper had published the BNP letter.[107] The letter writers declared, '[t]he normal rules of free speech and expression cannot possibly apply to those who aim to deny the most basic rights and freedoms to entire sections of the population'.[108] This was followed by a debate between Foot and Andrew Marr, a columnist for *The Independent*, in which Foot criticised the newspapers for being 'too uncritical of the BNP'.[109] An account in *The Independent* of the debate reported that Foot argued:

> the BNP had received a disproportionate amount of publicity and argued journalists should 'self-censor' on the basis of social consequences and ensure 'no platform for fascist propaganda' …
>
> The history of the 20th century showed the danger of providing the 'privilege' of free speech to a group which would 'wipe out free speech forever' should it gain power.[110]

Marr's response, similar to many in the press, was that the 'bad arguments and false logic' of the BNP could be dealt with and that this could be done with reporting and investigative journalism,[111] but overlooked the fact that anti-fascist campaigners did not want an end to reporting on the BNP and other fascist groups and instead wanted the media to not uncritically repeat assertions made by fascists, provide them with prominent interviews or invite them to participate in media debates.

Nigel Copsey suggests that for the most part, anti-fascist efforts to deny fascism a media platform 'proved futile' throughout the 1990s[112] and once the BNP gained some momentum in the 2000s, anti-fascists found it even harder to discourage the media from providing platforms to the revamped party under Nick Griffin (even though a number of critical exposés were broadcast and published at the same time). Daniel Trilling shows that the BBC in particular allowed Griffin and other BNP members to speak on television and radio throughout the 2000s, while also producing a documentary by an undercover journalist that provided 'compelling evidence' that the BNP 'remained a party which nurtured violence and racism'.[113] The dual approach by the media in Britain, giving airtime and column inches to the BNP's electoral messages, while producing highly critical pieces that poked holes in the BNP's attempts to soften its image, culminated in the invitation of Nick Griffin to appear on BBC's *Question Time* in late 2009 (which is discussed in more depth in Chapter 7). It has become somewhat of a liberal myth that Griffin's poor performance on the show revealed the true nature of the BNP and voters abandoned the party at the next election, overlooking the grassroots activism by anti-fascists to challenge the BNP in key battleground seats. The *Question Time* episode has become a liberal rebuttal against the tactic of 'no platform', arguing that the problems of fascism and racism can be exposed through reasoned debate and giving fascists enough rope to hang themselves.

Over the last decade, this argument has been replayed *ad infinitum*. As Nesrine Malik has written, the decade since Griffin's appearance has seen the expansion of what has been considered 'acceptable speech' and there has been a view by 'neutral' media outlets that 'every opinion must have a counter opinion'[114] – allowing the marketplace of ideas to determine what is reasonable and unreasonable. The main benefactor of this outlook has been the far right in its various guises.

With the decline of the BNP after the 2010 election, two groups occupied the void: the English Defence League (EDL) and the UK Independence Party (UKIP). The EDL was an anti-Muslim street movement, co-founded by Tommy Robinson, while UKIP was a right-wing Eurosceptic political party that, under the leadership of Nigel Farage, gained significant electoral influence (especially in the European Parliament) and corresponding media attention. Anti-fascist and anti-racist campaigners have argued that the mainstream media has given prominent attention to and platforms for Farage and Robinson (as well as others), which has contributed to a mainstreaming of far right politics. As Aurelien Mondon and Aaron Winter have noted, Farage has been 'a regular guest at BBC question time, but also was given a slot on LBC and regular columns in prominent newspapers', while Robinson has also been given a media platform on a number of occasions, such as on ITV's *Good Morning Britain*. [115]

This media coverage can translate into tangible political benefits for the far right. For example, a 2018 study by Justin Murphy and Daniel Devine found that 'media coverage may have played a unique causal role in increasing support for UKIP, in a fashion irreducible to previous levels of support or election outcomes'.[116] Furthermore, as Joe Mulhall has shown, Robinson's combination of anti-Muslim, pro-free speech and anti-elite rhetoric has attracted some of largest number of far right supporters since the 1930s.[117] Despite various campaigns, both online and on the streets, against the media platforms given to far right politicians like Farage or Robinson (or controversialists like disgraced columnist Katie Hopkins), the dominant view held by British media is that in a free society, extreme views on race, gender, homosexuality and trans rights (amongst other things) should, in the spirit of debate, be allowed to be heard, regardless of their offensiveness or inaccuracy. As a result, the media engages in the same combative spectacle as the debating societies in the student union buildings across the country's universities.

Some, such as Nesrine Malik, have suggested that the proliferation of social media and online platforms have aided this shift, writing that '[t]he expansion of media outlets meant that it was not only marginalised voices that secured access to the public, but also those with more extreme and fringe views'.[118] It has been well established that the growth of the internet (and in recent years, social media) has given the far right a massive boost and that online platforms have become more and more integral to far right organising, alongside the dissemination of far right ideas. As Stephen Albrecht, Maik Fielitz and Nick Thurston have written:

> Far-right movements from around the world have relentlessly intervened in both the private and public spheres of our digital worlds, from the deep web to the surface net, from public chat rooms to multi-player gaming environments.

> Digital platforms that bypass traditional editorial and governmental controls yet overlay our traditional political milieus have empowered such groups to directly broadcast their content globally to witting and unwitting audiences alike.[119]

The centrality of social media platforms to the far right has led some to call for the deplatforming of far right activists and trolls from these platforms, such as Facebook, Twitter and YouTube. In the wake of several right-wing terrorist attacks over the last few years, these calls have intensified. For example, the New Zealand government pushed for social media companies to take greater steps to limit violent far right content online.[120] In Britain, the campaign for deplatforming has been largely spearheaded by the anti-fascist organisation Hope Not Hate. Writing on the group's website, Joe Mulhall has argued that online hate, distributed via social media, had 'dangerous real-world effects' and to fight this, social media companies needed to be pressured to 'remove hate speech and hateful individuals'.[121] Citing the decline of Britain First and alt-right provocateur Milo Yiannopoulos after they were both banned from Facebook and Twitter, Mulhall declares that '[d]eplatforming works' and that the far right losing their social media platforms has greatly impacted their ability to organise in the 'real world'.[122] Unlike the initiatives of the New Zealand government and others, such as the Royal United Services Institute, who have called for government intervention to induce social media companies to remove violent far right content from their platforms,[123] the Hope Not Hate campaign is a traditional campaign to pressure social media providers to act. As Mulhall concludes:

> The last decade has seen far-right extremists attract audiences unthinkable for most of the postwar period, and the damage has been seen on our streets, in the polls, and in the rising death toll from far-right terrorists. Deplatforming is not straightforward, but it limits the reach of online hate, and social media companies have to do more and do more now.[124]

Although this may not be so straightforward, with Jeff Sparrow warning that '[i]t would be naïve … to expect reforms of the major social media corporations to provide an answer to [atrocities like] Christchurch'.[125] Sparrow argues that 'a thorough ban on fascist or far-right [social media] accounts seems unlikely' because: '[e]ven if they can be shamed by political outrage, they're ultimately driven by the pursuit of profit – and the inflammatory accounts of the far right deliver user engagement that can be monetised via advertising'.[126]

Nonetheless, for Hope Not Hate, deplatforming has become a central part of their anti-fascist activism, coming at a time when the organisation has moved away from the position of 'no platform for fascists', which had guided anti-fascist activism since the 1970s. Mulhall was quoted in *The Guardian* in 2018 as saying that the internet had 'fundamentally undermined "no platform" as a tactic' and that 'in the traditional sense, it doesn't work anymore'.[127] Physically 'no platforming' speakers and organisations from public and semi-public spaces wasn't seen as a priority, when the internet and social media allowed the far right access to much larger audience. Another piece published on the Hope Not Hate website by Safya Khan-Ruf expanded on this:

> Although no-platforming has expanded and remains controversial, the internet allows anyone – including far-right personalities – to create their own microphone. The power of social media has changed how opinions are shared and makes the tactic of no-platforming redundant to a certain degree.[128]

For Khan-Ruf and others at the organisation, there was an impression, shared by many of the centre left, that the current usage of 'no platform' as a tactic had strayed from its origins as an anti-fascist tool against the National Front and the British National Party and had been 'used to shut down legitimate viewpoints under false accusations'.[129] Although Khan-Ruf repeats the trope used by many from the conservative right to the centre left that 'no platform' had been employed in recent times 'as an excuse to shut down views some people don't like at universities', she does acknowledge that the expansion of the tactic has been 'in keeping with our better understanding of damage and harm that can be caused to vulnerable people by non-physical actions'.[130] While the internet and social media have, in the words of Richard Seymour, 'acquired jackboots'[131] and the need for pressure upon social media companies to act responsibly has been mounting, events over the last few years in Britain, as well as across the English speaking world, show that shutting down fascists and racists (as well as sexists, homophobes and transphobes) in the 'real world' remains vitally important. This is especially the case at universities and colleges, which are portrayed in Britain, North America and Australasia as the epicentres of the 'marketplace of ideas'.

The transnational spread of 'no platform' as a concept

In recent years, the term 'no platform' has spread across the English speaking world, with commentators, politicians, university officials and thinktanks raising concerns about the act of 'no platforming' by students. This is most noticeable in the United States. In the 1960s and 1970s, the left mobilised against the American Nazi Party (ANP) and the Ku Klux Klan (KKK), including protests against attempts by ANP leader George Lincoln Rockwell to speak at universities in the early-to-mid-1960s.[132] However it was only the small Trotskyist group, the Spartacist League (SL), which used the term 'no platform' back in the 1970s. In March 1975, the Spartacist Youth League held a demonstration, alongside the Progressive Labor Party and the Revolutionary Student Brigade, at the San Francisco State University against an invitation made to fascists to speak at the university.[133] Although the SL had not yet formed in Britain, the idea of 'no platform' (which had been a term used in the British Trotskyist milieu for the past few years) was promoted by the SL, calling for 'No Platform for Fascists'.[134] Calling for 'no platform' on university campuses as well as in street protests against the KKK, the SL declared:

> Our perspective must be the struggle to mobilize the mass organizations of the working class and black community for labor/black defense capable of smashing the fascist threats and defending the democratic rights of the oppressed ...
>
> - NO PLATFORM FOR FASCISTS!
> - FOR LABOR/BLACK DEFENSE AGAINST FASCIST TERROR![135]

The predominant Trotskyist group in the United States, the Socialist Workers Party (no relation to the SWP in Britain) responded to the SL, who accused the US SWP of defending the right of the American Nazis and the KKK to free speech, and argued that the 'no platform' tactic turned the struggle against racism and fascism 'into a sterile dispute over the "rights" of the fascists'.[136] The SWP dismissed the tactic because for them it gave 'the racists and fascists a new weapon to use against their opponents' and 'allow[ed] these thugs to pose as a persecuted minority or as defenders of democratic rights'.[137] The Spartacists continued to use the 'no platform' slogan into the 1980s, although other US groups eschewed the term. But as Shane Burley has shown, the notion of denying fascists the public space to assemble, on the streets or on campus, had just as long a history in the United States as it did in Britain.[138]

In the 1990s, the North American group Anti-Racist Action (ARA) also used the slogan, inspired by the British organisation Anti-Fascist Action (AFA), who they were in contact with.[139] Formed in Minneapolis in 1986, ARA spread across the United States and Canada in the late 1980s and 1990s and derived much of its politics from the world of anarchism, endorsing direct action against white supremacist and neo-Nazi groups.[140] A breakaway group from the Spartacist League, the International Bolshevik Tendency, reported on an ARA demonstration in Toronto in 1993 against the far right group, the Heritage Front, describing their tactics as 'no platforming'.[141]

In the last decade, various groups, such as the revitalised ARA and the International Socialist Organisation, have increasingly referred to the slogan of 'no platform' to describe their militant anti-fascist approach, on the streets and on campus.[142] But opponents of anti-fascism and free speech warriors have also latched onto the phrase to denounce the tactics of 'Antifa'. For example, the Foundation of Individual Rights in Education (FIRE) have railed against 'no platform' on US campuses since the mid-2010s, inspired by *Spiked Online*'s 2014 campaign, 'Just Say No to No Platform'.[143] In early 2019, even US President Donald Trump capitalised on this moral panic about 'no platform' and vowed to introduce an executive order to 'protect' free speech on campus, possibly denying funding to university and colleges that did not uphold it[144] – similar to the proposals made by the Thatcher government with the Education (No. 2) Act in 1986.

A similar concern about 'no platform' has led to other governments in the English speaking world to lead inquiries into the 'problem' of campus censorship. Sam Gyimah's predecessor as Universities Minister, Jo Johnson, launched a parliamentary inquiry into free speech at universities in late 2017, and in 2018 it concluded that the threat to free speech on campus was highly exaggerated (which was confirmed by a BBC investigation in the same year).[145] In Australia, the Liberal/National Party government also held an inquiry into free speech at Australian universities in late 2018, after some media outlets, such as Murdoch-owned newspaper *The Australian*, reported that students were involved in 'no platforming' on various campuses. Prior to this inquiry, the Institute of Public Affairs, a right-wing thinktank, had published two annual reports on free speech at Australian universities, influenced by similar free speech rankings by *Spiked* and FIRE (see Chapter 7). Like in Britain and the US, conservative and right libertarian commentators and politicians in Australia have indulged in creating a moral panic over a small number of incidents that have led to government interest and possible intervention.

Similar to the British inquiry, the Australian inquiry, which was chaired by former Chief Justice of the High Court Robert French, found that there were few actual incidents of free speech being hindered on campus, remarking that recent incidents reported in the press 'do not establish a systematic pattern of action by higher education providers or student representative bodies, adverse to freedom of speech or intellectual inquiry in the higher education sector'.[146] However, it argued that 'even a limited number of incidents … may have an adverse impact on public perception of the higher education sector which can feed into the political sphere',[147] which seems more of a condemnation of how the media has stoked this moral panic, rather than a criticism of the actions of students and universities. Nevertheless the French report still recommended a code of conduct for universities to commit to upholding free speech, which the re-elected Liberal/National Party government has since sought to legislate. Although Nick Reimer has recently suggested in *Overland* that 'as commentators endorse speech codes as a way to remove an imaginary left-wing threat to free expression on campus, the main effect is to reinforce the "extreme centre" in Australian politics'.[148]

In Canada, the provincial government in Ontario has bypassed the inquiry process and introduced legislation to 'protect' free speech on campus, after several years of agitation by free speech groups at Canadian universities. Zac Vescera has written about how the far right in Canada have used these free speech student groups as a place of recruitment and have been 'a magnet for extremists'.[149] Similar to the replication in the British discourse of past moral panics about free speech, Michael Bueckert has shown that today's concerns over left-wing students at Canadian universities repeat right-wing concerns from the 1980s, such as when anti-apartheid students protested against speakers from the South African Embassy.[150] But emboldened by a global surge by the populist right and in consultation with conservative and libertarian student groups,[151] Ontario Premier Doug Ford has created laws to link funding for universities with a duty to uphold free speech (again similar to the UK's Education (No. 2) Act 1986).

In March 2019, Donald Trump signed a similar executive order linking funding for higher education bodies with the protection of free speech on campus, declaring, 'If a college or university does not allow you to speak, we will not give them money. It's that simple.'[152] The move was celebrated by sections of the conservative and libertarian right, as well as the Foundation for Individual Rights in Education. However, critics have argued that the executive order is vague and already covered in many areas by existing arrangements.[153] Although there has been much crossover on both sides of the Atlantic around the topic of 'no platform', 'safe spaces' and 'trigger warnings', the situation in the United States, with the First Amendment, makes the translation from discourse into practical action less comparable with the United Kingdom.

The history of free speech at US universities and colleges has its own history, which is currently being explored by other scholars, particularly since the election of Donald Trump and disruptions on American campuses.[154] Nesrine Malik, citing research by the website *Vox*, writes that 'an entire genre' has developed regarding the 'US college campus free speech panic', which 'includes books, online magazines and is the theme of regular columns in the American press'.[155] While there have been numerous opinion pieces and new stories about this topic in the UK, there is not the same level of academic scholarship about 'no platforming' and free speech on British university campuses, and this book aims to rectify this.

A note on methodology

This book is primarily based on material published at the time, such as newspaper accounts, the student press, far left publications and parliamentary debates. Primary source material from university archives has been utilised when available. However archival records relating to student activism, including the student press, is fragmentary and is maintained at various levels across Britain. The archives of the National Union of Students are only partially catalogued and available via the Modern Records Centre at the University of Warwick, which predominantly holds material from the 1940s to the 1970s. Records of the NUS from the 1980s onwards have been held uncatalogued in Edinburgh and Manchester. Mike Day from the NUS was helpful in obtaining materials from this uncatalogued collection. Some of the episodes discussed in this book resulted in disciplinary procedures for students and inquiries by university administrations, which has meant that some university archives have been able to provide complementary archival materials to the contemporary student press accounts.

The publications of the far left groups, which were very influential in the student movement throughout the post-war period, have provided another source of accounts of the numerous student protests, as well as significant coverage of the debates around the tactic of 'no platform'. As I have written elsewhere with Matthew Worley, historians of the far left in Britain have benefitted greatly from the digitisation projects that have allowed researchers access to far left publications previously unavailable.[156] As much of the student press was wary of the far left groups involved in the student movement, such as the International Marxist Group and the International Socialists/Socialist Workers Party, the far left press provides a counter-narrative to help understand the tensions between the liberal centre and the Marxist left over the policy of 'no platform' in the student unions.

The accounts provided by the student and far left press are read against the versions of events provided by the mainstream press, particularly the newspapers. Although different episodes in the history of 'no platform' were covered by a range of newspapers over the years, from *The Guardian* to *The Times* and the *Daily Telegraph* to the *Daily Express* and the *Daily Mail*, the predominant framing of these episodes has been that students have unfairly silenced speakers at universities. These speakers, it has been argued, should be allowed to speak and are to be therefore debated, instead of shut down. Over the years, many of those who were 'no platformed' or protested against complained of being silenced or their views being suppressed, but it has mainly been the case that it is *their* versions of events that have been given prominence in the mainstream press, while students' point of view is marginalised. The voice of protesting students is relegated to the student press and the far left press, as well as some sympathetic accounts in newspapers such as *The Guardian* or *The Independent*.

Those who were protested against by students were often given a media platform to decry their 'silencing' (and hard right politicians also used Parliament to air their grievances against the reception they'd faced from hostile students), revealing that 'no platforming' these speakers on campus did not mean an end to their freedom of speech in other spheres. This is something which recurs in the present. As Sara Ahmed has written, controversial speakers have their views expressed 'as if they are being stifled' and repeated by the media while 'presented as prohibited'.[157] Ahmed elaborates on this how this narrative replicates the privileged voices who seek to use 'free speech' to further harmful views and ideologies: 'Whenever people keep being given a platform to say they have no platform, or whenever people speak endlessly about being silenced, you not only have a performative contradiction; you are witnessing a mechanism of power.'[158]

As a historian using mainstream media accounts of 'no platforming', one needs to be aware of how claims by speakers of being silenced or shut down feed into wider tropes of university students as censorious and hostile to different ideas. Using student, far left and other activist accounts of these episodes, one can read (in the words at Ann Laura Stoler)[159] 'against the grain' of these prevailing narratives to explore how students have used 'no platforming' to resist the hate speech on campus over the last four decades.

Book structure

The contemporary discourse around 'no platform' across the English speaking world makes understanding the concept's origins in Britain an important history to uncover and explore. The purpose of this book is not to be a polemic on the contemporary situation, but a historical intervention to trace how 'no platform' has developed as a political tactic amongst the British student movement, from its anti-fascist antecedents to the various ways it has been utilised in the twenty-first century. Its aim is not to cover every episode on university campuses where 'no platform' has been an issue over the last four decades, but to investigate some of the major flashpoints since 'no platform' became a tactic in the 1970s, as well as the factors that influenced the development of the tactic and the eventual NUS policy. This chapter has sought to outline the historical and contemporary context in which 'no platform' sits, with the following chapters exploring the history of 'no platform' in more detail.

Chapter 2 looks at the origins of 'no platform' in the anti-fascist activism of the 1930s and 1940s, showing how anti-fascists fought Oswald Mosley's British Union of Fascists during the inter-war years and then the Union Movement in the post-war period. It explores how anti-fascists sought to disrupt public meetings of the BUF and their speaking engagements through heckling, physical interruptions and mass blockings of access to public spaces. Then in the immediate years following the Second World War, various fascists attempted to revive their political associations and publicise their propaganda, using the events in British Palestine as well as the early days of the Cold War and decolonisation to attract people. Anti-fascists sought to shut down the fascist meetings, using the techniques developed in the 1930s.

This chapter also examines the ways in which student groups at various universities, including the Oxford and Cambridge Unions, invited far right speakers, primarily Oswald Mosley, to speak during the 1950s and 1960s. Often under the guise of free speech and debate, the invitation of Mosley (as well as Colin Jordan in the 1960s) is a precedent for the controversial far right and hard right speakers that continue to be invited by student groups to the present day.

Chapter 3 focuses on the student movement that arose in the late 1960s and how this era of radicalism preceded the formation of the National Union of Students' 'no platform' policy in the mid-1970s. In the late 1960s, students protested against Conservative MP Enoch Powell (who had just made his 'rivers of blood' speech) and representatives from the right-wing Monday Club at several universities and tried to disrupt their speeches. In the early 1970s, a small group of Maoists physically assaulted the racist psychologist Hans Eysenck at the London School of Economics, and US academic (and government adviser) Samuel Huntington was prevented from giving a lecture at the University of Sussex. These incidents, which sought to deny right-wing speakers (including the explicitly racist Powell) a chance to publicly speak, can be seen as instances of 'no platforming' before the policy was introduced and the term widely used. In many ways, the NUS' 'no platform' policy was the formalisation of the more ad hoc protests against right-wing speakers that had occurred over the previous half-decade.

Chapter 4 investigates the pivotal moment when the 'no platform' policy was introduced by the National Union of Students in 1974 in response to the threat of the National Front and other fascist groups. The chapter interrogates the debates that took place at the NUS conference that voted to implement the policy and the subsequent controversy. This includes the special NUS conference that was held two months later, which coincided with an unruly demonstration against the NF in Red Lion Square and the ensuing police violence contributing to the conference upholding the motion. The chapter also looks at the ways in which the 'no platform' policy controversially began to be used against other groups, in this case against pro-Israel student groups. While this use of the policy was eventually banned by the NUS and the policy itself was suspended for a short period in the late 1970s, the chapter shows that there was still significant support amongst the student movement for 'no platform' throughout the decade, and although modified, it remained in place as the 1980s began.

Chapter 5 outlines how 'no platform' shifted in the 1980s to be used against other speakers and groups besides the explicit racists and fascists mentioned in the original 1974 resolution. As feminism and gay rights became prominent issues within the student movement, some student groups and unions argued that 'no platform' should be extended to sexists and homophobes, as well as some anti-abortionists. This caused dissent amongst some who supported the original policy, as they felt it was diluting the intention and aim of 'no platform' as an anti-fascist tactic. The chapter contrasts this with the support for the 'no platforming' of Young National Front organiser, Patrick Harrington, who was the focus of a campaign to exclude him from the Polytechnic of North London in 1984–85. While this was a more straightforward use of the 'no platform' tactic, it attracted criticism and controversy due to the focus on a single individual (albeit an influential one within the NF) who was supposedly attending classes rather than speaking on campus.

Chapter 6 covers the period from the mid-to-late 1980s when the Thatcher government became concerned about free speech on campus after several hard right Conservative MPs (as well as Enoch Powell) were 'no platformed' at universities around the country between 1985 and 1987. The protests against these MPs were sometimes official implementations of a 'no platform' policy by student unions, and at other times were unofficial actions by left-wing student groups. But they were seen by the government as evidence of a culture of censorship amongst the student population. The chapter looks at how this concern led to the introduction of the Education (No. 2) Act in 1986 in an attempt to legally protect freedom of speech at British universities, and the difficulties that were encountered in enforcing this legal obligation, culminating in a court case involving the Conservative Association at the University of Liverpool in the late 1980s. By the time that a decision was reached in the case of *R v University of Liverpool ex parte Caesar-Gordon* in 1990, the 'no platform' policy had been in place for more than 15 years and despite government attempts to curtail the policy, it remained a significant weapon in the armament of the student movement against fascism and racism, as well as against sexism and homophobia.

Chapter 7 brings the story through the 1990s and into the twenty-first century. It examines how the revitalised threat of the British National Party in the 1990s saw the fascist party 'no platformed', but at the same time, the NUS and individual student unions used the policy to ban the Islamic fundamentalist group, Hizb ut-Tahrir, from campuses and the student union bureaucracy. As the BNP grew in the first decade of the 2000s and its leader Nick Griffin gained a media profile, there were pushes to 'no platform' him after he was invited to speak at several universities, including Oxford, Cambridge and St Andrews.

This chapter also analyses the resistance to 'no platform' that originated with the Revolutionary Communist Party, whose journal *Living Marxism* became a significant base for free speech absolutism and opposition to the NUS' 'no platform' policy. With some influence in the student movement, the RCP sought to contest 'no platform' through its student wing, the Revolutionary Communist Students. When the RCP and *Living Marxism* both folded in the late 1990s, their successor, *Spiked Online*, developed into a prominent online space that promoted absolute free speech and maintained that 'no platform' was a more significant problem than the BNP. This chapter outlines how this free speech absolutism fed its way into mainstream journalism and politics, significantly contributing to the contemporary moral panic about 'no platform', 'safe spaces' and 'trigger warnings'.

This chapter concludes with a brief assessment of this contemporary free speech 'crisis', looking at how the trans debate has reignited many of the concerns about the extension of 'no platform' beyond explicit fascists and racists, and how the outlook of student activists and their use of the tactic has shifted since the 1970s. The chapter argues that the reconsideration of the targets of 'no platform' is not a new phenomenon and can be seen in the debates that were had in the early 1980s, and that the application of the tactic to alleged transphobic speakers and groups must be seen within this historical framework.

Chapter 8 looks over the history laid out in the book and discusses why 'no platform' continues to matter. It argues that 'no platform' was developed as a tactic and as a policy to combat the problem of racism and fascism on campus at British universities, particularly the invitation of speakers from racist and fascist organisations. This problem has not gone away – and with the mounting transnational discourse of free speech absolutism, it seems to be more important than ever. But 'no platform' has also expanded and shifted over the last 40 years to address issues of sexism, homophobia and transphobia on campus. Understanding why and how the tactic has changed since the 1970s is key to contemporary debates over the endurance of the NUS policy and how students have utilised it as a tactic in the twenty-first century.

Although a number of commentators have contrasted the present day 'crisis' with the original implementation of 'no platform' in the mid-1970s, this book seeks to place the current debates over 'no platform' and the creation of the NUS policy in 1974 in a much longer historical context. This narrative starts with the protests against Oswald Mosley and the British Union of Fascists in the 1930s and traverses the twentieth century, intertwining the histories of fascism and anti-fascism, as well as the student movement and the rise of the new social movements (or identity politics). To understand how 'no platform' is being applied as a tactic and a student union policy in the present, we need to understand that it has a long and complicated history. The purpose of this book is to trace this history and to challenge the way in which 'no platform' has been framed in the present.

Notes

1 Sam Gyimah, 'Civility Under Threat', *Research Research*, 1 October, 2018, www.researchresearch.com/news/article/?articleId=1377459 (accessed 8 June, 2019).
2 Ibid.
3 Ibid.
4 Ibid.
5 Ibid.
6 Ibid.
7 Claire Fox, *I Find That Offensive!* (London: Biteback Publishing [epub version], 2016) p. 77, pp. 59–63.
8 Greg Lukianoff & Jonathan Haidt, *The Coddling of the American Mind: How Good Intentions and Bad Ideas Are Setting Up a Generation for Failure* (New York: Penguin Press, 2018) pp. 1–15.
9 Nick Cohen, 'What Could Be More Absurd Than Censorship on Campus?' *The Guardian*, 7 February, 2015, www.theguardian.com/commentisfree/2015/feb/07/censorship-campus-no-way-fight-fanatics (accessed 13 June, 2019).
10 Nigel Farage, 'Once and For All: Nigel Farage Debunks the Left's Big Lie About Nationalism', *Nigel Farage*, 19 May, 2019, www.nigelfaragemep.co.uk/once-for-all-nigel-farage-debunks-the-lefts-big-lie-about-nationalism/ (accessed 13 June, 2019).
11 Will Davies, *Nervous States: How Feeling Took Over the World* (London: Jonathan Cape, 2018) p. 209.
12 Tom Slater, 'Don't Blame the Students. They're a Product of a Britain That's Losing Its Love of Free Speech', *The Spectator*, 18 January, 2016, https://blogs.spectator.co.uk/2016/01/ban-happy-students-didnt-come-from-nowhere-theyre-a-product-of-our-illiberal-society/ (accessed 14 June, 2019).
13 See: Matt Myers, *Student Revolt: Voices of the Austerity Generation* (London: Pluto Press, 2017).
14 Thomas Simpson & Eric Kaufmann, *Academic Freedom in the UK* (London: Policy Exchange, 2019) p. 7.
15 *The Red Mole*, September 18, 1972, p. 1. For further history of the International Marxist Group, see: John Callaghan, *The Far Left in British Politics* (Oxford: Basil Blackwell, 1987) pp. 113–160; Evan Smith & Matthew Worley, 'Introduction: The Far Left in Britain from 1956', in Evan Smith & Matthew Worley (eds), *Against the Grain: The British Far Left from 1956* (Manchester: Manchester University Press, 2014) pp. 1–22.
16 NUS, *April Conference: Minutes and Summary of Proceedings* (London: NUS, 1974) p. 79.
17 See: Jeffrey Weeks, 'Value for Many', *Marxism Today* (December 1989) pp. 30–33.
18 The term 'hard right' is used to describe the politicians on the right-wing of the Conservative Party and the Ulster Unionist Party and distinguish them from the broader far right, which includes both fascist organisations, such as the National Front and the British National Party, and populist organisations, such as UKIP.
19 Kenneth Lasson, 'Racism in Great Britain: Drawing the Line on Free Speech', *Boston College Third World Law Journal*, 7/2 (1987) pp. 163–165; Iain Channing, 'Policing Extreme Political Protest: A Historical Evaluation of Police Prejudice', *Policing*, pay010, https://doi.org/10.1093/police/pay010, p. 12.
20 Lasson, 'Racism in Great Britain', pp. 165–166.
21 Paul Jackson, *Colin Jordan and Britain's Neo-Nazi Movement* (London: Bloomsbury, 2017) p. 110.
22 Evan Smith, *British Communism and the Politics of Race* (Leiden: Brill, 2018) pp. 80–82.
23 Race Relations Act 1965, s6(1).
24 Gavin Schaffer, 'Legislating Against Hatred: Meaning and Motive in Section Six of the Race Relations Act of 1965', *Twentieth Century British History*, 25/2 (2014) pp. 258–263; 269–273.

25 Simon Peplow, 'The "Linchpin of Success"? The Problematic Establishment of the 1965 Race Relations Act and Its Conciliation Board', *Contemporary British History*, 31/3 (2017) p. 443.
26 Lord Scarman, *The Red Lion Square Disorders of 15 June 1974: Report of Inquiry by the Rt. Hon. Lord Justice Scarman, O.B.E.* (London: HMSO, 1975) p. 35.
27 Schaffer, 'Legislating Against Hatred', pp. 263–268.
28 Ibid., p. 268.
29 Ibid., p. 274; Peplow, 'The "Linchpin of Success"?', pp. 443–444.
30 Chris Hilliard, 'Words That Disturb the State: Hate Speech and the Lessons of Fascism in Britain, 1930s–1960s', *Journal of Modern History*, 88/4 (2016) p. 795.
31 House of Commons, *Hansard*, 21 October, 1986, col. 1117.
32 Gavan Titley, *Racism and Media* (London: Sage, 2019) p. 2.
33 Alana Lentin, 'Beyond Denial: "Not Racism" as Racist Violence', *Continuum*, 32/4 (2018) p. 401.
34 Ibid.
35 Titley, *Racism and Media*, p. 151.
36 Malcolm Harris, 'What's a "Safe Space"? A Look at the Phrase's 50-Year History', *Splinter*, 11 November, 2015, https://splinternews.com/what-s-a-safe-space-a-look-at-the-phrases-50-year-hi-1793852786 (accessed 7 June, 2019).
37 Ibid.
38 Moira Kenney, *Mapping Gay LA: The Intersection of Place and Politics* (Philadelphia, PA: Temple University Press, 2001) p. 24.
39 Christina B. Hanhardt, *Safe Space: Gay Neighborhood History and the Politics of Violence* (Durham, NC: Duke University Press, 2013) pp. 29–30.
40 See: Matt Cook, *Queer Domesticities: Homosexuality and Home Life in Twentieth-Century Britain* (Houndmills: Palgrave Macmillan, 2014) pp. 199–225; Christine Wall, 'Sisterhood and Squatting in the 1970s: Feminism, Housing and Urban Change in Hackney', *History Workshop Journal*, 83/1 (2017) pp. 79–97; Florence Binard, 'The British Women's Liberation Movement in the 1970s: Redefining the Personal and the Political', *Revue Française de Civilisation Britannique/French Journal of British Studies*, 22 (2017) pp. 6–7.
41 See: Sonja J. Ellis, 'Diversity and Inclusivity at University: A Survey of the Experiences of Lesbian, Gay, Bisexual and Trans (LGBT) Students in the UK', *Higher Education*, 57/6 (June 2009) pp. 723–739.
42 Chris Waugh, 'In Defence of Safe Spaces: Subaltern Counterpublics and Vulnerable Politics in the Neoliberal University', in Maddie Breeze, Yvette Taylor & Cristina Costa (eds), *Time and Space in the Neoliberal University: Futures and Fractures in Higher Education* (Cham: Palgrave Macmillan, 2019) p. 145.
43 Francesca Laguardia, Venezia Michalsen & Holly Rider-Milkovich, 'Trigger Warnings: From Panic to Data', *Journal of Legal Education*, 66/4 (2017) pp. 882–883.
44 Clare Forstie, 'Trigger Warnings', in Nelson M. Rodriguez, Wayne J. Martino, Jennifer C. Ingrey & Edward Brockenbrough (eds), *Critical Concepts in Queer Studies and Education* (Houndmills: Palgrave Macmillan, 2016) p. 422.
45 Laguardia, Michalsen & Rider-Milkovich, 'Trigger Warnings', pp. 883–884.
46 *The Independent*, 9 October, 2016, www.independent.co.uk/news/uk/home-news/trigger-warnings-universities-students-us-uk-a7353061.html (accessed 17 June, 2019).
47 Tony Pollard, 'Offering Trigger Warnings to My Students Doesn't Make Me – Or Them – a Wuss', *International Business Times*, 30 September, 2016, www.ibtimes.co.uk/offering-trigger-warnings-my-students-doesnt-make-me-them-wuss-1584250 (accessed 17 June, 2019).
48 'Race Theorist Rejected', *Searchlight* (May 1986) p. 3.
49 'Professor Threatens Anti-Racist Students', *Searchlight* (December 1980) p. 8.
50 See: Helene Guldberg, 'Why Ban Racist Brand?', *Living Marxism* (June 1996) http://web.archive.org/web/20010521174518/www.informinc.co.uk/LM/LM91/LM91_Brand.html (accessed 30 January, 2020).

51 *The Guardian*, 24 March, 2006, www.theguardian.com/uk/2006/mar/24/raceineducation.highereducation (accessed 30 January, 2020).
52 *Red Weekly*, 29 March, 1974, p. 3.
53 Ibid.
54 Michael Billig, *Fascists: A Social Psychological View of the National Front* (London/New York: Academic Press, 1978).
55 Michael Billig 'Psychology, Racism and Fascism', *Searchlight* (1979).
56 Ibid., p. 34.
57 *The Independent*, 30 May, 2002, www.independent.co.uk/news/education/higher/free-to-speak-out-190617.html (accessed 16 October, 2019).
58 Ibid.
59 Cited in, Ibid.
60 Angela Saini, *Superior: The Return of Race Science* (Boston: Beacon Press, 2019) p. 83.
61 Ibid., p. 80.
62 *New York Times*, 8 May, 2018, www.nytimes.com/2018/05/08/opinion/intellectual-dark-web.html (accessed 14 November, 2019).
63 Gideon Rozner, 'Inside the Intellectual Dark Web', *IPA Review* (October 2018) pp. 7–8.
64 Aurelien Mondon & Aaron Winter, *Reactionary Democracy: How Racism and the Populist Far Right Became Mainstream* (London: Verso, 2020) p. 80.
65 *The Guardian*, 21 March, 2019, www.theguardian.com/education/2019/mar/20/cambridge-university-rescinds-jordan-peterson-invitation (accessed 18 October, 2019).
66 Jordan Peterson, 'Cambridge University Rescinds My Fellowship', *Jordan B. Peterson*, 20 March, 2019, www.jordanbpeterson.com/blog-posts/cambridge-university-rescinds-my-fellowship/ (accessed 17 October, 2019).
67 Noah Carl, 'How Stifling Debate Around Race, Genes and IQ Can Do Harm', *Evolutionary Psychological Science*, 4/4 (December 2018) pp. 399–407.
68 Cited in *The Guardian*, 1 May, 2019, www.theguardian.com/education/2019/may/01/cambridge-university-college-dismisses-researcher-far-right-links-noah-carl (accessed 17 October, 2019).
69 *Daily Mail*, 29 September, 2019, www.dailymail.co.uk/news/article-7516365/Cambridge-scientist-sacked-publishing-racist-research-reveals-suing-university.html (accessed 17 October, 2019).
70 Ibid.
71 Ibid.
72 Roger Eatwell & Matthew Goodwin, *National Populism: The Revolt Against Liberal Democracy* (London: Pelican Books, 2018)
73 Eric Kaufmann, *Whiteshift: Populism, Immigration and the Future of White Majorities* (London: Allen Lane, 2018).
74 Mondon & Winter, *Reactionary Democracy*.
75 Ibid.
76 'Framing Ethnic Diversity as a "Threat" Will Normalise Far-Right Hate, Says Academics', *Open Democracy*, 23 October, 2018, www.opendemocracy.net/en/opendemocracyuk/framing-ethnic-diversity-debate-as-about-threat-legitimises-hat-0/ (accessed 19 October, 2019).
77 Matthew Goodwin & Eric Kaufmann, 'What Happened When We Tried to Debate Immigration', *Quillette*, 8 December, 2018, https://quillette.com/2018/12/08/what-happened-when-we-tried-to-debate-immigration/ (accessed 20 October, 2019).
78 Ibid.
79 Kaufmann, *Whiteshift*.
80 Ibid.
81 *Bristol Post*, 5 April, 2019, www.bristolpost.co.uk/news/bristol-news/bristol-university-students-walk-out-2725051.amp (accessed 13 April, 2019).
82 Eric Kaufmann (@epkaufm), Twitter thread, 6 April, 2019, https://twitter.com/epkaufm/status/1114473894797299714 (accessed 13 April, 2019).

83 Priyamvada Gopal, *Insurgent Empire: Anticolonial Resistance and British Dissent* (London: Verso, 2019) p. viii.
84 For a discussion of the Ramsay Centre and the culture wars over academia in Australia, see: Patrick Stokes, 'Ramsay's Long March Backwards', *Alfred Deakin Institute for Citizenship and Globalisation*, https://adi.deakin.edu.au/news/ramsays-long-march-backwards (accessed 20 November, 2019).
85 For more on the 'Rhodes Must Fall' campaign, see: Rhodes Must Fall Oxford, *Rhodes Must Fall: The Struggle to Decolonise the Racist Heart of Empire* (London: Zed Books, 2018).
86 Nigel Biggar, 'Rhodes, Race and the Abuse of History', *Standpoint* (March 2016) p. 40.
87 *Ethics and Empire*, n.d., www.mcdonaldcentre.org.uk/ethics-and-empire (accessed 21 October, 2019).
88 Richard Drayton, 'Biggar vs Little Britain', in Stuart Ward & Astrid Rasch (eds), *Embers of Empire in Brexit Britain* (London: Bloomsbury, 2019) pp. 114; 146.
89 'Ethics and Empire: An Open Letter from Oxford Scholars', *The Conversation (UK)*, 20 December, 2017, http://theconversation.com/ethics-and-empire-an-open-letter-from-oxford-scholars-89333 (accessed 21 October, 2019).
90 Cited in, *Daily Mail*, 21 December, 2017, www.dailymail.co.uk/news/article-5200381/Oxford-academics-accused-bullying-Empire-defending-don.html (accessed 21 October, 2019).
91 *The Times*, 3 February, 2018, www.thetimes.co.uk/article/climate-of-fear-at-oxford-warns-colonialism-scholar-nigal-biggar-tjg633tv7 (accessed 21 October, 2019).
92 *The Times*, 8 October, 2018, www.thetimes.co.uk/article/campus-censorship-is-stalinist-says-oxford-professor-nigel-biggar-5870pt28f (accessed 21 October, 2019).
93 Toby Young, 'Free Speech Is Officially Dead in British Universities', *The Spectator*, www.spectator.co.uk/2018/11/free-speech-is-officially-dead-in-british-universities/ (accessed 1 December, 2019).
94 For a recent example of this, see: Simpson & Kaufmann, *Academic Freedom in the UK*.
95 Janet Dack, '"It Certainly Isn't Cricket!": Media Responses to Mosley and the BUF', in Nigel Copsey & Andrzdej Olechnowicz (eds), *Varieties of Anti-Fascism: Britain in the Inter-War Period* (Houndmills: Palgrave Macmillan, 2010) p. 154.
96 Ibid., p. 153.
97 Robert Skidelsky, *Oswald Mosley* (London: Papermac, 1990) p. 517.
98 *The Times*, 24 October, 2009, www.thetimes.co.uk/article/past-notes-sir-oswald-mosley-and-the-bbc-th6hb6lcdp3 (accessed 25 October, 2019).
99 Paul Jackson, *Colin Jordan and Britain's Neo-Nazi Movement* (London: Bloomsbury, 2017) p. 87.
100 Denis MacShane, *Black and Front: Journalists and Race Reporting* (London: NUJ pamphlet, 1978) pp. 6–7.
101 Barry Troyna, 'The Media and the Electoral Decline of the National Front', *Patterns of Prejudice*, 14/3 (1980) p. 26.
102 Nigel Copsey, *Anti-Fascism in Britain* (Abingdon: Routledge, 2017) p. 136.
103 MacShane, *Black and Front*, p. 20.
104 Ibid., pp. 15–16.
105 Copsey, *Anti-Fascism in Britain*, p. 138.
106 'The BBC and the BNP', *Searchlight* (February 1993) p. 24.
107 *The Independent*, 4 April 1994; *The Independent*, 13 April, 1994.
108 *The Independent*, 13 April, 1994.
109 *The Independent*, 11 May, 1994.
110 Ibid.
111 Ibid.
112 Copsey, *Anti-Fascism in Britain*, p. 179.
113 Daniel Trilling, *Bloody Nasty People: The Rise of Britain's Far Right* (London: Verso, 2013) pp. 122–123.

114 Nesrine Malik, *We Need New Stories: Challenging the Toxic Myths Behind Our Age of Discontent* (London: Weidenfeld & Nicolson, 2019) pp. 101–103.
115 Mondon & Winter, *Reactionary Democracy*, p. 143.
116 Justin Murphy & Daniel Devine, 'Does Media Coverage Drive Public Support for UKIP or Does Public Support for UKIP Drive Media Coverage?', *British Journal of Political Science*, 2018, DOI: 10.1017/S0007123418000145.
117 Joe Mulhall, 'Modernising and Mainstreaming: The Contemporary British Far Right', 19 July, 2019, www.gov.uk/government/publications/modernising-and-mainstreaming-the-contemporary-british-far-right (accessed 24 October, 2019).
118 Malik, *We Need New Stories*, p. 102.
119 Stephen Albrecht, Maik Fielitz & Nick Thurston, 'Introduction' in Maik Fielitz & Nick Thurston (eds), *Post-Digital Cultures of the Far Right: Online Actions and Offline Consequences in Europe and the US* (Bielefeld: transcript, 2019) p. 7.
120 *The Guardian*, 9 August, 2019, www.theguardian.com/world/2019/aug/09/new-zealand-telco-bans-8chan-as-chief-censor-calls-it-racist-killers-platform-of-choice (accessed 30 October, 2019).
121 Joe Mulhall, 'Deplatforming Works: Let's Get On With It', *Hope Not Hate*, 4 October, 2019, www.hopenothate.org.uk/2019/10/04/deplatforming-works-lets-get-on-with-it/ (accessed 30 October, 2019).
122 Ibid.
123 See: Lella Nouri, Nuria Lorenzo-Dus & Amy-Louise Watkin, *Following the Whack-A-Mole: Britain First's Visual Strategy From Facebook to Gab* (London: RUSI, 2019).
124 Mulhall, 'Deplatforming Works'.
125 Jeff Sparrow, *Fascists Among Us: Online Hate and the Christchurch Massacre* (Melbourne: Scribe, 2019) p. 123.
126 Ibid.
127 Cited in *The Guardian*, 26 October, 2018, www.theguardian.com/commentisfree/2018/oct/26/dont-normalise-far-right-sometimes-we-must-take-it-on (accessed 30 October, 2019).
128 Safya Khan-Ruf, 'The Mutating of No-Platform', *Hope Not Hate*, 18 May, 2018, www.hopenothate.org.uk/2018/05/18/mutation-no-platforming/ (accessed 30 October, 2019).
129 Ibid.
130 Ibid.
131 Richard Seymour, *The Twittering Machine* (London: Indigo Press, 2019) p. 191.
132 Frederick J. Simonelli, *American Fuehrer: George Lincoln Rockwell and the American Nazi Party* (Urbana/Chicago, IL: University of Illinois Press, 1999) pp. 128–129.
133 'Defense of Anti-Nazi Demonstrators Score Victory!', *Young Spartacist* (June 1975) p. 12.
134 Ibid.
135 'Spartacus Youth League Motions to the 19–21 November Conference of the NSCAR', *Young Spartacus* (December 1976) p. 9.
136 Malik Miah, 'Free Speech and the Fight Against the Ultraright', *International Socialist Review* (August 1975) p. 10.
137 Ibid., p. 17.
138 Shane Burley, *Fascism Today: What It Is and How to End It* (Chico, CA: AK Press, 2017) pp. 301–313.
139 See: Nigel Copsey, 'Crossing Borders: Anti-Fascist Action (UK) and Transnational Anti-Fascist Militancy in the 1990s', *Contemporary European History*, 25/4 (2016) pp. 707–727; Mark Bray, *Antifa: The Anti-Fascist Handbook* (Melbourne: Melbourne University Press, 2017) p. 67; Nigel Copsey, 'Militant Antifascism: An Alternative (Historical) Reading', *Society*, 55 (2018) pp. 243–247.
140 George Michael, 'Right-Wing Extremism in the Land of the Free: Repression and Toleration in the USA', in Roger Eatwell & Cas Mudde (eds), *Western Democracies and the New Extreme Right Challenge* (London: Routledge, 2004) pp. 174–175; Burley, *Fascism Today*, pp. 313–315.

141 IBT, 'No Illusions in Cops and Courts – No Platform for Fascists!', IBT leaflet (June 1993), www.bolshevik.org/Leaflets/No%20platform%20for%20fascists%201993.html (accessed 20 June, 2019).
142 Nell Gluckman, 'The Antifa Academic', *Chronicle of Higher Education*, 24 August, 2017, www.chronicle.com/article/The-Antifa-Academic/241002 (accessed 21 June, 2017).
143 Samantha Harris, '"Down with Campus Censorship!" Campaign Launched in Britain', *FIRE*, 5 March, 2014, www.thefire.org/down-with-campus-censorship-campaign-launched-in-britain/ (accessed 14 June, 2019); Rahul Truter, 'Don't Shout Down, Speak Up!', *FIRE*, 10 July, 2018, www.thefire.org/dont-shout-down-speak-up/ (accessed 19 June, 2018).
144 *CNN Politics*, 2 March, 2019, https://edition.cnn.com/2019/03/02/politics/trump-executive-order-colleges-free-speech/index.html (accessed 21 June, 2019).
145 Joint Committee on Human Rights, *Freedom of Speech in Universities: Fourth Report of Session 2017–19*, HC589/HL111, p. 44; Rachel Schraer & Ben Butcher, 'Universities: Is Free Speech Under Threat?', *BBC Reality Check*, 23 October, 2018, www.bbc.co.uk/news/education-45447938 (accessed 15 December, 2018).
146 Robert S. French, *Report of the Independent Review of Freedom of Speech in Australian Higher Education Providers* (Canberra: Department of Education, 2019) p. 217.
147 Ibid.
148 Nick Reimer, 'On Free Speech on Campus and Why the French Code Will Be No Help', *Overland*, 1 July, 2019, https://overland.org.au/2019/07/on-free-speech-on-campus-and-why-the-french-code-will-be-no-help/ (accessed 3 July, 2019).
149 Zac Vescera, 'A Splintered Movement: How the Far-Right Found a Foothold on Campus', *The Ubyssey*, 20 April, 2019, www.ubyssey.ca/features/a-splintered-movement-far-right-on-campus/ (accessed 3 July, 2019).
150 Michael Bueckert, 'No Platform for Apartheid', *Africa Is a Country*, 3 April, 2018, https://africasacountry.com/2018/04/no-platform-for-apartheid (accessed 29 June, 2019).
151 Michael Bueckert, 'Did Doug Ford Consult Any Students for His "For The Students" Plan?', *Medium*, 19 January, 2019, https://medium.com/@michael.bueckert/did-doug-ford-consult-any-students-for-his-for-the-students-plan-74327fc68fad (accessed 22 June, 2019).
152 Andrew Kreighbaum, 'Trump Signs Broad Executive Order', *Inside Higher Ed*, 22 March, 2019, www.insidehighered.com/news/2019/03/22/white-house-executive-order-prods-colleges-free-speech-program-level-data-and-risk (accessed 11 July, 2019).
153 Ibid.
154 See: Erwin Chemerinski & Howard Gillman, *Free Speech on Campus* (New Haven, CT/London: Yale University Press, 2017); Sigal R. Ben-Porath, *Free Speech on Campus* (Philadelphia, PA: University of Pennsylvania Press, 2017); Keith E. Whittington, *Speak Freely: Why Universities Must Defend Free Speech* (Princeton, NJ: Princeton University Press, 2018); Robert C. Post, 'The Classic First Amendment Tradition Under Stress: Freedom of Speech and the University', in Lee C. Bollinger & Geoffrey R. Stone (eds), *The Free Speech Century* (Oxford: Oxford University Press, 2019) pp. 106–122.
155 Malik, *We Need New Stories*, p. 120.
156 Evan Smith & Matthew Worley, 'Introduction: The Continuing Importance of the History of the British Far Left', in Evan Smith & Matthew Worley (eds), *Waiting for the Revolution: The British Far Left from 1956* (Manchester: Manchester University Press, 2017) pp. 4–5.
157 Sara Ahmed, 'You're Oppressing Us!', *Feminist Killjoys*, 15 February, 2015, https://feministkilljoys.com/2015/02/15/you-are-oppressing-us/ (accessed 6 November, 2019).
158 Ibid.
159 Ann Laura Stoler, 'Colonial Archives and the Arts of Governance', *Archival Science*, 2 (2002) pp. 99–100.

2

FASCISM, ANTI-FASCISM AND FREE SPEECH BEFORE 'NO PLATFORM'

'No platform' emerged out of a much longer anti-fascist tradition in Britain of denying a platform to fascists during the inter-war and early post-war periods. This chapter explores how anti-fascists responded to the threat of fascism in the 1930s and after the Second World War, which informed those who proposed the idea of 'no platform' in the 1970s. In the early days of anti-fascism in Britain, especially against Oswald Mosley's British Union of Fascists (BUF), militant anti-fascist activism often meant the physical denial of a platform for fascists by anti-fascist protestors. Anti-fascists in Britain looked to what was occurring in Italy, Germany and other parts of continental Europe and many came to the conclusion that fascists should not be given the space to organise, parade or espouse their ideology at any cost. Much of this militant anti-fascism was led by rank-and-file members of the Communist Party of Great Britain (CPGB), alongside some from the Independent Labour Party (ILP) and Jewish activists, which often involved combating the more moderate sections of the left and labour movement, as well as fighting Mosley's fascists.

After the hostility he faced in the early 1930s towards his New Party, Mosley had become convinced that these protests had had a severe impact on the fledgling party's electoral fortunes, and inspired by Mussolini in Fascist Italy, started to argue that the new form of politics that he proposed needed defending against communist subversives through physical force. The establishment of the BUF in late 1932 was accompanied by the creation of a unit of bodyguards that would protect the political party from alleged communist intimidation.

From the very beginning, the BUF presented themselves as the defenders of free speech and claimed that communists wanted to deny them a platform, which, to the BUF, meant using violence to counter the censorious 'Reds'. Those who opposed Mosley and the BUF pointed to what was occurring in Germany and Italy, arguing that fascism was the antithesis of free speech. The only way to protect free speech for all was to actively prevent the fascists from organising, recruiting and speaking in public. The militant anti-fascists who proposed this course of action used several tactics to deny the BUF a platform and the use of public space.

Throughout the BUF years, those who opposed Mosley would heckle the speakers and seek to be a disruptive element in the crowd, which would often lead to confrontations with Mosley supporters and bodyguards who were employed to 'protect' Mosley's speakers. This would sometimes escalate to involve the police.

An example of this tactic was in June 1934 at the Olympia Stadium in London, when around 500 communists entered a crowd of an estimated 10,000 BUF supporters and sought to disrupt the night's events, with large crowd of anti-fascist protestors also on the outside of the venue. Staggered throughout the evening for maximum effect, the disrupters were dealt with severely by BUF security and the police. This caused concern amongst politicians and the press about the violence of the BUF (and of the anti-fascists), as well as questions over whether anti-fascists were right to infringe upon Mosley's free speech. 'The opinions expressed, however,' wrote Robert Benwick, eventually 'favoured the anti-Fascists, for although they came determined to provoke disorder, the Blackshirts used unnecessary violence to maintain order'.[1]

Alongside the disruption of BUF meetings, another tactic used by anti-fascists in the 1930s was holding large counter-demonstrations and pickets to prevent fascists access to a particular space. The quintessential example of this was the 'Battle of Cable Street' in October 1936, which become central to the narrative of anti-fascist history in Britain. 'Cable Street' was used at the time and since then as a rousing story of anti-fascist resistance and an episode in which the BUF were physically denied their platform – a march through the East End of London. Over 100,000 people flocked the streets to stop Mosley from holding a provocative march through the area where a large Jewish population lived. Although historians and activists have debated the effectiveness of the protest (particularly in the long term), the 'Battle of Cable Street' was a demonstration of the popular resistance to fascism in Britain in the 1930s and has since served as an inspiration to anti-fascists. In the era of 'no platform' in the 1970s, the slogan of the protest, 'They Shall Not Pass', was evoked time and time again to draw an analogy between the fight against the BUF and the fight against the National Front.

But the 'Battle of Cable Street' and the public disorder that surrounded it brought into question the notion of free speech for the extremes of the political spectrum. Many politicians and journalists pronounced that they abhorred the BUF and Mosley, but defended the democratic right of Mosley to espouse fascist ideology in public. When there was opposition from below to Mosley and the BUF, the government and the police sought to intervene, suggesting that a line had been crossed between an acceptance of free speech for all and the concern over political violence. The aftermath of 'Cable Street' saw the introduction of the Public Order Act 1936, which was first used to crack down on the BUF, but was subsequently used over the next half-century to curtail the political activities of the left.

The BUF was banned by the British government at the beginning of the Second World War and Mosley, as well as other leading fascists, were interned. In the late 1940s, these fascists started to re-organise and formed informal groups before Mosley launched the Union Movement (UM) in 1948. The re-emergence of Mosley and the various fascist groups established in the late 1940s also led to a resurgence of anti-fascism in the post-war era. The Communist Party, the Association of Jewish Ex-Servicemen (AJEX) and the National Council for Civil Liberties (NCCL), as well as other more militant groups, such as the 43 Group and the Revolutionary Communist Party (RCP),[2] built upon tactics developed in the inter-war period to fight the revived fascist movement. These included heckling fascist speakers, breaking up and disrupting fascist meetings and physically occupying spaces to deny the fascists a platform. At the same time, most of these groups pushed for greater intervention by the state to outlaw anti-Semitism and for some, to ban fascist groups outright. These tactics helped diminish the appeal of the Union Movement and other fascist groups to the British public and led to Mosley fleeing temporarily to Ireland in 1951.

While Mosley's influence diminished considerably in the 1950s and other fascist groups contested the UM for the spotlight (with the neo-Nazi Colin Jordan being a prominent figure in several of these groups), Mosley was still sought after by various student groups to speak or debate. This included several invitations throughout the mid-to-late 1950s and early 1960s to speak at the Oxford and Cambridge unions that encouraged debates on controversial topics. Furthermore, as Jordan, by now leader of the infamous National Socialist Movement (NSM) gained notoriety and Mosley again moved away from the political spotlight in the mid-1960s, he was also invited to speak at universities and was interviewed by several student publications. Some student groups, seeking to be controversial, often invited Mosley and Jordan to speak or debate (a tactic that has been continued since then) and when these far right figures have been invited, there has been significant anti-fascist opposition. This has caused some invitations to be withdrawn and at other times led to protestors seeking to disrupt events. Through the period from the early 1930s to the mid-1960s, a pre-history to the tactic of 'no platform', eventually becoming the policy of the National Union of Students in 1974, can be traced, showing that the tactic was developed over three decades of varying anti-fascist activism. This chapter delves into this pre-history.

The advent of the BUF

First a Conservative, then an independent, then a Labour MP, Oswald Mosley resigned from the Labour government in 1930 after his proposals for dealing with the unemployment problem, partially inspired by Mussolini's corporatist approach in Italy, were rejected by the Cabinet. Out of this, Mosley formed the New Party. The New Party was not fascist in the same way that the BUF was, but it indicated the corporatist elements of Mosley's thinking at the time.

The New Party, in its attempts to be all things to all people, also attracted opposition from many different quarters. Dave Hann wrote: 'The Communist Party understood it as a fascist party in the making, while Labour Party members and trade unionists regarded Mosley as a traitor who split the working class vote.'[3]

Between the formation of the New Party in March 1931 and the General Election in October 1931, the New Party conducted a number of public meetings around the country, which became more and more violent as more anti-fascists (especially Communist Party members) sought to disrupt them. Although not reaching the same level of violence and mayhem that came with the BUF, Matthew Worley has shown that '[d]isruption and a degree of disorder appeared to characterise the New Party's public appearances from the outset', with significant incidents occurring during the Ashton-under-Lyne by-election in April 1931, in Glasgow in September 1931 and in Birmingham and Glasgow (again) during the General Election campaign in October 1931.[4]

The Communist Party members were more willing to be involved in physical violence, but were also joined by some Labour Party activists, who preferred, on the whole, to limit themselves to heckling and jeering. However, Mosley confused 'the vocal opposition of disgruntled Labour supporters with the rarer but more combative response of the CPGB' and as Worley has written, used his own bodyguards and New Party supporters to promote a 'wholly exaggerated' and violent retort that exacerbated tensions.[5] According to Worley, 'Mosley's decision to forge an increasingly disciplined extra-parliamentary force provided a stimulus rather than an antidote to political violence in Britain' and thus, he 'succeeded only in transforming verbal challenge into physical conflict and thereby helped formalise what became almost a ritual of confrontation'.[6]

These confrontations between anti-fascists and the New Party were used by Mosley as justification for his shift towards fascism and the formation of the BUF in late 1932, after a visit to Mussolini's Italy. From the very beginnings of the BUF, Mosley embraced militarism and violence as part of his political movement, with the Blackshirts organised as 'shock troops', called the Fascist Defence Force, to confront the 'Reds'.[7] Mosley formed the BUF in October 1932, preceded by the publishing of the tract *The Greater Britain*, which outlined Mosley's full conversion to fascism, predominantly inspired in the early years by Mussolini, but as the 1930s wore on, the influence of Nazi Germany became much more apparent.

Convinced of the failure of parliamentary democracy, the BUF did not contest elections until 1936,[8] preferring to build an extra-parliamentary movement. It grew exponentially in its first years, with nearly 50,000 members allegedly joining.[9] Enjoying support from Lord Rothermere's *Daily Mail* and other sections of the Conservative right, Mosley attempted to establish the BUF through a series of public meetings, demonstrating its supposed mass support at rallies, inspired by Mussolini and Hitler. There were frequent mobilisations by anti-fascists against these public meetings and rallies in the early years of the BUF, culminating in events in 1934 that solidified the militant anti-fascist approach of physical confrontation and also revealed the violent nature of the BUF.

Olympia, June 1934

Robert Skidelsky suggested that '[f]or both fascists and anti-fascists Olympia was the epic battle of the 1930s', explaining:

> Fascists looked back with satisfaction on the 'beating' they had given the 'Reds' and claimed that it had restored 'free speech' in Britain. Anti-fascists

> regarded it as the moment when they unambiguously exposed the brutal face of fascism and condemned it thereafter in the eyes of all decent Englishmen.[10]

Olympia was to be a demonstration of the strength of the British Union of Fascists. As mentioned previously, its membership growth had been strong throughout its first 18 months. After several well-attended meetings at the Albert Hall, Mosley believed that a larger venue, such as that of Olympia in west London, was necessary. Around 10,000 people filled the venue, with anti-fascists (primarily members of the Communist Party) securing around 500 tickets. The Communist Party portrayed Olympia as a chance to build the anti-fascist movement and confront the growing BUF. Regarding threats made in the run up to the meeting by Mosley, the *Daily Worker* declared:

> Already the Blackshirts have used provocative threats against the workers ...
>
> They have made such threats at many meetings, but [past] events have shown that all their thuggish methods were unable to prevent the workers having their say. To-night will again prove this rule ...
>
> [T]he workers' counter-section will cause them to tremble. All roads lead to Olympia to-night.[11]

A counter-demonstration by anti-fascists was held outside the venue, while anti-fascists heckled the speakers, including Mosley, and sought to disrupt the meeting. These disruptions were staggered over the evening, so to ensure the maximum disruptive effect. As *The Times* reported the following day, 'The campaign of interruption had been well planned so that it should affect every part of the meeting in the course of the evening.'[12]

BUF bodyguards violently ejected the anti-fascist protestors, with *The Times* stating that the constant interruptions were 'countered with similar thoroughness and with a uniformity of treatment which suggested a prescribed technique of violence'.[13] The newspaper continued:

> Stewards at once made for the offenders. If they resisted ejection the incident at once became an affair of fisticuffs and, if the victim remained standing at the end of his resistance he was seized ju-jitsu fashion and dragged out. Quite a number were borne out limp bodies after the frays.[14]

Once ejected, there were a number of arrests of anti-fascists outside the venue, where further violence was meted out by the police. The *Daily Worker* reported that outside Olympia, 'seething crowds of thousands of workers kept up a continual anti-Fascist uproar, despite the enormous special concentration of police forces which had been gathered ... for the Blackshirts' protection'.[15] The following day, the newspaper stated that 24 anti-fascists had been arrested, compared to one BUF supporter, claiming that this was 'a striking fact, which [spoke] volumes' about the differing treatment by the police towards the BUF and the CPGB.[16]

Mosley and the BUF complained about the tactics used by the anti-fascists, described as 'highly organized groups of Reds', to break up the public meeting. Quoted in *The Times*, Mosley claimed:

> For over three weeks certain Communist and Socialist papers have published incitements to their readers to attack this meeting. The result was that a large Red mob gathered outside the hall for the purpose of intimidating those who entered, and very many of the audience were in fact jostled before they managed to enter the meeting at all.[17]

In the BUF press, the violence was blamed on the Communists, but the fascist response was also celebrated, with A.K. Chesterton declaring it a 'fascist victory' and the 'Red Terror Smashed'.[18] On the other hand, the Communist Party also claimed a victory at Olympia, with the *Daily Worker* declaring the following day: 'Terrific scenes were witnessed at Olympia last night, when the workers of London staged a mighty counter-demonstration to the Mosley Fascists. Mosley's carefully planned arrangements were turned into a complete fiasco.'[19]

There was an outcry by some in the press and some politicians at the violence witnessed at Olympia, which has been documented by a number of scholars. For example, *The Times* quoted Conservative MP Geoffrey Lloyd as declaring, 'I am not very sympathetic to Communists who try to break up meetings, but I am bound to say that I was appalled by the brutal conduct of the Fascists last night.'[20] Although a number argued that the tactics of the anti-fascist protestors were just as deplorable as the actions of the BUF stewards. *The Times* reported on debates in the House of Commons in the aftermath of Olympia, summarising that 'members were about equally divided between unqualified condemnation of alleged Fascist brutality towards interrupters, and the feeling that allowances must be made for those who had been sorely provoked by Communists'.[21] Rajani Palme Dutt, a leading CPGB figure, wrote in his editorial for *Labour Monthly* that it was only because of the anti-fascist demonstrators that 'the eyes of millions' had been opened 'to the real character of Fascism'.[22] Dutt proclaimed, 'It is solely thanks to their stand that the present universal outcry against Fascism has developed, where before there was silence or indifference or amused toleration.'[23]

The violence meted out to anti-fascists who broke up the meeting at Olympia roused the anti-fascist movement. Dave Hann wrote, '[a]nti-fascists had certainly taken a beating at Olympia but their growing movement responded in force, with an increase in the number of BUF public appearances interrupted by anti-fascists and the number of people involved in anti-fascist activity'.[24]

The momentum shifted away from the BUF after 1934, towards the anti-fascist movement, but also to the National Government. As a number of a scholars have shown, the events of 1934 had led the National Government to debate laws regarding the policing of political meetings and public order, but which were shelved at the time. This was partly due to a reluctance by some politicians to curtail the freedom of political expression and partly because the BUF began to co-operate with the police.[25] Martin Pugh also suggests that the BUF avoided large urban areas where there was more likely to be an anti-fascist mobilisation, preferring to hold meetings across provincial England.[26] It was not until 1936, when Mosley and the BUF shifted tactics towards explicit anti-Semitism and trying to attract more working class supporters in the East End of London, that confrontations between anti-fascists, the police and the National Government reached a new crescendo.

The Battle of Cable Street, October 1936

Discussing the work of Nigel Copsey and others, Daniel Tilles has suggested that historians of British anti-fascism have concentrated on the events of 1934 and 1936, when there were mass mobilisations of anti-fascists, with co-operation between communists and Jewish activists.[27] For Tilles, focusing on these peaks in popular anti-fascism overlooks the other forms of anti-fascism and strategic positions taken up in opposition to the British Union of Fascists. For this book, the events of 1934 and the 'Battle of Cable Street' are important as they demonstrate the use of the tactic of physical disruption of fascist meetings and public gatherings. The purveyors of the tactic of 'no platform' harked back to Olympia and Cable Street when developing a response to the National Front in the 1970s.

'The Battle of Cable Street' is well-known and probably the most famous anti-fascist event in British history, although the events surrounding it, its impact on the BUF and its legacy are all hotly contested. On October 4, 1936, anti-fascists blockaded the East End of London against a march by the BUF through Cable Street and Gardiner's Corner, where a large Jewish population lived. For the Communist Party, it was a demonstration of the Popular Front in action, when a party that had around only 11,500 members in October 1936[28] could mobilise over 100,000 people in anti-fascist action.

Richard Thurlow has shown that this also revitalised the anti-fascist movement and in the lead up to Cable Street, anti-fascist activists had attempted to disrupt BUF meetings throughout 1936.[29] The most infamous incident was when anti-fascist activists had attempted to disrupt a meeting at the Royal Albert Hall, but were prevented by police from being in the vicinity of the venue. A crowd of around 3–5,000 amassed at the nearby Thurloe Square, and were subjected to baton charges by the police, resulting in 46 allegations of police brutality.[30]

Increasing confrontation between fascists and anti-fascists, as well as between anti-fascists and the police, set the stage for the clashes at Cable Street. The details of the day have been told by a number of scholars and need not be repeated here. Essentially, over 100,000 anti-fascist protestors blocked the East End of London and were confronted by around 6,000 police, with clashes leading to 79 arrests.[31] Around 3,000 fascists had assembled nearby, but surveying the anti-fascist crowds, the Metropolitan Police Commissioner, Sir Philip Game, requested that Mosley cancel the march, which he did.[32]

'Cable Street' reinvigorated the National Government's concern over political violence and public disorder in the late 1930s, with BUF and CPGB events both seen as provocative and potentially violent. Richard Thurlow describes 'Cable Street' as the 'straw that broke the camel's back'[33] and the Public Order Act 1936 was introduced shortly afterwards, greatly increasing police power over public demonstrations. The increased police pressure upon public BUF events, using the Public Order Act, adversely affected the group's fortunes and anti-fascist resistance meant that most BUF events were heavily policed. As Britain edged closer to war with Nazi Germany, focus upon Mosley and the BUF by the security services and the Metropolitan Police's Special Branch intensified, with the outbreak of the Second World War eventually leading to the end of the BUF after Mosley and other leading figures were interned. While mainstream revulsion and government intervention both impacted negatively upon the BUF, its demise was also significantly hastened by the anti-fascist movement that was mobilised against them throughout the 1930s. As Copsey has written:

> the general effect of popular anti-fascism was to spatially contain the BUF – not just on the streets or in meeting halls, but also in terms of inspiring a wider spatial imaginary where local and international contexts became intrinsically connected to developments overseas, whether in Nazi Germany, Fascist Italy, France, or Spain.[34]

This also (temporarily) concluded a long-running debate in Britain over free speech and the political (as well as physical) space afforded to fascism, with the National Government and anti-fascists squeezing this space. The debate had begun in 1933, and although it seemed to have been decided by the events of Cable Street and the Public Order Act, it did raise its head again after the war.

Fascism and free speech in the 1930s

Since the days of the BUF, fascists have attempted to portray themselves as the defenders of free speech. As meetings of the BUF were interrupted by anti-fascist activists, the BUF complained that 'the Reds' were trying to deny them their freedom of speech. In the first issue of *The Blackshirt* from February 1933, Mosley's front page article, quoting from the BUF's 1932 manifesto *The Greater Britain*, claimed that the anti-fascist campaigns against the newly established BUF had indicated that 'we have reached a point in this country in which free speech is a thing of the past'.[35] Mosley complained: 'Organised bands of "Reds," armed with sticks, bottles and razors, attend all important meetings which threaten their position in areas where they are strong, with the declared object of breaking them up'.[36]

Only the fascists, Mosley claimed in his newspaper, could 'hold open meetings in such areas without police protection', suggesting that the reason for this was that the 'Fascist Defence Force has been organised to protect free speech' which had 'often met and defeated "Red" violence'.[37] The trope of the far right being silenced by left-wing violence, which continued across the twentieth century and into the present, was first used by Mussolini and Hitler in the 1920s and explicitly used again by Mosley in the 1930s. The portrayal of the Fascist Defence Force as an organisation built to forcefully respond to the threats from the left indicates the early embrace of violence in the BUF, confident of its own strength and not needing to rely on the police. It was only after the disturbances at Olympia in June 1934 that the BUF moved to explicitly calling for the police to intervene against anti-fascist activists.

These were continued themes in the BUF propaganda throughout the 1930s. In the 1936 publication *Fascism: 100 Questions Asked and Answered*, Mosley made a distinction between indoor meetings, where BUF stewards were allegedly allowed 'to preserve order in accordance with the Law', which meant '[i]f the Chairman orders the removal of a persistent interrupter, it is [the stewards'] duty to eject him with the minimum of force necessary to secure his removal'[38] – even though it was evident from disturbances at Olympia and elsewhere that this was not the case. On the other hand, Mosley stated that for outdoor meetings, 'it is the duty under the Law of the police alone to preserve order, and Fascists do not attend for that purpose'.[39] However, various clashes between fascists and anti-fascists on the streets, especially in 1936 as the BUF started to intensify its anti-Semitic street campaigns, also show that this claim was false.

In March 1936, Mosley asserted that when the BUF had first emerged just over three years earlier, 'free speech in Britain had virtually come to an end' and that in 'great industrial centres Socialism could be vigorously attacked from the platform without the break-up of the meeting by highly organised bands of hooligans.'[40] He declared that the Blackshirts 'with their bare hands' had 'overcome red violence armed with razors, knives and every weapon known to the ghettoes of humanity', and thus pronounced, 'Their bodies bear the scars, but free speech is regained.'[41] Once again, Mosley portrayed the BUF as the defenders of free speech against communist violence and suggested that it was through violent self-defence that free speech was preserved.

Mosley complained elsewhere that the BUF were hindered in their pursuit of free speech by the government and the police who increasingly prevented BUF rallies and marches from occurring out of fear of violence. A few weeks after the 'Battle of Cable Street', Mosley lamented in the BUF weekly *Action* that the government did not use the law 'to deal with the assailants [i.e. the anti-fascist activists] but with the defenders of Free Speech', objecting:

> If trouble takes place at a meeting, Government and law now regard as the guilty party, not those who assemble with violence to prevent an opinion being stated, but those who peacefully assemble to state that opinion.[42]

However. Iain Channing has argued that the opposite was often the case, writing that 'it appears more common that it was audience members who heckled and showed their contempt for fascism to end up before a magistrate.'[43]

Elsewhere in their propaganda, the BUF argued that 'freedom of speech does not exist' and seemed nonplussed to actually hold up this freedom, especially if they came to power.[44] Mosley suggested that while 'anyone can carry a soap box to a street corner and … make any moderate noise that he sees fit to emit', there was no 'effective action following from his words'.[45] In the eyes of Mosley only the press and the party machine had a voice, and he wrote, 'in actual practice under this system freedom of speech is the freedom to be the servant of the financier.'[46] While the BUF claimed to be defenders of freedom of speech, the BUF programme envisaged 'freedom of speech' to be accessed via Corporate Life, the alleged 'machine for putting into practice the principle of freedom of speech'.[47] Mosley's convolutedly explained this process in *Action* in 1936:

> Every man and woman with any industry, profession, or interest in this country will be able to enter into the work of his or her corporation. There they will not only be permitted but invited to express their opinions. The ordinary man and woman drawn from the great majority, who cannot or do not care to talk at street corners, will be invited to express their opinion. They will be encouraged to do so because the expression of their opinions will affect the work of the Corporation, and through that definite machinery the opinion of the people will affect Government.[48]

So even though the BUF stressed the idea of free speech when discussing their public meetings and claimed that anti-fascists threatened their freedom of speech, the BUF did not foresee in their programme any freedom of speech outside the fascist corporate state.

This reinforced the idea for the Communist Party and other anti-fascist activist that the real threat to free speech and democracy was fascism, with them pointing to what had happened to the working class, trade unions and socialists in Fascist Italy and Nazi Germany. Arguing against the BBC giving airtime to Mosley, the *Daily Worker* put that 'Fascism is the same in all countries – there is no special British brand – it is a creed of murder and violence.'[49] Then in 1937, discussing the fascist breaking up of a Labour Party meeting being addressed by Clement Atlee, the same paper stated: 'Fascism, wherever, and in whatever form it raises its head, aims to destroy free speech, democracy, and every liberty which centuries of working-class endeavour have wrestled from the ruling class.'[50]

The Communist Party lambasted the Labour Party for its pleas to allow 'free speech' for Mosley and the BUF. For example, the *Daily Worker* criticised the short-lived Labour MP Fielding West for writing to the *Daily Herald* that 'the Labour Party do not fear the effect of Mosley's speeches. In any event, let him be heard, for free speech is still precious to-day.'[51] The Communist newspaper retorted that '[w]hile even Tory MPs were horror-stricken at the brutalities of Mosley, this Labour MP comes out attacking the Communists and pleading with the workers to give freedom to Fascism.'[52] The following month, Dutt wrote in *Labour Monthly* that the Labour Party leadership was too ready to defend the bourgeois concept of 'freedom of speech', but explained that this meant: 'the workers must listen like docile, obedient sheep in regimented silence whenever a noble, respected bourgeois chooses to get on his hindlegs to air his caste-theories and generally put them in their place'.[53]

Dutt claimed that 'freedom of speech' was allowed for proponents of ideologies that sought to inflict violence upon the working class, but often trade unionists and socialists were denied freedom of speech and on occasions, charged with sedition.[54] To prevent Britain allowing a fascist movement to rise like in Italy and Germany meant *practical* opposition to Mosley and this meant opposition to Mosley's ability to broadcast his message in public or semi-public places.

Fascism at universities in the 1930s

While the BUF were challenged by anti-fascists in public places and on the streets throughout the 1930s, one area where there was less confrontation was at the universities of Britain, particularly compared with the student reactions to fascism in the post-war period. Despite there being a significant communist presence at universities during the inter-war period, the British Union of Fascists also gained a foothold on campus (although Laurence Brown argues that the BUF were 'never a national presence, especially within British universities').[55] The pages of the BUF's *Blackshirt* and *Action* often reported on talks given to university groups by leading members of the BUF, such as A.K. Chesterton or Alexander Raven Thomson, and with little or no mention of hostility from protesting students. On the other hand, the *Daily Worker* also reported little resistance from students to fascist meetings on campus. An exception to this comes in November 1938, when 30 students walked out of a speech given by John Beckett to the Cambridge University Fascist Association, 'leaving four discommitted Fascists and Beckett'.[56]

One of the most active university fascist groups in the 1930s was the Oxford University Fascist Association (OUFA), which was established in early 1933. David Renton has written that the BUF branch in Oxford always gave 'a clear priority ... to organizing within the university' and '[o]f 27 members ... named in the *Oxford Mail* or *Oxford Times* between 1933 and 1939, at least 16 gave university addresses'.[57] Shortly after the formation of the OUFA, Mosley came to town to address the student group at the Carfax Assembly Rooms, a popular meeting place off-campus. *The Times* reported that Mosley was 'given a quiet hearing' and that the meeting was restricted to members of the university as a precaution against disruption.[58] Renton suggests that the relatively quiet reception that Mosley received at this time was due to the fact that much of the left in Oxford were meeting elsewhere that night.[59] However the Vice-Chancellor saw Mosley's visit (as well as a proposed visit by former Labour MP, Ellen Wilkinson to the Oxford University Labour Club) as evidence of 'too much political activity' amongst students and temporarily banned all meetings by political clubs at Oxford.[60]

While students from the OUFA dominated BUF activity in the city, the major flashpoints did happen away from the university. In May 1936, Mosley returned to Oxford and gave an address at the Carfax Assembly Rooms. Renton suggests that rather than students from the university, many of the anti-fascists who attended the meeting were workers who picketed the meeting and sought to disrupt it from inside, albeit not in a co-ordinated manner.[61] Mosley had repeatedly warned that hecklers would be ejected from the meeting, but he also proceeded to make inflammatory remarks in front of a crowd that was divided between fascists and anti-fascists. *The Times* described the events as the meeting became more confrontational:

> a young man who was asking questions was approached by two or three Blackshirts. Then a party of 20 Blackshirts went down the centre of the hall. People near intervened, and in a few seconds there was a fight in the centre of the hall. Several metal chairs were thrown about, and one woman was hurt.[62]

The 'Battle of Carfax', as Renton has called it, has been seen as similar to the events at Olympia two years earlier, highlighting the violence of the BUF and alienating potential supporters.[63] Like the debates over Olympia, historians have been divided over whether Mosley provoked a hostile reaction from the crowd and if the BUF stewards at the meeting violently overreacted to the disruptive elements inside.[64] However anti-fascists were able to use the events at the Carfax Assembly Rooms to highlight the violence of the BUF, and as Duncan Bowie has written, 'Mosley did not hold any further public meetings in Oxford' – although fascists did continue to hold some events in the city and at the university.[65] Renton shows that the BUF went into decline in Oxford after 1936, with the student mobilisation around the Spanish Civil War creating an unhospitable environment for fascist activity in the city in the late 1930s.[66] Similar to the BUF more broadly, the Second World War practically ended fascist politics in Oxford, including at the university, until the post-war period. However, fascism re-emerged at Oxford and Cambridge in the late 1940s, as well as in the East End of London, where the anti-fascist tactics of the 1930s were repurposed for a new era.

The revival of British fascism in the post-war era

Mark Neocleous has written that 'seeing fascism as a historical phenomenon that ended in 1945 or thereabouts … encourages a dangerous forgetting'.[67] Although Oswald Mosley and some of the leading figures of the British Union of Fascists, as well as Arnold Leese of the tiny Imperial Fascist League (IFL), were interned during the Second World War, many other fascists were not. The BUF became a proscribed organisation in 1940 and the IFL went into decline with Leese's internment, but a number of people that supported these fascist groups sought to revive similar organisations in the post-war period. A number of smaller groups run by ex-BUF members had started agitating around the time of the end of the war and were eventually brought together by Mosley under a new moniker, the Union Movement (UM). Although Mosley attempted to distance the UM from the BUF, much of its programme was similar, with an increased focus on Western Europe as a bloc against Soviet communism and for the maintenance of empire in Africa and

Asia. Campaigning against Zionism in British Palestine and the creation of Israel, the Union Movement, alongside other fascist groups and activists, revived a campaign of violence and intimidation. The Second World War and increasing knowledge by the British public of the horrors of the Holocaust meant that fascism remained deeply unpopular at this time, but in certain areas, such as London's East End, the Union Movement still looked to resume the BUF's pre-war campaign of anti-Semitism and provocative street activities.

The reawakening of British fascism in the mid-to-late 1940s saw a number of groups emerge to combat it, including the CPGB, the Trotskyist RCP, the NCCL, AJEX, the Board of Deputies of British Jews and the 43 Group. Like in the inter-war period, these groups worked separately and together at different times to counter the Union Movement, utilising a range of different tactics, including campaigns to prevent fascists from using public buildings and calls for the banning of these new fascist organisations, street fighting with fascists, heckling and the breaking up of fascist meetings. The latter tactics were developed by the 43 Group, which was made up of Jewish activists, primarily in the East End of London, and was involved in the direct action against Mosley's men on the streets.

Despite the internment of Mosley and the banning of the BUF during the war, the Atlee government was reluctant to ban the Union Movement and believed that the existing laws, primarily the Public Order Act 1936, were enough to contain the fascist elements that had emerged.[68] However several scholars have argued that in the late 1940s, the Communist Party was seen as a much more prominent threat and in policing the street battles between fascists and anti-fascists, the police were more likely to use the Public Order Act against anti-fascists. In a pamphlet written in 1947, E.P. Thompson wrote, 'It is quite clear that the fascists welcome the police at their meetings – not as a warning, but as protection from the justice of the people.'[69]

The Communist Party was divided over its approach to the Union Movement, carrying over tensions between the leadership and the local rank-and-file over the use of direct action against Mosley that were seen in the late 1930s. The leadership called for the Home Secretary to ban the Union Movement. In Thompson's pamphlet, the Party demanded that the 'spreading of specifically fascist doctrine … be outlawed', that the 'spreading of racial hatred and anti-Semitism … be made a crime' and that 'existing laws … be strictly enforced'.[70] Furthermore, the Party urged that other organisations 'go on record for the outlawing of fascism' and more immediately told readers of the pamphlet, 'If the fascists come into your locality, get all the inhabitants to sign a petition of protest to the Home Secretary.'[71]

In spite of the CPGB leadership's preference for the government and the police to intervene against the Union Movement, many in the rank-and-file ignored this approach and still pursued direct action against it. In March 1946, a number of Jewish activists formed the 43 Group, which included several Communist Party members.[72] The 43 Group was involved in street fighting with the fascists, breaking up (indoor and outdoor) meetings, heckling fascist speakers and disrupting paper sales. Disrupting meetings through heckling and physically denying the fascists to space to congregate were two tactics that were employed by anti-fascists in the inter-war period, and were used effectively by the 43 Group.

Prior to the formal establishment of the Union Movement, the 43 Group were disrupting meetings of Mosley sympathisers. Morris Beckman, a 43 Group activist and author of an activist history of the group, wrote that in the summer of 1946, 'between six and ten fascist meetings per week were being attacked by the Group'.[73] According to Beckman:

> A rough estimate showed that one third [of these meetings] were ended by the speakers' platform being knocked over, another third were closed down by the police to keep the peace, and the remaining third or so continued to the finish due to too heavy a presence of police or stewards.[74]

In his book, Beckman explains that the 43 Group first attempted to heckle fascist speakers but found that this was 'futile unless it prepared for the closing down of a meeting by knocking over a platform'. [75] As both the police and fascist stewards became increasingly aware of these disruptive tactics at indoor meetings, confrontations between fascists and anti-fascists, as well as the police, moved outside and also became increasingly violent. The police were more likely to arrest anti-fascists, but similar to the events in the 1930s, the constant chaos that surrounded fascist meetings increased the difficulty for fascists to publicly organise.

As more fascist meetings started to take place outside, the marketplace area on Ridley Road in Dalston, East London, became a contentious space, with '[p]itched battles … fought between fascists and anti-fascists on a regular basis throughout the summer and autumn of 1947'.[76] This involved anti-fascists physically occupying the space to prevent fascist speakers from using it, a tactic called 'jumping the pitch'. Dave Hann describes it:

> Jumping the pitch was such an accepted practice that the police would allow the first arrivals to occupy a speaker's spot regardless of any claim by their opponents. A kind of political musical chairs developed as fascists and anti-fascists vied with each other to be the first to occupy the most popular pitches. Members of the Hackney Trades Council, the AJEX, the RCP and all used this tactic, although it could involve arriving at the designated spot many hours beforehand or even sleeping out overnight.[77]

As mentioned previously, the breaking up of fascist meetings or physically denying them the space to organise were only some of the tactics involved in combating the resurgent fascist movement in the late 1940s. Another tactic was a campaign to make the production and dissemination of anti-Semitic material illegal, as well as public pronouncements of anti-Semitism. In the 1945 general election campaign, the Communist Party had proposed that anti-Semitism become a criminal offence, a propsal described by Henry Srebrnik as an attempt to attract support from the local Jewish circles and emphasise the Party's anti-fascist stance.[78] The 43 Group and the RCP made similar demands, as well as the more moderate organisations, such as the Board of Deputies and the NCCL. Despite this, the Labour government was unwilling to pursue legislation of this kind, relying on the Public Order Act to be used in the most provocative cases. When questioned about the public airing of anti-Semitism in parliament in 1949, Home Secretary Chuter Ede stated:

> I regret that this kind of speech should be made. Such speeches are carefully reported, and the observations made are submitted to the Director of Public Prosecutions. I was helped on one occasion when a prosecution was undertaken, by an hon. Member who sent a report of what he had heard, and on that occasion the prosecution was brought to a successful conclusion. If any other hon. Member feels that it is consistent with his public duty to render similar assistance, I shall be greatly obliged, because it is desirable, if possible, that corroboration of police evidence should be available.[79]

Despite police having these powers to make arrests under the Public Order Act, David Renton has shown that they were reluctant to do so.[80]

Similar calls were made for the Home Secretary and the police to ban fascist marches under the Public Order Act. However, while the government stressed that 'any legislation would apply equally to the Left as well as to the Right', in practice this legislation was used 'almost entirely … against anti-fascist protestors'.[81] Anti-fascists bore the brunt of the state's zeal to keep the status quo and as David Renton has written, the state frequently used its laws to harass the anti-fascists, particularly communists, while sympathising with the fascists.[82] When Ede was moved to use the Public Order Act, such as in mid-1948 shortly after Mosley formally announced the formation of the Union Movement, he implemented a ban on all political processions – first in East London, and then the rest of the London metropolitan area.[83] David Renton has written that the ban was only fully rescinded in April 1950.[84]

The Communist Party, and others, also argued for the outright banning of fascist organisations, just as had been used against the BUF in 1940. However there was resistance from the government, particularly from Chuter Ede, who believed that the Public Order Act (alongside monitoring by the Metropolitan Police and MI5) had been successful in the past and the fascists did not warrant further legislative attention. Responding in parliament to a request by Labour MP John Haire for an inquiry into fascism and anti-Semitism in 1947, Ede replied:

> The activities of these organisations are closely watched, and no special inquiry needs to be instituted for this purpose. Their influence is negligible and it would be an exaggeration of their importance to suggest that their activities have resulted in any significant increase of anti-Semitism.[85]

As Nigel Copsey has explained, for Ede, '[i]f existing legislation had proven sufficient in the 1930s, then there was surely no need to further restrict civil liberties when public opinion had become so resolutely opposed to fascism'. [86] The CPGB's *Daily*

Worker quoted Ede as stating at a public meeting in South Shields in December 1947, 'In this country you do not kill any idea by attempting to say that no one shall utter it … Ideas are only killed by better ideas.'[87]

A Mass Observation report in July 1946 on free speech and anti-Semitism found that 'one out of every two of those who said they were in favour of free speech, withdrew this in the case of fascism'.[88] However the same report found that nearly half of those interviewed agreed that public speeches against the Jews should be allowed as part of the upholding of free speech.[89] David Renton has suggested that public opinion seemed to be closer to the anti-fascist argument being put forward by the various groups, rather than the limited approach taken by the Home Secretary.[90]

Despite the fascists gaining momentum momentarily, reaching their peak with the pronouncement of the formal existence of the Union Movement in early 1948, the confrontational tactics of the 43 Group, coupled with the broader anti-fascism of the other groups mentioned previously and the public distaste for fascism, saw Mosley quickly go into retreat. By 1951, Mosley had left the remnants of the Union Movement in tatters and went into self-exile in Ireland until the late 1950s. However, while Mosley's influence on the British fascist movement declined in the 1950s, fascism did not go away and as will be discussed in Chapter 4, slowly developed over the next decade and half through various groups which eventually led to the formation of the National Front in 1967.

The fascists go to university

With the banning of the British Union of Fascists and the internment of fascists during the Second World War, reading circles and book clubs became integral to the informal fascist networks being put in place by ex-BUF and IFL members. Before the formation of the Union Movement in 1948, these informal groups were used to organise activists and disseminate fascist propaganda while attempting to avoid repercussions from anti-fascists and the state. These book clubs 'met behind closed curtains in the back rooms of public houses and in half-empty Church halls, booked under assumed names', and as Graham Macklin has written, 'served as a ready-made nucleus for branches of a new fascist movement'.[91] In September 1946, an editorial for the *Daily Worker* complained about these 'literary circles' that operated essentially as 'a new Fascist party', quipping 'The storm-troopers who burned the books have now become bookmen!'[92]

Some of these reading circles and book clubs were established at British universities, primarily at Oxford and Cambridge, where a new generation of fascists was being formed and recruited. At Oxford, a Corporate Club was established, while future neo-Nazi leader Colin Jordan started a Nationalist Club during his time at Cambridge, linked to the British People's Party (BPP).[93] The Oxford Corporate Club was founded in 1946 by two undergraduates, Desmond Steward and Philip Thomas, and produced a short-lived journal called *Avant Garde*, as well as organising a debate at Oxford in October 1947 which proposed the motion 'that this house would deplore legislation to curb fascist activities in this country'.[94] Macklin notes that the motion won by 350 votes to 178, but the Corporate Club did not live much longer.[95]

Each of these student groups attracted the ire of anti-fascists from inside the university and from outside. In a 1948 Revolutionary Communist Party pamphlet by future Militant leader Ted Grant, the Corporate Club was identified as an explicitly fascist group, alongside the British League of Ex-Servicemen and Women, Mosley's Book Club and Discussion Group, the Union of British Freedom, the Sons of St George, the Imperial Defence League and the British Workers' Party of National Unity.[96] The *Daily Worker* reported that the Club was involved in debates at the Oxford Union Society, where Mosleyite literature was sold outside.[97] While a student, Tony Benn, co-wrote an open letter in the student magazine *Isis* condemning the Corporate Club, and brought together a number of student groups from across the political spectrum to call for action against the Club.[98] The letter stated:

> It has come to our notice that a fascist organization under the name of the Corporate Club has been operating in the University for the last two terms …
>
> By the end of the Hilary Term it numbered approximately forty members spread over nine colleges. It is significant that one of their members wrote an article which appeared prominently in the Spanish press, boasting of the existence of 'a large reactionary movement in Oxford.'
>
> The organization is not recognized by the Proctors and works in and through existing political parties, clubs, newspapers and periodicals; also through discussion groups and non-political University or College societies.[99]

The letter writers urged 'all members of the University to exercise the utmost vigilance in the interest of the country and of the good name of the University' with regards to the Corporate Club,[100] although it is unclear whether there were any further student actions against the Club.

Paul Jackson has shown that the BPP had a presence at Cambridge (with a BPP candidate even running in the Combined Universities by-election in March 1946)[101] and representatives from the party, as well as Mosleyite Jeffrey Hamm, were invited by right-wing student groups to speak. In May 1948, protests against Hamm prevented him from speaking, while the Duke of Bedford, a leading member of the BPP, spoke at the university in February 1949, although the student newspaper, *Varsity*, reported little trouble.[102] John Beckett, the founder of the BPP who had previously been in Mosley's BUF in the inter-war period, alongside Jordan, spoke at a school in Cambridge in June 1949, which was picketed by Cambridge University's Jewish Society, Labour Club and Socialist Society.[103]

Jordan left Cambridge in 1949 and became more involved in political activities around Arnold Leese, while the Union Movement faded away after Mosley left for Ireland in 1951. This coincided with a drop in fascist appearances at British universities in the early 1950s, but from 1954 onwards and throughout the 1960s, Mosley and Jordan both made regular appearances at British universities, often accompanied by student protests.

In April 1954, Mosley was invited by Nicholas Tomalin, President of the Cambridge Union, to debate the programme of the Union Movement's attempt 'to advocate by legal means a complete change in the system of Government'.[104] Following a debate in the pages of *Varsity*, the student newspaper at Cambridge, a motion to censure Tomalin for inviting Mosley was debated by the Cambridge Union in the week before his visit, which led to scuffles between Labour and Conservative students at the special meeting.[105] Although the student paper gave significant airing to both sides of the debate over whether to invite the Union Movement leader, Mosley claimed that the paper had 'incited to violence quite deliberately' and that if it 'had not been a privileged undergraduate newspaper, [the editors] would have been run in under the Public Order Act'.[106]

On the day of Mosley's visit, the *Daily Mail* reported that 'special wooden barriers had been nailed up in the corridors … to restrain gatecrashers' and that extra police (including a plain clothes detective) had been drafted in.[107] But the paper claimed that these precautions were, in the end, 'hardly necessary' and that Mosley was a 'damp squib'.[108] The paper described (almost disappointingly) the reaction of students who opposed Mosley, but who were unable to disrupt the event: 'Undergraduates who failed to get in punctuated the opening speeches with loud assaults on the locked doors and the half-hearted explosion of one firework outside aroused expectations of excitement.'[109]

The *Daily Express* gave a slightly differing view to the level of disruption brought by the protesting students, reporting:

> UNDERGRADUATES hung on high window frames outside the crowded Cambridge Union last night or sneaked in by the fire escape … Some of the 750 students inside the chamber hissed when a party of Sir Oswald's friends and supports took their places in the gallery.
>
> And throughout the main speeches there were loud 'noises off' caused by students battering at the locked doors.[110]

An editorial for the *Daily Mirror* called the students that had invited Mosley as 'incredibly stupid' and asked, 'Why dig up this old dummy?'[111] The newspaper noted that the Cambridge Union regarded itself as 'a forcing house for the Front-Bench of the Commons' that schooled students in 'bright talk', but quipped 'their hospitality to Mosley was NOT a bright idea'.[112] The Cambridge Union replied to this editorial, retorting that they had 'accorded to Sir Oswald the right of free speech, and accorded it at the same time to one of Fascism's strongest enemies, the Rev. Dr. Donald Soper'.[113] The Union pointed to the fact that the vote went against Mosley and '[b]y an overwhelming majority of 650 we have shown our lack of confidence in the Mosleyites'.[114]

In October 1957, Mosley was invited by the Oxford Union to debate the possibility of a Soviet withdrawal from Eastern Europe, which attracted protests in the days leading up to the debate, but according to *The Times*, the debate 'although crowded, passed off quietly'.[115] The newspaper quoted the President of the Oxford

Union when defending the decision to invite Mosley after an undergraduate student questioned this: 'This society was founded many years ago to enshrine a very great principle, that of free speech. The society has had to fight against many authorities to ensure that minority points of view shall be put.'[116] This statement is similar to other statements by the Oxford Union and other groups since the 1950s that have invited fascists, racists and other far right figures to speak or debate at British universities.

In April 1960, Mosley was speaking about South Africa to the Cambridge University Conservative Association. A protesting student, Philip Gratier, 'slapped a jelly into the face' of Mosley as he addressed the Conservative student group, with *The Times* reporting that chants of 'Sharpeville, Notting Hill' being heard throughout the speech.[117] The student paper at Cambridge, *Varsity*, described the scene:

> Sir Oswald had been speaking for about five minutes when Gratier – himself one of the twenty-strong bodyguard the Conservative committee had placed at strategic points near the speaker's chair – made his gesture.
>
> He walked up to Sir Oswald and said: 'Have a jelly my friend.' Then he thrust the green jelly into his face.[118]

The Mosleyites tried to diminish the impact of the incident in their account on the front page of the UM newspaper, *Action*:

> A few beardie weirdies from the Lab-Comm ranks were present, and one of them expressed himself by the only method of which he was capable. He threw a small jelly at Mosley, who subsequently enjoyed more substantial fare during the agreeable evening with his hosts.[119]

Peter Temple Morris wrote to Mosley on behalf of the Conservative Association and apologised for the 'jelly incident', saying that it 'really was the most stupid thing and … none of the audience liked it'.[120] He praised Mosley for his speech and said amongst people he had spoken to, there was 'an overall admiration for the quite outstanding way in which you handled your audience'.[121] He also lamented that it was 'a pity that small concentrated heckling groups gave you so much trouble', but reassured Mosley that 'now that the meeting is over we have no doubt at all of your ability in dealing with them'.[122]

The following month, Mosley was invited again by the Oxford Union to debate whether apartheid South Africa's racialised policies were incompatible with membership in the British Commonwealth, with future Liberal leader Jeremy Thorpe being one of his opponents.[123] Hugo Young reported in the student paper *Cherwell* that 'no jellies and apparently no blousons noirs' were present at the debate and described Mosley's speech in quite favourable terms: 'A far cry from the jack-booted demagogue of the yellow Press [sic], he impressed the House with his sober debating skill (especially in a brilliant, and ultimately victorious, exchange with Mr. Thorpe), if not the solidity of his arguments.'[124]

This debate was repeated the following year, with both Mosley and Thorpe returning. Like Young's write up of the debate the previous year, there were some that fawned over Mosley's turn of phrase. For Mosley's future biographer, Robert Skidelsky, witnessing this debate was a life-changing moment:

> Mosley evidently had a hopeless task. His main point was that if we insisted on condemning every country which failed to live up to our particular moral requirements we would soon have no friends left in the world. But the highlight of the speech came when he trapped Mr Thorpe in a series of brilliantly timed and calculated exchanges which the Liberal M.P. seemed to have won completely till Mosley demolished him with a final crushing rejoinder. It was a superb example of the art of public debating, which failed to win the vote, but won for Mosley an ovation.[125]

The Union Movement's paper, *Action*, complained that '[t]he Left turned out in force in the desperate effort to prevent Mosley's case being heard again in Oxford … with ape-like grunts, yells, screams from hysterical females, and even rattles'.[126] The Mosleyites argued that the protestors did this because they were 'hopelessly defeated in argument, and once more resort[ed] to screaming'.[127]

A few days later, Mosley spoke again at Oxford, this time to the Humanist Group, debating Marxist scholar Raymond Williams.[128] *Cherwell* reported on the hostile reception that Mosley received:

> Heckling, hisses and boos swelled from an opening disturbance to an overwhelming uproar at Sir Oswald Mosley's address on 'Racial Purity' on Tuesday. Shouting at the top of his voice, Sir Oswald was finally drowned out by chants of 'Seig Heil', cheers for Hitler and choruses of booing …
>
> Violent protests and allegations from the largest-ever Humanity [sic] Group audience, packed into The Taylorian, interrupted Sir Oswald's speech constantly, and his voice was drowned in uproar …[129]

Several students from the women's college of Oxford, Somerville, wrote a letter to *Cherwell*, criticising the Oxford Union and the Humanist Group for 'us[ing] their positions irresponsibly to give a platform to a man whose views are not only scientifically and economically untenable, but positively abhorrent in human terms'.[130] The students warned that there was an impression in the press that Oxford was 'veering towards the extreme Right' and warned 'those who wish to be … Liberal-minded should guard against confirming this impression'.[131]

In fact, Mosley's son, Max, was Secretary of the Oxford Union at the time and was key to inviting his father, as well as becoming a touring speaker for the Union Movement in the early 1960s.[132] When Oswald Mosley came to Oxford in January 1961, Max came into conflict with editor of the student magazine *Isis*, Paul Foot (later to be a member of the International Socialists and Socialist Workers Party).[133] After Foot criticised the choice to allow Mosley to speak and alleged that

Mosley had 'done his best for 30 years to stir up racial violence', Mosley requested an apology from the magazine and publishers.[134] The publishers apologised, but Foot resigned as editor rather than apologise to Mosley.[135]

While receiving numerous opportunities to speak, particularly from Oxford and Cambridge, there were times when Mosley was prevented from speaking at universities. For example, in December 1960, the University Debates Union at the University College of North Staffordshire, Keele, voted by a small majority to withdraw an invitation for Mosley to debate on South Africa's readmission to the Commonwealth.[136] The editor of the student newspaper *Cygnet* moved the motion for the withdrawal of the invitation, saying 'there is no place for [Mosley] at Keele'.[137] *The Guardian* also quoted a member of the university's Liberal Society who supported maintaining the invitation as arguing, 'Every time you demonstrate against Mosley, boycott his meetings or ban him, you just enhance his reputation among his followers.'[138]

A few months later, the Vice-Chancellor of the University of Leicester banned Mosley from speaking at a debate on nuclear disarmament, after a vote to disinvite Mosley by the Leicester University Student Union Council, then a wider student vote in favour of inviting Mosley.[139] The Vice-Chancellor cited the possibility of disturbances if Mosley came to the university as one of the reasons to disinvite him, as well as 'the considerable offence he would give in the university'.[140] The *Daily Mail* reported that over 1,000 students held a protest meeting against the Vice-Chancellor's intervention[141] and an article in the student newspaper at Leicester, *The Ripple*, questioned the Vice-Chancellor's actions:

> surely the way in which the Vice-Chancellor acted leaves much to be desired. It seems autocratic to say the least … hasn't rather a dangerous precedent been established? Could not the Vice-Chancellor consider to a greater extent the express wishes of the Union? [142]

The newspaper's editorial in the same issue defended the Vice-Chancellor's position, asking why the student union did not ban Mosley themselves, claiming that the Vice-Chancellor 'showed more foresight, more humanity, than did the Union'.[143] However the President of the student union was quoted by *The Guardian* as arguing that Mosley should have been allowed to speak '[o]n the ground that a university is a bastion of freedom of speech' and that the student body had voted to invite him.[144] He further complained in *The Ripple* that the university 'could have expected … one of the best debates this Union has ever known' as Mosley was 'a speaker of outstanding brilliance' and the Campaign for Nuclear Disarmament would have provided another eloquent speaker to oppose him.[145]

It was not only Mosley who was invited to speak or debate at universities in the 1960s – Colin Jordan was also invited to speak at times, particularly as the notoriety of his National Socialist Movement (NSM) grew. The NSM had begun in the early 1960s as Jordan sought to move away from the other fascist groups that existed in the 1950s, such as A.K. Chesterton's League of Empire Loyalists or John

Bean's British National Party. Jordan was more interested in a transnational neo-Nazism, making connections with other Hitler worshippers in North America and Europe, than the other groups, who sought to promote the 'Britishness' of their fascism. Paul Jackson shows that Jordan was invited to speak at Southampton University in October 1965, addressing an audience of around 600 students.[146] The student newspaper at Southampton, *Wessex News*, reported that there was 'virtually no interruption' when Jordan first spoke, adding 'what heckling there was, was largely good-natured'.[147] However, the student paper described that during the Q&A session that followed, there were cries of 'Hitler Youth', 'a barrage of positive applause, which lasted for over half a minute' when a student questioned Jordan about white supremacy in Africa and a 'pale, and quivering with rage' student who called Jordan a 'human abomination'.[148] A final student turned his back on Jordan and 'told how three of his coloured worker friends had been beaten up by "Jordan's thugs"', which Jordan dismissed as 'nonsense' before winding up.[149]

Jordan was also invited to speak at the Oxford Union in January 1966, although, as Jackson notes, 'this event was subsequently cancelled as the organizers felt that the event would only end up being wrecked by opponents'.[150] As well as these invitations to speak, Jordan was also interviewed by several student newspapers (including student publications at the University of Manchester, the University of Warwick, Manchester Metropolitan University and Aberystwyth University).[151]

Of the various far right figures in post-war Britain, Oswald Mosley and Colin Jordan were probably the most famous and generated the most headlines, although Jeffrey Hamm, A.K. Chesterton, John Tyndall, John Bean and Martin Webster all received a fair amount of publicity from the press, particularly around the political stunts and public displays that these far right figures took part in. While the various student groups that invited Mosley and Jordan to speak or debate at various universities predominantly spruiked the principle of free speech and allowing 'minority' or controversial views to be heard, these two far right leaders were invited because of their notoriety. Although Mosley was described by many of those who invited him as a brilliant orator, it was the controversy and publicity that a Mosley speech would create that often drove people to book him for student union debates. Jordan was similar in this regard, as he had achieved national attention in the late 1950s and early 1960s. Not only was Jordan invited to speak at Southampton and Oxford (although this invitation was later withdrawn), several student newspapers published interviews with Jordan in the mid-1960s.

There are several possible reasons why the student press decided to interview Jordan, with one being a student indulgence in contrarianism and shock, particularly as there was a broader growth in student rebellion in the mid-to-late 1960s in Britain (and around the world). From the various student groups that invited Mosley and Jordan, it seems that in many instances, it was Conservative and Liberal groups which supported inviting them, while Labour and other communist or socialist groups opposed – although there were often divisions within these groups over these invitations. For example, the Cambridge University Conservative

Association was divided in 1961 over whether to invite Mosley to speak, with future ministers Kenneth Clarke and Michael Howard at odds over this (Clarke was for inviting Mosley and Howard opposed).[152]

Mosley and Jordan, who personally benefitted from these occasions, used these speaking events as opportunities to legitimise themselves and their ideologies. Mosley in particular believed that he had been denied his rightful place in British political leadership and craved legitimacy. Presenting himself at these debates as a person of interest worth engaging with, these student audiences reinforced Mosley's ego, while at the same time, Mosley relished the controversy that surrounded him.

There is some indication that the Union Movement saw the tactic of speaking at universities as a way to recruit youth, who they believed were rejecting 'the Old Gang' in the 1950s and supposedly looked to Mosley 'as a leader who can inspire'.[153] In the late 1950s and early 1960s, the Union Movement was frustrated at being banned from holding meetings in public halls in several London boroughs, and used university debates as alternative recruiting grounds.[154] After Mosley was banned from speaking at the University of Leicester, but allowed to speak at Oxford, *Action* declared that the 'Union Movement's progress in the universities is frightening the old parties' and that the 'old world fights back with the only weapon it possesses – suppression'. [155] But as the 1960s progressed, it became clear that the majority of youth were not willing to listen to Mosley and other far right cranks, as much as they looked to youth to regenerate their movements.

As the student movement started to grow in Britain in the mid-to-late 1960s, radicalised by the Vietnam War, increasing strike action by the trade unions, apartheid in South Africa and corresponding struggles in the United States, there were increased protests against various right-wing figures who spoke at universities, extending beyond protests against figures like Mosley or Jordan. For example, students at Essex University protested against Enoch Powell in March 1968 (weeks before his infamous 'Rivers of Blood' speech),[156] while an official from the US Embassy had paint thrown over him at the University of Sussex in February 1968 as part of a student protest against the war in Vietnam.[157] Student protests on campuses escalated in the late 1960s and early 1970s, with much ire directed towards politicians and other figures from the right who visited universities. It is within this context of a rising student radicalism that the framework for the creation of the 'no platform' policy was established.

Conclusion

At the emergency conference of the National Union of Students in June 1974 when students debated the recent introduction of the 'no platform' policy, John McGeown, a Trotskyist activist at the University of Kent, conjured up the past deeds of anti-fascists in order to provide a narrative for 'no platform' policy of the present. McGeown proposed a resolution declaring: 'Conference believes that no restrictions should be made in the fight against racialism and fascism, a tradition established by working people against the British Union of Fascists in the Battle of Cable Street.'[158]

The anti-fascist struggle of the 1930s provided inspiration as a triumphant moment for both the left and Jewish communities in the post-war era and as an example of successful anti-fascist techniques. In the era of 'no platform', which began nearly four decades later, the fight against fascism during the inter-war years was seen as the dawn of a struggle, beginning against the BUF, that continued into the 1970s, then against the National Front.

Oswald Mosley attempted to portray the BUF as the protectors of free speech against the 'Reds' and claimed that anti-fascists were an unruly mob that sought to shut down those who opposed them. Despite warnings from anti-fascists, a number of politicians and journalists stressed that the BUF and Mosley had a right to speak, and only started to walk back from this position when it was evident that the BUF was willing to use excessive force against its foes.

In reaction to the rise of the British Union of Fascists, the anti-fascist movement grew in Britain during the 1930s. With an eye to events on the continent, various sections of British society (including Communists, Jews and trade unionists, among others) came together to oppose Mosley and his Blackshirts. Several protest tactics were developed during this period that influenced the actions of anti-fascists and anti-racists in the post-war period, particularly evoked in the proposal of 'no platform' for fascists in the 1970s.

First, there was heckling of Mosley and his supporters, which began when he started the New Party in 1931 and continued all through the years that the BUF existed. The 'heckler's veto' was widely recognised as part of the democratic right to freedom of speech in Britain, although police had discretionary powers under the Public Meetings Act 1908 to prevent breaches of the peace.[159] Anti-fascists used this to great effect to disrupt public meetings of the New Party and the BUF. As the BUF's paramilitary tendencies came to the fore 1933–34, heckling often provoked a violent response and anti-fascists attempted to use this to further disrupt public BUF events.

Second, there were the more sustained disruptions by anti-fascists who sought to provoke increasingly violent confrontations with the BUF's paramilitary squads, who acted as Mosley's bodyguards. Historians have often seen the events at Olympia as part of a turning point in the fortunes of the BUF and Mosley, revealing that the BUF were not interested in free speech, but in the brutal putting down of any dissent.

David Renton has recently noted that while the term 'no platform' is usually used to mean any means by which to deny the far right the opportunity to spread its message, in the late 1940s, anti-fascists employed tactics that included physically denying fascists a platform, or removing them from it.[160] As shown in this chapter, this tactic was also known as 'jumping the pitch' and was used by militant anti-fascists, such as those who belonged to the 43 Group, as well as the CPGB and RCP. At a time when British fascism was possibly at its lowest ebb, fascists still attempted to provoke, recruit and organise across the country (particularly in the East End of London) and anti-fascists used several tactics to stop this, including physically disrupting fascist meetings, heckling fascist speakers and campaigning for laws to be implemented against anti-Semitism. This resistance to the re-emergence of fascism in the immediate post-war period helped lead to the virtual collapse of Mosley's Union Movement in the early 1950s.

During this period of fascist reconfiguration Mosley did not just disappear, but found notoriety in public speaking opportunities, particularly at student union debates. Mosley's invitations to speak or debate at numerous universities including Oxford and Cambridge during the late 1950s and early 1960s, fed into the far right's trope of him as a contrarian against the status quo. Mosley was not the only far right person to be invited, with Colin Jordan being invited in the mid-1960s to Oxford and Southampton, as well as being interviewed for several student publications. Often invited by Conservative or Liberal student groups, these speaking engagements drew considerable protest from Labour, Communist and Jewish student groups. In these student actions of the 1950s and 1960s, we can see the antecedents of the eventual 'no platform' strategy in the 1970s.

Notes

1 Robert Benwick, *The Fascist Movement in Britain* (London: Allen Lane, 1972) p. 170.
2 Note that this Revolutionary Communist Party is a different organisation to the one that existed in the 1980s and 1990s.
3 Dave Hann, *Physical Resistance: A Hundred Years of Anti-Fascism* (Winchester: Zero Books, 2013) p. 23.
4 Matthew Worley, *Oswald Mosley and the New Party* (Houndmills: Palgrave Macmillan, 2010) pp. 118–119.
5 Ibid., p. 123.
6 Ibid.
7 Stephen Dorril, *Blackshirt: Sir Oswald Mosley and British Fascism* (London: Penguin 2007) pp. 189–190.
8 Martin Pugh, *'Hurrah for the Blackshirts!': Fascists and Fascism in Britain Between the Wars* (London: Pimlico, 2005) p. 223.
9 Michael A. Spurr, '"Living the Blackshirt Life": Culture, Community and the British Union of Fascists, 1932–1940', *Contemporary European History*, 12/3 (2003) p. 309.
10 Robert Skidelsky, *Oswald Mosley* (London: Papermac, 1990) p. 365.
11 *Daily Worker*, 7 June, 1934, p. 1.
12 *The Times*, 8 June, 1934, p. 14.
13 Ibid.
14 Ibid.
15 *Daily Worker*, 8 June, 1934, p. 1.
16 Ibid.
17 *The Times*, 9 June, 1934, p. 11.
18 *The Blackshirt*, 15 June, 1934, p. 3.
19 *Daily Worker*, 8 June, 1934, p. 1.
20 *The Times*, 9 June, 1934, p. 11.
21 *The Times*, 12 June, 1934, p. 14.
22 R. Palme Dutt, 'Notes of the Month', *Labour Monthly* (July 1934) p. 390.
23 Dutt, 'Notes of the Month', p. 390.
24 Hann, *Physical Resistance*, p. 46.
25 Richard C. Thurlow, 'The Straw That Broke the Camel's Back: Public Order, Civil Liberties and the Battle of Cable Street', in Tony Kushner & Nadia Valman (eds), *Remembering Cable Street: Fascism and Anti-Fascism in British Society* (London: Valentine Mitchell, 2000) pp. 83–84; Lawrence, 'Fascist Violence and the Politics of Public Order in Inter-War Britain', p. 263,
26 Pugh, *'Hurrah for the Blackshirts!'*, pp. 169–170.
27 Daniel Tilles, *British Fascist Antisemitism and Jewish Responses, 1932–40* (London: Bloomsbury, 2015) pp. 96–97.

28 Willie Thompson, *The Good Old Cause: British Communism, 1920–1991* (London: Pluto Press, 1992) p. 218.
29 Thurlow, 'The Straw That Broke the Camel's Back', p. 88.
30 Nigel Copsey, *Anti-Fascism in Britain* (Abingdon: Routledge, 2017) p. 39.
31 Ibid., pp. 51–52.
32 Ibid., p. 52.
33 Thurlow, 'The Straw That Broke the Camel's Back', pp. 74–94.
34 Copsey, *Anti-Fascism in Britain*, p. 70.
35 *The Blackshirt*, 1 February, 1933, p. 1.
36 Ibid.
37 Ibid.
38 Oswald Mosley, *Fascism: 100 Questions Asked and Answered* (London: BUF Publications, 1936) p. 56.
39 Mosley, *Fascism*, p. 56.
40 Ibid., p. 57.
41 Ibid.
42 *Action*, 24 October, 1936, p. 9.
43 Iain Channing, 'Blackshirts and White Wigs: Reflections on Public Order Law and the Political Activism of the British Union of Fascists' (University of Plymouth: unpublished Ph.D. thesis, 2014) p. 170.
44 Oswald Mosley, *Tomorrow We Live* (London: BUF, 1938) p. 20.
45 Ibid., p. 20.
46 Ibid., p. 21.
47 Ibid., p. 22.
48 *Action*, 24 October, 1936, p. 9.
49 *Daily Worker*, 11 June, 1934, p. 3.
50 *Daily Worker*, 28 September, 1937, p. 5.
51 Cited in *Daily Worker*, 11 June, 1934, p. 3.
52 *Daily Worker*, 11 June, 1934, p. 3.
53 Dutt, 'Notes of the Month', pp. 398–399.
54 Ibid., p. 399.
55 Laurence Brown, 'Reactions in British and French Universities to the Spanish Civil War: A Comparative History' (University of York: unpublished Ph.D. thesis, 1998) p. 84.
56 *Daily Worker*, 23 November, 1938, p. 4.
57 Dave Renton, *Red Shirts and Black: Fascists and Anti-Fascists in Oxford in the 1930s* (Oxford: Ruskin College Library, 1996) p. 4.
58 *The Times*, 2 May, 1933, p. 11.
59 Renton, *Red Shirts and Black*, p. 10.
60 *The Times*, 5 May, 1933, p. 11.
61 Renton, *Red Shirts and Black*, pp. 38–39.
62 *The Times*, 26 May, 1936, p. 18.
63 Renton, *Red Shirts and Black*, p. 38.
64 See, Skidelsky, *Oswald Mosley*, pp. 412–415; Cullen, 'Political Violence', p. 259; Renton, *Red Shirts and Black*, pp. 38–41; Copsey, *Anti-Fascism in Britain*, p. 42.
65 Duncan Bowie, *Reform and Revolt in the City of Dreaming Spires: Radical, Socialist and Communist Politics in the City of Oxford, 1830–1980* (London: University of Westminster Press, 2018) p. 192.
66 Renton, *Red Shirts and Black*, pp. 42–46.
67 Mark Neocleous, *Fascism* (Milton Keynes: Open University Press, 1997) p. xi.
68 David Renton, *Fascism, Anti-Fascism and the State* (Houndmills: Palgrave Macmillan, 2000) p. 74.
69 Edward Thompson, *Fascist Threat to Britain* (London: CPGB pamphlet, 1947) p. 12.
70 Thompson, *Fascist Threat to Britain*, p. 14.
71 Ibid.

72 Daniel Sonabend, *We Fight Fascists: The 43 Group and the Their Forgotten Battle for Post-War Britain* (London: Verso, 2019) pp. 100–101. For further discussion of the relationship between the 43 Group and the Communist Party, see: Evan Smith, *British Communism and the Politics of Race* (Leiden: Brill, 2017) pp. 55–57.
73 Morris Beckman, *The 43 Group* (London: Centerprise Publications, 1993) p. 31.
74 Beckman, *The 43 Group*, p. 31.
75 Ibid., p. 32.
76 Dave Hann, *Physical Resistance: A Hundred Years of Anti-Fascism* (London: Zero Books, 2013) p. 172.
77 Ibid., pp. 172–173.
78 Henry Srebrnik, *London Jews and British Communism, 1935–1945* (London: Vallentine Mitchell, 1995, p. 75.
79 *Hansard*, 24 February, 1949, col. 2009.
80 Renton, *Fascism, Anti-Fascism and the State*, pp. 109–110.
81 Copsey, *Anti-Fascism in Britain*, p. 56; Richard C. Thurlow, 'The Straw That Broke the Camel's Back: Public Order, Civil Liberties and the Battle of Cable Street', in Kushner & Valman, *Remembering Cable Street*, p. 91.
82 Renton, *Fascism, Anti-Fascism and Britain in the 1940s*, pp. 101–129.
83 Copsey, *Anti-Fascism in Britain*, pp. 88–89; Renton, *Fascism, Anti-Fascism and Britain in the 1940s*, pp. 75–76.
84 Renton, *Fascism, Anti-Fascism and Britain in the 1940s*, p. 76.
85 *Hansard*, 31 July, 1947, col. 66w.
86 Copsey, *Anti-Fascism in Britain*, p. 83.
87 *Daily Worker*, 1 December, 1947, p. 6.
88 'Free Speech and Anti-Semitism', 25 July, 1946, p. 8, File Report 2411–2, Mass Observation Online Archive.
89 Ibid., pp. 14–15.
90 Renton, *Fascism, Anti-Fascism and Britain in the 1940s*, p. 83.
91 Graham Macklin, *Very Deeply Dyed in Black: Sir Oswald Mosley and the Resurrections of British Fascism after 1945* (London: I.B. Tauris, 2007) p. 37.
92 *Daily Worker*, 24 September, 1946, p. 1.
93 Renton, *Fascism, Anti-Fascism and Britain in the 1940s*, p. 58; Jackson, *Colin Jordan and Britain's Neo-Nazi Movement*, pp. 51–54.
94 Macklin, *Very Deeply Dyed in Black*, p. 37.
95 Ibid.
96 Ted Grant, *The Menace of Fascism: What It Is and How to Fight It* (London: RCP pamphlet, 1948) p. 5.
97 *Daily Worker*, 24 October, 1947, p. 1.
98 *Daily Worker*, 21 May, 1947, p. 6.
99 *Isis*, 14 May, 1947, p. 17.
100 Ibid.
101 *The Times*, 11 March, 1946, p. 2.
102 Jackson, *Colin Jordan and Britain's Neo-Nazi Movement*, pp. 48; 53.
103 Ibid., p. 54.
104 *Belfast Newsletter*, 10 May, 1954, p. 4.
105 *Varsity*, 8 May, 1954, pp 1; 16.
106 *Union*, 22 May, 1954, p. 3.
107 *Daily Mail*, 12 May, 1954, p. 3.
108 Ibid.
109 Ibid.
110 *Daily Express*, 12 May, 1954, p. 5.
111 *Daily Mirror*, 13 May, 1954, p. 2.
112 Ibid.
113 Ibid.
114 Ibid.

115 *The Times*, 25 October, 1957, p. 10.
116 Ibid.
117 *The Times*, 25 April, 1960, p. 7.
118 *Varsity*, 30 April, 1960, p. 1.
119 *Action* (May 1960) p. 12.
120 Letter from Peter Temple-Morris to Oswald Mosley, 25 April, 1960, OMD 1/1/4/10, Oswald Mosley Papers, University of Birmingham.
121 Ibid.
122 Ibid.
123 *The Times,* 20 May, 1960, p. 14.
124 *Cherwell*, 21 May, 1960, p. 4.
125 Skidelsky, *Oswald Mosley*, p. 15.
126 *Action*, 1 February, 1961, p. 12.
127 Ibid.
128 Ibid.
129 *Cherwell*, 28 January, 1961, p. 1.
130 *Cherwell*, 1 February, 1961, p. 1.
131 Ibid.
132 See: *Action*, 21 November, 1961, p. 2; *Action*, 15 November, 1962, p. 2.
133 Stephen Dorril, *Blackshirt: Sir Oswald Mosley and British Fascism* (London: Penguin Books, 2007) p. 622.
134 *The Times*, 1 March, 1961, p. 5.
135 Ibid.
136 *The Guardian*, 3 December, 1960, p. 12.
137 Ibid.
138 Ibid.
139 *The Guardian*, 21 February, 1961, p. 3.
140 Ibid.
141 *Daily Mail*, 22 February, 1961, p. 5.
142 *The Ripple*, 1 March, 1961, p. 1.
143 Ibid., p. 2.
144 *The Guardian*, 21 February, 1961, p. 3.
145 *The Ripple*, 1 March, 1961, p. 4.
146 Jackson, *Colin Jordan and Britain's Neo-Nazi Movement*, p. 134.
147 *Wessex News*, 11 November, 1965, p. 3.
148 Ibid.
149 Ibid.
150 Jackson, *Colin Jordan and Britain's Neo-Nazi Movement*, p. 134.
151 Ibid., pp. 134–135.
152 Kenneth Clarke, *Kind of Blue: A Political Memoir* (London: Macmillan, 2016) pp. 25–26.
153 *Union*, 29 May, 1954, p. 1.
154 *Action*, 27 February, 1959, p. 5; *Action*, December 1960, p. 6.
155 *Action*, 1 March, 1961, p. 12.
156 *The Times*, 16 March, 1968, p. 5.
157 John W. Young, *David Bruce and Diplomatic Practice: An American Ambassador in London, 1961–69* (London: Bloomsbury, 2014) p. 157.
158 NUS, *Minutes of Extraordinary Conference* (London: NUS, 1974) p. 35.
159 Iain Channing, 'Freedom of Expression from the "Age of Extremes" to the "Age of Terror": Reflections of Public Order Law and the Legal Responses to Political and Religious Extremism in 1930s Britain and the Post 9/11', *Law, Crime and History*, 1/2 (2011) p. 43.
160 David Renton, 'When No Platforming Really Meant No Platforms', *Lives; Running*, 7 December, 2018, https://livesrunning.wordpress.com/2018/12/07/when-no-platforming-really-did-mean-no-platforms/ (accessed 14 December, 2018).

3

THE STUDENT MOVEMENT AND THE PRELUDE TO 'NO PLATFORM'

As much as the policy of 'no platform' owed to the tradition of left-wing anti-fascism (as outlined in the previous chapter), it was developed in the context of the student movement in Britain that had grown since the mid-to-late 1960s. The student movement was part of a wider wave of industrial militancy and cultural radicalism that swept across the country at this time, responding to national and international factors. This included, but was not limited to, the far left that had historically been at the forefront of the struggle against fascism and racism in Britain. The previous chapter showed that socialists, Labour Party and Jewish students had often joined together to protest against fascist and far right speakers in the 1950s and early 1960s, following on from the anti-fascist action against Mosley and other fascists in the late 1940s. By the late 1960s, Mosley's public image had faded somewhat and other controversial speakers were invited to university campuses, in particular the Tory MP Enoch Powell, as well as Conservative politicians connected to the right-wing Monday Club. As Powell made a name for himself with his anti-immigrationist rhetoric, he was invited on several occasions by student Conservative associations to speak, which attracted significant student protest. Representatives from the Monday Club, such as Haltemprice MP Patrick Wall, were also invited onto campus and provoked student dissent. Unlike the protests of the 1950s and 1960s against Mosley, the resistance to Powell and Wall took place within a broader groundswell of student radicalism that drew greater numbers and sustained opposition, especially as the university authorities attempted to clamp down on protest activity, such as that against Powell. For example, the protest against a visit by Powell to Essex University in February 1968 was the catalyst for a lengthy period of radicalism on campus. This chapter outlines how the student movement reacted to the presence of Powell on campus in the late 1960s and how this contributed to the development of the tactics and rhetoric used in the opposition to the National Front and the Monday Club under the 'no platform' policy in the mid-1970s.

The chapter also explores other incidents towards the end of the radical era of the student movement, just prior to the creation of the 'no platform' policy. Before the NUS formalised the 'no platform' policy and put forward a strict position towards the invitation of fascist and far right speakers, the response to individual speakers was much more haphazard, with various student activist groups reacting in different ways. In the year leading up to the 1974 policy being introduced, there were two incidents that acted as a prelude to a formal policy needing to be implemented. The first was the protest against psychologist Hans Eysenck in May 1973 at the London School of Economics, which attracted student protests, but was marred by the violent actions from members of the tiny Maoist group, the Communist Party of England (Marxist-Leninist). The second was the successful occupation of a lecture theatre at the University of Sussex in June of the same year by student activists in opposition to American academic Samuel P. Huntington, who had previously advised the US government on Vietnam. Both events were portrayed as a serious threat to freedom of speech at British universities, but also met with resistance from within the student unions on both campuses. This chapter shows that before the National Union of Students eventually adopted the 'no platform' policy, student action against far right speakers on campus was much more varied, with these incidents at the beginning and the end of the era of heightened student radicalism highlighting the localised reactions to the invitation of these speakers.

The student movement in Britain

The emergence of the student movement in Britain in the mid-to-late 1960s was the result of a series of domestic and international factors. Crucially there was an expansion of the higher education sector in the post-war period and a larger cross-section of society could now afford to go to university. At the same time, there was generational shift in the country, with those born during and after the Second World War entering the universities. At the height of the post-war boom, the younger generation had witnessed Harold Wilson's Labour government take over after 13 years of Conservative rule, offering a new way forward and embracing the science and technology of the era (as demonstrated by his 'white heat' speech at the 1963 Labour Party conference)[1] – solidified by his second electoral victory in 1966 shortly after England won the World Cup. However, as Andrew Scott Crines has written, 'the future didn't materialise in the way Wilson expected or hoped for',[2] and many younger persons were disillusioned with the economic and social realities of Britain in the 1960s.

Students at British universities were also influenced by events happening elsewhere around the world. In particular, the students looked to the United States where the civil rights movement and the free speech movement at universities such as California–Berkeley were making international headlines, as well as the movement formed in opposition to the Vietnam War. On both sides of the Atlantic, the anti-Vietnam War movement had mobilised many young people and drawn them into the orbit of radical politics. As Martin Jacques wrote in *Marxism Today* in 1974:

> The Vietnam war in fact had two obvious consequences. Firstly, it was largely responsible for changing the international outlook of large sections of youth, at least in their view of imperialism and the third world, if not as yet in their view of the socialist world. Secondly, the example and methods of the Vietnamese struggle, particularly the Tet offensive, exercised a profound influence on the attitude of significant sections of students towards the nature of British capitalism and the forms which the revolutionary struggle at home might take.[3]

Closer to home, the civil rights movement in Northern Ireland was beginning to emerge in the mid-1960s and further afield, the first wave of the Cultural Revolution in China was underway. Both of these events were followed with interest by British students as the end of the decade neared. By 1968, the burgeoning student movement in Britain was invigorated by an upsurge in radicalism in both Western and Eastern Europe, as well as in North America, Asia and the Middle East.[4] As the front page of the radical journal *Black Dwarf* declared in June 1968, 'We Shall Fight, We Shall Win – Paris, London, Rome, Berlin'.[5]

Traditionally the National Union of Students had been the peak body for student representation in Britain, although as Jodi Burkett had noted, its constitution, until 1969, did not allow the NUS to engage in political activism outside of the realm of the specific concerns of students.[6] As Burkett has shown, the NUS, at times, circumvented these restrictions by actively campaigning around the concerns of international students in Britain and students internationally.[7] The long standing activism of the NUS with regards to the plight of international students is one of the reasons why the policy of 'no platform' was incorporated into a broader statement about combating the racism faced by international students in Britain in the early 1970s.

While individual universities had various left groups during the first half of the twentieth century, the emergence of the first new left in the late 1950s signalled the existence of a student left that existed beyond party structures. An example of this was the publication of the *Universities and Left Review*, edited by Stuart Hall, which merged with E.P. Thompson and John Saville's *The New Reasoner* in 1960 to become the *New Left Review*. Scholars, such as Paul Blackledge, have shown that the first new left occupied a space between the Communist Party, the Labour Party and the various Trotskyist groups, most prominently the Socialist Labour League (SLL), and was increasingly attracted to single-issue social movements, like the Campaign for Nuclear Disarmament, rather than party politics. However, Nick Thomas has argued against seeing the left and the student movement as synonymous, although there was much overlap between the two.[8] Students made up a significant section of the new left in the late 1950s and early 1960s and did so again in the mid-to-late 1960s, with the notion of 'student power' becoming a major theme of the '1968' generation.[9]

Member of the International Socialists (IS) and 1968-er David Widgery described the NUS as 'the student's muffler'[10] and the NUS was decried by many of the more radical students in the mid-to-late 1960s for its conservatism. A number of alternative student groups and publications emerged in this period that tapped into the growing disgruntlement with the NUS and budding radicalism of the era's social movements, with possibly the most important being the Radical Student Alliance (which brought together students from the left of the Labour Party and the Communist Party, as well as independent socialists). The RSA was created in February 1967 as an alternative to the NUS and rode the initial wave of student protest in Britain, but transformed into the Broad Left student alliance in 1969, while at the same time overtaken by the Revolutionary Socialist Student Federation (RSSF).[11] The RSSF was primarily a vehicle for International Socialists and the International Marxist Group, invigorated by the radicalism found in the Vietnam Solidarity Campaign (VSC), but also included other Trotskyists (such as those from Militant) and Maoists. Both the IS and IMG were enthusiastic about the revolutionary potential of the student movement, but the IMG was the left organisation that invested the most in its student activities. This is important, notably because in the lead up to the establishment of the 'no platform' policy in 1974, it was the IMG that drove this policy idea through the NUS.

Students and young people were heavily involved in the wider protest and radical movements of the mid-to-late 1960s and early 1970s, taking part in protest actions, such as demonstrations and marches on the streets, as well as on university campuses. Protest activity on campuses occurred during the early-to-mid-1960s, often around students' disagreement with the rules and traditions of the universities – the influx of students in the post-war era challenged the conservatism of the higher education system that had previously been for the privileged few. As Nick Thomas has argued, students, as well as young people more broadly, occupied a new economic and social space created by the post-war boom and became more willing to challenge authority and traditional societal values.[12] From protests against the regulation of university life, students across Britain became more willing to engage in other forms of protest and the university campus became another space of political contest.

In popular memory, the prevailing image of the student movement in Britain was the sit-in. Inspired by the civil rights and student movements in the United States (as well as the 'sit-downs' of the anti-nuclear Committee of 100 in the early 1960s), the sit-in was viewed as a non-violent tactic of civil disobedience that would bring attention to the violence of the authorities that attempted to move the protestors. As Caroline Hoefferle has written:

> Sit-ins required students to occupy part of the university continuously and involved considerably more planning and dedication than simply showing up at a demonstration or heckling a speaker ... More so than demonstration marches or pickets, they also represented a direct challenge to the authorities, who normally controlled university facilities, and as such demonstrate the increasingly confrontational nature of student rights protests in 1968.[13]

First used at a protest at the London School of Economics in March 1967 (against the suspension of students that had earlier in the year protested the appointment of the incoming LSE Director), the use of the tactic spread across British universities in the next year, with similar protests occurring at Aston, Essex, Hull, Hornsey, Leeds, Birmingham and Bristol throughout 1968.

These student protests were boosted by a wider surge in industrial militancy and cultural radicalism in Britain, described by Chris Harman as the 'British upturn',[14] as well as the radical social movements happening across the world at the time. The intersection of local university-specific concerns with the events occurring at the national and global level empowered students to feel that they were part of something much bigger, with Hoefferle writing: 'British students attempted to use their universities as bases for expressing their political dissent, but when university authorities reacted with tough disciplinary actions, students turned their protests toward demanding more freedom and power within the university itself'.[15]

Over the next half decade, student protests against university disciplinary procedures, as well as university governance and student living, mobilised several strikes and occupations on campuses and in halls of residence, tapping into the increased radicalism of the student movement of the era.

Protests against controversial speakers before 'no platform'

Protesting Powell and the Monday Club in the late 1960s

As demonstrated in the last chapter, protests against fascist and far right speakers occurred decades before the development of the 'no platform' policy by the NUS. In the heady days of the student movement in the late 1960s and early 1970s, there were numerous protests against controversial speakers from the right that preceded the official creation of the 'no platform' policy. This section will look at three examples of this – the protests against Enoch Powell and the Monday Club's Patrick Wall in the late 1960s, the protests against the psychologist Hans Eysenck at LSE in 1973 and those against American political scientist Samuel P. Huntington at the University of Sussex in the same year.

Enoch Powell was the Shadow Secretary for Defence in the mid-to-late 1960s, and during the 1967–68 period he started make several public pronouncements against Commonwealth migration. Shirin Hirsch has suggested that Powell looked at the increasing racial tensions in the United States and believed that immigration in Britain would replicate these tensions.[16] In December 1967, Powell complained that the BBC had broadcast an interview with the Black Power activist Stokely Carmichael and extracted an apology from the BBC's News and Current Affairs Editor.[17]

At the same time, the increase of South Asians being expelled from Kenya worried both the Conservative opposition and the Labour government. Powell, alongside fellow Tory MP Duncan Sandys, was instrumental in putting pressure on the Wilson government to rush through the Commonwealth Immigrants Act

1968,[18] which divided Commonwealth migrants into 'patrials' (those who had ancestral ties in Britain) and 'non-patrials' (those who did not). This led to Powell vocally opposing migration from the Caribbean, Africa and South Asia. Powell's speech in April 1968 in Birmingham, euphemistically titled the 'Rivers of Blood' speech, is seen as a turning point in British race relations, but two months before, he had made a similarly incendiary speech to the Walsall Conservative Association.[19] This preceded a visit he made to Essex University in February 1968, which provoked student protests.

In late February 1968, Enoch Powell and the local Conservative MP for Colchester, Antony Buck, visited Essex University, with Powell giving a private address to the university's Conservative Association and another public address on poetry for the Literary Society. A bomb threat was made prior to Powell's arrival, which did not deter Powell from speaking.[20] A number of students gathered around Powell and Buck as they left the university, damaging Buck's car in the process. Buck described the incident in Parliament:

> After a brief pause and a Press conference, my right hon. Friend and I went to my car, which was nearby … A hard core of students started to indulge in open violence, rocking my car and shouting obscenities. It was outrageous to hear anyone with a war record such as my right hon. Friend's described as a Fascist, interspersed with four-letter words. There was a noisy crash and a large, hard object descended on the bonnet of my car. I was livid; it was a new car. I was so angry that I got out of the car and it took a certain degree of self-restraint to prevent myself dealing summarily with the person who I thought, perhaps wrongly, threw the missile.
>
> Having restrained myself I got back into the car. Six people or so were on the bonnet rocking it up and down. I revved up the car with great caution because I did not want to harm these poor misguided and stupid people.[21]

While Powell's increasingly racist pronouncements on immigration were a cause for the students to protest, like other student protests at the time, the Vietnam War also became a factor in the protest. Andrew Mack, one of the radical students involved in the protest, wrote to the *Essex County Standard*, arguing that as Powell was a member of the Conservatives, he supported the American war in Vietnam and the propping up of South Vietnam.[22] Mack stated:

> By associating themselves with American policies, to us the Powells and the Wilsons of this country come to symbolise these policies. Thus when Mr Powell, in addressing us blandly talks of 'unavoidable inhumanities,' can he really be surprised that instead of gentlemanly debate he gets shouts of disgust and bitter derision?[23]

The university administration sought to discipline several students involved in this fracas, which led to further protests at the university, similar to responses by students at other institutions when the university administration had tried to reprimand protesting students. The *Daily Express* reported that more than 100 students 'trapped the Vice Chancellor … in his office', who were 'furious because six students had been threatened with punishment' following the confrontation the previous month with the Conservative MPs.[24] This action against the university administration stemmed from a feeling that the university should not interfere in matters in which the police had jurisdiction. An editorial in the student newspaper *Wyvern* explained that students 'protested strongly at the University's role as law enforcer' and argued that 'where necessary, the ordinary processes of law could be used to deal with alleged offences'.[25] Even the Conservative Association allegedly called for those students to be made to pay for any damage caused, but did 'not want a punishment affecting the academic career of any student'.[26]

In the end, there were no charges brought against the students involved in the protest against Powell, while three students were made to contribute to the costs of the repairs to Buck's car and to the Fire Brigade for setting off a fire alarm.[27] Buck complained about this and was quoted in the *Essex County Standard* as saying, 'It is an inadequate outcome for a matter involving violence' and declared that he would be bringing this up with the Vice-Chancellor.[28] In the aftermath of the protest against Powell and Buck, the university's Liberal Union complained that it regarded it 'as unsafe for visiting speakers to attend meetings', cancelling a speech by a representative from the South Vietnamese Embassy.[29]

The protests against Powell were at the beginning of a sustained period of radical activity at Essex University, with Powell's visit often overshadowed in histories of the university's student radicalism by the protests against Dr Thomas Inch, a chemical defence scientist from Porton Down, in May 1968 – at the height of the Vietnam War and the controversy over the United States' alleged use of chemical weapons. But Powell continued to be protested at other universities throughout 1968 and into the following year.

Powell was not the only right-wing MP who was vocal about immigration to be faced with student protests in the late 1960s. Patrick Wall was a leading figure in the Monday Club, a group of right-wing Conservative MPs that had formed in response to Harold Macmillan's 'Winds of Change' speech in 1960 and opposed British decolonisation in Africa. The Monday Club particularly campaigned around the issue of support for Rhodesia's Unilateral Declaration of Independence, as well as against continued Commonwealth immigration to Britain.[30] As Mark Pitchford and Camilla Schofield have shown, the positions held by the Monday Club, markedly by Wall himself, chimed closely with the British fascist groups, such as the League of Empire Loyalists and the National Front, and with Enoch Powell.[31] Powell's national notoriety, alongside the Monday Club's vocal campaigns inside and outside the Conservative Party and the establishment of the National Front, produced a moment in the late 1960s where a pro-empire and anti-immigration mood captured the national consciousness of the British right, further antagonised by the global events of '1968'. Like Powell, the Monday Club used speaking engagements at universities as opportunities to combat the changes of the time.

In May 1968, Wall and his wife were invited to the University of Leeds by the Conservative Association at the university, where Wall gave a talk on Rhodesia and British foreign policy. The *Daily Telegraph* reported that Wall was 'constantly heckled' during his talk before a scuffle broke out as the Walls tried to leave the meeting room while around 300 students 'ran riot'.[32] *The Times* described the incident in further detail:

> Ugly scenes developed as stewards intervened to protect the couple as they walked to the Students' Union refectory for lunch. The students blocked their way by lying down in their path.
>
> Shouting slogans, including 'Fascist pig', some students trampled over Mrs. Wall as she lay weeping on the steps of the refectory. Stewards linked arms and she was hustled to safety inside the building.[33]

While Sheila Wall put the commotion down to 'a case of pre-examination nerves and damn bad manners', Patrick Wall called the students' actions 'deplorable' and claimed that he had been spat at by the protesting students.[34]

In a letter to *The Times*, Mrs Wall argued that 'this kind of behaviour [was] designed to prevent Members of Parliament speaking at universities', and if these actions were successful, 'then a small minority of apparent anarchists will … have gained their objective in denying free speech'.[35] An editorial in *The Times* a few days later described the protests against Powell and Wall as 'the silencing of opponents by mob action' and lamented that the university was supposedly 'the breeding ground for this form of mindless opposition'.[36] Describing universities as places of 'intellectual liberty, critical inquiry, and free traffic in ideas', the editorial claimed that these places of higher learning failed 'if the young do not acquire … , or if they there unlearn, the habit of tolerating the expression of opinions contrary to their own'.[37] Similar to tropes that have been repeated over the last 50 years, students were seen as intolerant of contrasting opinions, with some carrying their intolerance 'to the borders of violence or anarchy'.[38]

Like the protests against Powell at Essex earlier in the year, the hostile reception that Wall faced at Leeds led to disciplinary actions taken against several students, which in turn led to wider 'critique (and action resulting in occupation) of the University institution itself, via the dissatisfaction of Leeds students with the actions of the university's security service'.[39] Wall was eventually invited (and allowed) to speak again later in the year, despite significant student dissent at this decision,[40] but protests followed both Wall and Powell around the country as they visited various universities over the next year.

In late October 1968, Powell made a visit to Exeter University to speak to the university's Conservative Association. The *Daily Telegraph* reported that 2,000 students attended the speech, but Powell had to abandon his talk after 15 minutes as around 30 to 40 protestors disrupted proceedings, when '[f]ighting broke out, banners were torn and Mr. Powell was pelted with paper darts and marbles'.[41] The

Daily Express claimed that this was 'the first time in his life' that Powell had been 'howled down by chanting'.[42] Powell was quoted by the newspaper as saying:

> I have never had to halt a speech at a university before. But this is a new technique – it is not just me. Over the last few months it has become almost routine for Ministers and other speakers to suffer this sort of behaviour.[43]

The *Daily Telegraph* reported that the university's Young Socialist Student Society and Marxist Society had called for students to 'silence Powell by mass heckling', but emphasised that any protest should be non-violent.[44] The President of the Guild of Students at Exeter stated afterwards that they 'deplore[d] the actions of a minority of its members', adding, 'All members of a university should be prepared to tolerate and indeed protect the expression of unpopular opinions.'[45]

However, the response to a campus visit by Powell did not always result in significant protest by students. *The Times* reported that there were 'more cheers than protests among the 500 Reading University students' who attended a speech by Powell to the university's Conservative Association, as Powell positively referred back to 'rivers of blood' speech.[46]

In February the following year, the Conservative Association at University College London invited Powell to speak to them. In the lead up to the event, the students at UCL arranged for a day long teach-in, organised primarily by the Anthropology Department.[47] Students also wrote to the student newspaper, *Pi*, to complain about the hosting of Powell at the university. Philosophy student Brian Klug argued that not allowing Powell to speak did not infringe his right to free speech because Powell was 'able to sit at his desk in London and address an audience located elsewhere, as he has free and easy access to the public media', assisted by the fact that Powell was invited to speak at many more meetings than an ordinary student.[48] Klug further argued that Powell was 'not a member of UC Students' Union – or UC Conservative Association – and therefore [had] no right to speak, no more than Harold Wilson, Ho Chi Minh, or Mrs Bloggs has.'[49]

Justifying Powell's invitation, the Chairman of the Conservative Association, Robert Orme, heavily suggested that while he did not agree with Powell's views on immigration, Powell 'did pinpoint the problem', further arguing: 'The whole issue could not be first shoved under the carpet and therefore while Powell's language may be deplored, his speeches and the subsequent reaction, has thankfully brought the subject out into the open'.[50] Another student replied that Powell's speeches did not 'publicise a hitherto obscure phenomenon', but did 'crystallise it, reinforce it, rationalise it and Establishment-ise it'.[51]

Powell spoke at the university, but the venue had to be kept secret by the organisers, with the *Daily Express* reporting that '[e]ven Mr Powell was not told where he was to present until the very last moment'.[52] The teach-in, organised for the day of Powell's visit, was well-attended, with up to 300 or 400 people attending many of the sessions and addressed by figures such as Robin Blackburn and Obi Egbuna.[53] One of the worrying developments at this protest was that it attracted members of the National Front, who attempted to intimidate the students – a tactic that would be replicated throughout the 1970s. About 30 NF members were ejected by the police for their efforts and an altercation broke out between the NF and the protesting students.[54] Writing about his memories of this protest, Klug wrote in *The Guardian* in 2007:

> I shall not forget the impression made on [me] by one member of the National Front who came uninvited to the evening session at Friends House and indulged in his own creative understanding of 'freedom of expression' – smashing me across the face.[55]

The evening event at Friends House had seen the NF members attend and be allowed to speak from the floor before being shut down by other students and then removed by the police. An account by a member of the UCL Socialist Society, Trevor Pateman, in *Pi* explained that the NF had been granted the opportunity to speak 'as part of a quite unprincipled deal: we let you speak, and then you shut up', but the NF did not adhere to this.[56] Pateman explained in 2016 on his blog:

> There were National Front members in the audience (and more in the streets outside) who began to interrupt and heckle. The Chair of the meeting responded by inviting one of the hecklers onto the platform where he was handed a microphone. At that point, I walked off and went to sit in the audience. I found a seat next to Jonathan Miller who chided me for walking off – Why not let him have a microphone? He will only discredit himself.
>
> I doubt I had a Mandate which required me to walk off in the circumstances I just described. I was more likely responding to a distinction which we regularly drew between those racists with whom it was worth trying to debate and those hard-core racists who had no interest in debate themselves and who might well be backed up by heavies waiting to beat you up. The man who got the microphone had supporters not only in the hall but outside, some of them carrying offensive weapons and waiting for the chance to beat someone up, probably a lone black person straying into a side street. (I am pretty sure that the audience at this meeting was warned when the meeting closed to stick together in groups). So the man who had got the microphone was someone you didn't debate with and walking off the platform was just a symbolic expression of that view.[57]

The two reports of the teach-in and the protest in *Pi* complained that there was little press coverage of the teach-in, while Pateman objected that what press coverage there was focused on the National Front.[58] At the time, this fascist intimidation was a new development, but it is possible that the media were less interested in student protests against Powell nearly 12 months after the 'rivers of blood' speech – although the media continued to be fascinated with Powell's pronouncements on immigration for quite a few years after.

Eysenck at LSE

These protests against Powell and the Monday Club coincided with the early height of the student movement in Britain in 1968–69, but it wasn't until 1973–74 that the issue of student protests against controversial speakers on campus reached another crescendo. By this time, the initial enthusiasm of the student movement in Britain and across the globe had waned and by the early 1970s, it seemed that the revolutionary politics of the late 1960s had transformed into a defensive battle against the Conservatives under Edward Heath. Even the *Daily Mail*'s education correspondent asked sarcastically, 'Remember the massive demonstrations? The tearing down of the LSE gates, the Manchester and Essex sit-ins, the Warwick Files? ... What happened to the Revolution?'[59] By the time that the 'no platform' policy was introduced, Britain had been plunged into an economic crisis and many on the left feared that this crisis would be used by sections of the right to launch an authoritarian offensive on the progressive elements that had emerged from '1968'.

In mid-1973, two incidents occurred that anticipated the 'no platform' position that was formally adopted the following year – the disruption of a speech by psychologist Hans Eysenck at LSE and the protest against American professor Samuel Huntington giving a lecture at Sussex. Eysenck, alongside Arthur Jensen, was part of a controversial circle of psychologists that worked in the area of 'race' and IQ, with Eysenck producing a book titled *Race, Intelligence and Education* in the early 1970s. This 'scientific racism', as criticised by radical scientists in *Socialist Register*, sought to argue that differences in IQ between 'races' was informed by genetics.[60] In May 1973, the Social Science Society at LSE invited Eysenck to speak, an invitation which was opposed by a number of student groups. One of the most vocal was the LSE Afro-Asian Society, which had links to the tiny Maoist Communist Party of England (Marxist-Leninist). As well as at LSE, the CPE (M-L) had a base at the University of Birmingham and students from these two universities were heavily involved in protesting against Eysenck's proposed lecture.

The Afro-Asian Society distributed a leaflet prior to the event, titled 'Fascist Eysenck has no right to speak', which declared:

> Today, fascist Eysenck has been sent by his masters, the British imperialists of the London School of Economics to spew out more of his fascist propaganda. This represents not only a brazen attack on the progressive masses of students and staff at LSE but represents another step in the insidious scheme of British imperialism to provide a rationale to unleash fascist and racist attacks on the broad masses of the English people including the various national minorities.[61]

The Afro-Asian Society characterised Eysenck as a fascist who had no right to speak and that he was using LSE 'as a platform for his attacks on the working and oppressed people not only of Asia and Africa but also of England, Ireland, Scotland and Wales'.[62] The Society saw the opposition to Eysenck as part of a wider struggle against British imperialism, arguing that 'the broader masses have every right to prevent fascists from doing propaganda for the ruling class' and called for 'the progressive LSE students and staff … to exercise their right to oppose the fascist propaganda of H.J. Eysenck', as well as 'to vigorously develop mass democracy and mass denounciation [sic] to expose the anti-people and anti-science theories of Eysenck'.[63]

On 8 May 1973, Eysenck rose to speak in front of a crowd of around 400 to 500 people at LSE, but as the *Daily Telegraph* reported, '[e]ven before Prof. Eysenck had a chance to begin, heckling, catcalls and obscenities were flung at him'.[64] A vote was taken by the Social Science Society to determine whether Eysenck was to continue, but a section of the crowd was still vocal in their opposition to Eysenck speaking. The President of the London University Conservative Association, who was in attendance, described what happened next for the *Daily Telegraph*: 'About 15 students from the front two rows jumped over the table and dived in with their fists flying. They were hitting out in all directions.'[65] The newspaper further reported that Eysenck had 'had his spectacles smashed, his nose cut and his hair pulled'.[66]

The actions by the protestors were quickly condemned on all sides, from the media, politicians, other far left groups and the student union. The Chairman of the LSE Social Science Society and former (and future) Labour MP, David Winnick, was quoted in *The Guardian* as saying, 'We all deplore the methods used to break up the meeting. They were Fascist-like tactics of hooliganism and physical violence.'[67] Digby Jacks, the President of the NUS and CPGB member, said afterwards, 'This kind of display will only achieve greater credibility for Eysenck's views.'[68] An editorial in the *Daily Mirror* proposed, '[a]ny university students who are not prepared to allow peaceful discussion of unpalatable views ought not to be at a university' and called the students who were involved in 'a group of hoodlums'.[69] The Under-Secretary of State for the Department of Education and Science, Norman St John-Stevas stated that disagreements with Eysenck needed to be wielded through 'the weapon of dialogue and rational discourse and not by the fist of the thug'.[70]

Soon after the events unfolded, it was widely conveyed that the Communist Party of England (M-L) were behind the violent disruption, with students allegedly from the University of Birmingham (as well as other Birmingham-based activists) joining the CPE (M-L) members at LSE for their protest – although *The Times Higher Education Supplement* claimed that the 'Afro-Asian Society was prominently represented but its members only shouted interruptions'.[71] The *Birmingham Evening Mail* reported that 'Communist revolutionaries at Birmingham University … admitted [their] involvement in the incident when a professor was attacked and prevented from speaking at the London School of Economics'.[72] The other groups on the left were quick to disassociate themselves from the CPE (M-L). In the *Morning Star*, the Communist Party of Great Britain railed against the 'gutter journalism' of *The Sun* and other tabloids that attempted to lump the CPGB in with the Maoists.[73] The CPGB newspaper proclaimed, 'Whoever the people were who ignored the wishes of the great majority of LSE students at Tuesday's meeting and broke it up by violence, they were not Communists.'[74] The International Socialists Society at LSE also condemned the CPE (M-L) in the LSE student newspaper, *The Beaver*, writing:

> According to their philosophy everyone except themselves (and perhaps THE National Front!) are fascists. Reformists are 'social-fascists'. IS are 'Trotsky-Fascists'. Heath is a fascist. Eysenck is a fascist. This would be laughable if it were not for the fact that these tactics and politics are a mirror image of those which enabled the Nazis in Germany to come to power, without any real opposition from the Germany [sic] CP. It is extremely lucky that the Maoists have no following in the working class because beneath their physical and verbal militancy they are pursuing a disastrous course.[75]

The *Sunday Telegraph* suggested that the CPE (M-L) had 'worried' other left groups and 'now found themselves daubed with the same brush as the CPE'.[76] Chiming with the criticisms made by the IS students at LSE, this newspaper article stated that the 'CPE's jargon is so absurd a parody of that of other Maoist organisations that it is widely believed among Left-wing students that its funds derive from the Central Intelligence Agency acting in the role of agent provocateur'.[77] Meanwhile the IMG contingent at LSE criticised the CPE (M-L)'s tactics against Eysenck as a premature anti-fascist reaction, as Eysenck was 'not organising such a movement in society around his views … and thus the question for many students is turned into a clash over intellectual ideas.'[78] A flyer produced by the LSE Red Mole qualified this by asserting: 'In such circumstances tactically, though not in principle it was incorrect to stop Eysenck from speaking as the physical act to prevent him from speaking is not understood by the mass of students at this stage.'[79]

There was a call for the universities to expel the students involved in the fracas and for the police to investigate. However there was division in the LSE student union over whether to assist with any university or police investigations. *The Times* reported that some students felt that 'since an inquiry was going to be held anyway it was best that the union should conduct it', but this argument was unsuccessful, with the university administration announcing that they were conducting their own inquiry.[80] After a heated internal debate, the LSE student union declared the following motion:

> Whilst deprecating the violence of the two meetings on Tuesday we should prevent any student from being victimised over the incident.
>
> The School is holding an enquiry into the matter; exaggerated press statements have already called for any students involved to be sent down.
>
> We ask every student to refuse to co-operate with the School and to give them absolutely no time at all, or to claim they know nothing about the incidents.[81]

John Carr, the Senior Treasurer of the student union, wrote in *The Beaver* that the students also sought for the union to apologise to Eysenck and condemn the violence, but this was resisted by the International Socialists present.[82] Tim Potter from the International Socialist Society replied to this, saying that the IS students refused to support a motion to apologise 'because he is a racist' and that such a motion 'would play into the hands of the right-wing reaction'.[83] The IS Society argued that even though they condemned the actions of the CPE (M-L), 'all socialists must defend them against the right-wing witch-hunt being whipped up by the Press and being put into practice by the College authorities.'[84] The IMG at LSE also warned of a 'renewed offensive' by universities and the Conservative government against left-wing students, warning that the Eysenck affair would be used to attack students and the student unions.[85] The IMG further lamented that 'the attitude of the NUS Executive, the LSE Executive and the Communist Party only reinforces this attack by playing into the hands of the right wing and confuses students as to what is going on'.[86] In the end, however, it seems as though there was no action taken by police with regards to the attack on Eysenck. The Director of LSE, Walter Adams, complained in a letter to the *Daily Telegraph* that police had investigated the incident, claiming that this was because Eysenck was 'not willing to bring charges of assault'.[87]

The protest against Eysenck at LSE was soon followed by another incident of the shutting down of a lecture by a controversial academic. This time it was American academic Samuel P. Huntington, who was denied access to a lecture hall to address a crowd at the University of Sussex in June 1973. These two incidents were portrayed as a worrying trend among British students and as a rejection of academic freedom and freedom of speech.

Huntington at Sussex

Mostly known nowadays for his post-Cold War 'clash of civilisations' thesis, Huntington was an academic but worked closely with the US Pentagon during the late 1960s at the height of the Vietnam War. One of the concepts that Huntington pushed was 'forced draft urbanisation', which meant coercing Vietnamese people out of the rural areas (where support for the Viet Cong was strongest) into the urban areas, where influence from the US-backed regime in Saigon was stronger. As he wrote in an article in *Foreign Affairs* in 1968, to eliminate the control of the Viet Cong in the rural areas 'would require a much larger and more intense military and pacification effort than is currently contemplated by Saigon and Washington'.[88] Despite its academic language, anti-war activists argued that what Huntington proposed was an intense escalation of the war in Vietnam and an attack on the Vietnamese countryside, which was an influential idea in the Pentagon and the US administration. As Roy Edgely, one of the academics at Sussex who opposed Huntington speaking on campus in June 1973, wrote for *Radical Philosophy* in the aftermath of the incident at the university:

> Huntington's theory about forced-draft urbanisation must be construed as prescriptive, as a strategic justification of the American attack on rural South Vietnam in the past, and advice on how to respond to wars of national liberation in the future ... Huntington formulated his theory of forced-draft urbanisation in his role of consultant or adviser to the American government. He was to this extent part of the collective agent prosecuting the war in Vietnam, an agent that put into action policies that it also worked out in speech and thought.[89]

For what it was worth, Huntington was reported in the *Daily Telegraph* as claiming that in 1968 he stated that his 'unequivocal position was that the bombing should stop immediately' and had been convinced after visiting Vietnam of 'the undesirability of the war'.[90]

Huntington was invited by the Institute of Development Studies and the School of English and American Studies to give seminars at Sussex during a visit in June 1973. This was opposed by some academics and students at Sussex, including the Sussex Indochina Solidarity Committee, which was composed largely of IMG and IS students. Although Huntington wasn't speaking on the Vietnam War directly for either of the seminars he was preparing to give at Sussex, the activists felt that he needed to be challenged on his involvement in the US war effort. As one of the activists later reported for US journal *Science for the People*, it was directed by the seminar organisers that 'discussion on Indochina would not be appropriate', but Huntington was 'prepared to meet two or three students, in private afterwards, to discuss Indochina'.[91] Those who opposed Huntington speaking 'were not impressed by this' and therefore 'decided that Professor Huntington wasn't going to give a lecture on the Soldier in American Society or anything else, for that matter'.[92] The topic of 'forced draft urbanisantion', they argued, 'didn't seem like the kind of issue one would settle by having a reasonable, gentlemanly "debate"' and to do so would further 'the liberal myth of the university as a "market-place of ideas"'.[93]

More than 500 students protested against Huntington on the day of his proposed lecture, both inside the lecture theatre and outside. According to the University of Sussex administration, 400 gained access to the theatre (with usual capacity for 350) and another 150 remained outside[94] – although the correspondent for *Science for the People* claimed that 200 of those that attended were in opposition to those attempting to stop Huntington from talking.[95] The *Daily Telegraph* described the scene:

> The students, waving a red flag and carrying pictures of Chairman Mao and placards declaring that Fascists had no right to speak, crowded into the lecture theatre 20 minutes before Prof. Huntington was due to begin.
>
> Pandemonium broke out as rival groups tried to make their voices heard through a loud-speaker and the university authorities called off the lecture at the last minute.[96]

The lecture and the other scheduled seminar were both cancelled. Although the occupation of the lecture was a non-violent action, the university administration called off the talk 'when it became clear that to give the lecture would have involved an unacceptable risk of physical violence'.[97] Coming a month after the physical disruption of Eysenck's lecture at LSE, it is understandable that the university was nervous about proceedings getting out of control, although there was no evidence that the activists were likely to engage in any form of violent protest. The Director of the Institute of Development Studies, which was to also hold a seminar by Huntington, claimed in *The Times* that they had 'received an explicit threat' from the Sussex Indochina Solidarity Committee that they would 'occupy the building, unless the meeting [was] cancelled' and suggested that there was 'no alternative to avoid further risk of extreme disruption and violence'.[98] A spokesperson for the Committee was quoted as saying, '[o]ur objective was to stop the lecture without using violence. We are pleased to announce that our objective has been fulfilled'.[99]

In a statement by the university, it was acknowledged that 'the visiting professor suffered no violence or other discomforts' and that 'there was no violence to persons or damage to property despite the existence of such a large crowd in a confined space', but maintained that there had been the possibility of violence and that the event was cancelled to ensure Huntington's safety.[100] Professor of American Studies at Sussex, Marcus Cunliffe, reportedly said to the protestors, 'You have won a disgraceful victory.'[101] In his *Radical Philosophy* article, Edgely wrote that those who opposed Huntington 'were commonly regarded as "extremists"', but the actions taken were actually 'extremely mild and moderate'.[102] *The Guardian* stated that the police attended the university for the entire day, 'but the only incident was a brief clash between students and supporters of the National Front',[103] which again highlights the issue that the NF were trying to antagonise protesting students at universities in the period before the 'no platform' policy.

The response by the student union at Sussex was set out in a motion that declared that freedom of speech was important to the union and the university, but 'the Union uphold the right of free speech for all, so that speakers must acknowledge the right of students in ordered debate to ask such questions and express such opinions'.[104] In other words, the union could not 'undertake to uphold the right of free speech to any who refuse the right of students to reply'[105] – which is what was proposed by the organisers of the Huntington seminars. Like the student union position at LSE after the Eysenck affair, the student union at Sussex also expressed 'opposition to any punitive measures that may be contemplated against those students and faculty who took part in the demonstration'.[106] With the protest against Huntington coming shortly after the disruption at LSE, there were rumours that students from the London School of Economics and the University of Birmingham were involved in the protest. However both LSE and Birmingham University denied these claims.[107]

However, for many, the two events were inextricably linked. Inches of column space were dedicated to the spectre of student violence and the apparent end of free speech at British universities. An editorial in the *Daily Telegraph* proclaimed, '[r]ecent events suggest that universities are no longer firmly wedded to free speech and free academic inquiry'.[108] Another editorial in *The Guardian* questioned:

> If in face of such threats [to freedom of speech] university authorities and academic staffs generally decide to do nothing, they should not be surprised when Parliament and the public begin to believe that 'academic freedom' is a term which has lost its meaning. If the universities cease to defend it, will anyone else?[109]

After a number of academics wrote a letter to *The Guardian* supporting the protest against Huntington, former Labour Cabinet Minister Richard Crossman wrote in *The Times* that he didn't think it was in the past 'possible for anyone to sign such a letter and remain senior members of a university', implying that in the future academics who supported protests against certain speakers should be fired.[110] *The Times* reported that the General Secretary of the Association of University Teachers, Laurie Sapper, said that university staff had a 'special duty' to make clear that 'the use of violence and the shouting down of an opposing party were alien to the purposes and method of university education'.[111]

Others suggested a tougher 'law and order' response to these forms of protest. A journalist for the *Daily Telegraph* suggested universities could employ CCTV to 'identify agitators at demonstrations', arguing that the technology was being employed by the British Army in Northern Ireland and that such technology 'could be concealed in lecture rooms or other places where trouble was expected'.[112] However the journalist also acknowledged that universities had been 'reluctant to use such equipment for surveillance purposes as are university staff to inform on students' and quoted a spokesperson for the Committee of University Vice-Chancellors as saying, 'I am sure that most members of the committee would regard [the use of CCTV] as repugnant'.[113] On the same day, the newspaper also reported that the Freedom Under Law Group, a right-wing organisation founded to support apartheid South Africa and the prosecution of anti-apartheid activist Peter Hain, announced that they would be setting up a 'free speech squad' in response to the recent incidents at universities.[114] These squads, it was purported, would consist of 'brawny young men' that could 'protect the right of speakers to be heard and audiences to hear them', as well as 'deal with would-be wreckers in an expert way'.[115] The same group had previously issued a leaflet with guidance for 'moderate students' who opposed sit-ins, claiming that students who had the right to use a room that was occupied could call the police and attempt to eject the protestors.[116] The leaflet gave the advice: 'If the sit-in happens, get as many opponents of it as possible to exert their rights, if necessary using such force as may be reasonably necessary as you are entitled in law to do.'[117]

However there is no evidence that these 'free speech squads' actually came to fruition, but the fact that a right-wing pressure group was able to get national press coverage around this proposal demonstrates the level of concern about student radicalism and political violence that was growing in the early 1970s. The description of student activists as either 'fascists' or 'Stalinists' in pursuit of ending free speech at British universities was one that preceded the establishment of the 'no platform' policy in 1974 and was one that was returned to continually throughout the 1970s by politicians, the press and right-wingers.

Conclusion

Before the formalisation of the 'no platform' policy at the NUS conference in April 1974, many of the arguments for such a tactical approach had been made by sections of the student movement who opposed fascist, racist and other right-wing speakers who came to British universities to speak. As this chapter demonstrates, the radicalism of the student movement in the late 1960s and early 1970s was just as important an incubator for the idea of 'no platform' as the traditions of militant anti-fascism of the British left. After Enoch Powell and Patrick Wall from the Monday Club were invited on several occasions by Conservative student groups to speak in the late 1960s, students at places like Essex, Leeds, Exeter and UCL, buoyed by the wider radicalism of the era, took part in extensive protests against his presence on campus. Compared with the protests against Oswald Mosley at various universities in the 1950s and early 1960s, those against Powell and Wall were larger and sustained by an air of rebellion generated by a rising student movement.

In the year before the 'no platform' policy was introduced, there were two further incidents that foreshadowed the eventual policy, but were implemented by student activists in different ways. In May 1973, there was a protest at LSE against the psychologist Hans Eysenck addressing the Social Science Society, which ended with a small group of Maoists attacking Eysenck as he began his talk. The following month, the Indochina Solidarity Committee occupied a lecture theatre at the University of Sussex to prevent visiting American academic Samuel P. Huntington from speaking. Although one incident involved violence and the other was a peaceful protest, together these events were portrayed as end to free speech on campus and an example of a violent turn within the student movement – coming at a time when the British authorities and press were becoming more alarmed about the spectre of political violence from the left.[118] As the 1970s wore on, the arbitrary nature of these protests would give way to a more formal approach by student unions, empowered by the 'no platform' policy at NUS level, as will be outlined in the following chapter.

Notes

1 Harold Wilson, *Labour's Plan for Science* (London: Labour Party pamphlet, 1963).
2 Andrew Scott Crines, 'Harold Wilson's Rhetoric', *Renewal*, 22/3–4 (2014) p. 134.
3 Martin Jacques, 'Trends in Youth Culture: Some Aspects', *Marxism Today* (September 1973) pp. 273–274.
4 For discussion on the 'global 1968' and its impact upon Britain, see: David Widgery, *The Left in Britain, 1956–1968* (Harmondsworth: Penguin, 1976) pp. 341–420; Chris Harman, *The Fire Last Time: 1968 and After* (London: Bookmarks, 1988); Arthur

Marwick, *The Sixties: Cultural Revolution in Britain, France, Italy and the United States, 1958–1974* (Oxford: Oxford University Press, 1998); Caroline Hoefferle, *British Student Activism in the Long Sixties* (Abingdon: Routledge, 2013); Jodi Burkett, 'The National Union of Students and Transnational Solidarity, 1958–1968', *European Review of History*, 21/4 (2014) pp. 539–555; Sam Blaxland, 'Re-Thinking Student Radicalism: The Case of a Provincial British University', *Espacio, Tiempo y Educación*, 6/1 (2019) pp. 29–39.

5 *Black Dwarf*, 1 June, 1968, p. 1.
6 Jodi Burkett, *Constructing Post-Imperial Britain: Britishness, 'Race' and the Radical Left in the 1960s* (Houndmills: Palgrave Macmillan, 2013) p. 14.
7 Burkett, *Constructing Post-Imperial Britain*, pp. 36–38.
8 Nick Thomas, 'Challenging the Myths of the 1960s: The Case of the Student Movement in Britain', *Twentieth Century British History*, 13/3 (2002) p. 281.
9 See: Alexander Cockburn & Robin Blackburn (eds), *Student Power: Problems, Diagnosis, Action* (Harmondsworth: Penguin Books, 1970).
10 David Widgery, 'NUS – The Student's Muffler', in Cockburn & Blackburn (eds), *Student Power*, p. 120.
11 Jodi Burkett, 'Revolutionary Vanguard or Agent Provocateur: Students and the Far Left on English University Campuses, c. 1970–1990', in Evan Smith & Matthew Worley (eds), *Waiting for the Revolution: The British Far Left from 1956* (Manchester: Manchester University Press, 2017) p. 20.
12 Thomas, 'Challenging the Myths of the 1960s', pp. 293–294.
13 Hoefferle, *British Student Activism in the Long Sixties*, p. 123.
14 Harman, *The Fire Last Time*, p. 226.
15 Hoefferle, *British Student Activism in the Long Sixties*, p. 129.
16 Shirin Hirsch, *In the Shadow of Enoch Powell: Race, Locality and Resistance* (Manchester: Manchester University Press, 2018) pp. 24–28.
17 *Daily Mirror*, 23 December, 1967, p. 1.
18 Paul Foot, *The Rise of Enoch Powell* (Harmondsworth: Penguin Books, 1969) pp. 110–111.
19 Enoch Powell, 'Walsall Speech', in Bill Smithies & Peter Fiddick (eds), *Enoch Powell on Immigration* (London: Sphere Books, 1969) pp. 19–22.
20 *Birmingham Evening Mail*, 20 February, 1968.
21 Hansard, 15 March, 1968, col. 1984.
22 *Essex County Standard*, 1 March, 1968, press cutting from University of Essex Archives.
23 Ibid.
24 *Daily Express*, 6 March, 1968, p. 1.
25 *Wyvern*, 26 April 1968, p. 2.
26 *Essex County Standard*, 1 March, 1968, press cutting from University of Essex Archives.
27 *Wyvern*, 26 April, 1968, p. 1.
28 *Essex County Standard*, 22 March, 1968, press cutting from University of Essex Archives.
29 *East Anglian Daily Times*, 6 March, 1968, press cutting from University of Essex Archives.
30 Mark Pitchford, *The Conservative Party and the Extreme Right* (Manchester: Manchester University Press, 2007) pp. 147–177.
31 Ibid., pp. 152–175; Camilla Schofield, *Enoch Powell and the Making of Postcolonial Britain* (Cambridge: Cambridge University Press, 2015) pp. 241–242. Also see: Daniel McNeil, '"The Rivers of Zimbabwe Will Run Red With Blood": Enoch Powell and the Post-Imperial Nostalgia of the Monday Club', *Journal of Southern African Studies*, 37/4 (2011) pp. 731–745.
32 *Daily Telegraph*, 4 May, 1968, p. 1.
33 *The Times*, 4 May, 1968, p. 1. Sheila Wall wrote to *The Times* to correct this report to state that she didn't weep, but 'may have used some strong language'. *The Times*, 6 May, 1968, p. 9.
34 *Daily Express*, 4 May, 1968, p. 11.

35 *The Times*, 6 May, 1968, p. 9.
36 *The Times*, 8 May, 1968, p. 11.
37 Ibid.
38 Ibid.
39 Esmée Sinéad Hanna, *Student Power! The Radical Days of English Universities* (Newcastle Upon Tyne: Cambridge Scholars Publishing, 2013) p. 43.
40 *Union News*, 1 November, 1968, p. 1; *Union News*, 15 November, 1968, p. 4.
41 *Daily Telegraph*, 24 October, 1968, pp. 1; 36.
42 *Daily Express*, 24 October, 1968, p. 9.
43 Ibid.
44 *Daily Telegraph*, 24 October, 1968, p. 36.
45 Ibid.
46 *The Times*, 26 October, 1968, p. 4.
47 *Pi*, 20 February, 1969, p. 1.
48 *Pi*, 6 February, 1969, p. 7.
49 Ibid.
50 *Pi*, 20 February, 1969, p. 2.
51 *Pi*, 6 March, 1969, p. 2.
52 *Daily Express*, 18 February, 1969, p. 9.
53 *Pi*, 20 February, 1969, p. 1.
54 *Daily Express*, 18 February, 1969, p. 9.
55 Brian Klug, 'Oxford in Wonderland', *The Guardian*, 27 November, 2007, www.theguardian.com/commentisfree/2007/nov/26/oxfordinwonderland (accessed 11 January, 2019).
56 *Pi*, 6 March, 1969, p. 3.
57 Trevor Pateman, 'No Platforming Then and Now: From Enoch Powell to Peter Tatchell', *The Best I Can Do*, www.trevorpatemanblog.com/2016/02/no-platforming-then-and-now-from-enoch.html (accessed 11 January, 2019).
58 *Pi*, 20 February, 1969, p. 1; *Pi*, 6 March, 1969, p. 3.
59 *Daily Mail*, 11 June, 1973, p. 6.
60 Steven Rose, John Hambley & Jeff Haywood, 'Science, Racism and Ideology', *Socialist Register*, 1973, p. 235.
61 LSE Afro-Asian Society flyer, 'Fascist Eysenck Has No Right to Speak', n.d., LSE/Student Union/24, LSE Student Union Papers, LSE Archives, London.
62 Ibid.
63 Ibid.
64 *Daily Telegraph*, 9 May, 1973, p. 1.
65 Ibid.
66 Ibid.
67 *The Guardian*, 9 May, 1973, p. 1.
68 *Guardian Weekly*, 19 June, 1973, press cutting held in LSE/Student Union/24, LSE Student Union Papers.
69 *Daily Mirror*, 10 May, 1973, p. 2.
70 *The Times*, 10 May, 1973, p. 2.
71 *The Times Higher Education Supplement*, 11 May, 1973, press cutting held in LSE/Student Union/24, LSE Student Union Papers.
72 *Birmingham Evening Mail*, 23 May, 1973, press cutting held in LSE/Student Union/24, LSE Student Union Papers.
73 *Morning Star*, 11 May, 1973, press cutting held in LSE/Student Union/24, LSE Student Union Papers.
74 Ibid.
75 *The Beaver* (June 1973) p. 10.
76 *Sunday Telegraph*, 24 June, 1973, p. 7.
77 Ibid.

78 LSE Red Mole flyer, 'Defend the Union! Defend the Afro-Asian Soc! Defend the CPE (M-L)!', n.d., LSE/Student Union/24, LSE Student Union Papers.
79 Ibid.
80 *The Times*, 11 May, 1973, p. 2.
81 Executive Committee of LSE Student Union, 'Eysenck', n.d., LSE/Student Union/24, LSE Student Union Papers.
82 *The Beaver* (June 1973) p. 10.
83 Ibid., p. 11.
84 Ibid., p. 10.
85 LSE Red Mole flyer, 'Defend the Union! Defend the Afro-Asian Soc! Defend the CPE (M-L)!'
86 Ibid.
87 *Daily Telegraph*, 14 June, 1973, p. 18.
88 Samuel P. Huntington, 'Bases of Accommodation', *Foreign Affairs*, 46/4 (July 1968) p. 467.
89 Roy Edgely, 'Freedom of Speech and Academic Freedom: Thought and Action in the Huntington Affair', *Radical Philosophy*, 10 (Spring 1975) pp. 15–16.
90 *Daily Telegraph*, 6 June, 1973, p. 19.
91 'Huntington at Sussex', *Science for the People* (November 1973) p. 45.
92 Ibid.
93 Ibid.
94 'Huntington – All the Statements', *University of Sussex Bulletin*, 20 June, 1973, p. 1.
95 'Huntington at Sussex', p. 45.
96 *Daily Telegraph*, 6 June, 1973, p. 19.
97 Ibid.
98 *The Times*, 6 June, 1973, p. 1.
99 *Daily Telegraph*, 6 June, 1973, p. 19.
100 'Huntington – All the Statements', p. 1.
101 *Daily Telegraph*, 6 June, 1973, p. 19.
102 Edgely, 'Freedom of Speech and Academic Freedom', p. 13.
103 *The Guardian*, 6 June, 1973, p. 1.
104 'Huntington – All the Statements', p. 1.
105 Ibid.
106 Ibid.
107 *Daily Telegraph*, 8 June, 1973, p. 9; *Birmingham Evening Mail*, 7 June, 1973, press cutting held in LSE/Student Union/24, LSE Student Union Papers.
108 *Daily Telegraph*, 5 June, 1973, p. 18.
109 *The Guardian*, 11 June, 1973, press cutting held in LSE/Student Union/24, LSE Student Union Papers.
110 *The Times*, 13 June, 1973, p. 16.
111 *The Times*, 11 June, 1973, p. 2.
112 *Daily Telegraph*, 13 June, 1973, p. 2.
113 Ibid.
114 Ibid.
115 Ibid.
116 *Daily Telegraph*, 16 May, 1973, p. 8.
117 Ibid.
118 J.D. Taylor, 'The Party's Over? The Angry Brigade, the Counterculture and the British New Left, 1967–72', *The Historical Journal*, 58/2 (2015) pp. 877–900.

4

THE NATIONAL UNION OF STUDENTS AND 'NO PLATFORM' IN THE 1970S

The policy of 'no platform' was formally adopted by the National Union of Students at its conference in April 1974, initiated by students linked to the International Marxist Group (IMG) and the International Socialists (IS), and also supported briefly by the Communist Party affiliated Broad Left. The policy, although controversial, was a formalisation of an approach that left-wing students had taken towards controversial speakers since the late 1960s, denying them the physical space and opportunity to speak. Citing Pamela J. Yettram, Dave Rich has written that 'from 1968 until 1970, efforts "to deny freedom of speech to those advocating what they saw as immoral policies" were the single most common form of student protest in Britain'.[1] While these efforts had taken on some extreme forms in the past, such as the assault on Hans Eysenck by Maoists at LSE in May 1973, most of the protests against right-wing speakers during the late 1960s and early 1970s had employed non-violent tactics, such as sit-ins and heckling. The 'no platform' resolution in 1974 attempted to co-ordinate anti-fascist and anti-racist actions against undesirable speakers that had been much more ad hoc and localised in the past. The resolution encouraged student unions to be proactive in this area and deny controversial speakers the opportunity to speak on campus, by disinvitation, denial of funds for groups that invited these speakers and by physical protest (if required). In the context of the previous chapter, the adoption of the policy in 1974 allowed a bureaucratic framework to be developed around spontaneous protest activities that taken place since the 1950s but heightened during the era of student radicalism.

The policy also tapped into a longer history of militant and left-wing anti-fascism that had been developed since the 1930s, reinvigorated by the rise of the National Front (NF) in the early 1970s. Between 1972 and 1974, the NF had made serious gains amongst disaffected Tories and exploited the Ugandan Asian 'crisis' by promoting a hardline anti-immigrationist line, with crossover between the NF and the Monday Club (a pro-empire and anti-immigration grouping within the Conservative Party).[2] Electoral performances by the NF (such as Martin Webster's sizeable share of the vote in West Bromwich in 1973) and the encroachment of the NF onto university campuses caused the student movement and the NUS to take fascism increasingly seriously. The 'no platform' policy was a marker of the hardening of left-wing student attitudes towards the NF and attempts to build the anti-fascist movement in Britain at a national level, throwing down the gauntlet to more moderate students regarding how to fight fascism and racism as Britain slipped into the crises of the mid-1970s.

Even after its introduction, the 'no platform' policy continued to be controversial and caused friction within the NUS. A few months after it was voted in, the NUS had to hold another extraordinary conference to re-debate the resolution, as the Broad Left coalition that had supported the resolution started to have second thoughts. However, this conference happened at the same time as a demonstration against the National Front in London's Red Lion Square, which was violently broken up by the police, resulting in the death of one anti-fascist protestor. The death and the actions of the police against the anti-fascist demonstration convinced many who supported the 'no platform' policy that it was necessary in the face of a rising far right.

The debate continued throughout the 1970s and the policy was hotly contested at NUS conferences in the mid-to-late 1970s. After the hard right Tory MP, Sir Keith Joseph, came to the University of Essex despite protests from the student union and was heckled heavily during a speech in early 1977, there was a push to revise the policy from 'no platform' to 'no invitation'. While this push for reform did not succeed in April 1977, the Broad Left coalition was able to get it through in the December 1977 conference under the stewardship of Communist Party and NUS President Sue Slipman. This reversal did not last long and by April 1978 the policy had been reinstated.

The same conference in December 1977 was also the site of a resolution deciding that 'no platform' could not be used to exclude Jewish and Zionist student groups from universities. The previous year had seen a number of student unions seek to use the 'no platform' policy to ban pro-Israel and Zionist groups after the 1975 United Nations resolution which declared that Zionism was a form of racism. The conflation of pro-Palestine/anti-Israel activism with the 'no platform' policy led to an application of the policy which divided the student body on many campuses and contributed to the temporary reversal of the policy in late 1977. Even though the 'no platform' policy was reintroduced the following year, the ban on it being used on Zionist and pro-Israel groups remained in place.

Despite the objections and controversies surrounding the policy of 'no platform' and its implementation, the policy endured as Britain headed into the 1980s (although it would continue to be seen as problematic throughout that decade). This chapter explores the creation of the 'no platform' policy in the early-to-mid-1970s and the battles it caused within the student movement during the 1970s.

The rise of the National Front

The strategy, and eventual policy, of 'no platform' was developed in response to the rise of the National Front in the early 1970s. The NF had formed in the late

1960s by bringing together a number of strands within the British far right that had developed during the late 1950s and early 1960s. Over the previous decade, a number of organisations had emerged out of a far right pressure group, the League of Empire Loyalists (LEL), which had been founded by the former BUF Director of Propaganda, A.K. Chesterton. Formed in 1954, the LEL was against decolonisation and Commonwealth immigration to Britain. The LEL made a name for itself by disrupting Conservative Party meetings, particularly at the annual Tory conference. Besides these protest spectacles, the LEL probably would have been forgotten, except that it became the conduit for most of the leading figures of the British far right for the next 20 years. Alongside Chesterton, the LEL saw Colin Jordan, John Tyndall, Martin Webster, John Bean and Andrew Fountaine go through the group in the 1950s before they all left (besides Chesterton).

The Notting Hill riots in August 1958, when white youths attacked Afro-Caribbean residents in West London, saw the first major fascist activity in Britain since the late 1940s. Jordan, who had left the LEL the previous year, used Arnold Leese House in the same borough as a base for his White Defence League (WDL), which provocatively patrolled the area and made public exhortations to 'Keep Britain White'. At the same time, Mosley's Union Movement (UM) started to campaign in the area and sought to rebrand the UM as an anti-immigration group, different from its anti-Semitic and fascist background. In the 1959 election, Mosley attempted to capitalise on this anti-immigration sentiment and ran as a candidate for Kensington North, but only gained 8 per cent of the vote.[3]

Between Jordan leaving to form the WDL in 1957 and the creation of the National Front (NF) ten years later, the far right in Britain continued to split and reform, often maintaining the same personnel, but with different names. Some of the splits were ideological (for example, Jordan was the most ardent National Socialist, compared with others who pushed for a more 'British' racialised nationalism), but many of ruptures were due to personality clashes between these leading figures. After Jordan formed the WDL, Bean and Fountaine left the LEL to form the National Labour Party (NLP), and the two merged in 1960 to create the British National Party (BNP). Jordan, along with Tyndall and Webster, established the National Socialist Movement (NSM) in 1962. However, Tyndall and Webster soon left, due to a mixture of political and personality differences, to form the Greater Britain Movement (GBM).

Despite its fractured nature in the early 1960s, the British far right focused largely on opposition to non-white Commonwealth migration and decolonisation (particularly after Harold Macmillan's 'Winds of Change' speech in 1960), with only Jordan's NSM continuing to emphasise its anti-Semitism. Although the Commonwealth Immigrants Act 1962 had been introduced by the Conservatives to limit Commonwealth migration, the far right groups called for restrictions upon non-white immigration to go much further and used it as an issue to distinguish between themselves and the Conservative right. The far right were also buoyed by Rhodesian Prime Minister Ian Smith's Unilateral Declaration of Independence in 1965, with the British groups seeing Rhodesia, alongside apartheid South Africa, as frontline states in a war against communism and multi-racial democracy.

Attempting to capitalise on this anti-immigrant and pro-imperial sentiment, the various forces of the British far right (the BNP, the GBM and the LEL, along with other groups such as the Racial Preservation Society) joined to form the National Front in 1967. Led by Chesterton and Bean, Tyndall and Webster were at first not allowed to join the NF, although the GBM membership were instructed to enter the NF. Only Jordan and his NSM were kept out of the merger. Tyndall and Webster were eventually welcomed into the organisation in the following year.

The NF were boosted at several points during the late 1960s and early 1970s by controversies over Commonwealth migration, siphoning off supporters and voters from disaffected Tories who felt that the Conservatives were not tough enough on immigration. After Enoch Powell's 'Rivers of Blood' speech in April 1968, the NF experienced an influx of new supporters, even though the NF stressed the differences between the Tory MP and themselves. Similarly, after the Conservative government agreed to the entry of Ugandan Asians after their expulsion by Idi Amin in 1972, the NF were able to appeal to disgruntled Conservative Party members, attracting several (including John Kingsley Read) from the Monday Club, a pressure group within the Tories.

From the very beginning, there were also tensions within the NF over its direction. Chesterton viewed it initially as a pressure group in the mould of the LEL, while others believed that the NF should be contesting elections or becoming involved in mass street politics. Chesterton resigned in 1970 in the wake of differences over how the NF should have reacted to the popular racism evoked by Enoch Powell. Furthermore, in the early 1970s, there were schisms between the 'authoritarians', those (like Tyndall and Webster) who had a background in explicit neo-Nazism, and the 'populists', who had been recruited from the hard right fringes of the Conservative Party, such as John O'Brien, John Kingsley Read and Roy Painter.[4]

By 1974, when the National Union of Students' policy of no platform was introduced, the NF had reached (and possibly passed) their peak in terms of membership and electoral presence. For example, Martin Webster had gained 16 per cent of the vote in a by-election in West Bromwich in 1973,[5] but at both elections in 1974, the NF had failed make much more of their voter base. After this time, there was a shift in the NF away from contesting electoral politics in the hope of attracting protest votes from traditional Conservative voters towards appealing to more working-class supporters who had previously backed Labour. This coincided with a greater emphasis on 'controlling the streets' and confrontational politics, similar to the shift by the BUF in the late 1930s. But as the NF moved in this direction, they encountered a growing anti-fascist movement – in the streets, in electoral politics, and most importantly for our purposes, in the universities.

The National Front Students Association

Alongside the broader growth of the National Front in the early 1970s, there was also a concern that the National Front were making their presence felt on university campuses around the country. As shown in the previous chapter, NF members had attempted to intimidate protesting students at universities and other places, but they also tried to organise on campus. In 1973, NF members at different universities sought to agitate against what they perceived to be the overwhelming Marxist influence at British universities. NF member Dave McCalden and Chris Morter formed the British Nationalist Society at Goldsmiths College and produced a journal, *Right On!*. The Society railed against the 'Socialist "Thought Police"' at Goldsmiths, which 'deliberately attacked' their stall at the college, complaining that they were denied their freedom of speech.[6] McCalden and Morter called for 'free debate' on several issues, including 'racialism', 'revolutionary nationalism' and the student union's policy on southern Africa, but complained that the student union had shut down this option.[7] McCalden ran for Union President, noting that 124 students voted for him and therefore 'registered their disgust at the corruption and mismanagement that has been a feature of Goldsmiths SU.'[8] When Hans Eysenck's speech at LSE was disrupted in May 1973, McCalden introduced a motion at the Goldsmith College Union Council condemning the attack on the psychologist.[9]

McCalden joined Richard Lawson and Denis Pirie, a veteran of the British far right by this time and a mature age student at the University of Sussex, to form the National Front Students Association (NFSA). The NFSA produced a newspaper called *Spark*, which appropriated the style of the student press at the time, and was first edited by Lawson and then McCalden. In the autumn of 1973, an editorial by Lawson claimed that 10,000 issues of the paper were circulated.[10] Writing in the NF newspaper *Britain First* (also edited by Lawson), McCalden declared that the NFSA 'refuse[d] to be intimidated by the thugs of the ultra-Left' and wrote of NF students disrupting anti-racist demonstrations and events.[11] This included distributing flyers at the Anti-Apartheid Movement's picket of a rugby match at Twickenham and disruption of a conference held by the Campaign on Racism, IQ and the Class Society at the Polytechnic of Central London.[12] McCalden called the NF's activities at the conference a 'resounding success', which 'showed how our mere presence at Leftist conferences can disrupt proceedings as Liberals and Marxists are amongst themselves' (over whether the NF should have been allowed to speak).[13]

Sussex University, where Pirie was based, also saw a short-term upswing in NF activism on campus during this period. The student newspaper at Sussex, *Unionews*, reported in February 1974 that four NF members came onto campus to put up NF posters and distribute copies of *Spark*.[14] When confronted by the student union president and the editor of *Unionews*, the NF members allegedly threatened the students.[15] In response, the Union President, Cam Matheson, stated, 'These people are extremely well organised and extremely dangerous, the way to beat them is not by false heroics but by being even better organised than they are.'[16] These kind of incidents were seen on several campuses in the early-to-mid-1970s and can be seen as one of the pressing concerns of the student movement in Britain which led to the NUS implementing the 'no platform' policy in 1974 – even though NFSA, in the long run, 'failed to make any wider impact' – and subsequently focusing on school students and young people who did not go on to higher education.[17]

The International Marxist Group and the concept of 'no platform'

The first use of the term 'no platform' was in 1972 in the IMG newspaper, *The Red Mole*. The IMG, as shown in the last chapter, was a Trotskyist organisation that had grown in the late 1960s as it became influential in the anti-Vietnam War and student movements. The IMG was, along with the International Socialists, the far left group that most embraced the counterculture and celebrated the revolutionary potential of youth. The IMG was also heavily involved in Irish solidarity in the early 1970s (it supported the Provisional IRA), as well as taking part in the anti-racist and women's liberation movements.[18] By 1972–73, there was an growing feeling amongst the IMG that Britain was heading towards crisis and the forthcoming revolution would follow, which encouraged an optimistic and ultra-left outlook to form. As Tariq Ali, one of the leading members of the IMG, wrote in his book *The Coming British Revolution*: 'The only real alternative to capitalist policies is provided by the revolutionary left groups as a whole. Despite their smallness and despite their many failings, they represent the only way forward.'[19]

As the Ugandan Asian controversy heightened in 1972 and the National Front (as well as the Monday Club) sought to mobilise disaffected Tories around this issue, the beginnings of a militant anti-racist and anti-fascist movement started forming, buoyed by the wider radicalism of the period. Both the IMG and IS were greatly involved in this.

In the issue for 18 September, 1972, the front page headline of *The Red Mole* declared 'NO PLATFORM FOR RACISTS'. It described the NF and the Monday Club as 'mortal enemies of the working class' and stated that these two groups 'must be stopped in their tracks'.[20] The newspaper argued that these groups needed to be confronted and were 'not going to be convinced by rational argument', calling for 'a concerted counter-attack' at meetings of both groups.[21]

The IMG proposed that groups like the NF could not be afforded 'free speech' because 'their racist campaigns are a means to destroy the organisations of the working class which defend such bourgeois democratic rights'. An editorial in the same issue claimed: 'the only way to deal with fascist type organisations like the National Front is to break up their activities before they grow to a size where they can begin to smash the activities of the working class'.[22]

While acknowledging that '[w]e are nowhere near a threatened Fascist coup yet', the article said 'the methods necessary on preventing such a threat must be explained and demonstrated in practice *now* ... We must begin to adopt the right tactics right from the start.'[23]

As shown in the previous chapter, before the term 'no platform' became common currency, there was already the idea amongst the left and the student movement that there were certain individuals and groups that were beyond the pale and had no right to espouse their views on university campuses. The concept of 'no platform' that had been developed in the pages of *The Red Mole* was formalised by the student movement and motivated by the IMG, shaping the nebulous protests that had occurred over the last half decade into a more coherent policy. This led to the implementation of the 'no platform' policy at the NUS conference in 1974 in Liverpool.

The 1974 NUS conference

The IMG was one of the most influential leftist groups amongst the student movement in Britain in the early 1970s, but competed with the International Socialists and the CPGB (who were part of the Broad Left group with students associated with the Labour left). It was through the student movement that the IMG pushed the policy of 'no platform'.

The NUS in 1974 was under the leadership of John Randall and Steve Parry, a member of the CPGB and the Broad Left, and were in broad agreement that a policy of 'no platform' should be applied to the NF and other fascist organisations attempting to recruit students on university campuses. At the Liverpool conference that year, the policy of 'no platform' was devised as part of a wider stance against racism, in particular the discrimination faced by international students in Britain. Amendment 4 of the resolution, moved by the student unions from Surrey, Reading, Hull, Sussex and Exeter, on the fight against racism stated:

> Conference recognises the need to refuse assistance (financial or otherwise) to openly racist or fascist organisations or societies ... and to deny them a platform. However conference believes that in order to counter these groups, it is also necessary to prevent any member of these organisations or individuals known to espouse similar views from speaking in colleges **by whatever means necessary** (including disrupting of the meeting).[24]

Student unions were also called upon to 'refuse any assistance to openly racist or fascist organisations or individuals', as well as 'prevent any racist or fascist propaganda being displayed, sold, distributed, or propagated through meetings by whatever means may be necessary'.[25]

There was resistance at the conference to this resolution when it was put forward. A representative from Bath University argued against the phrase 'by whatever means necessary', saying that violence was 'a denial of reason' and 'the weapon of the man who could not use reasoned argument'.[26] They warned that if this resolution was passed, the NUS would be 'sinking to the self same level as the fascists' and would give the right wing press 'the chance to discredit [the] NUS'.[27] Although another delegate from the same university 'stressed for the benefit of the minute-takers and conference that the majority of the Bath delegation totally rejected the last speech'.[28] A student from Manchester University called the resolution 'patronising paternalism at its worst' and suggested that if the NUS rejected 'the possibility ... that the mass of the people in Britain could be able to reject the fascists for what they were', then those within the NUS who pushed for the 'no platform' policy 'considered themselves intellectually superior to make decisions'.[29] Later in the debate, the same student declared that a '[b]an on any political group by another was a fascist act' and was contradictory to the 'interests of free speech'.[30] When the chairman told the student to 'shut up for goodness sake', he replied: 'Fascism was rearing its head in this meeting. He demanded freedom of speech for every group. If they wanted the capitalist Press to brand NUS as fascist, they were going the right way about it'.[31]

In response to criticisms of the resolution, particularly the appeal by some students for reasoned debate with fascists, a representative from the University of Reading quipped, 'Could the relatives of the 13,000 slaughtered comrades in Chile believe that fascism could be defeated by reason?'[32] Parry, as NUS Secretary, elaborated on this further, stating:

> Did reasoned argument stop the fascists led by Mosley in the East End in the 1930s? Of course, it did not. Had reasoned argument stopped Colin Jordan and his cronies in the Union movement having armed camps in Britain and working with ex-Nazis in Germany? Had reasoned argument stopped the junta in Chile killing thousands of people?[33]

The resolution was eventually passed by a vote of 204,619 to 182,760, with a number of student groups, including the Federation of Conservative Students (FCS), opposing it.[34] In the debate, a representative from Middlesex Polytechnic had exclaimed, 'Let us smash every manifestation of racialism and that's a warning to the Federation of Conservative Students',[35] which indicated the hardening of attitudes between the student left and the FCS, which would reach new heights in the 1980s.

Anticipating the controversy surrounding the passing of the resolution, the NUS issued a press release to clarify what 'no platform' meant. The press release stated the NUS were 'not going to send round a "heavy squad" to break up meetings' nor were they 'going to try to restrict activities of the Conservative Party'.[36] Instead, the NUS intended 'to deny platforms to the apostles of racial hatred',[37] presumably by not allowing student union buildings around the UK to be used by fascist groups. However, this was not clarified in the press release and open to interpretation by the various anti-fascist and far left groups.

A number of individual student unions, such as those from Keele University, Huddersfield Polytechnic, Queen Mary College, the University of Hull, St Hilda's College, St John's College and Balliol College at Oxford, Churchill College, Christ's College and Emmanuel College at Cambridge, opposed the resolution and wrote to the NUS to inform it that the 'no platform' policy would not be administered by the student unions.[38] Furthermore, representatives from the student unions of Balliol College and the Open University, as well as from the Monday Club's student association, the Army and Navy Club and LSE's Labour Society, condemned the policy in the letters pages of the *New Statesman*. [39] In the case of the latter, a former Labour MP who had been the Chairman of the LSE Social Science Society that had invited Hans Eysenck to speak in the previous year.

While the student union at the University of Warwick gave 'qualified support' to the policy, the students' newspaper, *The Warwick Boar*, reported that in a poll of students, only 12 per cent agreed with the policy.[40] 'The rest of the sample', the newspaper said, 'expressed personal repugnance over the views of many of the fascist groups [but] saw the motion as an unacceptable attack on the rights of free speech.'[41] In the University of Sheffield student newspaper *Darts*, a student protested against the 'no platform' policy, writing 'I, for one, refuse to be told which lectures I should or should not attend, or which way I should or should not think.'[42] The student union at Durham University described the policy as 'jackboot politics' and while the union 'recognise[d] that racist extremists [were] a threat to institutions of higher education and community relations in general', it proposed that 'the surest punch we can pull is a critical, logical and intelligent refutation of emotive racist credo'.[43]

The resolution was heavily criticised in the mainstream media, with even left-leaning *The Guardian*'s John Fairhall describing the move as a denial of free speech, voted for by students 'under the spell of Mr Parry's oratory'.[44] Fairhall predicted that '[t]rouble and violence seem inevitable' and warned: 'Students should perhaps remember that frustration which leads to a denial of the right of one section of society is not something new. It is classic pattern of fascism'.[45]

Parry replied in a letter to the newspaper, arguing:

> Our members overseas have been singled out for abuse, threats and outright economic attack by powerful extreme right-wingers during the time of the last Government. All our conference agreed was that at least they should not be subject to that abuse in our own student union.[46]

Applying the policy at Newcastle and Oxford

While the controversial aspects of the 'no platform' policy continued to be debated in the press and within student unions, there were instances where the policy was put into practice with varying results. In May 1974, the Deputy President of the Newcastle University Student Union, Paul Curran, invited Steve Parry to take part in a debate on freedom of speech, but he did not tell Parry that his opponent would be Martin Webster from the National Front.[47] The student newspaper at Newcastle explained what happened next:

> Since it was Parry who proposed the motion at NUS Conference that NUS give no platform to fascists, it was clear that he would never agree to speak on the same platform as Webster, and once informed (by a group of students who were worried that Union property may have damaged and Union staff hurt if Webster had appeared in the Union) Parry cancelled immediately, and the debate was called off.[48]

It was reported in *The Times* and the *Daily Telegraph* that this was the first time that the 'no platform' policy had been evoked since it was passed the previous month.[49] Curran complained that there was a 'security risk' as some student activists had warned that the meeting would be disrupted if the meeting went ahead.[50] He was quoted in the *Daily Telegraph* as saying:

> I am myself a Left-winger and do not agree with the policies of the Monday Club or the National Front, but I see no reason why they have less chance to be heard than the International Marxists [sic] or other extreme Left-wing groups.[51]

Curran's views were echoed by Diana Boyle, the student union president, who claimed that the debate was called off 'because left-wing students have threatened to organize a lot of trouble both inside and outside the union'.[52] The narrative that the media presented was that the new NUS policy had quickly led to left-wing students shutting down debate on campus, with both *The Times* and the *Daily Telegraph* giving column space for Richard Lawson from the National Front Students' Association, who described the episode as 'a typical example of the absolute gutlessness of the National Union of Students'.[53] Parry returned to Newcastle the following month to debate Brendan Barber, the student union president at City University London and leader of the 'Free Speech in NUS' campaign.[54] But the original Newcastle episode was soon overshadowed by a more high profile student protest against a right-wing speaker, this time at Oxford University.

Harold Soref, Vice-Chairman of the Monday Club, was invited to speak by the Oxford University Monday Club branch and in the lead up the event, the President of the Monday Club at Oxford, Andrew Bell, warned that students attempting to disrupt Soref's speech could be photographed or come to the attention of Special Branch police officers.[55] Bell declared: 'We have called this meeting to bring the issue [of 'no platform'] to a head. I believe we can stop the disruption of unpopular speakers from going any further if we can beat the disrupters at their own game.'[56]

However this did not go according to plan for Bell and Soref. Around 20 to 40 students disrupted Soref during his speech, smashing a window of a barricaded door to enter the Monday Club meeting.[57] The *Daily Telegraph* reported that while the audience tried to prevent the demonstrators from gaining access to the room, 'Mr Soref, escorted by a posse of students, fled down a back staircase, clambered over a six-foot wall and was driven off at high speed in a waiting yellow sports car'.[58] Soref, quoted in *The Times*, described his version of events:

> I spoke for forty minutes without any trouble. Then I heard a howling mob screaming and shouting outside, trying to break into the place.
>
> Thanks to a couple of resourceful undergraduates who smashed the padlock of an adjacent room, I was able to escape to the back of the building, … with this mob coming screaming and shouting after us.[59]

Both Soref and Bell criticised the student protestors as their stance was given a sympathetic portrayal in the press. Soref called those who protested against 'scum who have no place in a democratic society', while Bell stated that the Monday Club did 'not intend to be intimidated by such tactics'.[60] The new president of the Oxford University Student Union, the President of the Oxford Union and the student leaders of the three major political parties at Oxford all wrote a letter to *The Times* condemning the protests, stating that the student union at Oxford disapproved of the NUS' 'no platform' policy and that the disruption was 'the actions of a small and unrepresentative minority'.[61] Even John Randall seemed to distance the NUS from the protest, asserting '[w]e have made it clear that our active opposition to racialism should not be an excuse for individual acts of hooliganism'.[62]

The Soref incident occurred as debates swirled around the 'no platform' policy and opposition to the policy seemed to be gaining momentum in the lead up to a special NUS conference to be held in London in June. But while some of the moderate left-wing elements in the student movement looked to be having second thoughts, the far left called for the NUS to stay the course. For example a *Socialist Worker* editorial proposed, 'The soggy left needs to take a close look at the credentials of its "allies" in the current "free speech" campaign.'[63] For the far left groups, the 'no platform' policy within the NUS was only part of a wider struggle against fascism and racism in Britain.

The far left and 'no platform'

The policy of 'no platform' passed by the NUS in April 1974 needs to be understood within the broader anti-racist and anti-fascist activism undertaken by the far left in Britain at this time, particularly the students that belonged to the International Marxist Group, the International Socialists and the Communist Party, who all worked within the NUS. Although agreeing in principle the concept of 'no platform', the Communist Party, the IMG and the IS differed on the details of the resolution and how the strategy should be applied. The IMG warned that action needed to follow to ensure that the NUS resolution was used effectively and warned against left-wing sectarianism impeding joint action. Steve Webster wrote in *Red Weekly* (the renamed paper of the IMG):

> The fascists will not be defeated by resolutions or statements alone. There are three specific issues which face us immediately: the activity of the right in the colleges, the campaign against the reactionary anti-abortion group, SPUC [the Society for the Protection of Unborn Children], and the fight against racism. The other groups of the left rejected joint action around these issues. But it is only by such joint mobilisations, by confronting the right wing head-on, that the fascists and racists will be routed.[64]

In a newsletter titled *The Red Agitator*, the LSE branch of the International Socialists stated that the 'no platform' policy devised by the NUS was 'fundamentally correct' but took exception to the resolution lumping together fascism and racism, stressing that different tactics were to be used against fascists than those in the mainstream who promoted racist ideas. The case of Eysenck at LSE from the previous year was used to highlight the difference. For the IS, Eysenck was a racist, but not a fascist, and the IS suggested approaching his meetings in a slightly different way to how the Maoists had before:

> To debate with Eysenck, to treat him as a genuine scientist, is thus to indirectly legitimise Powellism. This is not to say that we should go out to break up meetings which he addresses – the real threat lies in organised fascist groups – but rather that we should picket them and organise counter-meetings in order to show up the real nature of his ideas.[65]

But on how to deal with the openly fascist NF, the IS agreed with the IMG. The *Red Agitator* newsletter finished with this:

> The racists and fascists of today are not something that we can ignore. They are a growing menace. The liberties we have today are worth defending, small though they are. Fascism aims to smash, racism creates the conditions for their destruction. We cannot allow the open fascist, or the concealed fascist working in the Monday Club or some similar organisation to gain a hearing. Every meeting that they hold gives them confidence. Every apologist for racism lends them comfort. Every liberal who debates with them gives them aid – much against their will.
>
> Every time they are stopped from meeting, every time their meetings are broken up, their task becomes harder and harder. The morale of the fascists falls. People turn away from them as a miserable and pathetic group with nothing to offer. Every success that we have demonstrates to the waverers that we are a better solution. That is the only way to fight fascism and racism.[66]

On the other hand, the Communist Party's National Student Organiser Dave Cook took exception with the supposedly broad nature of the 'no platform' resolution devised by the NUS. Writing in the CPGB's *Morning Star*, he pledged support for the NUS policy, stating that 'it is correct to argue that student unions should seek to deny racists a platform', but also argued that the phrase 'by any means necessary' could potentially isolate the more moderate and centrist elements in the NUS and endanger the resolution in its entirety.[67] Cook attempted to make clear that conservative or right-wing ideas, while 'repugnant', were 'political views which [students] can accept or reject', but racist attacks 'on the grounds of his or her colour' were 'against that person as a human being'.[68] Akin to the Communist Party's wider anti-fascist strategy in the 1970s, Cook also warned against the vanguardist approach of breaking up meetings by a minority of students, writing 'It is important that direct action does not become a substitute for the often more difficult task of winning the majority.'[69]

Unlike the position taken by Cook, NUS President and fellow CPGB member Steve Parry saw the matter as more straightforward and posed the question, 'What is the difference between the ideologies of the National Front and the Nazi party?' Responding to the claim that the notion of 'no platform' put restrictions on 'free speech', Parry answered at length:

> One must accept that to deny racists and fascists a platform is to 'limit freedom of speech' but one cannot see this freedom as something which exists in the abstract. It is a freedom which is already limited by such laws as the Race Relations Act and the law of libel, and must also be seen in the context of a class society in Britain which limits the freedom of speech for the vast majority of people ... In refusing to assist the spread of racism the NUS is fighting for a freedom of even greater importance: the freedom to live without discrimination on the basis of race. It is only in relation to reality that principles of freedom can be seen. It is not an abstract intellectual exercise.[70]

The IMG took exception to the Communist Party's seemingly qualified support of the 'no platform' strategy.[71] The Communist Party's anti-racist position in the 1960s and 1970s had focused largely on campaigning for the strengthening of the Race Relations Act to combat racial discrimination and racial hatred – a position that was criticised heavily by many of the other left-wing, black radical and migrant groups in this period.[72] 'The "no platform" position ... cannot be made dependent on the legal situation', argued the IMG's John Kilbane, reiterating that 'mass action will remain necessary'.[73] The argument for direct action, with the potential for physical confrontation, was also made by the International Socialists, who criticised the CPGB for 'talking of "peaceful pickets" and implying that the police can "stop the fascists"'.[74] For the IS, the 'peaceful picket, pious resolutions, rational arguments alone' would not stop the fascist threat, who had to be 'driven physically from the streets'.[75] The issue of 'no platform' and direct action, the far left, the police and the NF came to a head on 15 June 1974, when an anti-fascist demonstration in Red Lion Square in London ended in the death of a demonstrator, Kevin Gately.

The emergency conference and the death of Kevin Gately

Because of the controversial nature of the 'no platform' resolution passed earlier in the year, the NUS decided that the resolution would again be debated at a special emergency conference in London on 15 June, 1974. The IMG accused the Communist Party faction within the NUS, with Steve Parry in the secretary position, of wavering, suggesting that the Party 'began to tremble at the thought that they were losing support inside the NUS' and eventually 'cracked under the strain'.[76] In the lead up to the conference, the IMG warned that the Communist Party faction wanted to weaken the resolution and restrict 'no platform' to non-violent means only, effectively getting rid of the phrase 'by whatever means necessary'.[77]

At the June conference, the debate was over the application of the resolution. A motion was put forward by several student unions arguing that 'violent disruption of a meeting of a racialist speaker gives that speaker publicity which she or he would welcome' and that the NUS should have used 'any non-violent tactics necessary to combat racialism'.[78] The student union from City University, London had been significant in the lead up to the June conference in the campaign to revise the 'no platform' resolution, and a representative from this student union stressed that any action 'must be non-violent because violent disruption was unacceptable on a moral level and politically bankrupt and ineffective on a tactical level'.[79]

However, a number of representatives again defended the 'by whatever means necessary' part of the resolution. A representative from Portsmouth Polytechnic said that it didn't matter whether violent disruption received negative publicity in the press and that 'students should not be interested in winning this mythical idea that somewhere there was the average man or the average student who symbolised public opinion'.[80] Another representative from Birmingham Polytechnic argued that fascists 'were willing to use whatever means necessary to achieve their policies' and thus, '[t]heir opponents should be the same'.[81]

There was also a debate over the autonomy of individual student unions to implement the resolution as they saw fit. Dave Cook, writing in *Morning Star*, said that the IMG and the IS wanted to maintain the resolution as it was passed, 'which dictated a common response to all racist and fascist organisations in all situations'.[82] The Communist-affiliated Broad Left group opposed this, arguing that 'the best way to implement national policy was for decisions to be made by each individual union in accordance with its local situation'.[83] Put to a vote, both amendments suggested by Broad Left failed to get over the line and the resolution remained as it was, despite the Federation of Conservative Students seeking the opportunity to defeat the resolution in its entirety.

This was the same day that the NF attempted to hold a meeting at Conway Hall in Red Lion Square and a counter-demonstration was held by Liberation and other anti-fascists, including the IMG. The resulting melee between anti-fascists and the police led to the death of Warwick University student Kevin Gately.[84] Nigel Copsey has suggested that the IMG was determined to 'organise a mass picket at the main entrance of the hall thereby denying the NF access'.[85] The police attempted to disperse the IMG contingent that was blocking the NF's access to Conway Hall.[86] The IMG members refused to be dispersed and according to Lord Scarman's subsequent report on Gately's death, 'when the IMG assaulted the police cordon there began a riot, which it was the duty of the police to suppress, by force if necessary'.[87] It was in this initial violent clash between police and militant anti-fascists, lasting fewer than 15 minutes, that Kevin Gately was fatally injured. Gately died from a brain haemorrhage stemming from a blow to the head.[88] Further clashes between police and anti-fascist demonstrators occurred throughout the day, with the end result being that 'one person died, 46 policemen and at least 12 demonstrators were injured, 51 people arrested and the whole police operation had cost an estimated £15,000'.[89]

News of the police actions at Red Lion Square filtered back to the NUS conference. John McGeown, an IMG member and University of Kent representative, announced to the conference during the 'no platform' debate: 'Someone had just come to the rostrum with blood over his face and body. The wound had been inflicted by the police who were preventing people from demonstrating against the National Front.'[90]

McGeown linked the action at Red Lion Square to the debate being held at the conference, arguing that the violence experienced by the (largely student) demonstrators emphasised 'the importance of the debate today'.[91] He continued:

> While students were sitting here and liberals came to the rostrum and talked about free speech and the right to do this and to do that, student were actually being attacked by fascists in conjunction with, and in alliance with, the police force ... Such violence was being inflicted by the police force outside Conway Hall today in alliance with the fascists. Students had the opportunity to make a big contribution to the fight against the fascists today and they ought to be doing that by upholding the Liverpool conference resolution.[92]

The death of Gately at an anti-fascist demonstration bolstered the argument made by the Trotskyist groups – if fascism was not countered 'by any means necessary', then people on the left were to become targets of violence. As Dave Hann has shown, throughout the mid-1970s, NF activists violently broke a number of meetings by the left, leading to the need for meetings to be stewarded by militant anti-fascists.[93]

The NUS produced a pamphlet in the aftermath of Gately's death that called for a mobilisation of an anti-fascist movement against the National Front. Although it did not mention 'no platforming' on university campuses, the NUS did call for other institutions to implement their own 'no platform' policies. The pamphlet proclaimed:

> we call upon the government and local councils to recognise their responsibilities and ban further marches by the National Front and other fascist groups, and to deny them the use of public facilities. Such measures alone will not alone win the fight against racism and fascism, but will be an expression of the government's resolve to check its growth and to protect hard-won democratic rights of working people.[94]

'No platform' in the late 1970s

By the mid-1970s, the National Front was starting to change tactics. For most of the early 1970s, the NF had played up its 'respectability' and tried to attract disaffected Tory voters (particularly members of the Monday Club) who were anti-immigrant, pro-empire and anti-Common Market. 'No platform' was probably at its most controversial, but also very necessary, during this period, when a determined anti-fascist movement was needed to break the respectable veneer that the NF was putting forward while trying to woo the Tory right.

It reached its highest membership during this period and concentrated on electoral politics. The NF continued to contest elections from 1974 to 1977, but switched to an attempt to siphon off right-leaning Labour voters. In this process, the small electoral fortunes of the NF kickstarted the anti-fascist movement against them and the years from 1977 to 1979 saw increasing confrontation between the NF and anti-fascists on the streets. 1977 saw large scale anti-fascist demonstrations in Wood Green and Lewisham in London and in Hyde in Manchester, as well as the formation of the Anti-Nazi League in November of that year.[95]

By the late 1970s, militant anti-fascists had taken the principle of 'no platform' and applied it broadly, with the purpose of occupying the streets and the places where the NF sought to publicly assemble. Colin Sparks, from the Socialist Workers Party (the name of the International Socialists after 1977), explained:

> We do not engage in this sort of activity because we like violence or because the NF are reactionary. There are many other reactionary organisations around, for instance the Tory Party, which we do not attempt to smash up. The National Front differs from the Tories because their aims are precisely to control the streets, to build a mass fighting movement. In this, they need the marches and rallies.[96]

The Communist Party, which was largely critical of the SWP's 'adventurist' approach, also recognised the need to confront the NF, but argued that this needed to be done on a mass scale. But they also advocated using the machinery of the state, primarily the Race Relations Act, to combat the NF's 'claim to have a democratic right to flaunt their racism'.[97] In his pamphlet, *A Knife at the Throat of Us All*, Dave Cook, now the CPGB's National Organiser, wrote:

> Communists support, and will defend to the utmost, the right of people to freely speak their mind. But to attack people because they are black is not a political argument. People form their political views on the basis of conviction. They are born with their colour. That is why to attack someone because of his or her race is to attack that person as a human being. Their political views can change, colour cannot.
>
> To permit the NF the 'freedom' to be anti-human can end up destroying the freedom of us all. That is why incitement to racial hatred must have no place in a civilised society.[98]

Even the Labour Party accepted a form of 'no platform' for the National Front, when the Party's National Executive Committee declared: 'Labour candidates should not share platforms at meetings or appear on constituency programmes on radio or television with candidates or other members of the National Front'.[99] But while the success of the broader anti-fascist movement in Britain seemed to demonstrate general support for the principle of 'no platform' and the denial of space or opportunities for the NF to promote their views, the NUS policy was still being challenged within the student movement.

Student challenges to 'no platform'

Despite the original NUS resolution specifically targeting openly fascist and racist organisations, such as the NF and possibly the Monday Club, there were fears that the policy could be widened to be used against any political organisation and individual that fell foul of the NUS leadership. In their pamphlet, *Fascism: How to Smash It*, the IMG gave instances where 'no platform' had been applied to political 'enemies' who were not fascists:

> Racists like Powell or Harold Soref – who are not fascists – have often been driven off university campuses. This is because the effect these people can have is similar to fascists – that is, terrorising black people or others chosen as scapegoats for capitalism's social ills, and encouraging social violence, legal or otherwise, against them …
>
> 'No Platform' has been applied to many people by the workers' movement. Trade unionists, for example, would generally expel employees who attended their meetings. Print workers sometimes censor by blacking a newspaper editorial attacking the unions. When Mr. Godber, Tory Minister for Agriculture, [was] sent to Birmingham one day last year to do a public relations job for Tory price policy, he was mobbed off the street by angry housewives. All these actions are against 'free speech' and sometimes involve a physical struggle.[100]

An example of this were the protests against Sir Keith Joseph in 1977 and 1978. Joseph, a hardline neoliberal within the Conservatives and supporter of Margaret Thatcher, spoke at Essex University where flour bombs and eggs were thrown at him in front of an audience of around 500 students.[101] *The Times* reported that about 150 students crowded the entrance to the lecture theatre and yelled 'fascist' and 'racist' at Joseph during his speech.[102] The student union had issued a statement disassociating itself from the lecture organised by the Conservative Association and by organising a picket, had 'made it clear that Sir Keith's presence was not welcome'.[103] At the 1977 NUS conference a few months later, concerns were raised about demonstrations against Sir Keith Joseph speaking at Essex University. In *The Guardian*, John Fairhall wrote that the NUS Executive Committee felt that actions, such as the one against Joseph, were 'against the interest of the union, and damage an anti-racialism campaign'.[104] Alan Elsner, a member of the Union of Jewish Students, wrote in the *New Statesman* that the Joseph incident 'heightened the fear that "no platform" policy could be used as a means of silencing people whose views might be controversial or unpopular'.[105]

A possible example of this occurred the following year when the LSE Students' Union opposed Joseph speaking on the grounds that it was 'Union policy … that there was no platform for racists and fascists and that [LSE Student Union] policy stated that immigration controls were racist'.[106] Since immigration controls were central to Conservative Party policy, Joseph was not allowed to speak, unless he signed a statement opposing controls. *The Economist* reported that Joseph refused to sign any statement and was therefore stopped from speaking at the university.[107] In response, the magazine quipped: 'The students [at LSE] had better tighten their belts for a thin gruel of speakers from the fringe left: there is hardly anybody within the mainstream of British politics who favours no immigration controls.'[108]

There were some suggestions that the Federation of Conservative Students had encouraged the use of the student union policy of 'no platform' to be applied to Joseph in order to undermine the policy in general. *The Times* quoted a Conservative member of the LSE student union executive as alleging:

> I think the motive was to make the union look irresponsible and to help the campaign by the Federation of Conservative Students against the National Union of Student's [sic] policy of no platform for so-called racists and fascists.[109]

In the LSE student newspaper *The Beaver*, it was questioned whether the FCS were willing to be that manipulative of the situation, with the front page article posing, 'Surely it is not possible that it was the intention of the FCS to get Sir Keith banned in the hope of discrediting the "no platform" policy.'[110] While it cannot be proven one way or the other that the FCS cynically encouraged the policy to be rigidly enforced to create a backlash against 'no platform', it did engage in very controversial practices in the 1980s, particularly concerning the 'no platform' issue, which will be explored in Chapter 6.

Throughout the 1970s, the 'no platform' policy was challenged at the NUS annual conference. At the NUS conference in April 1977, John Fairhall reported for *The Guardian* that some on the NUS Executive Committee, supported by the Communists in the Broad Left coalition, wanted to change the policy from 'no platform' to 'no invitation', but this suggested change was defeated.[111] Future Labour MP Charles Clarke was, at the time, NUS President and a member of the Broad Left, but after the vote, defined the existing policy of 'no platform' as:

> A student union would do anything it could physically – such as picketing and demonstrating – to prevent people whom the student union decided by a general meeting vote were racists or fascists from speaking on a campus. But prevention would stop short of violence.[112]

The *Morning Star* quoted Clarke as being disappointed that the policy had not changed and that the NUS Executive Committee would 'continue to present this matter to national conferences because we believe that the "no platform" position is a barrier to strengthening the anti-racist campaign among our membership.'[113] The short-lived journal of the NUS, *National Student*, explained that while the policy remained unchanged, the campaign against racism and fascism (now in the era of Rock Against Racism and the Anti-Nazi League) would concentrate on:

- Setting up a network of anti-fascist committees in colleges to co-ordinate the campaign.
- Bringing together nationally overseas students to lead the campaign.
- Developing a cohesive policy and campaign, together with other education unions.
- Co-operation with external organisations campaigning against racism and fascism.[114]

This campaigning by the Broad Left eventually led to the policy being dropped by the NUS in December 1977. *The Courier* at Newcastle University reported that 'Communists, Conservatives, Labour and Liberal students united to reject the policy' and having 'turned its back on confrontation', the NUS policy '[left] the way open now for democratic discussion and action'.[115] However this change in policy did not last long and the 'no platform' resolution was reinstated at the 1978 NUS conference just four months later.[116] Although the moderate NUS leadership opposed it, the left-wing groups managed to get the policy reinstated. By this time, the broader anti-fascist movement had gained significant momentum and threatened to leave the NUS behind. The Anti-Nazi League had formed in late 1977 and at the time that the 'no platform' policy was reinstated, the first Anti-Nazi League/Rock Against Racism Carnival in Victoria Park was being organised.

Trevor Phillips, the incoming NUS President and who was personally against the policy, maintained that the policy would be used against the National Front, but 'would oppose any attempt to use it against Mrs Thatcher or other members of major political parties'.[117] The outgoing NUS President, Sue Slipman (who had presided over the momentary reversal of the policy) added, 'The new policy will not mean the infringement of the democratic right of any members'.[118] The *Glasgow University Guardian* reported that some elements of the left (such as the National Organisation of Labour Students) supported the policy of 'no platform' but made an amendment to the motion supporting this with the statement: 'that racists and fascists should be denied a platform wherever it is possible to do so through mass collective action, not through individual acts of violence.'[119] In response, the student newspaper questioned 'whether this watered-down version of "No Platform" will prevent the more extremist student elements from manipulating the policy to their own ends remains to be seen'.[120]

No platform for Zionists?

In his 1977 *New Statesman* article, Alan Elsner also raised the controversy over the use of 'no platform' against organisations that were explicitly Zionist or supporters of Israel.[121] This followed on from a wider global campaign (promoted by the Soviet Bloc and the Arab world) that equated Zionism with racism and apartheid, which reached its height with the UN resolution in 1975 that declared, 'Zionism is a form of racism and racial discrimination.'[122] David Cesarani wrote, 'The UN resolution made it possible to link popular mass-based anti-racist campaigns at home with palpably less relevant anti-Zionism.'[123]

Dave Rich, in his book *The Left's Jewish Problem*, has detailed the use of 'no platform' for Zionist student groups in the late 1970s, writing '[w]ithin eighteen months of the United Nations passing its "Zionism is racism" resolution, British Students' Unions began discussing motions to ban Zionism from campus'.[124] In late 1976, the student union at Salford University was the first to adopt an anti-Zionist policy, which brought it into conflict with the Jewish Society at the university, who were prevented from organising an 'Israel Week' in 1977.[125] Other Manchester Universities witnessed a similar divide between their student unions and Jewish societies (although the outcome was different to Salford at the University of Manchester and the University of Manchester Institute of Science and Technology).[126] Rich cites the Union of Jewish Students which asserted that by late March 1977:

> Motions equating Zionism with racism had been debated by at least seventeen Students' Unions, and York, Salford, Warwick and Lancaster University Students' unions had all passed motions 'expelling Jewish societies on the ground that they are Zionist and therefore racist.'[127]

These motions had attempted to distinguish between the cultural and religious aspects of the Jewish societies on one hand and the political aspects of the Jewish societies on the other, with the motions putting restrictions on Jewish students 'express[ing] their Jewishness in a political way through Zionism and support for Israel'.[128] In an interview with Rich, Sue Slipman said that 'campus anti-Zionists ended up banning Jewish societies "more by accident than design" without stopping to realise that "banning Jewish societies is in itself a racist act"'.[129]

At the same time as the NUS, under Slipman's helm, reconsidered the 'no platform' policy in full, the NUS Executive Committee attempted to quash the use of 'no platform' against Zionist and Jewish student groups – although a reversal of a number of these motions was already in action by the December 1977 conference.[130] Rich notes that a motion preventing the 'no platforming' of Zionist groups (while 'heavily critical of Israel') was passed, declaring: 'No limitations on the rights of Jewish or Palestinian student or Jewish or Palestinian societies whether they are religious, political or social groupings, should be contemplated.'[131]

Slipman stated at the time that she wanted 'to make it absolutely clear that what happened at Salford and York was corrupt and undemocratic' and announced that the NUS would 'fight it all down the line'.[132] While the 'no platform' policy was reintroduced at the NUS conference in April 1978, the ban on excluding Zionist and Jewish groups remained in place. Slipman, as outgoing President, asserted that the restoration of the 'no platform' policy 'definitely [did] not mean reraising the question of banning Jewish student organisations'.[133] Although the 'campus war' between pro-Israeli and pro-Palestinian groups was revived in the 1980s, particularly after invasion of Lebanon by Israel in 1982 and then in 1985 when the student union at Sunderland Polytechnic sought to deny funding to a newly formed Jewish Society.[134] The controversy at Sunderland Polytechnic did not reach the same heights as it did in the late 1970s and when the controversy broke, it was subsumed by a broader debate about the use of 'no platform' against non-fascist targets, such as hard right politicians (as discussed in Chapter 6).

Conclusion

The use of the 'no platform' policy was only part of the anti-racist struggle on university campuses during the 1970s. As David Renton has shown, 18 colleges or universities saw the formation of Anti-Nazi League groups, along with 12 national student groups.[135] With the anti-fascist movement against the National Front gaining momentum in the late 1970s, the NUS cited the anti-fascist stance being taken by the trade unions and implored students to do the same: 'It is now the duty of every student in the land to follow this example and speak, demonstrate and organise against these fascists each time they raise their banner of racism.'[136]

While the student movement had declined from the heights it reached in the late 1960s and early 1970s, students were an integral part of the anti-racist and anti-fascist movements that fought the National Front later in the decade. But while anti-racist and anti-fascist ideas perhaps spread further amongst the British population than previously, leaving fascists and explicit racists more and more isolated, the push by students to keep them off campus through the 'no platform' policy remained contentious.

This chapter explored how the 'no platform' policy was introduced, building on the activism of the student movement since the late 1960s, which had seen the opposition to several right-wing and controversial speakers over the years. The tactic had been developed by the far left, primarily the IMG and IS, and under the influence of these groups, 'no platform' became policy at the NUS conference in April 1974. At this critical juncture, the Communist Party affiliated Broad Left also supported the measure, but shortly afterwards, the Broad Left began to waver. This contributed to a debate throughout the 1970s over the application of the 'no platform' policy.

After the breaking up of an anti-fascist protest by the police at Red Lion Square in June 1974, many students were convinced of the necessity for taking a hard line against the National Front and other racists who attempted to speak or organise on university campuses. However, as the 1970s wore on, other uses of the policy caused concern amongst other student groups, with considerable media and political interest. In 1977, Keith Joseph was heckled relentlessly by protesting students at the University of Essex and then prevented from speaking entirely at the London School of Economics in 1978. This troubled some students as it seemed that the 'no platform' policy was being implemented against non-fascists, going beyond the original remit of the policy. Some student unions also used the 'no platform' policy to exclude pro-Israel and Zionist student groups in the wake of a UN resolution in 1975 that claimed that Zionism was a form of racism. Both of these issues came to a head at the NUS conference in December 1977, when the policy was actually overturned, while there was a resolution that precluded any bans on Jewish or pro-Israel student groups. In April 1978, 'no platform' was reintroduced, but the resolution regarding Jewish and pro-Israel groups remained in force.

By the end of the 1970s, the political landscape in Britain had changed. The National Front were roundly defeated at the 1979 general election, but Thatcher's incoming Conservative government had attracted much of the right-wing vote with overtures about severely decreasing immigration and a strict law and order agenda, which targeted Britain's multicultural inner cities. Thatcher and the Tories became the focal point of student protest over the next decade, with the cuts to higher education grants being the main site of political contest. While the threat of the NF declined in the 1980s, the 'no platform' policy stayed in place and was often applied to a number of different individuals and groups, which some saw as straying from the original intent of the 1970s policy. The next two chapters will explore this evolution of the 'no platform' policy in the decade of Thatcherism.

Notes

1 Dave Rich, 'Zionists and Anti-Zionists: Political Protest and Student Activism in Britain, 1968–1986' (Birkbeck College: unpublished Ph.D. thesis, 2015) p. 174.
2 See: M. Hanna, 'The National Front and Other Right-Wing Organisations', *Journal of Ethnic and Migration Studies*, 3/1–2 (1974) pp. 49–55; Mark Pitchford, *The Conservative Party and the Extreme Right, 1945–1975* (Manchester: Manchester University Press 2011) pp. 181–219.
3 Robert Skidelsky, *Oswald Mosley* (London: Papermac, 1990) p. 514.
4 Richard Thurlow, 'Authoritarians and Populists on the English Far Right', *Patterns of Prejudice*, 10/2 (1976) pp. 13–20; Martin Walker, *The National Front* (London: Fontana, 1977) pp. 133–177.
5 Nigel Copsey, 'Introduction: Contemporary Perspectives on the British National Party', in Nigel Copsey & Graham Macklin (eds), *The British National Party: Contemporary Perspectives* (Abingdon: Routledge, 2011) p. 5.
6 *Right On!*, 1, n.d. (c. 1973) p. 2, RH WL D6820, Kenneth Spencer Research Library, University of Kansas.
7 Ibid., p. 4.
8 *Right On!*, 2, n.d. (c. 1974) p. 2, RH WL D6820, Kenneth Spencer Research Library, University of Kansas.
9 *Spark*, 2 (Autumn 1973) p. 1.
10 Ibid., p. 2.
11 Dave McCalden, 'NF Students Refuse to be Intimidated', *Britain First*, 19 (April/May 1974) p. 4.
12 Ibid.
13 Ibid; For the view of these events from the IMG perspective, see *Red Weekly*, 29 March, 1974, p. 5.
14 *Unionews*, 6 February, 1974, p. 1.
15 Ibid.
16 Ibid.
17 Ryan Shaffer, *Music, Youth and International Links in Post-War British Fascism: The Transformation of Extremism* (Houndmills: Palgrave Macmillan, 2017) p. 70. For further discussion of the NF and youth, particularly the Young NF, see: Michael Brillig & Raymond Cochrane, 'The National Front and Youth', *Patterns of Prejudice*, 15/4 (1981) pp. 3–15; Matthew Worley & Nigel Copsey, 'White Youth: The Far Right, Punk and British Youth Culture, 1977–87', in Nigel Copsey & Matthew Worley (eds), *Tomorrow Belongs to Us: The British Far Right since 1967* (Abingdon: Routledge, 2017) pp. 113–131.
18 John Callaghan, *The Far Left in British Politics* (Oxford: Blackwell, 1987) pp. 113–160.

19 Tariq Ali, *The Coming British Revolution* (London: Jonathan Cape, 1972) p. 10.
20 *The Red Mole*, 18 September, 1972, p. 1.
21 Ibid.
22 Ibid.
23 Ibid. Italics in original text.
24 NUS, *April Conference: Minutes and Summary of Proceedings* (London: NUS, 1974) p. 79. Bold in original text.
25 Ibid., p. 79.
26 Ibid., p. 79.
27 Ibid., p. 79.
28 Ibid., p. 80.
29 Ibid., p. 80.
30 Ibid., p. 82.
31 Ibid., p. 82.
32 Ibid., p. 80.
33 Ibid., p. 80.
34 'The Dialectics of Freedom', *Patterns of Prejudice*, 8/3 (1974) pp. 12–13.
35 NUS, *April Conference*, p. 80.
36 NUS press release, 'NUS Statement on Racism', 16 April, 1974, MSS 280/54/1, NUS papers, Modern Records Centre, University of Warwick.
37 Ibid.
38 See correspondence to NUS President John Randall by various unions in the file MSS 280/54/1, NUS papers, MRC.
39 *New Statesman*, 10 May, 1974; 17 May, 1974.
40 *The Warwick Boar*, 2 May, 1974, p. 2.
41 Ibid., p. 2.
42 *Darts*, 374 (1974) p. 7.
43 *Palatinate*, 21 May, 1974, p. 2.
44 *The Guardian*, 9 April, 1974.
45 Ibid.
46 *The Guardian*, 16 April, 1974.
47 *The Courier*, 15 May, 1974, p. 3.
48 Ibid.
49 *The Times*, 2 May, 1974, p. 4; *Daily Telegraph*, 2 May, 1974, p. 8.
50 *Daily Telegraph*, 2 May, 1974, p. 8.
51 Ibid.
52 *The Times*, 2 May, 1974, p. 4.
53 Ibid.
54 *The Times Higher Education Supplement*, 14 June, 1974, p. 4.
55 *Daily Telegraph*, 10 May, 1974, p. 2.
56 Ibid.
57 *The Times*, 11 May, 1974, p. 3; *Daily Telegraph*, 10 May, 1974, p. 2.
58 *Daily Telegraph*, 10 May, 1974, p. 2.
59 *The Times*, 11 May, 1974, p. 3.
60 *Daily Telegraph*, 10 May, 1974, p. 2; *The Times*, 11 May, 1974, p. 3.
61 *The Times*, 13 May, 1974, p. 17.
62 *Daily Telegraph*, 14 May, 1974, p. 19.
63 *Socialist Worker*, 25 May, 1974, p. 3.
64 *Red Weekly*, 12 April, 1974, p. 13.
65 LSE International Socialists, *The Red Agitator* (London: LSE IS pamphlet, 1974) pp. 2–3.
66 Ibid., p. 6.
67 *Morning Star*, 24 May, 1974, p. 4.
68 Ibid.
69 Ibid.
70 Steve Parry, 'Students Against Racism and Fascism', *Labour Monthly* (June 1974) p. 259.

71 *Red Weekly*, 29 March, 1974.
72 Evan Smith, *British Communism and the Politics of Race* (Leiden: Brill, 2017) pp. 80–85; 109–112.
73 *Red Weekly*, 29 March, 1974.
74 'Fists Against Fascists', *International Socialism*, 1/70 (June 1974) p. 5.
75 Ibid.
76 *Red Weekly*, 31 October, 1974, p. 2.
77 *Red Weekly*, 23 May, 1974, p. 6.
78 NUS, *Minutes of Extraordinary Conference* (London: NUS, 1974) pp. 34–35.
79 Ibid., p. 35.
80 Ibid., p. 36.
81 Ibid., p. 36.
82 *Morning Star*, 21 June, 1974.
83 Ibid.
84 See: Copsey, *Anti-Fascism in Britain*, p. 120.
85 Ibid.
86 Lord Justice Scarman, *The Red Lion Square Disorders of 15 June 1974: Report of Inquiry by the Rt. Hon. Lord Justice Scarman, O.B.E.*, 1975, p. 8.
87 Ibid.
88 Copsey, *Anti-Fascism in Britain*, p. 120; Scarman, *The Red Lion Square Disorders of 15 June 1974*, p. 11.
89 Copsey, *Anti-Fascism in Britain*, p. 120.
90 NUS, *Minutes of Extraordinary Conference*, p. 36.
91 Ibid., p. 36.
92 Ibid., p. 36.
93 Dave Hann, *Physical Resistance: A Hundred Years of Anti-Fascism* (London: Zero Books, 2013) pp. 250–251.
94 NUS, *The Myth of Red Lion Square* (London: NUS pamphlet, 1974) pp. 21–22.
95 David Renton, *Never Again: Rock Against Racism and the Anti-Nazi League 1976–1982* (Abingdon: Routledge, 2018) pp. 69–103; David Renton, 'Anti-Fascism in the North West: 1976–1982', *North West Labour History Journal*, 27 (2002) pp. 17–28.
96 Colin Sparks, *Fascism and the National Front* (London: SWP pamphlet, 1978) p. 41.
97 Dave Cook, *A Knife at the Throat of Us All: Racism and the National Front* (London: CPGB pamphlet, 1978) p. 28.
98 Ibid.
99 Labour Party NEC *Statement by the National Executive Committee: Response to the National Front* (London: Labour Party pamphlet, 1978) p. 3.
100 IMG, *Fascism: How to Smash It* (London: IMG pamphlet, 1974) p. 11.
101 *The Times*, 12 February, 1977, p. 3.
102 Ibid.
103 Ibid.
104 *The Guardian*, 23 March, 1977.
105 Alan Elsner, 'Race, Tolerance and the NUS', *New Statesman*, 13 May, 1977 p. 638.
106 *The Beaver*, 3 May, 1978, p. 1.
107 *The Economist*, 29 April, 1978, p. 26.
108 Ibid.
109 *The Times*, 28 April, 1978, p. 4.
110 *The Beaver*, 3 May, 1978, p. 1.
111 *The Guardian*, 1 April, 1977.
112 Cited in ibid.
113 *Morning Star*, 1 April, 1977, p. 5.
114 'Racism', *National Student*, 2/3 (May 1977) p. 9.
115 *The Courier*, 7 December, 1977, p. 1.
116 *The Times*, 7 April, 1978.
117 Ibid.

118 Ibid.
119 *Glasgow University Guardian*, 22 April, 1978, p. 3.
120 Ibid.
121 Elsner, 'Race, Tolerance and the NUS', p. 638.
122 Bernard Lewis, 'The Anti-Zionist Resolution', *Foreign Affairs*, 55 (1976) p. 54.
123 David Cesarani, 'Anti-Zionism in Britain, 1922–2002: Continuities and Discontinuities', *Journal of Israeli History*, 25/1 (2006) p. 146.
124 Dave Rich, *The Left's Jewish Problem: Jeremy Corbyn, Israel and Anti-Semitism* (London: Biteback Publishing, 2018) p. 119.
125 Ibid., pp. 120–122.
126 Ibid., pp. 121–122.
127 Ibid., p. 122.
128 Ibid., pp. 122–123.
129 Cited in Rich, *The Left's Jewish Problem*, pp. 123–124.
130 Ann Hulbert & Peter Galison, 'Zionism, Racism and Free Speech', *Commentary*, 1 October, 1978, p. 73.
131 Rich, *The Left's Jewish Problem*, p. 135.
132 Cited in Hulbert & Galison, 'Zionism, Racism and Free Speech', p. 73.
133 *The Times*, 7 April, 1978.
134 Noah Lucas, 'Jewish Students, the Jewish Community and the "Campus War" in Britain', *Patterns of Prejudice*, 19/4 (1985) pp. 27–34; Rich, *The Left's Jewish Problem*, pp. 139–152.
135 Renton, *Never Again*, p. 97.
136 'The Fight Against Racism', *National Student*, 2/3 (May 1977) p. 3.

5

EXPANDING 'NO PLATFORM' IN THE 1980S

In the general election in May 1979, the National Front received only 1.3 per cent of the vote out of the 303 electorates challenged.[1] Margaret Thatcher and the Conservatives won the election convincingly and ushered in 18 years of Conservative rule. As Maurice Ludmer warned in an editorial for the anti-fascist magazine *Searchlight* the previous summer, 'The Front has suffered a major blow, but the racism on which it breeds is alive and well and living in Conservative Central Office.'[2] Alongside the important anti-fascist work done by the Anti-Nazi League, Rock Against Racism and the broader anti-racist movement, one of the other primary reasons for the demise of the NF at the general election was the appeal of Thatcher's right-wing populism to potential NF voters. As Richard Thurlow wrote, Thatcher's 'forceful aggressive leadership, her uncompromising stance on law and order, the stand against the unions and the illiberal attitude towards immigration' had demonstrated that Thatcherism was a powerful alternative to the dwindling fortunes of the National Front and thus, 'Attacked by the left, undermined by the state and having its appeal to patriotism made unnecessary by the actions of Mrs Thatcher, the racial populist neo-fascist right had nowhere to go.'[3] The NF split into three different factions, while the openly neo-Nazi British Movement (previously led by Colin Jordan) continued, recruiting heavily amongst the young skinheads left unemployed by Thatcher's economic policies.

The Anti-Nazi League had mobilised people on an unprecedented scale against the National Front (and against racism more broadly) and this was highly successful in arresting the electoral fortunes of the NF, as well as challenging their determination to win 'the streets'. The success of the ANL saw the NF perform very badly at the 1979 election, but anti-racist, as well as other, activists were confronted with a much more powerful threat – a combative Conservative government under Margaret Thatcher.

With the defeat of the National Front and its immediate threat declining in the eaarly 1980s, there was a rethink of the various strategies used to combat them and the new threats that presented themselves at the time. This included debates about the application of the tactic of 'no platform'. As well as targeting fascists and racists, the 'no platform' policy was also used at times to oppose speakers and groups that were sexist and homophobic. One of the reactions to the growth of the anti-racist movement in Britain was the questioning over whether the fights against sexism and gay oppression needed to taken more seriously. As David Renton notes, when Rock Against Racism was formed in 1976, there were a number of activists who argued that there should be a corresponding Rock Against Sexism.[4] Natalie Thomlinson has shown that within and around the women's liberation movement at the same time, there were Afro-Caribbean and Asian activists who argued that the movement often overlooked or downplayed issues of racism and the experiences of non-white women in Britain.[5] Looking at the example of the NUS' 'no platform' policy in the 1970s and the refusal to allow fascist and explicitly racist speakers to have a platform, inspired some feminist activists in the early 1980s to call for a 'no platform' for sexists as well. This also came as part of a broader campaign against sexism on campuses in the 1980s and critiques of the sexist aspects of student culture.

The 'no platform' tactic was also extended to some homophobic speakers. Coming at a time when the Conservatives stood steadfastly against gay rights and homophobia was the norm on the right, there were protests against some of the explicitly homophobic speakers who appeared on campuses. The most prominent example of this were the protests against a local Tory councillor with a record of homophobic remarks who was invited by the Conservative Association to speak at Swansea University in 1987. The councillor was banned by the student union from campus and the Conservative Association was briefly unaffiliated from the student union.

This led to a debate over the limits of 'no platform' as a tactic and who should be 'no platformed' throughout the 1980s (and which continues today). This debate coincided with a wider one about the relationship between traditional left-wing politics based around class and the new social movements that had emerged in the 1960s and 1970s, increasingly referred to as 'identity politics'. While the left in Britain continued to struggle around prioritising anti-racist politics,[6] anti-racism *in the form of anti-fascism* was taken very seriously by the left (including the student left),[7] which meant a forceful campaign against fascism and racism, such as the maintenance of the 'no platform' policy by the National Union of Students. There was an increasing opinion that sexists and homophobes should be 'no platformed' in the same way as racists and fascists, with many student unions adopting this stance during the 1980s.

However, at the same time, some of those who in the 1970s promoted the tactic of 'no platform' in the student movement, and within the anti-fascist movement more generally, disagreed with the expansion of the 'no platform' policy by some student unions in the 1980s. They argued that 'no platform' was created with the original purpose of opposing the threat of organised fascism on campus, such as that presented by the National Front, which had been involved in the breaking up of meetings at universities and intimidating student protests since the late 1960s (as discussed in the previous chapters). They felt that sexists and homophobes, while offensive, did not present the same kind of threat as the fascists that the policy was originally developed to combat. However, in making the distinction between the threat posed by fascists and organised racists and the 'lesser' threat posed by sexists and homophobes, these critics sometimes lapsed into broader critiques of 'identity politics' and used language that edged towards the right's dismissal of the 'loony left'.

Some of those who disagreed with the expansion of the 'no platorm' policy in the 1980s were more comfortable with the use of the 'no platform' policy against a leading National Front (NF) figure, Patrick Harrington, when he resumed his studies at North London Polytechnic (PNL) in 1984. Although he claimed that he was there to study, his public role in the NF concerned students on campus and soon there was a campaign to have Harrington removed from the campus. Involving the Socialist Workers' Student Society (SWSS), as well as other left-wing groups and non-affiliated students, the campaign continued throughout 1984 with Harrington attempting to use the courts to maintain his presence at PNL, as well as fight the students' campaign. While Harrington was a leading fascist in his organisation, some questioned whether this was an appropriate use of the 'no platform' tactic by students at PNL, and as things came to a head in late 1984, many of the protesting students felt let down by the reluctance of the NUS leadership to support them. Eventually the students essentially 'won' the campaign against Harrington and in early 1985, the PNL administration gave him the option of being taught privately off-campus. But some felt that this gave Harrington victim status and made the student left look intolerant and unreasonable – a complaint that had been made since the 1960s and continues into the twenty-first century.

By the mid-1980s, the application of the tactic of 'no platform' had widened in many circumstances and debates about its use to fight sexist and homophobic speakers, as well as individual students, meant that many felt that the policy had strayed from its original intention. This chapter looks at how these debates unfolded in the early-to-mid-1980s and how sexism and homophobia were presented as threats to students equally significant as racism and fascism, which demanded a similar tactic to prevent sexists and homophobes from airing their views at universities. Individual fascists, such as Patrick Harrington, were also seen as just as problematic as representatives of fascist groups invited to speak or allowed to organise on campus, even if they were there allegedly to study. This chapter will explore how 'no platform' was recalibrated in this period to combat other menaces to students after the initial threat of the National Front had waned by the early 1980s, indicating that debate around the repurposing of the tactic by students has endured for nearly 40 years.

'No platform' for sexists and homophobes

'No platform' for sexists

The history of the Women's Liberation Movement and feminism at British universities has yet to be written, although Sarah Browne has explored the WLM at Scottish universities in the 1960s and 1970s, arguing that the universities became 'a key site in the development of feminist thought and practice'.[8] Since the late 1960s, there had been a concerted effort by feminists at British universities to combat sexism, misogyny and patriarchal attitudes on campus, as well as in the wider world. Coming at the same time as the emergence of women's studies as an academic discipline in universities across the English-speaking world, primarily in Britain and the United States, universities and student politics became an important space for fostering feminist ideas and organising feminist activism. Like other social movements from the same period, the WLM possibly reached its radical peak in the early-to-mid-1970s, but did not disappear in the 1980s, and feminists continued to campaign on a number of fronts during the decade of Thatcherism, including at universities.

Concurrent with a wider campaign against sexism, sexual harassment and sexual violence on campus, there were efforts by some feminist activists at British universities to prevent sexists from publicly appearing or organising within these spaces. Possibly the most well-known of these efforts was at LSE in the early 1980s. In January 1981, a motion was proposed to the LSE student union on women's safety, highlighting attacks on women students and arguing that 'sexual attacks cannot be seen as an isolated phenomenon but rather as a brand of violence that is increased by an increasing wave of sexist ideas'.[9] As well as calls for support for a women's right to self defence (including self defence classes), adequate alarm systems in the halls of residence and NUS support for the Reclaim the Night demonstrations, the motion resolved that the union: 'maintain a "no platform" policy for sexist ideas, literature of any kind, etc., as this obviously contributes to the socialisation process which breeds violence against women'.[10]

This motion followed an earlier debate in March 1980 over the sexist (and racist) nature of rag mags at LSE and a resolution to cease distribution of the rag mag for that year after it was found have included sexist and racist jokes.[11] The protests against the distribution of rag mags occurred at several universities in the 1970s and 1980s due to their racist and sexist content.

Similar to the original introduction of the 'no platform' policy in a wider resolution on the discrimination and violence faced by international students in Britain, the 'no platform' for sexists needs to be seen in a wider context of a resolution explicitly addressing the sexual harassment and violence experienced by students, both on and off campus. Like the 'no platform' for fascists and racists line taken by the NUS, the LSE student union's 'no platform' for sexists was not just an action to be taken against certain types of speech, but saw these forms of speech as precursors to acts of violence which required a pre-emptive response.

The 'no platform for sexists' position at LSE is probably the best known of these kinds of policies, because of the controversy around a protest against the musical act Hot Gossip in 1981, shortly after the motion was proposed to the student union. In March 1981, a group of women occupied a theatre room to prevent the act from performing. The action wasn't completely successful as the act still played (albeit at a later time) after the protestors and those representing the act negotiated an end to the occupation. The student newspaper at LSE, *The Beaver*, reported that an ENTS person had told the paper that 'little disruption was caused as they had been able to work around the protestors'.[12] The feminist magazine *Spare Rib* gave some coverage to the controversy, reporting that the musical act, as well as the LSE's Union Secretary, 'failed to see that the group would be sexist or racist'.[13] The Union Secretary and the group's manager both argued that it was 'sexually liberated' and that 'black and white people dance[d] together'.[14] But the magazine retorted, 'What is so liberating about women in schoolgirls' outfits being whipped or men dragging them across the floor by their hair?'[15] *The Beaver* noted that while the occupation came to an end and the act was able to eventually perform, 'women's groups and Gay Soc staged a peaceful picket by the entrance to the concert' later in the evening.[16]

This particular event was used by future Conservative member of the House of Lords, Daniel Finkelstein, to push for the LSE student union to overturn their 'no platform' policy. The motion, proposed by Melanie Nazareth and seconded by Finkelstein, condemned the 'attempts to ban the dance group Hot Gossip from appearing at the LSE' and listed it alongside 'moves to prevent the Israeli Ambassador speaking', as well as the 'barracking and disruption of Timothy Raison [to be discussed in the next chapter] and Sir Keith Joseph, duly elected Government ministers, using this policy'.[17] The motion proposed:

1. That the 'no platform' policy is abused;
2. That a university is supposed to be a centre for the free exchange of ideas;
3. That there is no need for a 'no platform' policy at the LSE.[18]

Nazareth and Finkelstein succeeded in convincing the student union to temporarily revoke the policy of 'no platform', although it was reinstated (and then overturned again) over the next few years.[19] In recent years, Finkelstein has used the Hot Gossip incident, as well as attempts to 'no platform' Raison and the Israeli Ambassador, to celebrate his temporary revoking of the 'no platform' policy at LSE and campaign for the policy to be rejected in the present.[20]

'No platform' for pro-life speakers and groups

As part of a broader campaign to combat sexism on British campuses, there were also instances of 'no platforming' pro-life organisations and speakers. During the original 'no platform' debates in 1974, Steve Webster wrote in the IMG's *Red Weekly* that 'the campaign against the reactionary anti-abortion group, SPUC [the Society for the Protection of the Unborn Child]' was just as important as the campaign against racism and fascism at British universities and colleges.[21] Protests against SPUC, Life and other pro-life speakers at British universities continued through the 1970s and 1980s. For example, during the campaign against the Corrie Bill to amend the 1967 Abortion Act in 1979, the Women's Group at the University of Warwick protested against the distribution of anti-abortion leaflets in the Union Building.[22]

In late 1985, the Women's Group at Newcastle University called for a representative from SPUC to be disinvited from a debate on abortion which was positioned as 'This House believes that abortion is legalised killing'.[23] The Women's Group was reported as stating:

> We (the Women's Group) don't want the Society for the Protection of the Unborn Child (SPUC) to speak at Newcastle as their anti-abortion views are sexist; any speech made by them would be a platform for sexism. We are simply going along with the Student Union Policy on non-sexism, racism and fascism.[24]

This provoked condemnation from pro-life supporters in the pages of the student newspaper, *The Courier*, with one student writing:

> It is clear from their opposition to the invitation of a speaker, from the Society for the Protection of the Unborn Child, to a debate, that the Women's Group have little or no confidence in their arguments against abortion …
>
> Any group of people, sincere in their beliefs, would have welcomed the opportunity of putting forward their case in a debate with their opposition.
>
> Their action in trying to ban their adversaries from the Union is tantamount to saying, 'We believe in free speech, as long as we agree with the speaker.'[25]

Another student wrote a letter to *The Courier* arguing that banning SPUC for sexism made 'our Student Union's commitment to fighting for abortion rights into no more than a token gesture', calling for debate with SPUC because their ideas were 'commonly held by society at large and by many students'.[26] Opposing the 'technical response of "no platform"', the student declared:

> For those of us who are serious about fighting women's oppression, we should welcome any opportunity to debate with our opponents in order to win the arguments and convince more and more students of the need to fight for free abortion on demand.[27]

Earlier in the same year, feminists at the universities of Glasgow, Manchester and Sheffield had organised protests against pro-life campaigner Victoria Gillick, who at the time was campaigning for under-16s not be given the pill by doctors without parental consent (a final ruling was made by the House of Lords in October 1985). This came at the same time that Enoch Powell sought to push the Unborn Children (Protection) Bill through the House of Commons. In fact, Gillick had previously been part of a pro-Powell group, Powellight, in the 1970s.[28]

Gillick spoke at Glasgow University's Turnbull Hall in February 1985, which was picketed by over 100 demonstrators from various women's groups, with some of those protesting barred from entry by the police.[29] The *Glasgow Guardian*, the student newspaper at the university, reported: 'After being whisked in through a back entrance by plain clothed police, Mrs Gillick began a speech which was heckled from beginning to end.'[30]

This led to some protestors also being ejected from the venue by the police.[31] A letter to the student paper condemned the 'motley group of feminists and communists' who attempted to disrupt Gillick's speech.[32] The letter writer complained:

> It is one thing to picket a politician but quite another to harass a decent law-abiding citizen who desired to enter a place of worship. Fortunately, due to police help, the meeting went ahead as planned but the first few minutes were marred by loutish interruptions from opponents of Mrs Gillick who had entered the meeting with the sole objective of causing trouble.[33]

At the University of Manchester the following month, Gillick was taking part in a debate over the prescription of the pill to under-16s and there was planned action by various feminists to hold placards in the crowd.[34] However, the Revolutionary Communist Party (RCP), usually opposed to actions such as 'no platform',[35] rejected this approach and 'furiously heckl[ed]' Gillick, which was followed by a storming of the stage.[36] The RCP saw Gillick as part of a moralist campaign by crusaders 'whose object is to impose their particular version of Victorian values on the rest of us'.[37]

One protesting student wrote in *The Mancunion*, the student newspaper at Manchester University, that they thought that the student union's policy was 'anti-racist [and] anti-fascist' and alleged that Gillick was a 'member of the Powell-lite Group [sic] in the 1970's', which was a reason, according to the student, why the student union should not have allowed her a platform.[38] She claimed that she was actually asserting this policy when the other feminist protestors harangued them for the disruptive protest, writing:

> The irony was that myself and my comrades, who were upholding union policy by disrupting the meeting, were abused by all the 'right on' radicals present, and finally thrown out, our arguments drowned out by their frenzied demands to hear Gillick's amazing insights (?!)[39]

The feminists, linked to the Women's Group and Sexual Equality Group at Manchester, wrote a letter to *The Mancunion* saying that while they agreed with the RCP's criticisms of Gillick, they objected to the protestors 'who tried to stop her speaking by standing up and shouting "murderer" and hurling general abuse'.[40] The letter stated that they found 'a certain incongruity in the [RCP's] professing to be fighting for women's rights' and argued that the RCP protestors 'overrode the decisions' of the other women at the Gillick debate by 'refusing to leave, although the majority of women there wanted you to'.[41] The letter writers added that the 'violence' of the RCP protestors 'affected many of the women in the room' and their 'stinkbombs set fire to a chair, a potentially dangerous situation'.[42]

Two members of the Revolutionary Communist Students group, David Chandler and Lynn Revell, replied to this letter the following week, stating that they disrupted the Gillick debate 'not because we wanted to be kicked out, but because we wanted to initiate broader opposition to Gillick's victorian [sic] morality'.[43] Despite the RCP's general resistance to 'no platform', Chandler and Revell used it to defend their actions against Gillick, claiming:

> We don't allow fascists to speak on principle ... [W]e can not fight [Gillick's and Powell's] attacks through debate, only by showing we are serious in defending our rights – which means giving no lee-way to them – and doing everything we can do to prevent them from speaking.[44]

Sarah Webster suggests that this disruptive protest by the RCP students 'left student feminists determined not to work with RCP, but also deepened wider factional divides, scuppering organisational work by creating mistrust and ill feeling amongst activists and potential recruits'.[45]

Similar scenes happened when Gillick spoke at the University of Sheffield in October 1985. Both the Revolutionary Communist Students and the Socialist Workers' Student Society (SWSS) called for a mass picket against Gillick by the student union, which was rejected.[46] The Executive Committee of the Sheffield University Student Union instead called for 'a peaceful demonstration, a strong opposing speaker to be invited and that well-constructed arguments be prepared to put to Mrs Gillick'.[47] But both the SWSS and RCS planned to carry out some kind of protest action at Gillick's talk. *Darts*, the student newspaper at Sheffield University, reported:

> The demonstrators originally occupied the stage in an attempt to prevent the debate going ahead. They were persuaded to leave the stage on the agreement that an under-sixteen would be allowed to speak. However, when Gillick rose to speak, the 100 demonstrators gathered in one group to disrupt the debate. The RCS have admitted that they 'did go in there with the sole intention of stopping Gillick from speaking'.[48]

However, while demonstrators were reportedly 'hostile but not violent' at first, scuffles between security staff and protesting students soon occurred, with the student union and the protestors blaming each other for starting the trouble.[49]

Following this incident, the student union debated whether to deregister the RCS and ban the SWSS from making bookings at the university as a student organisation, as well as banning local representatives from the RCP and SWP from appearing on campus.[50] Tracy Nathan from the SWSS described the action taken by the student union as a 'witch hunt' and claimed that 'no solid evidence of [violent] activity has been cited against any SWSS or SWP member'.[51] The Liberal Society at the university criticised this decision and the Society's chair wrote that 'it should be the right of any individual (or group) to organise and campaign on any issue'.[52] Yet the SWSS declined this support from the Liberals as they felt that allowing every group to organise within the union could have been extended to racists and fascists, with Nathan asking 'Are we to extend democratic rights to those who are prepared to physically take them away from anyone who happens to be black or gay etc?'[53]

The final decision of the student union to deregister the RCS and ban both the RCS and SWSS 'from making block bookings in the Students' Union' was made in December.[54] The RCS collected enough signatures to challenge this decision at the next general meeting, but the decision to deregister the group until the end of the academic year was upheld.[55] The RCS tried to work around the ban by attempting to affiliate the RCP front group, Workers Against Racism (more in Chapter 7), to the student union, but this was rejected by the student union leadership.[56] This was during a time when there was a tension within the RCP over whether to protest forcefully against anti-abortionists like Gillick or to debate them (more in Chapter 7). By the late 1980s and into the 1990s, the RCP's attitude towards 'no platform' hardened and there was an increasing fetishisation of 'free speech', which would make future disruptions, like that against Gillick at Manchester in 1985, less likely.

By November 1985, the resistance that Gillick experienced during her speaking engagements led to her announcing her intention to cancel any speeches at universities due to a 'co-ordinated campaign against her being heard' by 'lunatic political elements'.[57]

Richard Lewis and 'no platform' for homophobes at Swansea

In January 1987, a local Conservative councillor in Swansea, Richard Lewis, was invited by the Conservative Association at the University College of Swansea (more commonly referred to as Swansea University) to speak. Lewis was well-known in the local media for his homophobic views and this was at a time when homophobia was widespread in British politics (particularly in the Conservative Party), with the concern about AIDS being used to promote anti-gay agendas. As Daryl Leeworthy has written, '[t]he emergence of HIV/AIDS provided an excuse for social conservatives to try and reverse the development of a public gay life in the 1970s and early 1980s' and that in 1987, several Conservative Party candidates and officials were involved in expressing 'overtly homophobic opinions', including Lewis.[58]

This incident occurred just prior to the Thatcher government starting to agitate against the 'promotion of homosexuality' by local governments (part of, as Anna Marie Smith points out, a wider attack on local governments during the 1980s), leading to the introduction of Section 28 the following year.[59] A column in *Bad Press*, the student newspaper at Swansea, noted that Lewis had 'called for a "Mary Whitehouse" type clean-up campaign for Swansea', 'labelled freedom fighters in Southern Africa as "terrorists"' and called AIDS a 'gay plague'.[60]

The student union at Swansea University had banned Lewis from entering the building, specifying that the Conservative Association had not given them the required four weeks' notice that Lewis was scheduled to speak, rather than 'actually refusing to let him speak' – although they did acknowledge that Lewis' views were 'very dangerous'.[61] But Lewis, supported by members of Conservative Association, attempted to proceed with coming to the university and giving his talk. *Bad Press* described the events:

> Accompanied by two bodyguards, Mr Lewis was met outside the Council Chambers by protestors who barred his entrance. Jon Lloyd-Owen, the Union Treasurer, informed Mr Lewis that he was not welcome in the building and had come uninvited. He was reluctant to leave, saying that he had every right to be there. However, led by Ms Pickett [the Chair of the Conservative Association] the entourage eventually moved out of the building and across to a lecture theatre, followed by some 60 protestors.
>
> Refusing to begin this meeting until everybody was 'sittign [sic] down properly', Ms Pickett looked on scornfully as [Mr Lewis'] speech was drowned by cries of 'OUT OUT' from angry students.[62]

The student newspaper reported that Lewis spoke about the evils of homosexuality and then 'condemned the behaviour of the S.U. members saying that it was an infringement of his freedom of speech'.[63] Lloyd-Owen replied that Lewis was 'a dangerous homophobic bigot, whose antics pose a threat to all students and in particular those already oppressed by racism and anti-gay hysteria'.[64] The student union president declared in *Bad Press* that Lewis was 'reactionary, opportunistic and misinformed' and that his 'ignorant views' were 'a danger to us all and generations to come'.[65]

In the aftermath of the protest against Lewis, the student union disaffiliated the Conservative Association and there was a fierce debate throughout the university about the protest.[66] There were letters in the student newspaper, as well as in the university newsletter, which both condemned and defended the actions of the protestors. One 'narked socialist' wrote to *Bad Press*, calling the protestors 'bloody thugs' and 'mindless', while ruminating that 'the days of peaceful, organised effective demonstration in Britain' were gone.[67] A protesting student replied the following week, countering:

> There was nothing 'thuggish'… about the behaviour displayed by those students who took part in the picket, … Lewis was met by a contingent of people who, not surprisingly, given the highly offensive nature of his views, weren't exactly prepared to roll out the red carpet for him. He received a noisy and hostile reception, it is true, but he was never at any point physically assaulted by a student.[68]

The letter writer also objected to the demonstrators being called 'mindless', stating that the protest was 'very effective' that had achieved its aim – 'the prevention from speaking (for very long) of a truly mindless man who denies freedom of speech to those whom he disagrees with'.[69]

Amidst the debate about the rights and wrongs of the protest, the university administration sought to take action against those involved in the protest, including two lecturers from the university.[70] The Principal at the university, Brian Clarkson, complained about the 'bad publicity' that had been attracted by the protest and proclaimed that he was 'particularly shocked to see that two members of the academic staff were associated with the disruption'.[71] After over 30 academics from across the university signed a letter defending the protest against Lewis, Clarkson stated that freedom of speech was 'the foundation of a University society and is not one which can be qualified in any way'.[72] But Colwyn Williamson, a philosophy lecturer at the university, asked 'is there anyone who honestly believes in an unqualified right of free speech?'[73] As the letter by the numerous academics pointed out, 'freedom of speech is not an absolute right in our society' and one that is legally curtailed on several levels.[74]

As the university administration deliberated over whether to discipline the staff members that had protested, particularly one drama lecturer who was also gay, the Association of University Teachers (AUT) and the student union publicly lambasted Clarkson.[75] The student union stated that it 'reject[ed] Clarksons [sic] unqualified statement on "freedom of speech"' and pushed to 'ensure that no-one [was] victimised by the Principal or College for their part in the demo'.[76] After Clarkson wrote in the university newsletter that it was 'not necessary for the College continually to have to dissociate itself from such views' as those professed by Lewis,[77] Dave Moxham, the student union President, argued that 'gay lecturers and students would still feel there was a lack of support because the College had in no way disassociated itself from Cllr. Lewis' "crusade"'.[78] In the wake of the Lewis incident, the student union implemented a formal 'no platform' policy, with *Bad Press* reporting that the union believed that 'positive action against bigots, racists and homophobes must have to be taken as their views [had] no place on a university campus'.[79] However, policies like the one introduced at Swansea caused concern amongst some of those who campaigned for 'no platform' in the previous decade.

Criticisms of the expansion of 'no platform' in the 1980s

Some of the original proponents of the 'no platform' approach in the 1970s were critical of the extension of its use in the 1980s against sexists and homophobes. For example, Lindsey German from the Socialist Workers Party wrote in *Socialist Worker Review* in 1986 that the policy had 'been used to deny a platform to a whole range of people whose ideas are very far from the original intention of the ban'.[80] German argued that while the call for its application against racists and sexists demonstrated 'the growing awareness among a layer of young people of the racist and sexist nature of capitalist society' and the urge 'to take quite radical action', it led to 'a growth in the level of tokenism about how to deal with the issues'.[81] German complained:

> By the early eighties, NUS conferences were riddled with points of order objecting to remarks supposedly discriminating against women, blacks, gays, disabled people and so on. Most of the objections were trivial and a few downright stupid. Nearly all could have been dealt with by argument, not no platform.[82]

Although coming from the left, and on the whole, supportive of campaigns around these issues, German's rhetoric here somewhat mirrored complaints from the right about 'sensitive' students in the 1980s (what would be labelled 'political correctness' in the 1990s and 'snowflake' culture in the 2010s) and the broader 'loony left'.[83] Part of German's criticisms of the student left in the 1980s possibly stemmed from the scepticism within the SWP over 'identity politics' at this time, with a view that some aspects of the struggles against sexism, racism and homophobia were distractions from the class struggle.[84]

A similar argument was made by the CARF (Campaign Against Racism and Fascism) collective. CARF had been a London based anti-racist organisation in the late 1970s, and in the 1980s had a monthly newsletter in the pages of anti-fascist magazine *Searchlight*. [85] CARF argued that the left, including the student left, had often articulated an anti-fascist outlook at the expense of broader anti-racist action, but at the same time, anti-fascism had sought to bring in a range of groups (such as gays, lesbians and feminists) to 'form the base of the anti-fascist constituency'.[86] CARF suggested, however, that 'equating different oppressions equally in the need to build an anti-fascist movement often has disastrous effects in terms of fighting racism' and claimed that this had happened with regards to the expansion of 'no platform' in the 1980s.[87]

CARF complained that the tactic used to be 'applied very seriously and carefully to *known* fascists and *active* racists', but now it was 'used to censor practically everyone – fascists, racists, sexists, heterosexualists – in a way that detracts from its original intention'.[88] This, CARF asserted, allowed the fascists to portray themselves as purveyors of 'free speech' and as 'victims of the loony left'.[89]

On the other side of the political divide, Paul Johnson, writing in *The Spectator* in 1986, bemoaned that '[a]n awful lot of banning, boycotting, vetoing and blacklisting' happened on campus and that '[w]hen not banning, students [were] worrying'.[90] Johnson trivialised the things that students were allegedly worrying about, mocked them for having anxiety over the cost of campus driers or the lack of vegetarian options in the student union, alongside concerns over AIDS and environmental cancers.[91]

For German, protests against hard right Tory MPs or pro-lifers like Victoria Gillick were sometimes necessary, but 'should not be graced with the title of "no platform"', which meant challenging racist and sexist ideas instead of instigating 'a blanket ban'.[92] German argued:

> the policy often means little in confronting racism and sexism on more than an individual level. But what is more, it broadens the definition of no platform to an almost unworkable degree. The original no platform went for stopping organised fascists and racists, because their organisation was such as threat. That is not the case with individual members of the rugby club, however noxious

they might be. These people have to be defeated politically, in open and hopefully large union meetings.[93]

While the targets of the tactic of 'no platform' for sexists may have differed from the organised fascist groups that the policy had originally been implemented for, German's description of how 'no platform' was being applied was not what was actually occurring in most instances. The application of 'no platform' was still primarily against those addressing an audience and using a platform to disseminate their ideas. 'No platform' was reserved, for the most part, for preventing racists, sexists and homophobes from speaking *from a platform*, not being used against individuals in a less public setting.

Patrick Harrington at North London Poly

German was more agreeable to other uses of 'no platform' in the 1980s, such as in the campaign against the National Front's Patrick Harrington at North London Polytechnic in 1984. Although the campaign centred on an individual, German maintained '[w]e deny the right of free speech to those who want to destroy free speech altogether' – people like Harrington.[94]

Patrick Harrington was a leading figure in the National Front in the early-to-mid-1980s. After the electoral defeat of the NF at the 1979 election, the organisation split into several different groups. John Tyndall formed the New National Front in 1980 and in 1982, transformed this into the British National Party (BNP). The remnants of the NF in the 1980s became divided between the 'Political Soldiers' and the NF Flag Group,[95] which competed with the more outwardly neo-Nazi British Movement and the BNP for support, primarily amongst football hooligans and skinheads,[96] in the Thatcher years. Both the wings of the NF, first under Martin Webster and then Andrew Brons, flirted with Strasserism (emphasising the 'left-wing' and 'anti-capitalist' aspects of national socialism), with some, such as Harrington, Nick Griffin, Joe Pearce and Derek Holland, combining this with the idea of the 'political soldier' and eschewing the electoralism of the NF of the 1970s.

The protests against Harrington should be seen in the context of the longer campaign against Andrew Brons, who had been a politics lecturer at the Harrogate College of Further Education since the 1970s. Once Brons became leader of the National Front in late 1980, there was a campaign against his role as a teacher at the college, even though the Principal supported Brons. This campaign was one of the last by the Anti-Nazi League before it wound up in 1982, but also brought together other anti-fascist activists in the North of England, as well as local Asian youth from Bradford and Leeds.[97] In May 1981, students at the college voted for Brons to be suspended, and the following month over 500 students and anti-racist protestors marched through Harrogate to demand his resignation.[98] *Searchlight* suggested at the time that anti-fascists were 'turning the tide against Andrew Brons and his thugs', so much so that 'the Students' Union [was] confident that Principal Peter Drake [could] no longer continue to cover up and excuse Brons' activites'.[99]

By early 1982, *Searchlight* was reporting that 11 Labour MPs had joined the campaign against Brons and that further demonstrations were to be held.[100] The issue, the anti-fascist magazine editorialised, went further than Brons because he had started to attract several Young NF members at Harrogate.[101] The editorial proclaimed:

> Brons has always been very careful to be seen as a moderate, democratic, mild-mannered man. But what Mr Drake and others who support the right of racists and fascists to teach politics are overlooking [is] the fact that he is not just a member, but the *leader* of a party which is doing its best to stir up racial violence … Now Brons is attracting young racists and fascists into the college where he supposedly leaves his politics outside the door.[102]

The magazine called for 'everyone who sympathises with the students who simply don't want to be taught by the leader of the NF' to write to the Principal of Harrogate College 'explaining why Brons is not fit to be a teacher'.[103]

The protests against Brons intensified at this time. In the lead up to a demonstration outside Harrogate College in February 1982, students announced in *Searchlight* that '[i]ndividual students have been threatened for organising against Brons and some have been sent threatening letters'.[104] The militant anti-fascist journal, *Red Action*, claimed that Brons was wary of these protests and was 'always escorted home by some NF students who have enrolled at the college'.[105] When over 500 people picketed the college at the time, they were confronted by around 40 fascists, which led to 2 anti-fascist protestors being stabbed.[106] However the campaign was unsuccessful and focus shifted elsewhere, especially after the Anti-Nazi League wound down. *The Times Higher Education Supplement* reported in 1985 that there was still student pressure on Brons to resign or be sacked, even after he stepped down from leadership of the NF.[107]

While the campaign against Brons was unsuccessful, anti-fascist students, after a long struggle, were eventually more fortunate in the campaign against Patrick Harrington. During the early 1980s, Harrington was deputy editor of the National Front's newspaper *NF News*, and in 1984 he re-enrolled as a student at the Polytechnic of North London (PNL). He had previously been identified the previous year as a student at PNL while attempting to sell *NF News* to students.[108] It has been suggested that Harrington re-enrolled at PNL, a notoriously left-wing campus at the time, as a deliberate provocation to the radical student body and to generate publicity for the NF.[109] Harrington was also not just a rank-and-file NF member who happened to be a student, but was a central figure in the organisation at the time. Nigel Copsey explains the significance of Harrington within the NF when he enrolled at PNL:

> he was a leading activist – the treasurer of Kensington/Chelsea NF, a student and Young National Front organiser, assistant editor of *National Front News*, and an officer in the NF's Publicity Department. Moreover, there were allegations that he was a former editor of *South London News*, a publication that had featured hit-lists of anti-fascists alongside details of how to send opponents

> faeces in the post as well as advice on how to tape razor blades to envelopes. Harrington had also been suspected of organising attacks on anti-fascists in Islington in 1981 and allegedly advocated the use of firebombing in a conversation recorded on tape by an ANL member.[110]

Susan Gardiner, who worked in the library at PNL at the time, has written in her recollections of the period that the mainstream press seldom mentioned that Harrington 'very rarely came to PNL alone' and was 'often accompanied by a small entourage who had no business in the building and many people felt that they were quite intimidating'.[111]

Protests began in the spring term of 1984 and gathered momentum when the Socialist Workers' Student Society became involved. As an article in *Socialist Worker* explained: 'When it became known Harrington was a student at the poly, black students began picketing his lectures. They rightly said that the presence of a Nazi organiser in the college would lead to a rise in racism'.[112]

There had been criticisms at the time (and in subsequent histories of militant anti-fascism) from those involved in the Anarcho-Trotskyist group Red Action (who were heavily involved in physical anti-fascism in the 1980s and 1990s) of the SWP's anti-fascism, which allegedly evaporated after the NF's electoral defeat in 1979 and the winding up of the Anti-Nazi League. But Dave Hann, who was involved in Red Action and its offshoot, Anti-Fascist Action, wrote that it would be 'wrong to assume that the SWP entirely abandoned the anti-fascist cause', highlighting the role that the SWSS played in mobilising an anti-fascist campaign to oust Harrington from the PNL campus.[113]

Harrington sought an injunction against the SWSS and identified a black SWSS member, Steve Phillips, within it, trying to ban PNL students from demonstrating against his presence on campus.[114] This led to mass picket in early May 1984, which was in breach of the injunction. Harrington persisted with his attendance at the Polytechnic, 'with considerable police protection', and continued with his pursuit of protesting students through the court system.[115] In response, students occupied buildings at PNL and after their removal by the police, another occupation of the library and canteen by 300 students commenced as Harrington arrived at college (with another 400 students protesting outside).[116]

Once the next academic year resumed in the autumn, the protests also recurred. *Socialist Worker* reported in October 1984 that 200 students had demonstrated outside the PNL, despite the on-going injunction.[117] By the end of the month, Harrington had been moved to another PNL campus (the Marlborough building on Holloway Road), which the SWP claimed 'has shown that mass activity by students is the only way to keep Harrington out of the Poly'.[118] Students continued to ignore the court orders to not picket against Harrington on PNL grounds and there was an occupation of the Marlborough building in November 1984.[119] *Socialist Worker* quoted several students involved in the occupation, writing:

> Contempt for the courts' injunctions grows at each picket. Val, one of the students who has become involved this term said: 'If our slogan is "Nazis Out", then we have to take the action needed to keep him out.'
>
> Steve Tusane [sic], one of the students threatened with jail, added: 'If there's enough support from PNL and other students, we can hold the occupation till we next appear in court.'[120]

However at this next court appearance, Steven Tisane and another student, John Leatham, were 'imprisoned for refusing to give an undertaking that they would stop trying to prevent Harrington from attending the Polytechnic'.[121]

Throughout the 10-month campaign, some of the protesting students complained that the NUS was not doing enough to help the students' protest against Harrington, despite the maintenance of the 'no platform' policy in the 1980s. There were several calls for the NUS to include the campaign against Harrington in their nationwide actions against cuts to grants.[122] When the occupations in contravention of the court injunctions were underway, the SWP criticised the NUS for not supporting them, writing:

> The behaviour of the National Union of Students has been just as bad. They say that they will not support the illegal actions. Even the most left wing member of the executive, Karen Talbot of the Socialist Students in NOLS grouping, refuses to stand out against the rest, hiding behind the 'complexity of the situation'.[123]

Maggie Mellon, a member of the Revolutionary Communist Group, objected that the NUS had 'not only failed to defend the North London Poly students but actively attempted to undermine their struggle', citing an alleged refusal by the NUS Executive to give students from PNL a platform during a national demonstration against grant cuts and the circulation of a letter advising students not to picket after the release of Tisane and Leatham from jail.[124] The SWP also condemned the NUS for not calling for the release of Tisane and Leatham while they spent their fortnight in prison[125] and reported that at the NUS' December conference, there was vocal grassroots opposition to the NUS leadership in support of the 'Harrington Out' campaign.[126] A report in *Socialist Worker* declared:

> During the campaign against nazi [sic] Harrington students at PNL have been amazed and disgusted at the behaviour of NUS executive who have consistently undermined and attacked the campaign. SWSS delegates at the recent NUS national conference successfully moved a vote of censure on the NUS executive on two occasions.
>
> Over two thirds of conference delegates censured the executive for their appalling behaviour towards PNL students.[127]

Grant Keir, writing in *Socialist Action* (the successor journal to the IMG's *Red Weekly* after it dissolved into an entrist group inside the Labour Party), accused the NUS leadership of 'organising a campaign of lies and slurs' against the PNL students.[128]

Phil Woolas, President of the NUS at the time, was quoted in the *Morning Star* as saying, '[v]iolence is the trademark of groups like the National Front' and that the 'case against the National Front is a just one, best served by peaceful protest'.[129] Anne McNaught, writing in the student newspaper at the University of Edinburgh, reported that a Joint Committee formed between the PNL student union, the NUS and various education unions described confrontations by protesting students with the police and the courts as 'counter-productive', which 'threaten[ed] staff and students' and 'could jeopardise the continued operation of the Polytechnic'.[130] The Joint Committee, McNaught wrote, were attempting to persuade the PNL Director to 'adopt the policy that no student should be forced against their will to share tutorials or seminars with a known racist or fascist' and that Harrington should be taught in isolation, which he had refused to do so far.[131]

Harrington attempted to cultivate his status as a victim of an intolerant student left and used the court system and police to maintain his presence on campus. But this image was hindered by the fact that he went on television in November 1984 and made racist remarks. This led to the Inner London Education Authority (ILEA) pressuring the administration at PNL to draw the controversy to a close, with the PNL Director, Dr David MacDowall, resigning shortly after.[132] The following month, the new Director arranged for Harrington to 'be taught in isolation in a small Polytechnic house away from the main sites', while students agreed to end the picket.[133] Students claimed this was 'a 90 percent victory', with *Socialist Worker* stating:

> This is a very important step forward for the Harrington Out campaign compared with what was on offer previously. It means Harrington will not, in any way, be able to organise for the NF in the college. It means that other students will be removed from the intimidating effect of his presence.[134]

Copsey has noted that some suggested that 'this "victory" came at too great a cost, with the media reporting Harrington and not his objectors as the injured party'.[135] Reports in the mainstream press did focus on Harrington and helped position him as the victim of a repressive left-wing student culture. An editorial for *The Times* demonstrates succinctly how this was framed by the press, in which it argued:

> The PNL harbours a cadre of young and not so youthful extremists, some identifiably members of the Socialist Workers' Party, others not; their brethren are responsible for much of the disruption that bedevils schools and municipal administration elsewhere in inner London. These leaders have followers: for too many of the polytechnic's lecturers teaching is a political game and their institutional obligations nil; for too long the absence of academic discipline has encouraged unaffiliated students to believe they can demonstrate and disrupt at no cost. These elements in the polytechnic gave Mr Patrick Harrington and his National Front friends their chance.[136]

But *Socialist Worker* argued that in the end, Harrington was 'unable to fulfil either of the NF's aims in sending him to the college – organising other students and intimidating black students'.[137] As Copsey notes, the NF's membership had fallen rapidly over the last five years (from around 10,000 in 1979 to just below 1,000 in January 1985) and Harrington's stunt could not arrest this decline.[138]

Unlike the 'Battle of Lewisham' in 1977 and the success of the Anti-Nazi League in the late 1970s and early 1980s, the protest against Harrington, led largely (but not wholly) by the SWSS, seems quickly forgotten in the SWP's remembrance of its anti-fascist history. Despite claiming a '90 percent victory' at the time, the Harrington affair has been portrayed since as a pyrrhic victory – the students may have won the battle to remove Harrington from the main PNL sites, but the optics of the controversy allowed Harrington to portray himself as a victim of a censorious student body.

This tapped into a wider concern about students' lack of tolerance for opposing ideas. While in the 1970s, the students involved in these kinds of protests and supporting the 'no platform' policy were portrayed by many as violent extremists (called 'red fascists' on occasions), by the 1980s, students were increasingly seen as over-sensitive, rather than dangerous, being linked to the wider tabloid disapproval of the 'loony left' in the 1980s.

Conclusion

The policy of 'no platform' was originally introduced to combat the threat of fascism and racism at British universities in the 1970s, and was particularly aimed at the National Front when the organisation seemed to be in the ascendance. By the late 1970s, the NF looked to be in decline, which was the result of a large scale anti-fascist campaign by the Anti-Nazi League and the rise of Margaret Thatcher as a hard right (and electable) alternative to the NF. At the 1979 election the NF vote was very low (despite its contesting over 300 seats) and in the aftermath of the electoral defeat the NF split into several different organisations.

The decline of the pressing threat of the NF left the anti-fascist and anti-racist movements in Britain with the question of how to adapt to the new realities of the 1980s, when the Conservative government was the most immediate threat of racism directed against Britain's ethnic minority communities. This required alternative methods to the tactics used to combat the NF. As Paul Gilroy wrote in *There Ain't No Black in the Union Jack* in the mid-1980s:

> The incoming Conservative administration had played the race card as part of its own populist electoral strategy. This altered the configurations of racial politics, further de-emphasizing the role of the neo-fascist parties. Anti-racism therefore acquired a party political connotation. The [Anti-Nazi] League's single issue orientation became harder to sustain and looked out of place when the Prime Minister elect made remarks about British people 'feeling rather swamped'.[139]

Alongside calls for a broader anti-racist movement, there were also a number of activists who felt that the anti-fascist cause was emphasised at the expense of campaigns for women's liberation and gay rights. The left took anti-fascism seriously – it needed to take the fight against sexism and homophobia just as seriously.

Against this background of shifting concerns in the early days of Thatcherism and debates around the left's relationship with identity politics and new social movements, there were pushes to widen the policy of 'no platform' by individual student unions to ban sexists and homophobes, alongside fascists and racists. An early example of this was at LSE in 1980–81, where an explicit 'no platform for sexists' policy was introduced. Although this policy was initially short-lived (being overturned after 18 months), by the mid-1980s a similar policy had been adopted by several student unions. As seen in the next chapter, the student unions at the University of East Anglia and University College Cardiff both had 'no platform' policies that included bans on sexist speakers.[140]

There were also efforts to 'no platform' pro-life speakers and organisations on campus, although this was not official student union policy in most instances. In 1985, students at Newcastle and Manchester universities protested against the Society for the Protection of the Unborn Child and pro-life campaigner Victoria Gillick respectively. This drew criticism from other feminists at the university, who disagreed with their tactics and encouraged debate with the pro-life lobby.

The policy of 'no platform' was also extended to homophobic speakers at some universities, with the student union at University College Swansea attempting to prevent a local Conservative councillor, Richard Lewis, from speaking to the university's Conservative Association. Lewis was infamous in the local area for his anti-gay attitudes and his hard right political outlook.

This expansion of the 'no platform' tactic to include action against sexists and homophobes caused some of those originally wedded to the idea to object to its use beyond the original targets – organised racists and fascists. They felt that sexists and homophobes, while offensive, did not present the same kind of threat as the fascists that the policy was originally developed to combat. However the 'no platform' for sexists and homophobes needs to be seen in a wider context of the student unions attempting to address the sexual and homophobic harassment and violence experienced by students. The policy of 'no platform' for sexists and homophobes was not just an action to be taken against certain types of speech, but saw these forms of speech as precursors to acts of violence which required a pre-emptive response.

Those who criticised the expansion of the 'no platform' policy were more comfortable with its use at the Polytechnic of North London in 1984, when students opposed the fascist Patrick Harrington's presence on campus. Harrington was a leading figure in the National Front, one of the groups that had emerged out of the splits in the NF after 1979, and enrolled at PNL as a student. Some students saw Harrington as an intimidating presence, particularly with regards to ethnic minority and overseas students, and he allegedly was involved in selling and distributing NF material while on campus. Students, including a contingent from the Socialist Workers' Student Society, launched a campaign against Harrington which lasted nearly a year. The polytechnic and the

NUS did little to help the protesting students and Harrington pursued the protestors through the courts. After ten months, the PNL administration arranged for Harrington to be taught privately off-campus and the students declared a 90 per cent victory, but the incident was seen by many as a pyrrhic victory for the students, that only allowed Harrington to portray himself as a victim of an intolerant student cohort denying him the freedom of speech.

These issues about the use of 'no platform' in the 1980s only heightened throughout the 1980s and as will be shown in the next chapter, the years from 1985 to 1987 saw the policy used against a variety of speakers who were not explicit fascists. This caused much concern about the supposed lack of free speech at British universities and was used by the Thatcher government to introduce legislation in late 1986 to 'protect' free speech on campus.

Notes

1 Christopher Husbands, 'Extreme Right-Wing Politics in Great Britain', *West European Politics*, 11/2 (1988) p. 67.
2 'Editorial', *Searchlight*, 36 (June 1978) p. 2.
3 Richard Thurlow, *Fascism in Britain: A History 1918–1985* (Oxford: Basil Blackwell, 1987) p. 286.
4 David Renton, *Never Again: Rock Against Racism and the Anti-Nazi League, 1976–1982* (Abingdon: Routledge, 2018) pp. 118–122.
5 Natalie Thomlinson, *Race, Ethnicity and the Women's Movement in England, 1968–1993* (Houndmills: Palgrave Macmillan, 2016).
6 See: Trevor Carter, *Shattering Illusions: West Indians in British Politics* (London: Lawrence & Wishart, 1986); Evan Smith, *British Communism and the Politics of Race* (Leiden: Brill, 2018).
7 For a discussion of how anti-racism was subsumed by left-wing anti-fascism in the 1970s and 1980s, see: Paul Gilroy, *There Ain't No Black in the Union Jack: The Cultural Politics of Race and Nation* (London: Routledge, 2002) pp. 151–156; Jenny Bourne, '*CARF*: The Life and Times of a Frontline Magazine', *Race and Class*, 59/3 (2018) pp. 92–95.
8 Sarah Browne, '"Women Are Far Too Sweet for This Kind of Game": Women, Feminism and Student Politics in Scotland, c. 1968–1979', in Jodi Burkett (ed.), *Students in Twentieth-Century Britain and Ireland*, p. 279. Also see, Sarah Browne, '"A Veritable Hotbed of Feminism": Women's Liberation in St Andrews, Scotland, c. 1968–1979', *Twentieth Century British History*, 23/1 (2012) pp. 100–123; Celia Hughes, *Young Lives on the Left: Sixties Activism and the Liberation of the Self* (Manchester: Manchester University Press, 2015) pp. 120–130.
9 'Agenda for Union General Meeting to be Held on 29.1.81', LSE/STUDENTS UNION/23, LSE Student Union Papers, LSE.
10 Ibid.
11 'Minutes of Executive Meeting', 5 March, 1980, LSE/STUDENT UNIONS/4, LSE Student Union Papers.
12 *The Beaver*, 11 March, 1981, p. 3.
13 Mary Middleton, 'Not So Hot …', *Spare Rib* (May 1981) p. 17.
14 Ibid.
15 Ibid.
16 *The Beaver*, 11 March, 1981, p. 3.
17 'Business Motion I: Freedom of Speech', 15 October, 1981, LSE/STUDENT UNIONS/35, LSE Student Union Papers.

18 Ibid.
19 *The Beaver*, 5 November, 1984, p. 8.
20 Warwick Smith, 'Mediating the Media: Daniel Finkelstein', *LSE Magazine* (Winter 2008) p. 19; Daniel Finkelstein, 'Free Speech Is Still Important', *Jewish Chronicle*, 12 March, 2010, p. 34; *The Times*, 16 October, 2013, www.thetimes.co.uk/article/never-empower-people-who-hate-freedom-0l0c3hs3qj0 (accessed 16 March, 2019).
21 *Red Weekly*, 12 April, 1974, p. 6.
22 *The Warwick Boar*, 16 May, 1979, p. 6.
23 *The Courier*, 21 November, 1985, p. 1.
24 Ibid.
25 *The Courier*, 5 December, 1985, p. 9.
26 Ibid.
27 Ibid.
28 Martin Durham, *Sex and Politics: Family and Morality in the Thatcher Years* (Houndmills: Macmillan, 1991) p. 50.
29 *Glasgow Guardian*, 7 March, 1985, p. 4.
30 Ibid.
31 Ibid.
32 Ibid., p. 6.
33 Ibid.
34 Sarah Webster, 'Protest Activity in the British Student Movement, 1945 to 2011' (University of Manchester: unpublished Ph.D. thesis, 2015) pp. 198–199.
35 'Fight Racism, Not Idiots', *The Next Step*, October 1984, p. 6; 'No Platform?', *The Next Step*, 3 May, 1985, p. 2.
36 Ibid., p. 199.
37 Kate Marshall, *Moral Panics and Victorian Values: Women and the Family in Thatcher's Britain* (London: Junius Publications, 1985) p. 32.
38 *The Mancunion*, 6 March, 1985, p. 4.
39 Ibid.
40 Ibid.
41 Ibid.
42 Ibid.
43 *The Mancunion*, 13 March, 1985, p. 5.
44 Ibid.
45 Webster, 'Protest Activity in the British Student Movement', p. 199.
46 *Darts*, 30 October, 1985, p. 2.
47 Ibid.
48 *Darts*, 13 November, 1985, p. 8.
49 Ibid.
50 Ibid., p. 1.
51 *Darts*, 27 November, 1985, p. 6.
52 *Darts*, 22 January, 1986, p. 7.
53 *Darts*, 5 February, 1986, p. 5.
54 *Darts*, 11 December, 1985, p. 1.
55 *Darts*, 22 January, 1986, p. 3; *Darts*, 5 February, 1986, p. 2.
56 *Darts*, 5 March, 1986, p. 1.
57 *The Times Higher Education Supplement*, 15 November, 1985, p. 1.
58 Daryl Leeworthy, *A Little Gay History of Wales* (Cardiff: University of Wales Press, 2019) pp. 122–123.
59 Anna Marie Smith, *New Right Discourses on Race and Sexuality: Britain, 1968–1990* (Cambridge: Cambridge University Press, 1994) pp. 15–22.
60 *Bad Press*, 3 February, 1987, p. 3.
61 Ibid., p. 1.
62 Ibid.
63 Ibid.

64 Ibid.
65 Ibid., p. 3.
66 *Bad Press*, 10 February, 1987, p. 3.
67 *Bad Press*, 3 February, 1987, p. 5.
68 *Bad Press*, 10 February, 1987, p. 5.
69 Ibid.
70 *Bad Press*, 10 February, 1987, p. 3.
71 *Newsletter/Newyddiun*, 5 February, 1987, p. 1.
72 *Newsletter/Newyddiun*, 26 February, 1987, p. 10.
73 Ibid.; Emphasis in original text.
74 Ibid., p. 9.
75 *Bad Press*, 10 February, 1987, p. 1; *Bad Press*, 24 February, 1987, p. 1.
76 *Bad Press*, 24 February, 1987, p. 1
77 *Newsletter/Newyddiun*, 26 February, 1987, p. 10.
78 *Bad Press*, 10 March, 1987, p. 1.
79 *Bad Press*, 24 February, 1987, p. 1.
80 Lindsey German, 'No Platform: Free Speech for All?' *Socialist Worker Review* (April 1986) p. 11.
81 Ibid.
82 Ibid.
83 For further information on the right-wing idea of the 'loony left', see: James Curran, Ivor Gaber & Julian Petley, *Culture Wars: The Media and the British Left* (Abingdon: Routledge, 2019).
84 See: Ian Birchall, *Tony Cliff: A Marxist For His Time* (London: Bookmarks, 2011) pp. 463–474.
85 Bourne, '*CARF*', p. 93.
86 CARF, 'Challenging the New Racist Culture … Part Two', *Searchlight* (July 1986) p. 17; Bourne, '*CARF*', p. 92.
87 CARF, 'Challenging the New Racist Culture', p. 17.
88 Ibid.
89 Ibid.
90 Paul Johnson, 'Negative Impressions', *The Spectator*, 15 February, 1986, p. 17.
91 Ibid.
92 German, 'No Platform', p. 12.
93 Ibid.
94 Ibid.
95 Nigel Copsey. *Contemporary British Fascism: The British National Party and the Quest for Legitimacy* (Houndmills: Palgrave Macmillan, 2004) pp. 36–46.
96 See: Anti-Nazi League, *British Movement: Nazis on Our Streets* (London: ANL pamphlet, 1981) pp. 12–13; Roger Eatwell, *Fascism: A History* (London: Pimlico, 2003) p. 343.
97 Sean Birchall, *Beating the Fascists: The Untold Story of Anti-Fascist Action* (London: Freedom Press, 2010) p. 53.
98 'Beating the Brons Brigade', *Searchlight* (August 1981) p. 12.
99 Ibid.
100 'Editorial', *Searchlight* (March 1982) p. 2.
101 Ibid.
102 Ibid.
103 Ibid.
104 'Demonstrate Against Racism', *Searchlight* (February 1982) p. 20.
105 *Red Action* (April 1982) p. 4.
106 Ibid.; *The Times*, 18 February, 1982, p. 3.
107 *The Times Higher Education Supplement*, 29 March, 1985, p. 4.
108 Nigel Copsey, *Anti-Fascism in Britain* (Abingdon: Routledge, 2017) pp. 153–154.
109 Ibid., p. 154.

110 Ibid., p. 154.
111 Susan Gardiner, 'Rioting in the Library: The Far Right and Men', *Chronicles of the British Far Right*, 1 April, 2019, https://chroniclesofthebritishfarright.wordpress.com/2019/04/01/rioting-in-the-library-the-far-right-and-me-draft/ (accessed 8 April, 2019).
112 *Socialist Worker*, 29 April, 1984, p. 14.
113 Dave Hann, *Physical Resistance: A Hundred Years of Anti-Fascism* (London: Zero Books, 2013) p. 321.
114 Copsey, *Anti-Fascism in Britain*, p. 154; *Socialist Worker*, 29 April, 1984, p. 14.
115 Copsey, *Anti-Fascism in Britain*, pp. 154–155.
116 *Socialist Worker*, 26 May, 1984, p. 16.
117 *Socialist Worker*, 13 October, 1984, p. 15.
118 *Socialist Worker*, 27 October, 1984, p. 15.
119 *Socialist Worker*, 24 November, 1984, p. 14.
120 Ibid.
121 Copsey, *Anti-Fascism in Britain*, p. 155.
122 *Socialist Worker*, 12 May, 1984, p. 14.
123 *Socialist Worker*, 20 October, 1984, p. 15.
124 Maggie Mellon, 'No NF Organisers', *Fight Racism! Fight Imperialism!* (January 1985) p. 4.
125 *Socialist Worker*, 7 December, 1984, p. 16.
126 *Socialist Worker*, 15 December, 1984, p. 15.
127 *Socialist Worker*, 22 December, 1984, p. 15.
128 Grant Keir, 'Students Back on the Streets!' *Socialist Action*, 7 December, 1984, p. 10.
129 *Morning Star*, 6 October, 1984, p. 6.
130 *The Student*, 8 November, 1984, p. 3.
131 Ibid.
132 *The Times*, 8 December, 1984, p. 2.
133 Copsey, *Anti-Fascism in Britain*, p. 155.
134 *Socialist Worker*, 12 January, 1985, p. 2.
135 Copsey, *Anti-Fascism in Britain*, p. 155.
136 *The Times*, 13 December, 1984, p. 15.
137 *Socialist Worker*, 19 January, 1985, p. 14.
138 Copsey, *Anti-Fascism in Britain*, p. 156.
139 Gilroy, *There Ain't No Black in the Union Jack*, p. 177.
140 Ian McKenzie, 'Confidential Report to the Vice-Chancellor on the Visit of John Carlisle MP to the University of East Anglia on 24th April 1986' (July 1986) appendix 2(i), UEA/GRAY/1/3, UEA archives; *Gair Rhydd*, 19 November, 1986, p. 3.

6

HARD RIGHT POLITICIANS AND STUDENT PROTESTS AT UNIVERSITIES IN THE 1980S

After the electoral defeat of the National Front at the 1979 election, the NF went into decline and it looked as if the pressing threat of fascism had reduced the need for the National Union of Students' 'no platform' policy. However there were students who argued that the policy needed to be expanded to deny a platform to sexists and homophobes, as well as racists and fascists. This led to much debate on the student left, but also opened up the student movement to criticism from both the left and the right for shutting down free speech and not engaging in reasoned debate with their opponents.

At the same time, hard right politicians and speakers, encouraged by the right libertarian Federation of Conservative Students (FCS), attempted to exacerbate hostilities around the 'no platform' policy of individual student unions by trying to speak at universities. While the Tories under Thatcher pushed an often racist law and order agenda (which culminated in riots in 1980, 1981 and 1985), as well as maintaining the racist and sexist immigration control system, it was not a fascist organisation. This led to a debate over the right tactics to be used to oppose these speakers. Student unions were divided over whether to apply their version of the 'no platform' policy to speakers or whether to allow them to speak, but mount protests against them.

The NUS argued against applying the 'no platform' policy to these MPs, such as Enoch Powell, John Carlisle and Harvey Proctor, stating:

> Odious though [government] policy may be, we do not achieve anything if we attempt to try and stop them speaking. Legitimate demonstrative action, pickets etc. should focus on the damage Government policies are doing to our society. Lock them in debate, show there is an alternative.
>
> A central tenet of the NUS 'No Platform' policy is that the abuse of the policy against those who are not declared racists or fascists brings the whole policy into disrepute.[1]

However, individual student unions and student groups were much more willing to use tactics to deny these speakers a platform, either by picketing the buildings to prevent entry or by disrupting the meetings through heckling, throwing stuff or storming the stage. Throughout the mid-1980s, numerous incidents on university campuses across the country demonstrated the opposition by some students to these hard right speakers and the tensions between some radical students and the often more moderate student union leaderships. This also led to differences of opinion over what actually constituted 'no platforming', rather than just a protest. To the right, large protests outside venues and heckling within were viewed as instances of the denial of free speech and the pursuit of a 'no platform' agenda. However some student activists differentiated between protests, to be used against the right in general, and the actual invocation of 'no platform', to be used against *organised* racists and fascists, such as the bureaucratic cancellation of speaking engagements or the physical denial of space.[2]

After some disruptive protests throughout 1985 and 1986, often when the policy of 'no platform' was not actually used, Conservative MPs sought to bring in legislation to outlaw 'no platforming' and to 'protect' freedom of speech on campus. First introduced as a Private Members' Bill by backbencher Fred Silvester, the legislation requiring universities to take 'reasonable steps' to ensure free speech at their institutions was pushed through in October 1986 with the Education (No. 2) Act. But this was not the magic bullet to dampen student protest that some Tories had hoped for and within a few years, the hard and libertarian right were still complaining about the 'uncontrollable terror' of 'tiny totalitarians' to deny free speech.[3]

This fight by the Thatcher government against 'no platforming' was part of a broader attack on progressive and left-wing students in the 1980s. Although the student movement was smaller than that which had existed in the late 1960s and early 1970s, students in the 1980s were heavily involved in campaigns against the Thatcher government's higher education policies, such as the cuts to student support grants and the introduction of fees for some higher education programmes, as well as against the broader government policies of the day, such as opposition to the Falklands War, support for the Miners' Strike, and opposition to the poll tax and to Clause 28. In the final decade of the Cold War, students were also heavily involved in campaigns regarding international politics and solidarity with political movements abroad, such as the revival of the Campaign for Nuclear Disarmament (CND), the Nicaragua Solidarity Campaign (NSC) and the Anti-Apartheid Movement (AAM).

The AAM, which had grown susbtantially by the 1980s, often overlapped with protests against racists and fascists at universities and also coincided with the broader 'boycott South Africa' movement promoted by both the AAM and the NUS. As well as protesting against pro-South Africa MPs like John Carlisle and the provocations of the Federation of Conservative Students, students were also involved in protests against representatives of the apartheid regime in South Africa speaking on campus. Throughout the 1980s, there were instances of protests being used successfully to deny South African diplomats and other representatives the opportunity to speak.

However in 1988, concerns about the large protests that were being generated at universities around the issue of South Africa led to the University of Liverpool cancelling an invitation by the university's Conservative Association of two South African diplomats, using the legislation brought in with the 1986 Act. The Liverpool University Conservative Association, supported by various right libertarian pressure groups within the Conservative Party, launched legal proceedings aginst the university, arguing that the legislation was being improperly used by the university administration to eschew their duties under the 1986 Act. This led to a High Court ruling which found that universities could prevent events from occruing if there was the risk of public disorder or violence, but that there were also limits on this application of the 1986 Act.

As seen in the previous chapter, the 1980s became a time of flux for the student movement in Britain, and the implementation of the tactic of 'no platforming' was a substantial part of this. While the previous chapter looked at how the tactic was used against speakers who were identified as sexist or homophobic and as a signficant risk to students as racists and fascists, this chapter looks at how the tactic was used against hard right politicians who straddled the political space between the mainstream and the far right. Ultimately it was the challenge that students presented to these politicians that saw the Thatcher government mobilise around the issue of freedom of speech on campus and deliver the Education (No. 2) Act in 1986.

The Federation of Conservative Students

Tensions around the use of the 'no platform' policy by individual student unions were aggravated by the FCS, who sought to combat the supposed 'Marxist' composition of student politics in the 1980s. The Federation of Conservative Students was founded in the 1930s, but in the late 1970s and early 1980s, it transformed into a particularly notorious organisation, with a strong right-libertarian outlook. After Margaret Thatcher became leader of the Conservative Party, the FCS became enthusiastic supporters of Thatcher and her key ally, Sir Keith Joseph. After Thatcher was elected in 1979, the FCS had come to combine Thatcherism with a hard libertarian streak. If Thatcher represented a reaction to the social forces unleashed by '1968',[4] then the FCS represented a reaction to the radicalism of the student movement in the 1970s, even if the student movement was in decline by this time. Former FCS members describe it as to the left of the Conservative Party in the late 1970s and claim that it altered its outlook once Peter Young became Chairman in 1980,[5] but it had already acquired a confrontational position vis-à-vis the rest of the student movement by this time. Ian Bradley noted in *The Spectator* in late 1976 that it had started campaigning on an explicit 'free enterprise' platform and against the student left, as well against the pro-Heath elements amongst Conservative students.[6] The FCS flirted with the idea of disaffiliation from time to time in the 1970s (and even into the 1980s)[7] but concerted efforts were also made to further enter the student unions at this time, attempting to rebuff the left-wing slant of the student body across Britain. The FCS saw the NUS as 'run by left-wing extremists for their own sectarian ends' and proposed that this needed to be countered by the FCS.[8]

As mentioned in Chapter 4, the FCS had opposed the original 'no platform' policy at the 1974 NUS conference and had attempted to use it as a wedge issue when it was again debated in April 1977, although its proposed amendments were defeated.[9] The FCS listed the 'banning of free speech' by the NUS alongside the alleged 'siphoning of public funds to the IRA' and 'attacks on senior statemen and politicians' as examples of the power of the left inside the NUS, which the FCS claimed to fighting against.[10] When the FCS invited Joseph to speak at LSE in 1978, he was not allowed to speak due to the student union's 'no platform' policy. This was shortly after the reinstatement of the 'no platform' policy at the April 1978 NUS conference. There were several accusations that the FCS had deliberately invited Joseph to speak and encouraged the use of the 'no platform' policy by the student union to draw attention to it. When the idea of disaffiliation was raised shortly after the 1978 conference, the FCS cited the 'no platform' policy was a factor, arguing that the policy might mean 'student unions banning leading Tory politicians, including Margaret Thatcher'.[11] The Joseph invitation might have been a test of this policy by the FCS.

After Young's ascension to Chairman in 1980, the FCS pursued an increasingly libertarian and controversial agenda, dominated by support for cuts to student funding, voluntary student unionism and scrutiny of the use of student unions' funds, support for anti-communist forces across the globe and extensive privatisation. The FCS saw itself as the vanguard of the 'Thatcherite Revolution' and on 'the political front line of vehement anti-Thatcherite hostility' that was supposedly pervasive at British universities in the 1980s.[12] As Timothy Evans has written:

> At campus level the FCS set out to carry on guerrilla warfare. The imagery of an FCS branch was deliberately designed to offend the student left and break its hegemony in student affairs by provoking riots, bans, public denunciations and general disruption.[13]

This included confrontation with the student movement over their anti-racist and anti-apartheid campaigning. Although the FCS had ostensibly supported an anti-racist campaign against the NF in the late 1970s,[14] there were a number of accusations in the early 1980s of links between the FCS and the NF, as well as with the BNP and the British Movement.[15] *Searchlight* raised the issue of NF and BM infiltration of the FCS in 1982 and 1983 and reported that this was of concern to the Conservative Party leadership.[16] In 1986, the same magazine ran another story of the defection of two FCS members from the University of Essex to the BNP and a BNP sympathiser who was also an FCS Publicity Officer at North Staffs Polytechnic.[17] One of the defectors, Stuart Millson, was quoted in *The Guardian* as saying that he joined the BNP 'because the Conservative Party – while, he claimed, containing many covert racialists – had cynically adopted a soft and hypocritical attitude to race relations to appease black communities and bid for their votes'.[18] *The Guardian* reported the other defecting FCS member, Allan Robertson, as saying, 'Quite a few of my members do support the BNP. I support the BNP on most issues, including law and order and race relations and immigration.'[19]

In the same year, another FCS member was reported to have written to the BNP, allegedly in an effort to forge links with the fascist organisation, although the member claimed 'he wrote the letter in an attempt to dupe the BNP into giving him the names of BNP supporters within the FCS'.[20] The student, Paul Delarie-Staines, wrote to the BNP organiser in Hull and suggested working together to disrupt left-wing meetings and exacerbate the political divisions on campuses,[21] a tactic that the FCS had also been pursuing with its invitation of controversial speakers. Delarie-Staines wrote, according to *The Guardian*:

> [E]ven though we have our differences, I know a lot of BNP people at college do support the FCS (some are members of the FCS). I can certainly envisage some degree of cooperation.
>
> For instance, we are moving away from just the normal political debate and towards more direct action – anti-Communist slogans on bridges, disrupting the leftist meetings by posing as leftists and then causing trouble, and also convincing individual leftists of the error oif their ways.
>
> Perhaps members of the BNP would care to join us in our anti-leftist activities ...[22]

Nowadays, the FCS is probably most remembered for its campaign against Nelson Mandela and the African National Congress. At the 1983 NUS conference, FCS members distributed stickers supporting the apartheid regime in South Africa, alongside anti-CND material.[23] Although they were reprimanded by the FCS Chairman, some FCS members displayed 'Hang Nelson Mandela' stickers when they got up to speak at the conference.[24] University of Warwick student David Hoile wore one of the offensive stickers on his tie while standing for a post on the NUS' European Delegation.[25] *Leeds Student* described the reaction by the other students:

> as the information rapidly spread to the back of the hall, where the delegates had difficulty distinguishing Mr Hoile, let alone the wording of his sticker, the uproar began. Led notably and vociferously by the SWP soon the chants of 'No platform for Fascists!' drowned out whatever Mr Hoile was trying to say.[26]

Hoile was 'eventually scuttled away surrounded by security staff', but he was not the only FCS member to brandish the sticker at the conference, with another speaker sporting one the next day.[27] *Searchlight* reported that '[t]his calculated insult was too much to stomach and black students lined up in front of the conference with their backs to the platform', noting that the student body 'made it quite clear it would not tolerate racist behaviour'.[28]

The FCS continued to campaign against 'no platform' during the 1980s, often as part of a wider campaign against the 'closed shop' of the NUS.[29] Future Speaker of the House John Bercow debated the policy at the University of Leeds shortly before the FCS was disbanded, arguing that the policy was 'dangerous' because 'it enable[d] cowardly student unions to use the policy against any people to whom they object'.[30] When asked whether he would allow the NF to campaign on campus, Bercow said he would, but claimed that 'No Platform is designed solely to exclude Conservative MPs' (despite evidence that fascists were still active on campuses across the country in the early 1980s).[31] Following on from the furore surrounding an invitation extended to Sir Keith Joseph by the FCS to speak at LSE in 1978, the FCS used a similar tactic to highlight what they perceived as the oppressive nature of the 'no platform' policy in the 1980s – inviting hard right Tory MPs to speak at universities, provoking student reactions. Invitations to MPs, such as the pro-apartheid John Carlisle, led to a major debate about freedom of speech at British universities in the mid-1980s.

Tories on tour

Timothy Raison at LSE

Protests against visiting MPs, particularly those on the hard right of the Conservative Party, were not new. As the previous chapters have shown, there were significant protests against Enoch Powell in the late 1960s and the 'no platform' policy was used at LSE against Sir Keith Joseph in 1978. This continued into the 1980s. In late November 1980, Conservative MP Timothy Raison was invited to speak at LSE by the Grimshaw Club, an international relations student group. Raison was Minister for Immigration at a time when the Thatcher government were pushing through the revised British Nationality Bill, and had been recently embroiled in the controversy over the denial of Anwar Ditta's children to be allowed to enter the country.[32]

The student newspaper *The Beaver* reported that a meeting of some student union members voted favourably on an emergency motion to interrupt Raison's talk, despite opposition from an FCS member.[33] But while this emergency motion was being debated, 'Mr Raison had already been heckled by a multi-racial audience', in what was described by the newspaper as 'an extremely hostile atmosphere' where the 'cries of "No to racist immigration laws" and "Out with the racist Tories" followed his every comment'.[34] After ten minutes, around 100 students from the student union entered and did not allow Raison, who had abandoned his talk, to continue.[35] The newspaper quipped that 'Raison left the LSE with a clear picture of left-student activism at work', but posited:

> Following the introduction of the government's Nationality bill and the accusations of racism that have been levelled against it, it seems unlikely that any serving Conservative minister will be able to take up invitations to speak at the LSE without similar disruption ensuing.[36]

Some students complained that the demonstrators (from the 'non-democratic Left') wasted everyone's time and sullied the reputation of LSE,[37] while others reminded the newspaper that the student union had 'made the decision … that we didn't want racialism as an acceptable philosophy at the LSE and were prepared to act in defence of that'.[38] In reply to the original newspaper article, Kelvin Baynton pilloried the 'free speech' defence of Raison, arguing:

> Putting the cosy world aside, we live in an increasingly violent and repressive country where many people are liable to be attacked or harassed because of the colour of their skins. Thankfully, for the most part, explicit racialism isn't a feature of life at the LSE …[39]

Baynton pointed out that the Home Office were responsible for several different racist practices regarding the control of immigration and the policing of migrant communities,[40] which meant that Raison, as Immigration Minister, was partly responsible for this. There were further debates back and forth over the next few weeks in the pages of *The Beaver*, but the incident was used as an example in the aforementioned motion to overturn the student union's 'no platform' policy by Melanie Nazareth and Daniel Finkelstein (see previous chapter). When this motion was passed by the student union, one student, Kofi Dwinfour, complained that 'our misguided guardians of "free speech"' had '[left] black students naked in front of attack', protesting:

> You can bash blacks as long as you are a Government Minister, newspaper editor, journalist, school-teacher or lawyer, or a qualified professional, or even just a poor working-class white man who happens to think that all these 'wogs' bring down the tone of the area.[41]

Dwinfour questioned why a small minority of those who preached a 'free for all' for the proponents of racist ideologies outweighed '[t]he number of those opposed to racist ideas and racist violence in this University'.[42] Apart from this, there was little coverage in *The Beaver* of the change in policy, which remained in place before being overturned (and overturned again) in the mid-1980s. By this time, the 'no platform' policy was being challenged at more universities, particularly when being applied in some instances to visiting Members of Parliament.

Leon Brittan at Manchester

There seemed to be a significant increase in the number of protests against visiting MPs to university campuses between 1985 and 1987, with several notorious hard right Tories, as well as Enoch Powell (now an Ulster Unionist MP), attempting to speak on campuses throughout this period. By 1985, students had been locked in a four-year battle with the Thatcher government over funding for higher education, with cuts to student grants and plans to introduce fees for higher education.[43] As Richard Aldrich has written, 'the more market-led, free-enterprise approach to society and the economy which characterized the premiership of Margaret

Thatcher' influenced the education reforms of the 1980s,[44] which led to confrontations with students, just as the government had in their battles with other sections of society such as the trade unions, peace campaigners or Britain's ethnic minority communities. The period of confrontation with MPs on campus came at the end of the Miners' Strike, which had polarised British society and generated a strong oppositional movement to the Thatcher government.

In March 1985, the Home Secretary Leon Brittan, who was ultimately responsible for both the police and the immigration control system, came to the University of Manchester to speak. Brittan was invited by the Manchester University Conservative Association and there was resistance within the student union to Brittan's invitation, but the student union executive voted 4–2 to allow Brittan's speech to go ahead.[45] It was reported in the *The Mancunion* that those who voted for Brittan to speak stressed 'the importance of "Free Speech" and maintained that it was safer for the visit to go ahead'.[46] An independent inquiry by the Manchester City Council noted that the Executive Committee of the student union looked into 'whether the visit was in any way in conflict with the policy of the Union which was that no platform should be given to a fascist', but noted that '[i]t was decided that this visit did not breach such a policy'.[47]

On the day of the speech, Manchester Police's Tactical Aid Group assembled outside the university in expectation of a large demonstration by students. The Secretary of the Conservative Association wrote a letter to the student newspaper that suggested due to the poster campaign across campus in the lead up to event, 'the police, not altogether unreasonably, assumed that there would be a violent demonstration outside the Union'.[48] Brian Pullan has explained that to many students, the police seemed to have 'applied their training in riot control although they had no riot to contend with, and set out to occupy the Union building and its surroundings in the manner of a besieging army'.[49]

The Mancunion described the events outside the Union building as the police confronted around 500 protesting students:

> At 7.15 p.m. a column of about forty officers from the Tactical Aid Group marched three abreast in military fashion out of Dover Street and towards the demonstration. In spearhead formation they ploughed into the main body of the crowd. This was quickly followed by two further waves of Tactical Aid officers. There was no chance to escape as demonstrators were pinned against the building by the force of the police onslaught.
>
> Many students were hurled down the union steps as police fought to clear a pathway to the main door. Many sustained injuries as a direct result of these tactics.[50]

As a result of the police actions, around 40 people were injured, while 33 were charged with public order offences.[51] Meanwhile inside, an increasingly vocal crowd attempted to shout down Brittan and although a number had originally planned a silent protest inside the venue, 'demonstrators entered the meeting and loudly voiced their anger and shock at what had happened outside'.[52] A report from *The Mancunion* stated that Brittan's speech 'quickly turned into an improvised rant', with 'many references to the right to freedom of speech'.[53]

The Secretary of the Conservative Association blamed a 'handful of left-wing activists who messed things up for everybody' and commended the student union executive 'for allowing freedom of speech in the Union'.[54] Indeed, as Mike Day and Jim Dickinson have noted, 'the students' union did all it could to ensure the meeting went ahead'.[55] Phil Woolas, as President of the NUS, criticised the police for 'acting irresponsibly' on the day, rather than the protesting students.[56] However in the subsequent discourse, the incident was used, particularly in the debate over the Education Bill the following year, as evidence of the intolerance of students on campus to right-wing and controversial ideas, coupled with other incidents over the next year and a half.

There were calls for an independent inquiry into the police actions, which were denied by the Home Secretary (who was at the centre of the controversial incident), but the police launched an internal investigation and another was conducted by the Manchester City Council – however, Pullan claimed, the police refused to co-operate with the Council's inquiry and the student union refused to co-operate with the police inquiry.[57] The student union explained, via *The Mancunion*, that they refused to co-operate to prevent statements collected by the police inquiry being used in prosecutions against the students charged with offences on the day.[58] In the end, 19 students were convicted (some had their convictions quashed on appeal) and 14 were found not guilty.[59]

The independent inquiry by Manchester City Council stated that they were 'left with little doubt that the action of some police officers was unnecessarily forceful' and that while there was some 'physical and violence resistance' to the police by protestors, it did not excuse the conduct of the police, particularly when some of the violence was directed at 'passive demonstrators who offered no resistance'.[60] The report found that: 'Practically all of 102 eye witnesses claimed that the policing was aggressive or witnessed police-initiated violence; and nearly half of these (48) claimed they were assaulted in some way by a police officer or officers.'[61]

It further concluded that the policing of the demonstration against Brittan 'involved unacceptable use of force and abusive language by police officers well-trained in public order policing, against innocent civilians participating in a peaceful demonstration'.[62] In an era of increasingly confrontational public order policing (as demonstrated by the policing of riots in Britain's inner cities, of the Miners' Strike and of football crowds, for example), the panel openly wondered whether 'this sort of conduct forms part of the training of these officers' and if it was 'now considered an acceptable part of this type of policing'.[63]

John Carlisle on tour

Leon Brittan was the most senior politician to attract student protests on campus in a battle over 'free speech' on campus in the mid-1980s. But it was the Tory backbencher John Carlisle who generated significant controversy during his tour of universities the following year, with several student unions invoking the 'no platform' policy against his visits. Carlisle was a prominent member of both the Monday Club and Federation of Conservative Students, and was a hard right figure within the Conservative Party. In the 1980s, he was most well-known for his support for apartheid South Africa and his condemnation of the African National Congress, including the imprisoned Nelson Mandela. Matthew P. Llewellyn and Toby C. Rider have described Carlisle as a 'fierce pro-Pretoria spokesman'[64] and it was on this topic that he frequently spoke at public meetings, including at universities.

In February 1986, Carlisle attempted to address meetings at Bradford and Oxford universities on the subject of sport and South Africa. Carlisle was invited to speak by the FCS at Bradford. The student union at the University of Bradford had a policy of 'no platform', but in a flyer distributed before the event, claimed 'the Union has been told that any student demonstrating against the meeting could face disciplinary action'.[65] Despite this, the union still called 'all students who object[ed] to John Carlisle's extremist views to take part' in a peaceful protest, stating that the union was 'receiving support from other student Unions, NUS, local community groups and individuals'.[66] Some of those involved in the protest were from the local Asian Youth Movement (AYM), a group established in the late 1970s in Bradford (as well as in several other northern cities) by South Asian youth to campaign against racism and participate in community self-defence.[67]

When Carlisle attempted to speak, he was allegedly attacked by protestors. *Fleece*, the student newspaper at the University of Bradford, reported at the time:

> According to an eye witness up to three Asians and a West Indian, none of whom were students, were involved in the attack on Mr Carlisle. Fighting started when Anti-Apartheid slogans that had been written on the blackboard were removed by Conservative student, Ian Gibb. When Mr Carlisle was identified the fighting quickly escalated.
>
> Mr Carlisle was punched in the face, fell to the ground and was punched again repeatedly in both the face and stomach as student stewards stepped in to break up the fighting. A number of students were hurt. Mr Carlisle was quickly hussled [sic] out of the room by security guards through the hostile crowd that had gathered for the advertised peaceful demonstration.[68]

The Asian Youth Movement in Bradford denied involvement in the fracas.[69] A press release issued by the AYM stated:

> Members of our organisation did attend the meeting. Our members did not orchestrate the violence that took place, and were not involved in any attack directed towards the MP …
>
> We do not agree with Mr Carlisle's views. However, we can fully understand the rage of those people he has attacked and insulted.[70]

Similar to the attack on Hans Eysenck at LSE over a decade before, there were condemnations from the press and from politicians. The *Daily Express* said '[p]hysically preventing a man from expressing his views is a particularly nasty form of censorship' and called for the Asian community in Bradford to 'root out the hooligans in their midst and deliver them to the authorities for proper punishment'.[71] Margaret Thatcher stated that the whole of Parliament 'sympathize[d] with him on the very nasty incident which he experienced'.[72] While the President of the student union at Bradford, John Renshaw, condemned the violence, he also 'questioned the motives of the FCS and right wing conservative MPs in coming to speak at Bradford and in other multi-racial areas', arguing that it was 'clearly intended to be provocative'.[73]

Coming at the beginning of a year of debate about 'no platform' policies, the student newspaper reported that the incident brought into question the 'effectiveness of the Union's no platform policy' and Renshaw admitted to the paper that 'the Union would come under increasing pressure to abandon the policy'.[74] While some students supported the continuation of the 'no platform' policy and chose not to condemn the youth involved in the protest, Renshaw himself stated that the 'no platform' policy was 'counter-productive' and 'succeeded only in giving undue publicity to tory [sic] MPs on the "lunatic fringe" of the party'.[75] As demonstrated throughout this book, this has been a constant refrain from those who have opposed 'no platform' and was a sentiment frequently expressed during 1986 as the debate over the policy heightened.

A few days later, Carlisle attempted to speak at Oxford University's Oriel College, invited by the university's Monday Club. With Carlisle scheduled to speak in the 'Nelson Mandela' room at Oriel, the room was occupied by about 120 protestors from the SWP, the Labour Club, Oxford Against Racism and the Oxford Anti-Apartheid group.[76] Upon advice from the police, the Monday Club decided to cancel Carlisle's talk at the university and under police escort, travelled to the city centre, where Carlisle addressed a very small audience.[77] Speaking to the student newspaper, *Cherwell*, Carlisle complained: 'It's a sad day when Oxford University students prevent an MP from putting his views forward. What worries me about tonight is that it's a copycat demonstration – just mimicking Bradford.'[78]

The President of Oxford University's Monday Club, Simon Clow, criticised the police for being 'too eager to avoid trouble rather than protect free speech'.[79] The *Daily Express* claimed that Carlisle had 'barricaded himself in an Oxford restaurant with aides as protestors marched up and down outside hurling abuse at him' and that '[p]olice rushed to rescue the MP'.[80] The newspaper quoted one policeman as saying, 'He did a runner – and fast.'[81]

Carlisle had planned to visit Leeds Polytechnic, having been invited by the FCS. However, following the events at Bradford and Oxford, his speaking engagement was cancelled, with the Polytechnic suggesting that there was 'no suitable venue where the meeting could be held in "a safe and orderly manner"'.[82] John Bercow, as President of the FCS, was quoted in *Leeds Student* as saying the cancelling of the event by the Polytechnic showed that the 'Left wing can't engage successfully in the intellectual battle', but the West Yorkshire NUS Area Convenor alleged that it was FCS that was to blame, declaring that the FCS was 'deliberately using speakers on the far Right with well-known contentious views on immotive [sic] subjects to stir up trouble in Student Unions'.[83]

The following month, Carlisle was invited to speak by the Conservative Association at the University of East Anglia (UEA). The student union at UEA had a 'no platform' policy that expressed:

> Union Clubs and Societies should not invite known fascists, racists, sexists or anti gay speakers with the deliberate intention of violating Union policy and antagonising minority groups. Such action will be regarded as intentional provocation and intimidation. Student's Council shall have the authority to take severe sanctions against Clubs and Societies who do so, such as freezing or suspending their Constitution.[84]

Part of the student union's policy on 'no platform' stated that 'Union resources and facilities must not be used for the propagation of defamatory sexist, racist, fascist or anti-gay views',[85] and after Carlisle's invitation by the Conservative Association, the union froze their funds and suspended their constitution.[86] The student newspaper at UEA, *Phoenix*, reported that the Conservative Association 'had been trying to keep the date of the visit a secret' in order to 'make it difficult for anyone to try and prevent the visit'.[87] Once the date of Carlisle's visit was known, the student union voted to 'stage a mass "silent vigil" in memory of those black people murdered in South Africa by the racist apartheid regime'.[88] This method of protest was chosen as the student union believed that 'both Carlisle and the Tory association [were] hoping that there [would] be violence during his visit' in a provocative campaign against the student union's 'no platform' policy.[89] However, the Socialist Workers' Student Society opposed this method, preferring a blockade of the proposed venue.[90]

On the day, a picket by around 50 to 60 people was formed, while a separate vigil of several hundred attendees was organised by the student union, with a local representative of the ANC speaking.[91] A report by the President of the student union to the university blamed the university administration of hindering the vigil and allowing Carlisle to enter the proposed venue and asking the vigil to clear so Carlisle could leave (while viewing the vigil).[92] This was opposed by the vigil organisers and eventually Carlisle was escorted by police via an alternative exit. The report by the student union president suggested that the university narrowly avoided a disorderly outcome, 'in spite of the conditions imposed by a combination of the ultra-right, ultra-left and the university authorities'.[93]

The report concluded that in the future, the university, rather than the student union, should make it clear that controversial speakers, such as Carlisle, were not welcome at the university or risk 'the prospect of certain disruption'.[94] The university would have to do this or else, the report claimed, they would have 'no remaining defence against either the ultra-right or the ultra-left'.[95] This reiterates a certain tension in the student movement since the 1970s, with the leadership of the student unions often at odds with the more radical elements of the student body. In many instances, episodes of disruption of certain speakers by students had been condemned by the student union, either in the lead up to the event or in its aftermath. In the case of the UEA student union, the President raised the spectre of direct action by radical student groups as the alternative to the orderly protest actions of the student union – if the university administration did not assist the student union in enforcing the 'no platform' policy, it would allow the radical left to seize the initiative (and allow the hard right to portray themselves as victims). With the introduction of the Education (No. 2) Act 1986 a few months later, this intervention by a university administration would be made more difficult and potentially unlawful.

Enoch Powell at Cardiff and Bristol

As Camilla Schofield has argued, Enoch Powell had an influence on the hard right forces in the Conservative Party that developed Thatcherism in the 1980s,[96] but during Thatcher's prime ministership, Powell himself remained a critic on the right for Thatcher. He had left the Tories just prior to the 1974 election over the issue of British membership of the European Economic Community and joined the Ulster Unionist Party (UUP). As the 'Troubles' continued into the 1980s, Powell frequently spoke about the issue of Northern Ireland. The other major topic that Powell spoke on in the 1980s was 'race relations' and immigration, a topic that had originally brought him notoriety in the late 1960s. Powell used the 1980–81 and 1985 riots as vindication of his racist pronouncements on Commonwealth immigration and challenged Thatcher to clarify her position on non-white immigration in the wake of the 1985 riots.[97] Despite no longer being a member of the Conservative Party, Powell was still a drawcard for the right and he was invited on a number of occasions to address Conservative Associations at various universities around the country. While he had to cancel a speaking event at Leeds University in January 1985 after a proposed protest,[98] he had still spoken at Cambridge later in the year with little protest, but after the actions against John Carlisle at a number of universities, Powell's campus visits drew a renewed level of opposition.

In October 1986, Powell was invited by the Conservative Association at the University of Wales Institute of Science and Technology (UWIST) to speak, using a lecture theatre at University College Cardiff (UCC) (both UWIST and UCC merged in 1988 to become the University of Wales, Cardiff). This was opposed by some students, including those in the Socialist Workers' Student Society, as well as the student union at UCC. The student union had an explicit anti-racist policy, with the student union's spokesperson on racism, Pat Younge, writing in the student newspaper, *Gair Rhydd*:

> UCC Students Union has the responsibility to take positive action in support of black, Jewish and Overseas Students and to ensure that at least their college environment is free from fear and intimidation … If the college grant Powell

> or any other racist the right to speak then they immediately deny the rights of blacks, Jews and Overseas Students to study in an environment free of intimidation and prejudice …
>
> [W]hy should we support a racist speaking in a multi-racial environment?[99]

Students from the SWSS, as well as the UCC Labour Club, the UCC Women's Group and the UCC Union of Liberal Students (several of which were leading members of the UCC student union),[100] launched a protest to prevent Powell from speaking. The front page of *Gair Rhydd* described the protest:

> Trouble began almost before the meeting had started when Socialist Worker Students, angered at the prospect of the controversial right-winger speaking at UCC, mounted a picket outside room 22 of the Law building.
>
> When this failed to stop the meeting they attempted to enter themselves … After ten minutes of argument [sic] most of the protestors were kept out.
>
> Trouble flared up again, however, when Mr Powell began speaking. A group of protestors flung open the doors and occupied the platform on which Mr Powell stood. Mr Powell then faced a barrage of abuse and chanting of 'No free speech for racists' …
>
> As it became more and more obvious that the protestors had no intention of leaving until Mr Powell did, the UWIST College Secretary made an appeal to the demonstrators to stop chanting of face disciplinary action. He was unable to finish his announcement before being drowned out by further chanting.
>
> Mr Powell then left with the words 'Thank you for your courtesy', and beat a hasty retreat to a waiting car.[101]

Ten students were eventually identified and faced disciplinary proceedings brought by the College, but the student union argued that the College had failed to inform the student union in a timely manner of Powell's proposed visit.[102] The student union declared, 'College denied us the right to organise and orderly protest … The spontaneous nature of the demonstration was due to College's negligence.'[103] As protests against the disciplinary actions grew in the weeks that followed, the student union's Communications Officer, Jake Lynch, claimed that the College had 'ridden roughshod over the Unions [sic] No Platform policy'.[104] This disciplinary charges were dropped after a negotiated settlement between the student union and the UCC administration, which also led to a revised version of the 'no platform' policy at UCC.[105]

The week after the Cardiff incident, Powell was scheduled to speak at the University of Bristol, invited by the Bristol University Conservative Association. The student union at the University of Bristol did not have a formal 'no platform' policy in place (in fact a referendum on whether to introduce such a policy was being held during the Powell debacle) and the student union instead urged a silent protest.[106] Similar to when John Carlisle visited Oxford, Leeds and Bradford earlier in the year, the President of the student union suggested that the Conservative

Association was being provocative with their invitation of Powell.[107] An editorial in the student newspaper *Bacus* questioned the motives of the Conservative Association in inviting Powell, asking:

> Do they hope for interesting speeches, or for the sort of protest which will give Fleet Street the chance to run yet more 'left wing thug' stories?[108]

Bacus also reported that the University was reluctant to intervene in the case, even though the Committee of Vice-Chancellors and Principals had previously recommended that 'speakers in possible danger should be barred' (especially after the incidents involving Carlisle a few months prior), while the student union president stated that he did not expect any trouble from students regarding Powell's visit.[109] The editorial in the student paper implored students to be peaceful in their demonstrations, pleading:

> Any sort of violent demonstrations will discredit all opposition groups in the eyes of those who read such reports [from Fleet Street].
>
> Don't play into the hands of the Tories and right-wing press by resorting to violence.
>
> We will suffer the consequences if you do.[110]

While around 200 students had attended a peaceful protest against Powell in the foyer of the building where Powell was speaking, a smaller group of protestors violently confronted Powell shortly after he began. The front page of *Bacus* described the incident:

> Around 30 demonstrators, mostly anarchists from outside the University, gathered at the front of the hall hurling abuse and spitting at Mr. Powell. They blew whistles, let off stink and smoke bombs and at one point threw a ham salad sandwich at him …
>
> Mr. Powell left the stage after only ten minutes when the protestors began shaking the crash barriers in front of the stage.
>
> Three of the demonstrators then climbed onto the stage, overturned tables and chairs and snapped the microphone stand. Two of them gave mock Nazi salutes to the audience.
>
> Others tried to chase Mr. Powell but were met by a locked door which one protestor kicked in.[111]

The actions by the anarchists were condemned widely. Phillip Malcom, the Chairman of the Conservative Association, described the events as 'worse than I could ever have imagined' and called for legal action to be taken against those who disrupted Powell.[112] An editorial in *Bacus* declared that the anarchist protestors had 'discredited everybody who had made an effort to provide a forum for those who find the views of Powell and his ilk abhorrent'.[113] In the *Daily Express*, Lord

Chalfont called those who disrupted Powell 'a mob of illiterate morons'.[114] Even the SWP criticised the anarchists for their 'tactical suicide',[115] suggesting that 'the event was marred by the Anarchists'.[116]

The anarchists themselves wrote to *Bacus* justifying their position. Alongside affirmation of the broader 'no platform' position shared by the SWP and others that 'it should not be used as an inalienable right to allow a racist a platform', the anarchists argued that '[s]ymbolic demonstrations do nothing to prevent racist attacks or the spread of racist propaganda.'[117] They rationalised their tactics by claiming: 'In the absence of an effective anti-racist policy in this Students Union there was no other way of preventing Powell and what he represents from speaking'.[118]

A week later, two figures from the 'new right' centred around the journal *Salisbury Review*, John Savery and Ray Honeyford, spoke at Bristol University, alongside John Bercow from the FCS. The student union had significantly increased security for the event in the light of the Powell protests.[119] Bercow commented on the disruption of the Powell speech the previous week, calling it 'a disgrace to a free society and to the very concept of an academy where debate and free speech occur'.[120] The student newspaper stated that there only three hecklers inside the venue and once the event had ended, Honeyford was 'jostled and pushed by about fifty demonstrators'.[121] One protestor attempted to throw yellow paint over Honeyford but missed, hitting a car, other protestors and a policeman.[122]

Harvey Proctor at Hull

Although the Education (No. 2) Act came in late 1986 with legislation requiring universities to ensure freedom of speech on campus (as discussed later in this chapter) in an attempt to prevent the disruptions that occurred in 1985 and 1986, similar disruptive protests still followed. One of those involved Harvey Proctor at the University of Hull in March 1987.

Like John Carlisle, Harvey Proctor was a backbench Conservative MP who was also a member of the Monday Club. In the early 1980s, Proctor had written a tract for the Monday Club calling for the repatriation of Commonwealth immigrants[123] and proposed at the 1983 Conservative Party conference an 'end to all permanent immigration from the New Commonwealth and Pakistan', as well as an increase in 'the financial and material provision for voluntary repatriation'.[124] Although at that time he was at the centre of a tabloid scandal, the Conservative Association at Hull invited Proctor to speak, which generated considerable protest (including from the Socialist Workers' Student Society). On the day, according to the student newspaper *Hullfire*, 500 students had gathered outside the building where Proctor was to give his speech, preventing him from gaining access.[125] To avoid the crowd, Proctor attempted to enter the building via a side entrance, which started the chaos. *Hullfire* described in detail the events that followed:

> The demonstrators ran from the front of the Lecture Theatre to the side entrance to find a white-faced Proctor, flanked by security men, attempting to enter the building. The sudden arrival of the main core of protestors caught Proctor and the few security men off guard. He had no time to climb into his chauffeur driven car.
>
> Students then forced Proctor against a wall and jeered and spat at him. Although at first there was no violence escalation was inevitable. Trouble started when a demonstrator climbed on the wall and started stamping on his head. Security Guards started hitting out at students as they struggled to get Proctor back to the car.
>
> As Proctor was hustled through the shouting crowd he was hit from behind by demonstrators and his hair was grabbed.[126]

As Proctor attempted to get away from the protestors, the car that he was being driven in ran into the crowd and injured eight students.[127]

Proctor was quoted in the *Daily Mirror* as saying that 15 students had cornered him and were 'punching, kicking and spitting', as well as jumping on his back.[128] In his memoirs, Proctor claimed 'I was in physical danger, and the car manoeuvred to get me to safety', adding 'I was being driven by security guards employed by the university. They had been in danger too.'[129] A representative from the student union at Hull said, according to the *Daily Express*, that the students had intended to hold a peaceful protest and that the driver of the car acted 'like the A Team': 'The car was in such a confined space, and there were so many bodies packed together, it reversed far too quickly – around 20mph.'[130]

The student union argued that 'the University did not adequately prepare for Proctor's visit' and the Conservative Association conceded that 'security was totally inadequate' on the day.[131] A member of the SWSS was paraphrased by *Hullfire* as saying that 'it was "unfortunate" that people were injured but it was a result of Conservatives being allowed to speak on campus'.[132] Similar to events at Bradford the previous year, the university's Information Officer blamed outside agitators for the disruptive protest, claiming, 'About half the people were outsiders, and it was them who were behaving in a violent manner.'[133]

An investigation was launched by the university into the events that day. Quoted by *Hullfire*, the report found:

> the description of events given to us leaves us in no doubt that Proctor and the security staff were ambushed by a well-organised group of persons, many of whom appeared not to be students of the University, or residents of Hull.[134]

The report also found that the venue chosen for the event was unsuitable and criticised 'the decision of the police not to come on campus until trouble occurred, and only at such time as necessary, to send a reconnaissance party'.[135] The report recommended that the university develop a code of practice for future events similar to Proctor's visit, and engage with the police early in the planning process.[136]

Revising 'no platform' policies

In the midst of these visits, several of the student unions revised their 'no platform' policies, especially as the student unions became divided between the far left students who pushed for militant direct action and the more moderate elements in the student union (often in leadership positions). In February 1986, Oxford University's student union held a referendum on their 'no platform' policy. In November the previous year, the Brasenose Debating Society had invited Patrick Harrington to speak, which caused the student union to invoke a 'no platform' policy.[137] Prior to Harrington's invitation, there was no formal 'no platform' policy at Oxford, although there was opposition to Harrington coming to the university, with a spokesperson from the Socialist Workers' Student Society stating, 'There is no way we will let Harrington even enter BNC [Brasenose College].'[138] The Oxford University Student Union's Anti-Racist Committee argued that Harrington's 'mere presence [was] an insult to students, especially non-whites' and that '[t]here should be no racist platforms in the University – they lend enormous credibility to such views'.[139] In an instance where the NUS policy was more radical than the student union's, the NUS Press Officer was quoted in the student newspaper, *Cherwell*: 'However academic the debate in Brasenose may be, the fact is that Harrington has been on record as endorsing firebombing attacks on NF opponents and shouldn't be given any platform at all.'[140]

In response, the Oxford University Conservative Association organised a petition of nearly 700 names calling for an overhaul of the policy.[141] The President of the Conservative Association, Nick Levy, described the 'no platform' policy as 'a serious infringement of the basic democratic right to freedom of speech'.[142] The number of signatures gathered by the Conservative Association triggered student union rules to hold a referendum on the policy, which was held in late February 1986 (a week after the Carlisle protest).

While the Oxford University Conservative Association led the charge against the policy, it was the Oxford Against Racism (OAR) organisation that spearheaded the campaign for retention of the policy. The student magazine *Isis* described Oxford Against Racism as 'an umbrella organisation of members of the town, University and Polytechnic' and one that argued that the issue over the 'no platform' policy was 'not one of the right to freedom of speech', but concerned 'the right of people to live in peace free from racial attacks and discrimination on the basis of the colour of their skin'.[143] OAR had allegedly gathered a larger number of signatures than the petition that had triggered the referendum, but enthusiasm for the referendum was mixed.[144] A poll by *Cherwell* the week before found that 42.6 per cent of those polled were in favour of the 'no platform' policy, while 44.8 per cent wanted it removed.[145] However, the following week the student paper reported a much more decisive result: 'OUSU's "No Platform" policy was heavily defeated in the referendum as expected. Only six colleges provided a "Yes" majority, the final result being 2,246 in favour of "No Platform" (41% of the vote) and 3,152 against.'[146]

The Guardian quoted the student union president, who was from the Liberal/SDP Alliance, as welcoming the result, saying 'I would not have wanted to implement the "no platform" policy … I think most students are aware of the need to combat racism but also to preserve free speech'.[147] In the wake of the referendum, the Monday Club declared that they would re-invite John Carlisle, but his rescheduled visit later in the year was cancelled due to sickness.[148]

A similar referendum was held at the University of Bristol in late 1986, sparked by disruptions that had occurred earlier in the year, starting with a campaign against Professor John Vincent. Vincent, a Professor of modern history, became a target for protesting students who objected to his columns for *The Times* and *The Sun*. Vincent was considered part of a cohort of 'new right' intellectuals, who 'skilfully adapt[ed] the cultural racism of the "New Right" circles into a populist format', namely the mainstream press.[149] Vincent had written some inflammatory columns for *The Sun*, such as one in July 1985 in which he blamed the death of a black toddler on Lambeth Council's belief in 'separate treatment' for black people.[150] Cited by Paul Gordon, 'The anti-racist "mumbo jumbo about black identity", Vincent wrote, had overridden the safety of the child and had led to disaster'.[151]

A campaign to boycott Vincent's lectures started in 1985 and escalated in early 1986, coinciding with the beginning of the Wapping Strike, when Rupert Murdoch moved his printworks and instigated a long-running battle with several trade unions (months after the Miners' Strike ended). In late February 1986, students disrupted a lecture by Vincent and this was repeated the following week. The *Daily Telegraph* described the second incident:

> Prof. John Vincent … was escorted by police through a mob of angry students yesterday after giving a lecture at Bristol University.
>
> Mr Vincent … left the arts faculty building after a two-hour siege by about 300 students while he gave a history lecture abandoned last week due to protests.[152]

The newspaper cited the university's Information Officer who claimed that the protest was 'orchestrated by the Socialist Workers Party and anarchist elements determined to widen the dispute over the printing of Mr Rupert Murdoch's newspapers at Wapping'.[153]

The disruption of Vincent's lectures was condemned in the media. An editorial for *The Times* declared:

> An academic lecture has an absolute privilege. Disruption is an act of intellectual vandalism as dangerous as any other effort to truncate learning and the exchange of opinion …
>
> Professor Vincent's extra-curricular activities are irrelevant. Prveenting his teaching about late nineteenth century politics was to disrupt the instrument of higher education itself, the academic lecture.[154]

In the same newspaper, Lord Beloff stated that the disruption of lectures due to the lecturer's external activities 'must be regarded as conduct so irreconcilable with the idea of a university that its perpetrators must, after due warning, face expulsion'.[155]

Fifteen students originally faced disciplinary proceedings as a result of the disruptions,[156] but this grew to 19 by May 1986, when nine were acquitted, two had the charges against them dropped and seven were found guilty.[157] Baroness Cox, during parliamentary debates about the introduction of legislation to protect free speech on campuses, complained that the penalties for those found guilty were too mild.[158] John Carlisle, who faced violent protests on various campuses around the same time, also criticised the leniency shown to the protesting students. In the House of Commons in June 1986, he said:

> The students who came before the court were merely fined and slapped on the wrist. They were not expelled from the university. The taxpayer has the right to ask whether such students should be able to continue their studies at the taxpayers' expense when they are intent on disrupting meetings.[159]

Eventually the seven students who were found guilty had their convictions quashed on a technicality.[160] Meanwhile John Vincent took a leave of absence from his teaching role after the disruptions, but continued to write.

But the troubles didn't stop after this. A day after Carlisle's aborted visit to the University of East Anglia (discussed earlier in this chapter), Carlisle arrived to speak at Bristol University, invited by the Conservative Association. He was joined by fellow Tory MP Fred Silvester, who had recently introduced a private members' bill to ensure free speech on campus[161] – an idea that had been raised by Sir Keith Joseph's green paper on higher education the previous year and would become part of the Education (No. 2) Act 1986 by the end of the year (after pressure from the House of Lords).[162] Unlike many of his previous attempts to speak at universities that spring, Carlisle was able to address a crowd, despite significant student protests. *The Times* reported that 'more than 100 left-wing students attempted to disrupt a meeting on free speech' and that both MPs faced 'a barrage of screaming, foot stamping and obscenities'.[163] The newspaper further described the protest with the following:

> Ignoring cries of 'fascist' and 'racist', Mr Carlisle said he was pleased that in Bristol at least he had been allowed to address a meeting…
>
> Making himself heard through a microphone in spite of a fire alarm being activated, Mr Carlisle shouted: 'You won't stop us because we believe in the fundamental principle of democracy.'[164]

Using the trope of the 'red fascist', Carlisle said that the reaction by the protesting students reminded him of 'what happened in Nazi Germany in the 1930s'.[165]

In the wake of these incidents at Bristol, the student union held a vote on whether a 'no platform' should be introduced at the university, which coincided with Enoch Powell and Ray Honeyford's earlier mentioned visits. According to *Bacus*, students were to vote 'either to allow all freedom of expression within the law, or to ban organisations such as the National Front and the British Movement and their members' (with the vote requiring support from 500 students to be binding).[166] But the NF and BM were not the target of the recent protests against Carlisle, Powell and Honeyford and the student union stressed that '[n]o platform would not be used to ban Conservative MPs unless they are declared members of the National Front or like organisations'.[167]

For the anarchists and Trotskyists who disrupted Vincent and Powell, whether a formal 'no platform' policy applied to Tory MPs was a moot point – the NUS-endorsed 'no platform' policy at the national level made a distinction between fascists (who were to be 'no platformed') and hard right politicians (who were to be allowed to speak), but was often ignored by more militant protestors from the left. The Powell incident showed that disruptive protests happened outside the bounds of the politics of the student union, often at odds with the wishes of the student union itself. As one of the protestors wrote in a letter to *Bacus*:

> When we sent [Harvey] Proctor, Vincent and Powell packing we were not simply silencing racists. We were saying an emphatic 'No!' to the lie that our 'free speech' has anything to do with real freedom or power over our own lives.
>
> The right must continue spouting its cliches [sic], and in such a white and middle class university as Bristol it can be no surprise that so many are willing to swallow them at face value. But, make no mistake about it, the only freedom that the brats in BUCA really care about is the freedom to stay rich and become powerful, and that means that the rest of us must stay poor and powerless.
>
> We can talk about it as much as we like. That's our freedom of speech. Unless we back our words up with action nothing will ever change.[168]

An editorial for *Bacus* in the week of the vote begged for a more civilised discourse around politics at the university:

> Whether we get No Platform or not, let common sense be the guiding instinct to those on both sides of the political divide. We do not want a repeat of the scenes at the Powell meeting ...[169]

This was a sentiment expressed by moderate student union leaders and student newspaper editors across the country in the mid-1980s (and is something that is still mentioned today) – that the far/hard right and the far/hard left were at each other's throats and left no room for civility. The eventual outcome of the vote was a rejection of a formal 'no platform' policy at the university, with just over 1,200 students voting for the option 'which compelled the Union to adopt a policy of freedom of expression for all views within the law'.[170]

In contrast with what happened at Oxford and Bristol universities, University College Cardiff saw the formalisation of the 'no platform' policy in the aftermath of the Powell disruption. As part of the agreement reached between the student union and the university administration, a new 'no platform' policy was devised, which had four main points:

- College should let the Union know formally of the identity of visiting speakers of a political nature.
- In the light of this information, if a speaker is controversial in respect of union policy, the Union will advise that the meeting be cancelled.
- If this advice is not taken, the Union will channel protest into an orderly counter-demonstration outside the meeting. When the meeting is about to begin, demonstrators will enter the meeting in an orderly fashion under official Union supervision.
- Should a speaker make comments which contravene, directly or by implication, the Union's democratically adopted policy of 'No Platform' for racism or sexism, (s)he will be heckled by Union sponsored demonstrators. Should (s)he persist in making such comments, chanting will take place.[171]

This policy, reportedly hailed by the NUS as 'a model "No Platform" policy',[172] was comprehensive in how the student union would react if a controversial speaker did attempt to speak at the university (which was often not explicitly stated in other student union policies), but it still remained unclear of how the student union would prevent an incident like the Powell demonstration if protestors ignored the directions of the union leadership. However, it was seen as a successful compromise at the time. An editorial in the student newspaper, *Gair Rhydd* (which was usually hostile to the notion of 'no platform') praised the new policy, saying it was 'as far as possible, cut[ting] down the potential abuse of the policy, by allowing freedom of speech as the government and law insists, but recognising the right to protest and disrupt if a speaker makes racist or sexist remarks'.[173]

However, these individual efforts by student unions to negotiate the terms and limits of their 'no platform' policies were disrupted by the energies of the Thatcher government, which sought to introduce legal restraints on the use of 'no platform' as a tactic on campus. This eventually became the Education (No. 2) Act in late 1986.

Government intervention and the Education (No. 2) Act 1986

There had long been calls for government intervention around the issue of freedom of speech at universities. In May 1970, Labour's Education Secretary Edward Short stated that he did not consider the topic of freedom of speech at universities 'an appropriate subject for legislation'.[174] After the introduction of the 'no platform' policy by the NUS in 1974, the Conservative MP Norman St John-Stevas asked the then Labour Education Secretary Reg Prentice whether he would publish a list of the student unions that had rejected the 'no platform' policy, to which Prentice responded:

> As for publishing a list of certain student unions, I do not have that information available and I do not think it would be right for anyone to seek such information. It is for the student unions to run their own affairs. It is not for us to compile lists. If I receive an invitation to speak to a students' union, I inquire from those issuing the invitation what is the attitude of the union to the ban.[175]

As the controversy surrounding the bans on pro-Zionist groups by some student unions raged in late 1977, Conservative MP Anthony Steen called for the defunding of student unions who upheld this ban. Steen suggested that the Labour Education Secretary Gordon Oakes 'warn unions which have passed disgraceful motions that the Government will not tolerate this action and that if they pursue them he will take steps to take the money away'.[176] Oakes replied that 'Ministers have no powers to intervene in the conduct of student union affairs', and added:

> There are many difficulties in relation to grants. Many universities are not involved in this matter. There would be great difficulty in trying to withdraw or discriminate with regard to grants. I do not want to take that course of action. I want students themselves to put this matter right in their national body, the NUS, and in their individual democratic student union bodies at particular universities.[177]

This would remain the consensus of the British government until the mid-1980s when Sir Keith Joseph as Education Secretary sought to fundamentally reform the higher education sector in line with the Thatcher government's neoliberal agenda. In 1985, the Green Paper *The Development of Higher Education into the 1990s* was presented by Joseph with a wide range of suggested reforms. Coming shortly after the protest against Leon Brittan at the University of Manchester, the Green Paper listed freedom of speech at British universities under the government's 'main concerns', stating:

> 1.10 All institutions, at all times, have a responsibility to ensure that their affairs are conducted as befits a liberal institution. In particular, they have a responsibility to protect freedom of speech within the law, even for those with widely unpopular views: this is essential, as part of a free society, for critical thought and the liberal education which it underpins.[178]

The Green Paper took up the argument that the funding given to student unions should not be given those unions that enforced the policy of 'no platform' – an argument also made by the Federation of Conservative Students about the alleged misuse of student union money to fund left-wing causes. Universities were called 'a natural home of free speech' and the policy of 'no platform' was described as the signal of 'the withering away of the university … as part of a free society in which all views may find free expression within the law'.[179] The Green Paper argued that 'taxpayer's money should not be used to fund unions that refuse a platform to speakers whose views are objectionable to some students although others wish to invite them', as well as to fund unions 'that prevent invited speakers from gaining a hearing, or that permit violence or the threat of violence to that end'.[180] This seemed to blame violent protests on the student unions even though in most instances, as demonstrated in this book, the student unions distanced themselves from any protest action deemed violent and often promoted peaceful protests at odds with the more militant actions taken.

At this stage, the Green Paper suggested that 'maintenance of freedom of speech will continue to be the duty of each institution' and encouraged the Committees of Vice-Chancellors and Principals (CVCP) and of Directors of Polytechnics to produce their own guidelines.[181] The Green Paper ended with a warning: 'The Government will watch to see the results and, should unsatisfactory incidents continue to occur, will consider what further may be done, either at a general level or through approaches by the Education Departments to individual institutions.'[182]

Attempting to stave off any future government intervention around this issue, the National Union of Students, the National Association of Teachers in Further and Higher Education and other peak bodies tried to formulate a charter that would indicate 'a commitment to the principle of independent and democratic student unions', including the freedom of speech and political activity on campus.[183] But agreement to the charter by all of the bodies involved could not be achieved and later in the year, the Committee of Vice-Chancellors and Principals developed their own guidelines 'in an attempt to preempt [sic] any plans the Government might have [had] to introduce legislation' around the issue of free speech.[184] The code circulated by the Committee made it clear that 'freedom of speech [was] not an absolute right at all times' and proposed that 'university authorities should have the right to stop meetings or visits by controversial figures if there is any threat to their safety'.[185]

This code was proposed by the Committee of Vice-Chancellors and Principals at the same time as Home Office minister David Waddington faced a disruptive protest at the University of Manchester, shortly after the riots in London and Birmingham and only several months after the protests against Leon Brittan at the same university. Invited by the Federation of Conservative Students, Waddington faced about 100 students who 'began stamping their feet and shouting "Racist" and "Deport Waddington"'.[186] The *Daily Telegraph* reported that 'protesting students jeered, spat and threw water' at Waddington, while the *Daily Express* claimed that he was punched and had beer thrown at him.[187] He was quoted by the *Daily Telegraph* as shouting at the protesting students:

> As long as I've got breath in my body I will defend freedom of speech against people like you. You want to turn this country into a socialist bloc. You are showing your contempt for democracy. However [sic] loud you shout, you will not be able to stop freedom of speech in Britain.[188]

Scheduled to speak for half an hour, he had to leave the stage after ten minutes and allegedly said, 'Those students were not fit to be educated at the country's expense.'[189]

The incident was brought up in parliament a few days later with Conservative MP Fred Silvester asking during Prime Minister's Questions:

> Is it not depressing that students at Manchester university should have attacked and abused the Minister of State, Home Office, my hon. and learned Friend the Member for Ribble Valley [Mr Waddington]? Does my right hon. Friend agree that it is about time that people inside and outside universities stood up to be counted on whether they are prepared to defend the right of free speech?[190]

The Prime Minister replied, 'Yes I agree … Universities are places where, above all, free speech should be honoured, not prevented'.[191] By February, Silvester had introduced a private member's bill to protect freedom of speech at universities, citing the protests against Brittan and Waddington at Manchester University amongst others.[192] In the days before presenting the bill in the House of Commons, Silvester told the *Times Higher Education Supplement*, 'In a student union it is very easy to raise the temperature and threaten disruption. This is a huge loophole.'[193] One that he intended to close.

Silvester's private member's bill was 'to safeguard the right of free speech and institutions of higher education, including student unions, to establish the duties and powers necessary for the enforcement of this right'.[194] Silvester criticised the guidelines devised by the Committee of Vice-Chancellors and Principals the previous year as having 'too many doors through which the activists can bolt', particularly criticising the notion that universities could use the threat of disorder as reason to prevent someone from speaking.[195] He argued that this 'would be an open invitation to those who adopt no platform policies to threaten disruption as a means of preventing the meeting from taking place' and to prevent university administrations from taking this option, Silvester's proposed bill sought to impose a duty upon university authorities to ensure that 'they had taken all reasonable steps' to maintain the right of free speech.[196] Silvester explained:

> Those steps should include a proper disciplinary code, adequate action against offenders, fines on student unions, where appropriate, arrangements properly made with the organisers of meetings and arrangements for the admission of the police, where necessary. Non-discrimination in the use of facilities by persons of different shades of opinion should also be included.[197]

The Times Higher Education Supplement reported that the chances of the bill passing were 'slim', but there some in the Conservative Party who hoped 'to use the occasion to prise some form of commitment from the Government to introduce its own legislation'.[198] Its second reading was delayed twice and after wrangling between several MPs and the House of Lords, the bill was dropped and eventually incorporated into the Education (No. 2) Bill, pushed through parliament by Sir Keith Joseph's successor as Education Secretary, Kenneth Baker.

The Education (No. 2) Bill was wide-ranging and sought to introduce many of the proposals put forward in the Green Paper from the previous year. Originally slated as clause 41 of the Bill, the section relating to 'no platform' was debated at length in the House of Commons in late October 1986, just days after Enoch Powell had faced disruptive protests at Cardiff and Bristol. The Under-Secretary for Education, George Walden, explained the purpose of the clause:

> the clause will require authorities to exercise judgment, sometimes as to whether a meeting should proceed at all. It will not prevent them from concluding in the last resort, although they would do well to consult the police before reaching such a conclusion, that a meeting should be cancelled or at least postponed because the threat of a breach of the peace was too substantial. But the clause will be beneficial in requiring them to weigh the situation most carefully before reaching a decision, rather than simply taking the line of least resistance.[199]

Most of those in favour of the Bill argued that the legislation would send a signal to the university administrations that measures to protect freedom of speech on campus had to be taken seriously. Backbencher David Crouch stated that the clause 'puts into law what the CVCP put in a letter', acting as 'belt and braces' for the Committee's previous guidelines.[200] Tory MP for Bristol North West, Michael Stern, furthered this sentiment by saying:

> The clause is necessary to get the CVCP to commit itself to something which most of us regard as important in our civilisation, instead of simply sitting on the sidelines saying that it deplores what is happening but unfortunately it cannot do anything about it.[201]

John Biggs-Davison, a prominent member of the Monday Club, claimed that the legislation was needed because the universities 'have shown themselves impotent to make available free speech to visiting speakers'.[202] John Carlisle, having been at the centre of these protests at universities, welcomed the Bill and declared that it sent 'a strong message' to Vice-Chancellors 'to firm up their own organisations and to become far more personally involved'.[203] Carlisle also argued that it sent a message to student unions that 'the British taxpayer will not tolerate no-platform policies', which 'should not be a part of any university'.[204]

However, at the same time many of those who supported the Bill conceded that it had its limits and that universities might not be able to stop disruptive protests altogether. As George Walden stated, 'I should like to stress that this legislation is by no means a panacea … [The] law, by its very nature, cannot be impregnable. We have been reminded of that by events in Bristol last week.'[205] John Carlisle acknowledged that 'those extremists who are intent on wrecking meetings … will not be put off by the clause', but argued that '[t]he message is that we will not tolerate violence on our campuses'.[206]

Liberal and Labour MPs opposed the legislation, questioning whether it was necessary to compel universities by law to enforce free speech. While declaring that Labour was 'totally against the no-platform policy', Labour MP Giles Radice suggested that it was uncertain whether the legislation would help foster free speech.[207] Radice claimed that Vice-Chancellors were worried about a number of things:

> Demarcation is an issue, as is judging in advance that which is lawful. There is a problem about the conflict of duties …
>
> Vice-chancellors [sic] are worried that they might have to be judges and police. They are worried about vexatious legislation.[208]

Instead of a legislative approach, Radice proposed that 'the best way forward … [was] through a code of practice'.[209]

In a last ditch attempt to avoid the legislative measures of the Bill, the NUS put forward a six-point charter that would uphold free speech at universities while providing protection for minorities who might not feel safe. The charter proposed:

- Black, Asian, Jewish and gay students should have the right to study free from fear of racial harassment, intimidation and violence;
- Women should have the right to study free from sexual harassment;
- Visiting speakers should have the right to free speech on campus providing they do not breach the rights of others outlined in the charter;
- The right to legitimate, non-violent protest should be maintained;
- Students should have the right to examine their personal record files;
- Students should be represented on all major college decision-making bodies.[210]

But this did not deter the government and the Education (no. 2) Act passed into law in November 1986. Section 43 of the Act demanded that universities, polytechnics and colleges 'shall take such steps as are reasonably practicable to ensure that freedom of speech within the law is secured for members, students and employees of the establishment and for visiting speakers'.[211] The last clause of section 43 stated that the Act applied to 'premises occupied by the students' union', but student unions contested that as they were separate legal entities, the Act did not apply to them. As Ian Cram and Helen Fenwick have shown, as 'section 43 does not directly cover student unions', the stance taken by student unions has been contested for the last 30 years.[212]

By 1989, there were calls for the laws around universities and freedom of speech to be strengthened, after Conservatives complained that universities were avoiding their responsibilities under the Education (No. 2) Act. The Conservative Collegiate Forum, a successor organisation to the Federation of Conservative Students, released a report in March 1989 which claimed that a 'survey of 97 sets of guidelines issued by higher education institutions' showed many were 'flawed', as they 'fail[ed] to guarantee sufficient security' and did 'not threaten penalties harsh enough to deter demonstrators bent on wrecking meetings'.[213] Looking at the report in detail, *Times* journalist Bernard Levin wrote of the 97 guidelines surveyed, 'Fifty three codes throw upon the student bodies the cost of stewarding the meetings', with 'eight of them demanding payment in advance or a deposit'.[214] In addition, '[n]ine codes insist that any loss or damage is to be made good, not by those who have caused it, but by the organizers of the meeting', while 'four require the holders of the meeting to bear the whole cost or part of any extra insurance required' and another ten 'limit[ed] the number of meetings where "designated" speakers are to appear'.[215] Lastly, Levin complained:

> Another, and wider, gap in the net is a clause in at least 27 codes; a meeting may be cancelled if it is likely 'to incite those attending to commit a criminal act' or 'lead to the expression of views in manner contrary to the criminal law' ...[216]

Levin claimed that this was 'another, and more serious, example of the victim being held responsible for the actions of the victimizer'.[217]

The Conservative Collegiate Forum report and the media used these guidelines as examples of 'campus cowardice' and suggested that the laws drawn up in 1986 had 'failed', or were being 'shirked, evaded and ignored'.[218] However, these arguments seem to assume that freedom of speech only existed for the speaker and the organisations that have invited them, disregarding that part of the freedom of speech was the right to vocally object and demonstrate. A university would have to weigh up these competing notions of freedom of speech when looking at events of campus and security at these events played a significant factor in whether they allowed these to go ahead. This is what 'reasonable steps' meant in section 43 of the 1986 Act. In response to criticism from Conservatives on this issue, the Committee of Vice-Chancellors and Principals replied that disruptions occurred at only a small number of meetings and 'large numbers of highly controversial meetings and classes took place within their institutions every week without disruption'.[219]

But a case in late 1988 launched by the Conservative Association at the University of Liverpool, when the university prevented a South African diplomat from speaking, tested the boundaries of how far the university could go in stopping events due to public order and safety concerns.

The Anti-Apartheid Movement and the Caesar-Gordon case

As well as the 'no platforming' of pro-South Africa speakers, such as John Carlisle, students protested against representatives of the apartheid government from speaking on campus throughout the 1980s, as part of the broader Anti-Apartheid Movement (AAM) in Britain. Although it had existed since the 1960s, the AAM grew exponentially after the Soweto Uprising in 1976, and by the 1980s it had become a significant social movement, including many young people and mobilising students on campuses across Britain.[220] In the early 1980s, the NUS and

AAM developed a number of joint campaigns which helped build anti-apartheid work as an important part of the student movement.[221] The 'no platforming' of pro-South Africa speakers and government representatives gained traction at British universities in the 1980s, building on previous anti-apartheid work on campus, such as the NUS boycott of Barclays for their investments in South Africa.[222]

In February 1982, students at the University of Bath, in the words of the Anti-Apartheid Movement Annual Report, 'provided an angry reception' for Dr Roy McNab, 'a former information attaché at the South African embassy in Paris and [then] the London Director of the South Africa Foundation'.[223] Later in the year, students at Bath University protested against the invitation by the Centre for Development Studies of Professor Jan Coetzee from the University of Bloemfontein.[224] *Anti-Apartheid News* reported that 'in the face of anti-apartheid action', Coetzee's status was shifted from 'official guest' of the Centre to 'personal guest' and as picket was mounted outside the Centre, Coetzee 'left a day earlier than planned'.[225]

In November 1983, the South African ambassador Marais Steyn encountered large student demonstrations at the universities of Nottingham and Cambridge, having to cancel one. Invited by the Conservative Association at Nottingham University, anti-apartheid protestors 'took over the room in which ambassador Steyn had been due to speak, forcing him to abandon his speech for "security reasons"'.[226] Speaking at the local Conservative Party headquarters in Nottingham, Steyn described the students as a 'jackbooted mob', claiming insincerely that '[i]n South Africa we certainly have free speech and believe in equality'.[227] In the same month, Steyn faced around 300 protestors at Cambridge after the Union Society invited him, alongside John Carlisle, to debate the sporting boycott of South Africa. *Anti-Apartheid News* reported:

> Waving banners and shouting anti-apartheid slogans, the protestors made clear their anger at the opportunity given to the ambassador to air his views on sporting links between Britain and South Africa. Their shouts could be clearly heard inside the debating chamber, where Steyn was joined by apartheid's old ally John Carlisle …[228]

In March 1985, Steyn's successor Denis Worrall was invited to a debate on South Africa by the Oxford Union, alongside the South African 'coloured' cabinet minister Allan Hendrickse and Bantustan leader, Chief Gatsha Buthelezi.[229] Following a protest by Oxford students and the local branch of the AAM, all three withdrew from the debate, which was subsequently cancelled.[230]

In September 1986, the South African Consul-General in Scotland, Dr James Alexander Shaw, was invited by the Federation of Conservative Students to speak at the University of Stirling, but was allegedly opposed by a number of students. *The Times Higher Education Supplement* reported that Shaw claimed: 'when he arrived at the campus gates, he was met by around 20 students who warned him that 150 students had been brought in from outside by the Socialist Workers Party and others, and were picketing the hall'.[231]

He further asserted that he had been told that 'the protestors had said they would not permit him to use the campus as a platform for racism, and had threatened violence if necessary'.[232] Shaw condemned the students who protested against him, declaring: 'Those students who believe their views should prevail and that the views of others should be suppressed are the step-children of Hitler, and epitomize the evil that is inherent in totalitarian systems of government.'[233]

The President of the Students' Association at Stirling University, Ian Robertson, disputed Shaw's version of events, saying 'there were between 40 and 50 students, who were intent on peaceful action' and that Shaw had only heard about the protest from FCS representatives (which Shaw conceded).[234] Robertson rebutted Shaw's characterisation of protestors as well and was quoted in the student newspaper at Stirling saying:

> For a representative of a racist regime which is involved in the brutal oppression of the majority of the South African population to equate peaceful protest with the action of Hitler and the Nazis would be laughable if it were not so disgusting.[235]

The Principal at the University of Stirling also queried Shaw's claims, replying that 'there were no groups of students from any other university on campus' and that 'Dr Shaw's allegations against the University of Stirling students are … based solely on a supposition of possible violence and not on fact'.[236] The Principal, Professor John Forty, also responded that the FCS had not informed the university of the impending visit and had not sought advice on potential security concerns.[237]

Even though Ian Robertson claimed that the protest was 'not a no-platform issue', a general meeting of the Stirling University Students' Association shortly afterwards 're-affirmed SUSA policy of no platform for racists or fascists in the light of the recent attempt by the FCS to bring the South-African [sic] Consul-General to speak at the University'.[238]

In October 1988, the Liverpool University Conservative Association invited two representatives from the South African embassy to speak at the university. After initially allowing the proposed event to go ahead under strict provisions (including no advertising of the event, restriction of entry to students only and the reservation of the right to charge the Conservative Association for any additional security costs),[239] the university administration cancelled the meeting after discussion with the Merseyside Police.[240] This was contested by the Conservative Association and after wrangling between the student group and the university, the proposed meeting was rescheduled for January 1989.[241] The Conservative Association's newsletter stated that the banning confirmed that 'the University's commitment to free speech was at best questionable' and that the action was 'totally without justification'.[242] The newsletter called the rescheduled meeting 'a considerable moral victory for the association [sic]'.[243]

However the January meeting was again cancelled after consultation with the police. In the ensuing legal case, the High Court judge stated that '[t]he police were very concerned about what in particular might happen in nearby Toxteth with its large coloured population'.[244] There was also concern about public disorder at the university after a visit by the Northern Ireland Secretary Tom King had led to 'widespread disturbance', when six arrests were made.[245] The university argued that they cancelled the meeting as a 'last resort' because 'the threat of a breach of the peace was too substantial', as outlined under section 43 of the Education (No. 2) Act 1986.[246]

Some right-wing columnists, politicians and activists complained about this move by the university. Conservative MP and Monday Club supporter, Sir Rhodes Boyson, wrote a letter with Norris McWhirter, chairman of the neoliberal group, the Freedom Association, to *The Times* condemning both the disturbances during the King visit to the university and the subsequent banning of the South African diplomats, seeing it as part of a wider trend for universities to use the 1986 Act draconianly:

> Liverpool University has classified visiting speakers, such as the Foreign Secretary and others, as 'controversial' and therefore likely to provoke violence or public disorder. Thus ministers of the Crown, elected MPs, and others are likely to be subject to the same arbitrary treatment as that given to the diplomat in question. Full censorship of visiting speakers by unrepresentative groups becomes possible by the expedient of issuing threats, as has happened at Liverpool.[247]

Also in *The Times*, columnist Bernard Levin argued that the Vice-Chancellor at the University of Liverpool, Graeme Davies, had failed in his moral and legal duty to uphold free speech at the university and had 'surrendered' to the 'barbarians' (echoing a term earlier used by Sir Keith Joseph to describe students in 1986).[248] Levin purported: 'Liverpool's preference for a ban on a meeting rather than on those who wish to disrupt it shows that some would take the practice of surrender even further'.[249]

The out-going Chairman of the Conservative Association at Liverpool University, Joe Baldwin, accused Davies of 'moral cowardice' and blasted the university for the decision to force the cancellation of the meeting in December 1988: 'I am totally outraged that the university has taken this decision. It has absolutely no legal or moral basis. It is abundantly clear that the University of Liverpool has flagrantly disregarded the duty laid upon it by the Act.'[250]

Although Baldwin was a member of the Conservative Collegiate Forum, a successor organisation to the FCS in the late 1980s and as *The Times* reported, 'appea[ring] to have stepped up controversial speaker visits in order to provoke left-wing students', he also suggested: 'This is a scandalous denial of free speech, which sets a disgraceful precedent and has handed extremists on both the left *and the right* [my emphasis] a licence to intimidate not just at Liverpool, but thoughout the country.'[251]

But the invitation and the subsequent legal case was largely seen in the mainstream and student press as a chance sought by the Conservative Association to test section 43 of the Education (No. 2) Act. As an editorial in the student newspaper at the University of Liverpool, *Gazette*, claimed:

> The highly provocative invitation was intended to serve a purpose. LUCA claim that they were testing the 1986 Education Act (no. 2) which requires Universities and others to take steps which are 'reasonably practicable' to ensure freedom of speech within the law is secured.[252]

In May 1989, the incoming Chairman of the Liverpool University Conservative Association, Andrew Caesar-Gordon, launched legal proceedings against the university, arguing that the banning of the event was *ultra vires* of the university's responsibilities under the 1986 Act, particularly with regards to the police suggestion that the event might have caused disorder in nearby Toxteth. The costs for the Conservative Association's case were being supported by a right libertarian group called the Campaign for a Free Britain (sometimes called the Committee for a Free Britain), headed by journalist David Hart,[253] but also included long-standing opponent of 'no platform' and radical student politics, Baroness Cox. Lawyers for the Conservative Association argued that the university was 'not entitled to take into consideration threats of disorder outside the university by persons not in statu pupillari' (students of the university) and while the university could 'take advice on the risk where there is a risk within the purview of the university', it could not 'take account of a substantial risk of riot elsewhere'.[254]

The university's legal representatives baulked at this division of risk, arguing:

> It is illogical, artificial and irresponsible to take into account of the risk of serious public disorder on university or outside the university involving its personnel but ignore other risks of disorder. Large-scale disorder was expected. A university cannot be expected to isolate itself from what is happening off its premises ... The court should say that reasonable practicality entitles the respondents to take into account of the possibility of injury to persons or damage to property in the local community.[255]

For the university, to ignore what the police had warned may occur if the event went ahead would be a dereliction of duty to its surrounding community. The university's lawyers suggested that with the introduction of section 43 of the 1986 Act, 'Parliament cannot have expected universities to place themselves in an ivory tower' and the university had performed the 'balancing exercise' between free speech and public order as required by the Act.[256]

In May 1990, the High Court noted that the 'university authorities acted with the best possible motives to prevent breaches of the peace which they had good reason to believe would occur on and off their premises', but stated that section 43 of the 1986 Act only pertained to 'good order within the precincts of the university'.[257] The High Court found that 'the university is not enjoined or entitled to take into account threats of "public disorder" outside the confines of the university by persons within its control', with Lord Justice Watkins quipping:

> Were it otherwise, the purpose of the section to ensure freedom of speech could be defeated since the university might feel obliged to cancel a meeting

> in Liverpool on the threat of public violence as far away as, for example, London, which it could not possibly have any power to prevent.[258]

The High Court suggested that if the university had simply refused permission for the event with regards to concerns about the risk of disorder within the university, they would have been within the law regarding section 43, but because 'the threat was of public disorder without the university, then, unless the threat was posed by members of the university, the matter was … entirely for the police'.[259] This meant that the Conservative Association won the case, but because the university had acted reasonably and in good faith, the court refused to order the university pay the student group's legal costs, which were being paid for by the Campaign for a Free Britain.[260]

While the university wholeheartedly welcomed the court's decision,[261] the response by the Liverpool University Conservative Association and its supporters was mixed. Caesar-Gordon himself called it 'victory at a price', but hoped that the court had 'handed a message to both left and right extremists that the threat of public disorder will not now be sufficient grounds for trying to halt a meeting taking place off a university campus'.[262] Although this overlooked the fact that the High Court ruled that this was only insufficient grounds if the possible disorder was to take place off campus and without the involvement of university students. Caesar-Gordon also raised the issue that the court did not object to the university's insistence on extra security for controversial speakers, arguing that it was 'still open for the university to charge what it wants for security measures, which could price clubs out of existence'.[263] This was a concern raised by the Conservative Collegiate Forum the previous year and remained a point of contention amongst Conservative students who criticised universities using the 1986 Act to cancel meetings on public order grounds.

Since 1990, this case has been used to argue that universities can cancel events due to public order concerns,[264] but that there are some limits to this with regards to risks outside the university – although in *R (Ben-Dor) v University of Southampton*, Justice Whipple ruled that outside factors could impact whether an event should be allowed as these 'might lead to disorder or violence *within* the confines of the university'.[265]

Conclusion

The 1980s saw an expansion of the uses of 'no platform' as a tactic by student activists. As shown in the previous chapter, an argument was made that the fight against sexism and homophobia was just as important as the fight against racism and fascism, and therefore sexists and homophobes were to be denied a platform, alongside racists and fascists. This led to criticism from some of the veterans of the student movement of the 1970s that the policy of 'no platform' had strayed from its original purpose.

As confrontations with the Thatcher government increased as the decade went on, Members of Parliament, particularly those from the hard right, became focal points of protest when they visited universities and polytechnics. As a number of them, such as John Carlisle, Harvey Proctor and Enoch Powell, espoused racist sentiments, there were debates over whether to apply the policy of 'no platform' to them. While discouraged by the NUS leadership at the national level, some individual student unions sought to 'no platform' these hard right speakers. But even in these cases, there was regularly a divide between the moderate students (often in leadership roles within the student union) and more radical student groups, particularly those aligned to the Socialist Workers' Student Society and anarchist groups.

Throughout the mid-1980s, there was a series of protests against hard right speakers on campuses across the country. Some were successful in preventing the speaker from visiting, some organised protests to demonstrate opposition to the speakers and some ended with the physical disruption of the event. Although there were a range of outcomes arising from these protests, it was portrayed by right wing politicians and the press as a crisis of free speech within the university system. Students were seen as intolerant and totalitarian enemies of freedom, a major buzzword for the Thatcher government and its supporters during the 1980s.

This led to the government eventually introducing legislation as part of the Education (No. 2) Act 1986 to demand that higher education institutions ensure freedom of speech and take 'reasonable steps' to guarantee speakers be allowed to address audiences, if within the law. However it was recognised that the university could cancel an event if there was a risk of public disorder or violence, and after the Act came into effect in 1987 there were still complaints for the next few years, accusing university administrators of circumventing their responsibilities by claiming that controversial speakers were a threat to public safety on campus.

This was challenged by the Liverpool University Conservative Association in the High Court, with their case funded by the right libertarian pressure group Campaign for a Free Britain, citing the university's cancellation of an event involving two South African diplomats due to fears of unrest in the nearby area of Toxteth. Although the ruling actually went against the university, the judgment handed down in 1990 has been used since to determine that there are limits to protection of the freedom of speech legislated for by section 43 of the 1986 Act. Originally seen as a way to hit back against the perceived power of the student unions, who were seen as the main instigator of the shutting down of free speech on campus, the 1986 Act put the powers to decide who could speak in the hands of the university authorities, which was largely reinforced by the High Court ruling. It has been evident since the late 1980s that universities have had to consider competing demands and legal requirements when allowing or not allowing events to take place or speakers to visit. As the next chapter will show, the 1990s and 2000s saw new challenges for the student movement and 'no platform' was again repurposed to contend with the new political and socio-economic landscape of a post-Thatcher Britain.

Notes

1 NUS, *Defend Your Union: The Education Bill 1986 and Its Effects on Student Union Operations and Policies* (London: NUS document, 1986) p. 15, NUS Archives, Scotland.
2 For example, see: *Socialist Worker*, 26 October, 1986, p. 15.
3 *The Times*, 31 May, 1990, p. 10.
4 Stuart Hall, 'The Great Moving Right Show', *Marxism Today* (January 1979) p. 16.
5 Harry Phibbs, 'FCS Twenty Years On', *Social Affairs Unit Blog*, 30 October, 2006, www.socialaffairsunit.org.uk/blog/archives/001216.php (accessed 26 March, 2019).
6 Ian Bradley, 'Students Move Right', *The Spectator*, 30 October, 1976, p. 10.
7 Ibid.; *The Sunday Times*, 9 April, 1978, p. 5; 'Student Politicians: Right Wing Moves to Disaffiliate from NUS', *Searchlight* (April 1980) p. 5.
8 FCS, *The Truth About NUS: A Report by the Federation of Conservative Students on the National Union of Students* (London: FCS pamphlet, n.d.) p. 1.
9 'The Dialectics of Freedom', *Patterns of Prejudice*, 8/3 (1974) p. 13; *The Times*, 1 April, 1977, p. 7.
10 *The Times*, 11 May, 1977, p. 19.
11 *The Sunday Times*, 9 April, 1978, p. 5
12 Timothy Evans, *Conservative Radicalism: A Sociology of Conservative Party Youth Structures and Libertarianism 1970–1992* (Providence, RI/Oxford: Berghahn, 1996) p. 65.
13 Ibid., p. 69.
14 See: 'Minutes of the National Committee Planning Conference Held at Conservative Central Office', 27 June, 1978, p. 8, CCO 506/32/3, Conservative Party Archives, University of Oxford.
15 Ruth Levitas, 'Tory Students and the New Right', *Youth and Policy*, 16 (1986) p. 4.
16 'Tory Party Probes Right-Wing Students', *Searchlight* (July 1982) p. 4; 'The Influences of the Racist Tory Right', *Searchlight* (January 1983) p. 11.
17 'Tyndall's Nazis Recruit FCS Activists', *Searchlight* (August 1986) p. 6.
18 *The Guardian*, 5 July, 1986, p. 4.
19 Ibid.
20 *Leeds Student*, 5 June, 1986, p. 3.
21 *The Guardian*, 31 May, 1986, p. 28.
22 Ibid.
23 'Ultra-Right Tory Students Show Their True Colours', *Searchlight* (June 1983) p. 20.
24 Ibid.
25 Ibid.
26 *Leeds Student*, 29 April, 1983, p. 8.
27 'Ultra-Right Tory Students Show Their True Colours', p. 20.
28 Ibid.
29 Levitas, 'Tory Students and the New Right', p. 4.
30 *Leeds Student*, 5 June, 1986, p. 3.
31 Ibid.
32 Evan Smith & Marinella Marmo, *Race, Gender and the Body in British Immigration Control: Subject to Examination* (Houndmills: Palgrave Macmillan, 2014) pp. 156–157.
33 *The Beaver*, 3 December, 1980, p. 3. Keir Hopley, editor of *The Beaver*, later stated in an article that the student union 'did not (repeat, not) vote to disrupt the meeting' and that a student 'merely moved a procedural motion to adjourn, and he even said that he only wanted to picket the meeting'. *The Beaver*, 10 February, 1981, p. 7.
34 Ibid.
35 Ibid.
36 Ibid.
37 *The Beaver*, 20 January, 1981, p. 2.
38 Ibid., p. 4.
39 Ibid.

40 Ibid.
41 *The Beaver*, 3 November, 1981, p. 5.
42 Ibid.
43 David Watson & Rachel Bowden, 'Why Did They Do It? The Conservatives and Mass Higher Education, 1979–97', *Journal of Education Policy*, 14/3 (1999) p. 244.
44 Richard Aldrich, 'Educational Legislation of the 1980s in England: An Historical Analysis', *History of Education*, 21/1 (1992) p. 59.
45 *The Mancunion*, 13 March, 1985, p. 4.
46 *The Mancunion*, 6 March, 1985, p. 1.
47 Manchester City Council, *Leon Brittan's Visit to Manchester University Students' Union, 1st March 1985: Report on the Independent Inquiry Panel* (Manchester: Manchester City Council, 1985) p. 9.
48 *The Mancunion*, 13 March, 1985, p. 4.
49 Brian Pullan with Michele Abendstern, *A History of the University of Manchester, 1973–90* (Manchester: Manchester University Press, 2013) p. 200.
50 *The Mancunion*, 6 March, 1985, p. 1.
51 Pullan, *A History of the University of Manchester*, p. 201.
52 *The Mancunion*, 6 March, 1985, p. 2.
53 Ibid.
54 *The Mancunion*, 13 March, 1985, p. 4.
55 Mike Day & Jim Dickinson, *David Versus Goliath: The Past, Present and Future of Students' Unions in the UK* (Oxford: Higher Education Policy Institute, 2018) p. 35.
56 *The Times Higher Education Supplement*, 15 March, 1985, p. 4.
57 Pullan, *A History of the University of Manchester*, p. 202.
58 *The Mancunion*, n.d. (May 1985) p. 1.
59 Pullan, *A History of the University of Manchester*, p. 202.
60 Manchester City Council, *Leon Brittan's Visit to Manchester University Students' Union*, pp. 14–15.
61 Ibid., p. 19.
62 Ibid., p. 59.
63 Ibid.
64 Matthew P. Llewellyn & Toby C. Rider, 'Sport, Thatcher and Apartheid Politics', *Journal of Southern African Studies*, 44/4 (2018) p. 579.
65 Student union flyer, n.d., Tandana Online Archive, www.tandana.org/pg/PDF/SC/SC101.PDF (accessed 31 March, 2019).
66 Ibid.
67 See: Anandi Ramamurthy, *Black Star: Britain's Asian Youth Movements* (London: Pluto Press, 2013).
68 'Carlisle: Safe in Our Hands', *Fleece*, 34 (February 1986) p. 3.
69 Ibid.
70 AYM, 'Press Statement', n.d., Tandana Online Archive, www.tandana.org/pg/PDF/SC/SC91.PDF (accessed 1 June, 2019).
71 *Daily Express*, 15 February, 1986, p. 8.
72 *The Times*, 19 February, 1986, p. 4.
73 'Carlisle', p. 3.
74 Ibid., p. 26.
75 Ibid.
76 *Cherwell*, 21 February, 1986, p. 1.
77 Ibid.
78 Ibid.
79 Ibid.
80 *Daily Express*, 18 February, 1986, p. 2.
81 Ibid.
82 *Leeds Student*, 21 February, 1986, p. 1.
83 Ibid.

84 Ian McKenzie, 'Confidential Report to the Vice-Chancellor on the Visit of John Carlisle MP to the University of East Anglia on 24th April 1986' (July 1986) appendix 2(i), UEA/GRAY/1/3, UEA archives. Emphasis in original text.
85 Ibid.
86 *Phoenix*, 13 March, 1986, p. 1.
87 Ibid.
88 McKenzie, 'Confidential Report to the Vice-Chancellor ...', appendix 2(ii).
89 *Phoenix*, 24 April, 1986, p. 1.
90 McKenzie, 'Confidential Report to the Vice-Chancellor ...', p. 4.
91 *Phoenix*, 1 May, 1986, p. 1; McKenzie, 'Confidential Report to the Vice-Chancellor ...', pp. 10–11.
92 McKenzie, 'Confidential Report to the Vice-Chancellor ...', pp. 11–12.
93 Ibid., p. 13.
94 Ibid., p. 19.
95 Ibid.
96 Camilla Schofield, *Enoch Powell and the Making of Postcolonial Britain* (Cambridge: Cambridge University Press, 2013) p. 330.
97 'Speech by the Rt. Hon. J. Enoch Powell, MBE, MP to the Birkenhead Conservative Women's Luncheon, at the Masonic Hall, Birkenhead, at 1pm, Friday, 20th September, 1985', PREM 19/1521, National Archives.
98 *Leeds Student*, 25 January, 1985, p. 1; *Leeds Student*, 1 February, 1985, p. 3.
99 *Gair Rhydd*, 29 October, 1986, p. 5.
100 *Gair Rhydd*, 22 October, 1986, p. 1.
101 *Gair Rhydd*, 15 October, 1986, p. 1.
102 *Gair Rhydd*, 22 October, 1986, p. 1.
103 Ibid.
104 *Gair Rhydd*, 5 November, 1986, p. 2.
105 *Gair Rhydd*, 19 November, 1986, p. 1.
106 *Bacus*, 3 October, 1986, p. 1.
107 Ibid.
108 Ibid., p. 2.
109 Ibid., p. 1.
110 Ibid., p. 2.
111 *Bacus*, 24 October, 1986, p. 1.
112 Ibid.
113 Ibid., p. 2.
114 *Daily Express*, 28 October, 1986, p. 8.
115 Ibid., p. 1.
116 *Socialist Worker*, 25 October, 1986, p. 15.
117 *Bacus*, 24 October, 1986, p. 2.
118 Ibid.
119 *Bacus*, 24 October, 1986, p. 12.
120 Ibid.
121 Ibid.
122 Ibid.
123 Paul B. Rich, 'Conservative Ideology and Race in Modern British Politics', in Zig Layton-Henry & Paul B. Rich (eds), *Race, Government and Politics in Britain* (Houndmills: Macmillan, 1986) p. 62.
124 Cited in, Zig Layton-Henry, 'The Conservative Party and the Far Right: Political Aspects', *Journal of Ethnic and Migration Studies*, 11/3 (1984) p. 324.
125 *Hullfire*, 16 March, 1987, p. 1.
126 Ibid.
127 Ibid.
128 *Daily Mirror*, 16 March, 1987, p. 11.

129 K. Harvey Proctor, *Credible and True: The Political and Personal Memoir of K. Harvey Proctor* (London: Biteback Publishing, 2016) p. 143.
130 *Daily Express*, 14 March, 1987, pp. 1–2.
131 *Hullfire*, 16 March, 1987, p. 2.
132 Ibid.
133 *Daily Express*, 14 March, 1987, p. 2.
134 Cited in, *Hullfire*, 5 October, 1987, p. 1.
135 Ibid.
136 Ibid.
137 *Cherwell*, 29 November, 1985, p. 1.
138 Ibid.
139 Ibid.
140 Ibid.
141 *Cherwell*, 21 February, 1986, p. 2.
142 *Cherwell*, 24 January, 1986, p. 1.
143 *Isis*, 4 March, 1986, p. 5.
144 Ibid.
145 *Cherwell*, 21 February, 1986, p. 2.
146 *Cherwell*, 28 February, 1986, p. 1.
147 *The Guardian*, 1 March, 1986, p. 1.
148 Ibid.; *Cherwell*, 24 October, 1986, p. 1.
149 Neil MacMaster, *Racism in Europe 1870–2000* (Houndmills: Palgrave, 2001) p. 197.
150 Paul Gordon, 'A Dirty War: The New Right and Local Authority Anti-Racism', in Wendy Ball & John Solomos (eds), *Race and Local Politics* (Houndmills: Macmillan, 1990) pp. 184–185.
151 Ibid., p. 185.
152 *Daily Telegraph*, 5 March, 1986, p. 1.
153 Ibid.
154 *The Times*, 28 February, 1986, p. 17.
155 *The Times*, 21 June, 1986, p. 8.
156 *The Times*, 23 April, 1986, p. 2.
157 *The Times*, 10 May, 1986, p. 16.
158 *The Times*, 28 May, 1986, p. 1.
159 House of Commons, *Hansard*, 10 June, 1986, col. 215.
160 *The Times*, 5 September, 1986, p. 2.
161 *The Times Higher Education Supplement*, 7 February, 1986, p. 1.
162 Secretary of State for Education and Science, *The Development of Higher Education into the 1990s* (London: HMSO, 1985); *The Times Higher Education Supplement*, 6 June, 1986, p. 3.
163 *The Times*, 26 April, 1986, p. 2.
164 Ibid.
165 *Daily Express*, 26 April, 1986, p. 7.
166 *Bacus*, 7 November, 1986, p. 1.
167 Ibid.
168 Ibid., p. 2.
169 Ibid.
170 *University of Bristol Newsletter*, 27 November, 1986, p. 1.
171 *Gair Rhydd*, 19 November, 1986, p. 3.
172 Ibid.
173 Ibid.
174 *Hansard*, 27 May, 1970, col. 477w.
175 *Hansard*, 23 July, 1974, col. 1283.
176 *Hansard*, 25 November, 1977, col. 2066.
177 Ibid., col. 2068; col. 2072.

178 UK Government, *The Development of Higher Education into the 1990s* (London: HMSO, 1985) p. 5.
179 Ibid., pp. 33–34.
180 Ibid., p. 33.
181 Ibid., p. 34.
182 Ibid., p. 34.
183 *The Times Higher Education Supplement*, 24 May, 1985, p. 3.
184 *The Times Higher Education Supplement*, 11 October, 1985, p. 4.
185 *The Times Higher Education Supplement*, 15 November, 1985, p. 1.
186 *Daily Telegraph*, 9 November, 1985, p. 1.
187 Ibid.; *Daily Express*, 9 November, 1985, p. 2.
188 *Daily Telegraph*, 9 November, 1985, p. 1.
189 Ibid.
190 House of Commons, *Hansard*, 12 November, 1985, col. 423.
191 Ibid.
192 House of Commons, *Hansard*, 11 February, 1985, col. 793.
193 *The Times Higher Education Supplement*, 7 February, 1986, p. 1.
194 House of Commons, *Hansard*, 11 February, 1985, col. 793.
195 Ibid., col. 794.
196 Ibid., col. 795.
197 Ibid.
198 *The Times Higher Education Supplement*, 14 March, 1986, p. 3.
199 House of Commons, *Hansard*, 21 October, 1986, col. 1120.
200 Ibid., col. 1109.
201 Ibid., col. 1111.
202 Ibid.
203 Ibid., col. 1114.
204 Ibid.
205 Ibid., col. 1119–1120.
206 Ibid., col. 1113–1114.
207 Ibid., col. 1118.
208 Ibid.
209 Ibid.
210 *The Times Higher Education Supplement*, 16 October, 1986, p. 4.
211 Education (No. 2) Act 1986, s43.
212 Ian Cram & Helen Fenwick, 'Protecting Free Speech and Academic Freedom in Universities', *Modern Law Review*, 81/5 (2018) pp. 856–858. For an example of the contested stance on the application of section 43 to student unions, see: Universities UK, *Freedom of Speech on Campus*, Parliamentary Briefing, 23 November, 2015, ss. 22–29, www.universitiesuk.ac.uk/our-work-in-parliament/Documents/freedom-of-speech-on-campus.pdf (accessed 1 May, 2019).
213 *The Sunday Times*, 19 March, 1989, p. A3.
214 *The Times*, 1 June, 1989, p. 14.
215 Ibid.
216 Ibid.
217 Ibid.
218 *The Sunday Times*, 19 March, 1989, p. A3; *The Times*, 1 June, 1989, p. 14.
219 *Daily Telegraph*, 4 May, 1989, p. 2.
220 Gavin Brown & Helen Yaffe, *Youth Activism and Solidarity: The Non-Stop Picket Against Apartheid* (Abingdon: Routledge, 2018) p. 6.
221 Roger Fieldhouse, *Anti-Apartheid: A History of the Movement in Britain* (London: Merlin Press, 2005) p. 334.
222 Jodi Burkett, '"Don't Bank on Apartheid": The National Union of Students and the Barclays Boycott Campaign', in Jodi Burkett (ed.), *Students in Twentieth-Century Britain and Ireland* (Houndmills: Palgrave Macmillan, 2017) pp. 225–248.

223 Anti-Apartheid Movement, *AAM Annual Report*, 1982, http://psimg.jstor.org/fsi/img/pdf/t0/10.5555/al.sff.document.aam00060_final.pdf (accessed 4 May, 2019).
224 *Anti-Apartheid News* (July/August 1982) p. 2.
225 Ibid.; Anti-Apartheid Movement, *AAM Annual Report*.
226 *Anti-Apartheid News* (January/February 1984) p. 2.
227 Ibid.
228 Ibid.
229 *The Times*, 7 March, 1985, p. 2.
230 Ibid.; Anti-Apartheid Movement, *AAM Annual Report*, 1985, http://psimg.jstor.org/fsi/img/pdf/t0/10.5555/al.sff.document.aam00063_final.pdf (accessed 5 May, 2019).
231 *The Times Higher Education Supplement*, 3 October, 1986, p. 5.
232 Ibid.
233 Ibid.
234 Ibid.
235 *Brig* (October 1986) p. 2.
236 *The Times Higher Education Supplement*, 24 October, 1986, p. 3.
237 Ibid.
238 *The Times Higher Education Supplement*, 3 October, 1986, p. 5; *Brig* (October 1986) pp. 2–3.
239 *Daily Telegraph*, 26 May, 1990, p. 8.
240 *R v University of Liverpool ex parte Caesar-Gordon* (1990) 3 All ER 821.
241 Ibid.
242 Liverpool University Conservative Association, *Society Newsletter*, January 1989, A161/52, Liverpool University Archives.
243 Ibid.
244 Ibid.
245 *The Times*, 2 December, 1988, p. 17; *Daily Telegraph*, 16 December, 1988, p. 2.
246 *The Times*, 2 December, 1988, p. 17
247 *The Times*, 22 November, 1988, p. 17.
248 *The Times*, 8 December, 1988, p. 16; *Daily Mail*, 16 May, 1986, p. 8.
249 *The Times*, 8 December, 1988, p. 16.
250 *The Times*, 5 December, 1988, p. 29.
251 Ibid.
252 *Gazette*, 24 November, 1988, p. 6.
253 *The Guardian*, 26 May, 1990, p. 4.
254 *Regina v University of Liverpool, Ex parte Caesar-Gordon* (1991) QB 124.
255 Ibid.
256 Ibid.
257 *R v University of Liverpool ex parte Caesar-Gordon* (1990) 3 All ER 821.
258 Ibid.
259 Ibid.
260 *Daily Telegraph*, 26 May, 1990, p. 8.
261 *The Times*, 26 May, 1990, p. 6.
262 Ibid.
263 *The Guardian*, 26 May, 1990, p. 4.
264 Ian Cram, 'The "War on Terror" on Campus: Some Free Speech Issues Around Anti-Radicalization Law and Policy in the United Kingdom', *Journal for the Study of Radicalism*, 6/1 (2012) p. 17.
265 *R (Ben-Dor) v University of Southampton* (2016) EWHC 953 (Admin). Italics are in the original text.

7

INTO THE TWENTY-FIRST CENTURY

In the 1980s, it was hoped by many on the right that the introduction of the Education (No. 2) Act 1986 would help curtail instances of 'no platforming' on campuses and discourage students from partaking in disruptive protests. However, the 1990s and 2000s showed that this would not be the case and over the next two decades, there were a number of instances of 'no platforming', as well as the use of the tactic to prevent different speakers from having a platform. But this also brought renewed and intense opposition to the use of the tactic.

In the 1990s, the British National Party (BNP) started to make incremental gains, feeding off discontent in post-Thatcher Britain, with a candidate winning a seat in a local election in East London in 1993. The increasing presence of the BNP in the electoral sphere and on the streets reinvigorated the anti-fascist movement, including amongst the National Union of Students, who supported student protests against the BNP and reaffirmed the stance of 'no platform' for the BNP. This culminated in Campus Watch, a short-lived joint venture with the Union of Jewish Students and the anti-fascist magazine *Searchlight*, that ran a 24/7 hotline for students to call to report instances of extremism on campus. Running for around two years, the majority of calls, it was reported in 1996, did not regard the BNP, but Islamic fundamentalist groups.

The most prominent Islamic group amongst students in Britain was Hizb ut-Tahrir. Beginning in the late 1980s in Britain, there was a concerted push by the group to attract students at universities, which led to a number of universities and student unions to ban them from university or student union premises on the grounds of anti-Semitism, racism, sexism and homophobia. Many student unions across the country banned Hizb ut-Tahrir in the mid-1990s, while the NUS barred them, along with other extremists, from holding student office positions. Opposing this move were many on the left, including the Socialist Workers' Student Society, which had been at the forefront of 'no platforming' in the previous decade, as well as the Revolutionary Communist Party (RCP).

Although a small group compared to other parties on the British left, the RCP became important as it was a highly vocal organisation that opposed 'no platform' in all its forms, arguing that both the BNP and Hizb ut-Tahrir should be allowed to speak and organise at British universities. In the 1990s, the RCP quickly embraced internet and media culture, becoming a prominent proponent of free speech absolutism, which over the next two decades permeated into mainstream political opinion. The RCP wound up in 1996 and became the *Living Marxism* network, then *Spiked Online*, which has had an enormous influence on debates about free speech in Britain (and all over the globe) – their libertarian contrarianism chiming with right-wing discourses on identity politics and 'political correctness'.

The RCP and its successors promoted the idea of absolute free speech on campus, and at several universities in the 1990s and 2000s student groups dedicated to free speech were established. One example of this was the Free Speech Society at the University of Leeds. In 2000–01, the Free Speech Society was taken over by two BNP members, who used it to invite new leader of the party, Nick Griffin to speak at the university. This led to a sustained campaign by anti-racists and anti-fascists at Leeds University to 'no platform' the BNP and exclude the two BNP members from the student union, which was ultimately unsuccessful.

This came at the beginning of further electoral breakthroughs for the BNP. Between 2002 and 2009, the BNP grew in stature at the electoral level, with both council and European Parliament members. This also meant that Griffin, who shaped himself after Front National's Jean-Marie Le Pen in France and other 'modern' far right leaders in continental Europe, became an infamous political figure and thus invited to speak by the media and by student groups. Over a five-year period between 2002 and 2007, Griffin was invited by several different student groups in England and Scotland to speak or debate, which led to high profile instances of 'no platforming' by anti-fascist students. While mostly successful, student protestors were unable to prevent Griffin, as well as Holocaust denier David Irving, from speaking at the Oxford Union in late 2007.

Griffin was increasingly seen in the media as a political figure worth engaging with and after he became an MEP in 2009, was invited onto the BBC's *Question Time*, despite significant protests against this. Griffin's poor performance on television was viewed, particularly after BNP's electoral losses over the next few years, as a vindication of allowing him a platform and engaging with fascists in 'debate'. Overlooking the groundwork done by anti-fascists to convince voters to shun the BNP, Griffin's televisual failure has become part of a liberal myth that 'no platform' was an outmoded concept and that the only way to defeat fascism was by taking them on in the 'marketplace of ideas'.

This fetishisation of debate as an anti-fascist weapon was used by some student unions to oppose 'no platform' as a policy, which occurred, for example, at the University of East Anglia in 2007, and by the media to give airtime and column space to other far- and populist right figures, such as UKIP's Nigel Farage and the English Defence League's Tommy Robinson (Stephen Yaxley-Lennon) – which has been an increasingly significant problem in the last few years.

This push for 'debate' and the celebration of the 'marketplace of ideas' has been disseminated widely by the successors of the RCP and *Living Marxism*, the *Spiked Online* website and its multitude of authors, such as Mick Hume, Tom Slater and Brendan O'Neill (amongst others). *Spiked* has been at the forefront of a campaign against 'no platform' and for absolute free speech on campus, with the website creating the Free Speech University Rankings in 2015. Running until 2018, these rankings alleged that there was a mass campaign of censorship engulfing British universities, but there have been a number of criticisms of the methodology and analysis, as well as the ideological outlook, of the report and its authors. This has not, however, stopped the rankings and the authors at *Spiked* from having a significant influence in the press and political sphere, amplifying the notion that free speech was endangered in the British higher education system.

Another source of concern over 'no platform' has emerged from reactions to the high-profile application of the tactic to others, particularly radical feminists who have been accused of transphobia, such as Julie Bindel and Germaine Greer. The 'no platforming' of 'gender critical' feminists has caused many to argue that 'no platform' has deviated too far from its original anti-fascist intention. But this debate is reminiscent of the debates over the use of the tactic to 'no platform' sexists and homophobes in the 1980s.

This chapter brings the history of 'no platform' through the 1990s and into the twenty-first century. It shows that 'no platform' remains a shifting tactic, used by different activists to prevent a variety of speakers and groups from having a platform to promote their views, which are deemed by some to be harmful. Similar to reactions against 'no platform' in the 1970s and 1980s, the continued use of the tactic has also seen a backlash, which combines the conservative right and libertarians. As this chapter will show, 'no platform' continued to be a contested concept and activity over the last 30 years, on from the apparent 'heyday' of 'no platform' in the 1970s and 1980s.

The rise of the British National Party

The British National Party entered the 1990s with a certain degree of notoriety and small number of active members. The BNP had emerged out of the decline of the National Front in the early 1980s as the political vehicle of former NF leader, John Tyndall. Roger Eatwell wrote that in many ways, 'the BNP was an extension of the 1970s NF' and under Tyndall, continued the NF's strategy of contesting elections, while engaging in street politics through provocative marches.[1] Faced with competition for the disaffected youth of the 1980s from the British Movement and then the 'political soldiers' of the National Front, the BNP attempted to attract disillusioned Conservatives (as the NF had done in the early 1970s).[2] The links between the Federation of Conservative Students and the BNP, as discussed in the previous chapter, is an example of this strategy. However, the BNP remained a small group centred around Tyndall that, on the surface, presented little chance of electoral breakthrough or extra-parliamentary political success.

In September 1993, a BNP candidate, Derek Beackon, won a by-election for a local council seat in the London borough of Tower Hamlets, which shocked mainstream politics, as well as anti-racists, in Britain. The area where Beacon won was the Isle of Dogs, an area of London that was undergoing significant socio-economic change and still feeling the effects of nearly a decade and a half of Conservative rule. As Daniel Trilling has written, the area represented 'a total breakdown of mainstream politics', with 'a Labour-run neighbourhood, in a Lib Dem-run borough, under a Tory Government – and nobody seemed able to provide the basic necessities'.[3] The BNP tapped into a wide discontentment with the local situation and also exploited the animosity between Labour and the Liberal Democrats in the ward to edge a narrow electoral victory.

Beackon's electoral win was preceded by a BNP campaign of 'Rights for Whites', which presented the white working class as a group that was discriminated against in the local political environment and 'left behind' in a post-Thatcherite Britain – a sentiment that the BNP sought to make use of throughout the rest of the 1990s and into the 2000s. As James Rhodes (citing Nigel Copsey) wrote, '[t]he BNP effectively latched on to local concerns regarding the allocation of public housing to Bangladeshi families and the closure of public facilities' and used the 'Rights for Whites' slogan to invoke 'a sense of the minority status of whites'.[4] This campaign, alongside the council seat win, presented the twin threat, a groundswell of discontent being tapped into by the BNP within the communities of East London and an electoral breakthrough that drew upon this discontent. Even though Beackon lost his seat the following year, the BNP's relative success was a wake-up call to many anti-fascists and anti-racists in the early 1990s.

The BNP's campaign happened at the same time as the rise of the skinhead group Combat 18 and the Blood and Honour network, established around a growing racist Oi music scene. This had evoked a response by various anti-fascist and anti-racist groups across the country in the early 1990s. Anti-Fascist Action, the militant anti-fascist organisation which had been assembled in 1986, was involved in much of the street fighting with Blood and Honour, Combat 18 and the BNP during this period.[5] In late 1991, a number of Labour MPs, including Ken Livingstone and Dianne Abbott, and trade union figures helped launched the Anti-Racist Alliance (ARA), which sought to combat the rising far right, as well as other forms of racism in British society.[6] Led ostensibly by black Labour Party activist Marc Wadsworth, the ARA was 'on the moderate wing of the anti-fascist movement' and advocated 'a legal policy of pressure group tactics' rather than the physical confrontation promoted by the AFA.[7] The Socialist Workers Party and the Labour MPs which had formed the Anti-Nazi League in 1977 revived the ANL in January 1992, which campaigned against the BNP in a similar manner to the 1970s ANL, with a combination of marches and electoral campaigning.[8] Although all three of these groups disagreed with each other about their tactics and there was particular criticism of the AFA for their confrontational strategy and of the ANL's lack of a local response to the BNP in East London,[9] but the increased attention by the anti-fascist movement, in its various guises, contributed to Beackon losing his seat in the May 1994 local elections.

The NUS supported both the ARA and the ANL, and while many students were involved in the anti-racist campaigns against the BNP in the early 1990s, concentrated anti-fascist activism on campuses directed at the BNP was not as strong as previous anti-fascist activities by the NUS. Like the approach taken by the ARA, opposition to the BNP was incorporated into a wider anti-racist approach taken by student unions across the country. Coming at a time when the Conservatives were attempting to legislate against the political activism of the NUS, the peak student body supported broad anti-fascist actions, such as the march past the BNP headquarters in East London in October 1993, which were compiled in a 'diary against fascism',[10] but with the BNP already subject to the policy of 'no platform', student unions focused on broader anti-racist actions.

One action that the NUS undertook, in conjunction with the Union of Jewish Students and the anti-fascist magazine *Searchlight* was the Campus Watch initiative. In December 1994, the three organisations came together over concern that a 'small but growing number of BNP and other fascist activists [were] now operating on campuses over much of the country' and established Campus Watch, 'a hotline to monitor racial attacks'.[11] The 24/7 hotline ran throughout 1995–96 and was described by NUS President Douglas Trainer as a 'massively important project'.[12] In a report released in October 1996, the first year of the hotline saw 381 calls made, although 271 (or 71 per cent) related to Islamic extremists (primarily Hizb ut-Tahrir).[13]

One of the predominant critics of the Campus Watch and of the NUS' approach towards the BNP was the Revolutionary Communist Party. The RCP, as discussed in Chapter 5, had long been considered a disruptive influence on campus through its student wing, Revolutionary Communist Students (RCS), and since the mid-1980s the RCS had been opposed to any formal 'no platform' policies. In the RCP's magazine *Living Marxism*, Jennie Bristow complained that the Campus Watch initiative was established 'to combat the (virtually non-existent) activity of the BNP on campus.'[14] The previous year, Juliet Connor objected to the focused anti-fascist response (what she called 'the "No Platform" lobby') to the BNP, arguing that the BNP was 'a small organisation of a couple of hundred people, a combination of social misfits and skinheads, concentrated in a handful of places'.[15] For Connor, the BNP had 'no platform in any real sense' and it was the anti-fascists that were giving them publicity.[16] Instead of enforcing the NUS' 'no platform' policy, Bristow suggested that student unions should have allowed the BNP to speak on campus, writing:

> If there is a conflict of ideas, and if we accept that some ideas are right and others are wrong, there are two possible ways of dealing with this situation. One way is to attempt to stifle the opinions which you believe to be wrong, by imposing bans and censorship. The other is to challenge the ideas you believe to be wrong in open argument.[17]

At this time, those writing for *Living Marxism* seemed to be suggesting that the BNP needed to be debated, rather than demonstrated against, moving away from the confrontational protest tactics used by the RCP in the 1980s, but maintaining the stance of opposing 'no platform'. This was part of a wider trajectory of the RCP (and its successors) from ultra-left Trotskyist group to libertarian contrarianism.

The Revolutionary Communist Party/*Living Marxism* and free speech absolutism

Originally a splinter group called the Revolutionary Communist Tendency (until 1981), the Revolutionary Communist Party gained a reputation on the British left in the 1980s as sectarian and controversialist, with some arguing that the RCP indulged in cult-like behaviour.[18] The RCT had originally broken away from the Revolutionary Communist Group (RCG) in the late 1970s, particularly over their approach to South Africa and the role of the African National Congress/South African Communist Party, although wider disagreements emerged. The RCG was itself a split from the International Socialists in the mid-1970s, before the IS became the Socialist Workers Party in 1977. The RCT/RCP formed several front groups around single issues during the late 1970s and early 1980s, with the most prominent being the Irish Freedom Movement and Workers Against Racism (WAR). John Kelly has written,

> Thanks to a combination of lively publications, particularly its weekly newspaper *the next step* [sic], popular anti-racist campaigning and extensive recruitment on university campuses, the RCP grew steadily into the 1980s and beyond.[19]

Being known by other left groups as promoting an ultra-left agenda, the RCP stood out from the rest of the left at this stage, even compared to other Trotskyist and Leninist groups that were around during the 1980s. As well as disagreeing with several groups over the Falklands War and balloting during the Miners' Strike, the RCP also argued that the Labour Party no longer represented the British working class and admonished the rest of the British far left for calling for a vote for Labour in general elections. While some of their ultra-left policies may have resonated with the rest of the far left, there were others that demonstrated the significant differences between the RCP and its rivals. This was particularly the case with regards to their views on social and equality issues (for example, their attitude towards AIDS awareness), which became more pronounced in the late 1980s and early 1990s.

By the early 1990s, the party had eschewed the other left-wing parties at the time and amplified its self-identification as the contrarian Robinson Crusoes of the British left. In his account of the life of the RCP, leading member Michael Fitzpatrick says that during the first half of the 1990s, the RCP argued that 'the working class had disappeared as a political force' and deeming that the revolutionary party was redundant, emphasised a shift 'towards advancing an intellectual rather than a practical alternative'.[20]

This shift upended its anti-racist outlook, which had previously been highly militant, but its attitude towards the far right (often minimising the threat that it posed) had existed for much longer. WAR had originally proposed that the 'most effective response to racism is the formation of workers' defence groups' and the mobilisation of workers against the racism of the state, portrayed as the opposite to the left's 'staple diet of petitions, lobbies and paper campaigns'.[21] This position meant that the RCP and WAR always looked to emphasise the fight against state racism, which sometimes undermined any anti-fascist actions as the NF and BNP were seen as the smaller threat. For WAR, anti-fascism against the NF was 'a convenient diversion' from the anti-racist struggle.[22] Even before the establishment of WAR, this position held by the RCT/RCP had led to criticism of 'no platform' as a tactic as it focused on the NF as a 'violent and racist organisation', but 'separate[d] the nationalism and racism of the NF from the nationalism and racism of reformism'.[23]

As the militancy of the RCP dwindled from the late 1980s to the early 1990s, WAR's street-based anti-racism faded and underestimation of the threat of the far right remained. But while it had previously argued that '[t]he fight against racism cannot be restricted to a campaign against racist ideas' and that '[r]acism cannot be fought with "facts"',[24] the RCP in the pages of *Living Marxism* now privileged debate over other forms of anti-racist activism. This fed into the party's approach to 'no platform', which had evolved over the 1980s towards free speech absolutism and a rejection of the anti-fascist consensus that had been built over the last two decades.

While the RCT had criticised 'no platform' in the late 1970s for its focus on the fascism of the National Front, the RCP's opposition to 'no platform' in the 1980s stemmed from the group's opposition to calls for the state to fight racism and fascism, eventually developing into a fetishism of free speech (including for racists and fascists). After a number of bans on demonstrations under the Public Order Act in the first half of 1981, the RCP condemned those on the left who seemed to condone bans of fascist demonstrations, declaring: 'Whether or not they are justified as measures aimed against fascists, *all* state restrictions of the freedom of speech, assembly and press are ultimately directed against the working class.'[25]

During the demonstrations against Patrick Harrington at the Polytechnic of North London, the RCP saw the call for Harrington to be excluded from the campus as a similar call for the authorities to intervene under the guise of anti-racism. Kirk Williams wrote:

> instead of simply beating Harrington off the campus, the campaign asked the college authorities to expel him and argued its case in the courts. The left's reliance on the law rather than direct action to deal with Harrington only encouraged other college authorities to introduce new powers of suspension, aimed at anybody expressing 'radical views'.[26]

It was actually Harrington that brought the case before the courts and the students were the defendants, but for the RCP, the broader demand for Harrington to be expelled was one of the primary problems with the campaign. Again Williams argued that Harrington was 'a soft target for the liberal left casting around for an issue on which to prove its anti-racist credentials' and instead '[a]nti-racist students should have been campaigning against state attacks on overseas students'.[27]

By 1985, the RCP's argument against 'no platform' was starting to solidify and in reply to a letter about the 'no platforming' of the Jewish Society at Sunderland Polytechnic, *The Next Step*'s editors stated, 'bureaucratic bans can never be an effective substitute for political struggle against racists or anybody else'.[28] The following month, the editorial in *The Next Step* wavered between the argument put forward by WAR that racism needed to be forcefully and physically confronted on one hand and on the other proposing that 'physical measures are no substitute for a political struggle against the influence of nationalist and racist ideas within the working class movement'.[29] The RCP still retreated from arguing that fascists should be debated, but suggested that other chauvinist ideas needed to be challenged in a non-physical manner.[30]

The editorial, written in May 1985, seemed to condemn left-wingers who 'indulge[d] their personal distaste' for anti-abortionists by 'breaking up meetings or suppressing student societies', writing that '[s]uch measures do nothing to combat the growing influence of these views'.[31] However, this was only a short time after a group of Revolutionary Communist Students attempted to disrupt a speech by pro-life speaker Victoria Gillick at the University of Manchester (as discussed in Chapter 5). The journal was celebrating a picket of another Gillick's talks in Edinburgh in December 1985,[32] but by early 1987, the RCP was encouraging an opposite approach, proposing '[w]e should organise public debates with the anti-abortionists and put them on the spot in front if a wide audience'.[33] The reasoning put forward by Frank Richards (a pseudonym for RCP leader Frank Furedi) was a precursor of the arguments made in *Living Marxism* in the 1990s:

> In the past left-wingers have criticised our party for taking the same platform as the anti-abortionists. But this only shows that the left lacks confidence in its arguments. We cannot afford to ignore our opponents if we are to defeat their ideas.[34]

As politicians and the media became increasingly concerned about 'no platform' and free speech at British universities during 1986, the RCP further denounced the tactic of 'no platform'. Beyond its principal argument that 'no platforming' fascists was a distraction from the primary fight against the racism of the state, the RCP now argued that the way that 'no platform' was being applied at universities in the mid-1980s was 'an impulsive outburst of liberal moralism which seeks to sweep away distasteful views, rather than confront them politically'.[35] Another editorial in *The Next Step* criticised the tactic of 'no platform' for giving 'exaggerated importance to a few eccentrics in idiot organisations which have virtually no influence' and playing into the hands of the right, who were pushing a 'free speech' agenda to combat broader student radicalism.[36] For the RCP, 'no platform' was 'an attempt to wish away a problem that must be confronted politically' and 'invite[d] the state to take repressive measures against the right which can easily be extended for use against the left'.[37]

The RCP's claim that 'no platform' was 'an evasion of the real problem of racism' and a token gesture against the far right seemed to suggest that 'no platform' was the only anti-fascist and anti-racist strategy being pursued by the student left in the 1980s.[38] While the left was in retreat during the 1980s (including on the anti-racist front), anti-racist and anti-fascist activism was still pursued by students and the left in a number of areas, including anti-deportation campaigns, campaigns against police racism and street campaigns against the National Front and the BNP. The RCP liked to portray itself as the only real anti-racist force in Britain and this often meant depicting the rest of the left as failing to take racism seriously. By focusing on 'no platform' at the expense of all other anti-racist and anti-fascist activism being conducted in the 1980s, the RCP could attempt to distinguish itself as the only group involved in the 'real struggle against racism in the workplace and on the estates'.[39]

The RCP also condemned 'no platform' for 'leav[ing] it up to the authorities, courts and the police to judge who should be censored',[40] but this overlooked the fact that most of the 'no platform' actions by students during the 1980s were in the face of pressure from the universities and student union leadership to allow controversial speakers to be heard. Even when student unions were involved in 'no platform' actions (such as at University College Swansea in 1987), there were few appeals to the university administration or the police, and instead the student union was used as a organising force for grassroots student activism. This was also partly a suspicion of the student unions by the RCP in the mid-to-late 1980s. Between 1988 and 1990, as the student unions came under a renewed attack by the Thatcher government, the RCP argued that the student unions were 'appendages of the institutions of higher education, not independent organisations of students' and therefore allegedly unwilling to adequately confront (in the eyes of the RCP) the universities and the government.[41] For the RCP, the NUS in particular was 'ill-placed to lead a student fightback because it [was] part of the system' that was attacking students.[42]

The formalisation of the RCP's opposition to 'no platform' during the late 1980s and early 1990s came also at a time when the RCP was increasingly concerned about censorship, defending Salman Rushdie, as well as fighting the broadcast ban on Irish Republicans and the 'Christian morality' of the Conservatives and the religious right.[43] However, by lumping 'no platform' together with these other forms of censorship, the RCP made no distinction between the censorship conducted by the state and by the media, and the denial of a platform by student groups. These student groups, in almost all instances, did not appeal to university authorities to ban certain speakers, but through the student union (or other student organisations) made a public (and often physical) demonstration that certain speakers were not welcome. For the RCP, there was no difference. This was made clear by Juliet Connor when discussing the anti-fascist campaign in the early 1990s calling for the media to refuse to provide a platform for the BNP:

> Many might think that it's all right to call for censorship of racists so long as the government is not invited to do the banning. Anti-fascists argue that it's up to ordinary people to demand 'No platform' for fascists in colleges, in the press and in their workplaces. But it makes no difference who does it. Whether the appeal for censorship is addressed to the government, media barons or trade unions, calling for a ban on the BNP can only reinforce an already censorious climate.[44]

The RCP steadfastly conflated calls for the state (through legislation, the police or discrete government bodies) with campaigns for the media to deny a platform to fascists and for student unions to refuse to allow racists or fascists to speak. The distinction between calls for a top down approach and a bottom up approach was non-existent. And as the militancy of the RCP faded and the 'marketplace of ideas' was increasingly fetishised by those centred around *Living Marxism*, debate became the primary battleground for the remnants of the party. Despite arguing ten years earlier that direct action against racism was needed and that arguments could not adequately fight racism, the RCP in its later days now argued the opposite – which would echo through its successor projects.

'No platform' and Hizb ut-Tahrir

As well as defending the BNP's right to free speech on campus, Jennie Bristow in her article for *Living Marxism* in 1995 also defended the Islamist group Hizb ut-Tahrir's right to organise at British universities.[45] As mentioned previously, over 70 per cent of calls made to the Campus Watch hotline set up by the NUS, UJS and *Searchlight* concerned Islamist groups, rather than far right organisations.

Hizb ut-Tahrir is a pan-Islamist organisation that began in Jordan in the 1950s, seeking to re-establish the caliphate through armed insurrection or military coup, with several unsuccessful coups d'état occurring in the Middle East and North Africa between the 1950s and the 1970s. Although it projects a highly conservative version of Islam, Hizb ut-Tahrir is not a jihadist organisation like Al Qaeda and while it has been suggested that the organisation has been linked to civil uprisings in the Caucasus region and Central Asia, it has not been associated with Islamist terrorism.

Establishing localised groups across the world, Hizb ut-Tahrir emerged in Britain in the early 1990s, with a concerted recruitment effort amongst Muslim youth and international students at British universities, especially in inner London. This led to complaints from some groups, such as the gay rights group OutRage! and the Union of Jewish Students, about the homophobic and anti-Semitic pronouncements of the Islamist group. There were also complaints in the student press from the various London universities about the presence of Hizb ut-Tahrir on campus and on the streets in the vicinity of the universities. At LSE in March 1994, an attempt by Hizb ut-Tahrir to set up a student society was rejected 'when it was realised that few of the required twenty signatures were of LSE students'.[46] In October 1995, the student newspaper at Imperial College, *Felix*, reported that Hizb ut-Tahrir had been 'caught illegally exhibiting at Freshers' Fair' and were 'attempting to distribute unsolicited leaflets through departmental pigeon holes as well as putting leaflets under students' doors'.[47]

The student unions at several universities in London and around the country used the 'no platform' policy to ban Hizb ut-Tahrir from organising and speaking on campus, including the University of Birmingham, Middlesex University, University College London, the University of Leeds and LSE.[48] For example, Nicola Hobday, editor of the student newspaper at LSE, *The Beaver*, explained in October 1996:

> At present Hizb-ut-Tahrir is banned from the LSE because its doctrine goes against the LSESU policy on Equal Opportunities. Believe me when I say that these people are very extremist and their views could be offensive to many of the minorities (and majorities) whom they are against; gays, jews [sic], blacks, democrats, socialists, women, or indeed anyone who doesn't agree with them.[49]

The Times reported in October 1995 that '[i]ncidents of verbal and physical assaults [had] led more than 100 student unions to ban the group'.[50] The NUS supported the actions by these student unions, after having monitored the activities of Hizb ut-Tahrir for several years in the lead up to these bans and blaming the Islamist group for 'a rise in racial tension on campuses'.[51] At the NUS conference in March 1996, a code of conduct was agreed to with the Committee of Vice-Chancellors and Principals that banned 'extremists' from standing for full-time representative posts in student unions.[52] *The Times* explained that the code 'would stop short of banning such groups [as Hizb ut-Tahrir] from campuses', but its 'members would be barred from elections for sabbatical office'.[53] Low voter turn-out at student elections made the NUS wary that Islamist groups, amongst other 'extremists', could exploit this to take positions of influence in the student unions.[54] While Hizb ut-Tahrir was the primary target of this code of conduct, some were wary that the language made it possible that it would be used against left-wing students, with a representative from Goldsmiths saying: 'All this stuff about extremism is rubbish. On the one hand, NUS talks about student apathy but then it makes out that students are all running around promoting extreme political views. They can't have it both ways.'[55]

But this pressure from the NUS and UJS did not always work. At the School of Oriental and African Studies (SOAS), part of the University of London, a student group linked to Hizb ut-Tahrir, the 1924 Committee, had held meetings on the subject of Israel, which were protested by Jewish students. Initially, according to the *British Muslim Monthly Survey*, '[o]fficials at SOAS said that members of the 1924 Committee had not broken any law or college regulation and therefore were free to continue to hold their meetings', but after a picket by Jewish students in

October 1994 to which police were called to maintain a distance between the two groups, SOAS authorities acted.[56] A few days after the picket, the administration at SOAS banned speakers from Hizb ut-Tahrir from future 1924 Committee meetings.[57] The Board of Deputies of British Jews gave a 'restrained welcome' to SOAS' decision, noting that the authorities only took action once students 'felt threatened', rather than seeing that views promoted by the 1924 Committee were, in the eyes of the Board of Deputies, 'an affront to the very fabric of university life'.[58] On the other hand, members of Hizb ut-Tahrir were outraged by this decision and retorted:

> SOAS has finally exposed its long-standing, hidden agenda of deep hatred for Islam by banning speakers invited who present Islam as an ideological alternative …
>
> The west and universities such as SOAS espouse ideas such as freedom of speech, but these become redundant when Muslims want to express their views.[59]

The banning by SOAS led to the student union at the school holding an urgent general meeting, attended to by around 400 people, including many Muslim students.[60] The student union passed a resolution 'which opposed "any attempt by college management to restrict what SOAS students can think, argue or organise"'.[61] According to a letter wrriten by a member of SOAS' Jewish Society to the student newspaper at SOAS, the student union allegedly 'called for the unconditional reinstitution of hizb 'ut tahrir [sic] as a legitimate society under the umbrella of the SOAS Students' Union'.[62] This stance by the student union was thus criticised by the Jewish Society for not taking into account 'either the concerns of the students who have felt intimidated, or of any willingness on the part of hizb 'ut tahrir [sic] and 1924 Committee spokespersons to in some way regulate their own activities'.[63] This led to wider disagreements with the NUS and the University of London Union, but the attention on Hizb ut-Tahrir from the press and student unions made them withdraw from their recruitment campaign at University of London campuses, including SOAS.[64]

While generally supportive of the tactic of 'no platform' for racists and fascists, most of the student left groups opposed the bans on Hizb ut-Tahrir, although the SWP did claim that they were 'the only group arguing consistently against the banning of Hizb Ut Tahrir [sic] and against their reactionary politics'.[65] The SWP argued that the NUS focused on Hizb ut-Tahrir without similar attention on the BNP, claiming: 'NUS does NOTHING to campaign on the ground against the BNP's attempts to gain support in elections, but finds the time to ban a Muslim organisation'.[66]

Although the SWP stated that they were 'completely opposed to the politics of Hizb ut-Tahrir', they 'refuse[d] to join in the call for the banning of this organisation'.[67] In opposing the ban, the SWP used similar arguments to that increasingly used by the RCP in the early 1990s to defend freedom of speech for the BNP.

While the RCP argued that a focus on the BNP ignored the larger threat of state racism, the SWP argued that banning the Islamic organisation 'misse[d] the real enemy – the racism endemic in British society'.[68] Juliet Connor wrote in *Living Marxism* that the anti-fascist campaign against the BNP 'elevated this little collection of scumbags into a recognised party that can even attract some protest votes' and a similar rhetoric was used by the SWP, who suggested that a ban would not stop Hizb ut-Tahrir growing and would only 'increase their attraction in the same measure as it alienates Muslim students from NUS'.[69] But unlike the RCP, the SWP saw a clear distinction between 'no platforming' the BNP and 'no platforming' Hizb ut-Tahrir. In a pre-conference bulletin from 1995, the Socialist Workers' Student Society declared:

> no matter how much we are against religious ideas, and the prejudices that often go along with them, we reject the equation of any Muslim group with the BNP. The BNP would happily slaughter Muslims along with gays, Jews and others. And to equate a tiny group like Hizb Ut-Tahrir with the BNP who have polling up to 44 percent in local elections, and are responsible for a string of racist murders, is a disgrace. It trivialises the real threat posed by the Nazis and makes 'fascism' a mere word to be thrown at anything we find offensive.[70]

Both the SWP and RCP suggested that the bans on Hizb ut-Tahrir reflected a growing Islamophobia in British society, which became much more acute in the post-9/11 era.

After the bans from campuses in the mid-1990s, Hizb ut-Tahrir sought to soften its image and promote its ideas through Islamic student groups at select universities, rather than explicitly as Hizb ut-Tahrir.[71] Sadek Hamid has written that the organisation 'attempted to rebrand itself as a moderate Islamist movement and made efforts to tone down its anti-Western rhetoric',[72] particularly in the heightened atmosphere following the September 11 attacks. At this time, the group also sought to make inroads into the anti-Iraq War movement but were sidelined by organisations such as the Stop the War Coalition.[73] With concerns about the radicalisation of Muslim students in Britain during the 'War on Terror' years, the NUS eventually banned Hizb ut-Tahrir in its entirety in 2004.[74] As Katherine E. Brown and Tania Saeed have written, universities were seen in this period as 'a significant meeting point, trigger or birthplace of radicalization' for Muslims in Britain[75] and the counter-terrorism concerns of the state filtered down through the university system, primarily the 'Prevent' strategy which sought to combat religious and political extremism in educational establishments.[76] This also filtered down through the National Union of Students. As in the 1990s, the Union of Jewish Students was instrumental in building support for the NUS applying its 'no platform' policy to Hizb ut-Tahrir and it was implemented at the NUS conference in Blackpool in April 2004, alongside the smaller Al Muhajiroun and the Muslim Public Affairs Committee.[77]

The discourse around the 'no platforming' of Islamist groups is often overshadowed by the implementation and practice of the Prevent strategy on campuses, which has been a major part of the government's counter-terrorism approach since the July 2005 bombings. When criticised for its 'no platform' policy, the NUS has been keen to stress that as well as banning the far right, the policy also applied to three Islamist groups and that the NUS took a similar approach to both far right and Islamist extremists.[78] A reason for this oversight may be that the 'no platforming' of Hizb ut-Tahrir and other groups fits into a broader Islamophobia that exists in Britain (and elsewhere around the world) where Muslims are seen as a 'suspect community'.[79]

As the landmark report by the Runnymede Trust showed in 1997,[80] Islamophobia was already widespread in Britain prior to 9/11 and the 'War on Terror'. One of the groups to exploit this was the British National Party, which, under new leader Nick Griffin, tapped into wider prejudices against Muslims to generate support for the far right party, and throughout the first decade of the twenty-first century developed this support into a number of electoral victories and prominent publicity for the BNP – resulting in a new wave of anti-fascist calls for 'no platform' and opposition to these calls grounded in free speech absolutism.

The British National Party under Nick Griffin

After Derek Beackon's electoral win in 1993, the BNP under John Tyndall looked to capitalise on this, but after some stronger showings by BNP candidates in local elections, the party stalled again. There was increasing frustration by a section of the party with Tyndall's leadership and Nick Griffin, formerly a leading figure in the Official National Front in the 1980s, became an influential challenger within the party. Griffin had joined the BNP in the early 1990s and was heavily involved in the BNP's 'Rights for Whites' campaign. But Griffin also looked to the rise of Jean-Marie Le Pen's Front National in France in the 1990s and believed that their shift towards conveying themselves as a professional and 'respectable' party showed a way forward for the BNP. As Steven Woodbridge has shown, the debate between 'ideological purity and electoral respectability' had gone on inside the party for a number of years before Griffin's ascendancy,[81] but by the late 1990s, the electoral gains being made by far right parties on the continent encouraged the BNP to move in this direction.

Despite Griffin's past anti-Semitic pamphleteering and Holocaust denial (which resulted in a conviction in 1998 under the Race Relations Act), Griffin was seen as a more electable option that Tyndall and in 1999, he was elected by the party membership as leader with around 70 per cent of the vote.[82] He sought to 'modernise' the party and avoid some of the traditional racist and fascist language used in the Tyndall years. The BNP often talked about the threats to (white) British national identity and the British 'way of life' – asylum seekers, Muslims, multiculturalism and the European Union – which took right-wing talking points shared by others, such as UKIP and the hard right of the Conservative Party, and promoted the BNP as the 'real' nationalist alternative. The populism of the BNP exploited the anxieties of sections of the population about neoliberal Britain in the twenty-first century and fuelled the idea that these people (predominantly described as the 'white working class') had been marginalised or 'left behind'. As James Rhodes wrote, the BNP:

> sought to cultivate and assume ownership of a widespread sense of resentment amongst sections of the 'indigenous' white, English population, particularly, though certainly not exclusively, the working classes ... This sense of marginalisation relates to both to the allocation of material resources, and a growing cultural anxiety regarding the 'plight' of English identity – in the context of declining national power, the rise of the European Union, perceived unmanageable levels of immigration, the spread of global capitalism, the perceived terrorist threat, devolution within the UK, and the apparent abandonment of the 'indigenous' population by the political establishment.[83]

The BNP also tapped into the growth of Islamophobia in Britain during the 1990s and even before 9/11, the party under Griffin used this hostility towards Muslims in Britain to generate publicity. Members of the BNP were involved in the riots in Oldham in the summer of 2001 and at the 2001 General Election, Griffin won 16 per cent of the vote in the seat of Oldham West and Royton.[84] This was only heightened over the next few years, especially in the wake of the bombings in London in July 2005.[85]

The BNP made its greatest impact in local elections. In 2002, it won five council seats and the following year, it won another 13 seats.[86] In 2006, the BNP won 12 seats on the Barking and Dagenham Council, which, as Robert Ford noted, made 'the BNP the second largest party represented on the council'.[87] In 2008, Richard Barnbrook was elected as a BNP candidate to the London Assembly, with over five per cent of the vote.[88] By the end of the decade, the BNP held over 50 local council seats across the country.[89] But the most significant electoral gain for the BNP came in 2009 when Nick Griffin and Andrew Brons (a former chairman of the National Front during the early 1980s) both became Members of the European Parliament. While the growth of the BNP had been a rising concern for anti-fascists for the last decade, the European election wins galvanised a broader response to combat the BNP.

Before this broad response, Griffin enjoyed both the notoriety of being the leader of the BNP and the 'respectability' of the BNP's electoral achievements. This led to Griffin being invited to speak and debate by various groups, including on university campuses. And these invitations led to student protests and calls for Griffin (as well as other BNP figures) to be 'no platformed'. One of the earlier instances was in 2001 at Leeds University involving the Free Speech Society.

Leeds University and the Free Speech Society

In early 2001, two young BNP members, Mark Collett and Chris Beverley, took over the Free Speech Society at the University of Leeds. Collett explained in an interview with *The Guardian*:

> When I came to Leeds University I joined the Free Speech Society to fight against political correctness. Then a BNP speaker got expelled, which I thought was absurd. He invited me to a BNP meeting in Burnley and I felt right at home. They were my kind of people – families, not loony Nazis of media hysteria.[90]

The Free Speech Society had existed for at least few years prior to Collett and Beverly joining it. There have been suggestions that the Free Speech Society was connected to the *Living Marxism* network, which existed after the Revolutionary Communist Party dissolved itself in 1996, but whether this was actually the case is unclear.[91] In October 1998, one of thc previous presidents of the Free Speech Society wrote an opinion piece for the *Living Marxism* website on the pulping of GQ magazine at Leeds University.[92] The former Treasurer of the Free Speech Society, Rosemary Schofield, wrote in the student newspaper, *Leeds Student*, that she was from 'the Mick Hume school, editor of *Living Marxism*, in that I believe that, "The best way to deal with prejudice is through more speech, not less ..."'.[93] This was also just a few years after Patrick Harrington, the National Front member who had been 'no platformed' at the Polytechnic of North London in 1984, had been invited to speak at a symposium on censorship organised by the *Living Marxism* network.[94]

When Collett became President of the Free Speech Society, it attempted to overturn the student union's 'no platform' policy, just as his ties to the BNP were confirmed by *Searchlight*.[95] However, as *Leeds Student* reported, many students 'were scared that if the No Platform policy was abolished racism and fascism would threaten minorities on campus every day'.[96] According to *Searchlight*, between 600 and 700 students attended the AGM, but Collett and Beverley could only muster 15 votes for their motion to overturn the 'no platform' policy, with a further 15 abstentions.[97] But this did not end the battle between Collett and anti-fascist students at the university, as well as in the student union and student press.

Rosemary Schofield, who had left the society when Collett took charge, wrote in the student newspaper that while she opposed the policy of 'no platform', the society under Collett 'no longer stood for free speech in action, it only stood for the abstract right of racists to speak freely, minus criticism'.[98] While refusing to confirm or deny his BNP membership, Collett spoke at a BNP rally in March 2001.[99] Although the student union overwhelmingly voted in favour of retaining the 'no platform' policy, the student union also decided not to exclude Collett from the union.[100] Ruth Clarke, the student union's Communications Officer, stated, 'the No Platform Policy does not apply to what members do in their spare time or political parties they affiliate to'.[101]

The same month, the Free Speech Society invited Nick Griffin to speak on campus, but, as reported in *Leeds Student*, 'the University refused permission for the possibly volatile meeting to be held on University premises on what Roger Gair, University Secretary stated were, "grounds of public safety"'.[102] According to the student paper, the meeting did go ahead, despite permission not being granted, with a 'spontaneous meeting' taking place to avoid protestors.[103]

Members of the Socialist Workers Party and Anti-Nazi League applied pressure within the student union to maintain the 'no platform' policy as Collett and Beverley refused to budge. When the Free Speech Society attempted to hold its AGM in May 2001, it was picketed by about 80 students, with Christian Høgsbjerg from the SWP and ANL declaring that 'it [was] up to the students' to fight the BNP and uphold the 'no platform' policy.[104] Other students tried a different tactic, 'joining the Free Speech Society just before the AGM to utilise their vote against Collett when the elections for the new president went ahead'.[105] But the student protests allowed the police to call off the meeting, with the society members escorted off campus.[106]

When the new academic year started in October, there were renewed calls for Collett to be excluded from the student union, with an open letter by a number of student union officers being published in *Leeds Student*. The letter proclaimed:

> We … are shocked and appalled that a student at Leeds University, Mark Collett, is now the fuhrer of the youth wing of the British National Party. While the BNP may be currently trying to cultivate a veneer of respectability, the fact is that they remain a neo-Nazi group whose members admire Hitler, deny the horror of the Holocaust, and stir up race hatred wherever they organise. We therefore demand the following,
>
> - That Collett is expelled from Leeds University Union (LUU).
> - That *Leeds Student* adheres to the LUU policy of No Platform for racists and fascists.
> - That *Leeds Student* takes a stand and supports our campaign to rid our campus of the BNP's politics of fear and hatred.[107]

Collett responded with his own letter to the student paper, calling his critics 'politically correct fascists'.[108] Arguing that he had 'never harassed anyone … [or] broken the law' and belonged to 'a 100% legal and fully registered political party', Collett claimed that there were no grounds to exclude him from the student union and that the 'whole farcical No Platform policy is an invention to stifle any ideas or speech that can pull apart the warped ideology of Socialism'.[109]

In February 2002, there were further attempts to exclude Collett from the student union, as Collett was announced as a candidate for the BNP in the local elections.[110] Collett was eventually suspended by the union pending an investigation in March 2002, 'following an alleged attack by him on members of the anti-Nazi league'.[111] Collett failed to win his council seat in the May local elections and in November of that year, he was temporarily expelled from the BNP following a documentary titled *Young, Nazi and Proud* being aired on Channel 4.

While Collett and Beverley's reign over the Free Speech Society ended and the issue died down at the University of Leeds, invitations by student groups to the BNP's Nick Griffin continued throughout the 2000s, which saw significant anti-fascist campaigns mounted by students, coinciding with broader anti-fascist actions led by groups such as Unite Against Fascism (UAF).

'No platforming' Nick Griffin

Alongside his invitation in 2001 to Leeds University, Griffin was invited to speak or debate at several other universities over the course of the decade. In late 2002, he was twice invited to debate at Cambridge. In November, the press reported that the Cambridge Union had invited Griffin and Islamic fundamentalist cleric, Abu Hamza Al-Masri, to debate in January of the following year.[112] Al-Masri and Griffin had already debated on BBC Radio 4, invited by *Today* programme editor Rod Liddle. The President Elect of the Cambridge Union, Shaphur Kabraji, stated that the invitations were 'not proving a point about freedom of speech', but maintained that it was 'the union's tradition to have a broad range of opinion, not all of which we're comfortable with'.[113] Kabraji added: 'We're not providing an unnecessary platform, but asking our members to make a value judgment, based on the evidence. We host the debates and ask the questions that others are afraid to ask'.[114]

However, *The Guardian* also reported that two others who had been invited to debate hadn't been told of the invitations to Griffin or Al-Masri, with Dr Azzam Tamimi of the Islamic Institute of Political Thought stating, after enquiries by the paper:

> I wouldn't share a platform with either of them … I think this is the wrong way of going about organising the debate. This is a very serious matter they are discussing. It's disgraceful that Cambridge would entertain such people. No respectable person would share a platform with them.[115]

The other invitee, Dr Tim Winter from the Cambridge Faculty of Divinity, was quoted in the paper as saying, 'I don't believe you can have a serious debate with those people present … It will merely be a repetition of slogans'.[116] The Islamic and Jewish Societies at Cambridge also condemned the invitations, while the NUS' anti-racism convenor, Daniel Rose, declared, 'Racism and fascism have no place on campus … If Nick Griffin can speak in the bastion of British academia, if he can conquer that, he can conquer anywhere.'[117]

Before this debate could take place (with Al-Masri's involvement not confirmed), Griffin was invited by the Cambridge Forum in early December 2002 to debate multiculturalism with Lembit Opik from the Liberal Democrats. While Lib Dem leader Charles Kennedy faced calls to sanction Opik, a spokesperson for Opik was defiant, reportedly stating:

> Lembit says there is no need to be defensive about this subject. We should be able to take the argument to those whose views are unpalatable and win that by reason and logic …
>
> Lembit does not accept the view that sharing a platform gives credibility to extremist organisations. You create legitimacy by the strength of your argument.[118]

However, on advice from the police, the debate was cancelled at the last minute. The President of the Cambridge Forum, Chris Paley, suggested that there had been intimidation by anti-fascist protestors and that he had 'very good reason to believe there would be significant confrontation outside'.[119] Paley described the cancellation of the debate as 'a sad day for democracy', adding '[f]reedom of speech is fundamental to democracy and has today been subjected to violent intimidation'.[120] However, Kimberly Chong, the student union's anti-racism officer at Cambridge, countered:

> Allowing Griffin to share a platform with a speaker from a mainstream political party, such as Lembit Opik, gives his extremist arguments the legitimacy and respectability which he and the BNP crave …
>
> The forum's decision to hold such a debate is not in the interest of intellectual discourse, but rather seeks to create scandal at the cost of the welfare and safety of Cambridge students, who are all living in a climate of rising racial and religious tensions.[121]

The arguments and counter-arguments used to defend or criticise the invitation of Griffin to speak at Cambridge were replicated over the next five years, with Griffin being prevented from speaking at some places and allowed to speak at others. In February 2005, Griffin was invited to take part in a debate at St Andrews University in Scotland, with the President of the Debating Society proposing:

> We believe that the only way to get to the truth of what the BNP are saying and to combat them is to do it in public in a debate.
>
> It is very dangerous to ignore them. They have had electoral success and people ignoring them won't help. If people want to challenge their ways, a debate is how to do it.[122]

The university administration refused to ban Griffin from speaking, with a spokesperson suggesting that they were 'not in the business of censorship',[123] even though they had to take section 43 of the Education (No. 2) Act 1986 into consideration. According to the student newspaper at the University of St Andrews, *The Mitre*, the university did send a message to staff and students stating that the proposed visit by Griffin was 'likely to be damaging to our efforts to promote diversity' and encouraged the Debating Society to 'reconsider this invitation'.[124] After pressure from the university and the NUS, as well as condemnation from the floor of Scottish Parliament,[125] the invitation was withdrawn. An editorial in *The Mitre* called the Debating Society 'heroic' in 'the face of intolerable pressure' from the 'heavy hands of highly-organised pressure groups', but suggested that it was the announcement by leftist groups that 'they would travel to St Andrews to disrupt the debate', as well as the requirement of 'a strong police presence' that made the Society eventually cancel the event.[126]

In May 2007, the head of the Young BNP, Daniel Lake, invited Griffin to speak at the University of Bath, where Lake was a student. This led to major condemnation from the National Union of Students and the University College Union (UCU), as well as anti-fascist groups such as Unite Against Fascism. The Joint General Secretary of the UCU, Sally Hunt, questioned the motives of Griffin's invitation by Lake, saying 'This was not an innocent politics student inviting him, but two senior BNP officials to promote their party'.[127] Hunt stressed that inviting the BNP onto campus would violate the notion of the university as 'a safe space … for people to work and study', arguing that universities were 'rightly held up as examples to the rest of society because of their diversity and tolerance' and that the BNP had 'no interest in sharing those values'.[128]

The campaign by UAF, the UCU and NUS generated significant pressure upon the university to cancel the event. *Socialist Worker* quoted Jen Russ from Bath UCU on the extent of the campaign, stating '[o]ver 700 complaints showered into the university from national trade unions, the National Union of Students (NUS), shocked individuals and anti-racist groups'.[129] Based on the large expected number of protests to descend on the university, the university administration cancelled the event. The Vice-Chancellor and the University Secretary released a joint statement pronouncing that while '[f]reedom of speech is a principle to be highly cherished by academic institutions', this needed to be balanced with other concerns about the safety of staff and students at the university.[130] In addition, the statement claimed:

> The university has … now learned that a very large number of protestors intend to arrive on campus. This creates the likelihood of substantial public order problems and the real possibility of disruption of the essential activities of the university community, making it impractical for the university to allow the event to go ahead.[131]

Regional Assistant General Secretary for the UCU, John Perry, claimed this a victory, telling *Socialist Worker*, 'The police were monitoring our protest – they knew how many coaches were coming. The cancellation was the result of our pressure, our unity and our show of strength.'[132] The president of the student union at Bath University claimed that this campaign and the cancellation by the university sent 'a clear message that students do not want the BNP on university campuses'.[133] Although Lake complained that the university's decision was 'a knee-jerk reaction to threats made by the undemocratic left'.[134]

While both the Cambridge Union and Cambridge Forum had to cancel their debates involving Griffin in late 2002 and early 2003, the Oxford Union invited Griffin to debate alongside Holocaust denier David Irving in 2007, who had previously been invited to debate by the same student group in 2001. This caused major concern amongst students at Oxford and amongst anti-racist and anti-fascist campaigners more broadly. President of the Oxford University Student Union, Martin McClusky, strongly argued against the invitations and called them 'utterly appalling', adding:

> It sets a really disturbing precedent. The Union being a student run society, it sends out the wrong sort of message. All this is doing is giving them a platform in a prestigious arena …
>
> I think as a Union member it's despicable that my membership fee and the membership fees of hundreds of freshers will be paying for hospitality for Holocaust deniers.[135]

Julian Lewis, a Tory MP, renounced his life-time membership to the union in protest, while Liberal Democrat MP Evan Harris agreed to debate Griffin and Irving, arguing that while he found the views of the BNP and Irving 'awful and abhorrent', the Liberal Democrats 'agreed that the best way to beat extremism is through debate'.[136]

On the night of the debate, protestors forced their way into the building where the debate was taking place in an attempt to disrupt the event. *The Guardian* described the events of the evening:

> A debate on free speech at the Oxford Union descended into chaos last night after scores of demonstrators broke through a security cordon and staged a sit-down protest in the union's famous chamber.
>
> Scuffles broke out in the hall as the demonstrators – there to voice their opposition to the presence of discredited historian David Irving and BNP leader Nick Griffin – clashed with organisers and security guards.
>
> Order was eventually restored and the event went ahead with Griffin and Irving forced to speak in separate rooms as hundreds of students and anti-fascist campaigners surrounded the venue chanting and singing.[137]

While students had previously had success with 'no platforming' Griffin at various universities, they were not able to successfully disrupt the event at Oxford. But despite the incremental success of the BNP throughout the 2000s, there was a general optimism about the use of tactic. Although, as will be shown further on, there was also a pushback against it in some student unions, with the University of East Anglia being the most prominent case.

'No platform' and the University of East Anglia

General Secretary of the Manchester University Student Union and member elect of the NUS National Executive, Rob Owen, argued after the successful campaign to prevent Griffin from speaking at Bath University that victories like this would encourage other students to implement 'no platform' policies, suggesting:

> No platform is a tactic based on mobilising the mass revulsion against fascism into a force which can shut fascists out of mainstream debate and campus life …

> In this environment the argument for no platform for the fascists is clear, We are the democratic anti-fascist majority – and we have the right to exclude organisations from our movement who would wish to see us destroyed.[138]

However this was not necessarily the case and similar to what occurred in the mid-1980s, some student unions pushed back against the NUS policy of 'no platform'. Coming in 2007 between the effective protest against Griffin at Bath University and the attempts to disrupt Griffin and Irving at Oxford, the student union at the University of East Anglia reconsidered its position on 'no platform'.

At the first Union Council meeting of the academic year, a representative from the Athletics Club, Joe Conboy, put forward a motion for the student union at UEA to prevent the implementation of the policy of 'no platform' at the university (despite one not being in force at the time) and encourage the NUS to do similar.[139] Conboy, who had previously written for the Trotskyist website *Socialist Appeal*,[140] described the policy of 'no platform' as 'cowardly and an affront to freedom of speech – especially as it allowed the small steering committee of NUS Conference to decide who to ban'.[141] This led to a motion being narrowly passed that expressed that 'in order to discredit illiberal, extremist or racist ideologies it is necessary to openly confront these ideas and not merely pretend they do not exist', calling for the complete abolition of 'no platform'.[142]

Despite being first proposed by Conboy, one of the key driving forces behind the campaign to overturn the 'no platform' policy was the News Editor of the student newspaper *Concrete*, Richard Reynolds, who was also the founder of Student Academics for Academic Freedom, an organisation linked to the *Spiked Online* network. In the pages of *Concrete*, Reynolds referred to the NUS leadership as 'nothing more than moral cowards' and proclaimed that '[a]s long as NUS feels it can "no platform" some groups, none of us are free', before adding '[w]e are under licence to speak only from a position that the NUS executive does not find too offensive'.[143] Reynolds suggested that 'no platform' was 'deeply patronising' to some student groups, including women, LGBT students and ethnic minorities, who, he believed, 'should easily be able to argue down, in alliance with the rest of us, the drivel that groups like the BNP and Hizb ut-Tahrir spout'.[144]

It was decided after this motion was passed that the policy would be the topic of a campus-wide ballot in late November 2007, with Reynolds leading the campaign against the policy.[145] Campaigning for the policy to be retained was Danny Turner, who argued:

> We are not trying to ban the BNP, we stand for the NUS' values of representation, equality and opportunity. My campaign is not run because of my opinion of racists and fascists. I am for No Platform because the aims of these people completely contradict what the NUS is there for.[146]

However, Reynolds countered:

> You do not win against fascist groups by banning them. I believe we can take these people in free debate. I believe we will win that debate and to ban the BNP is to say we are too scared to try …
>
> Absolute freedom of speech is the foundations of democracy. Banning groups makes us fascist and not them.[147]

This was a distillation of the idea that 'no platform' was a form of fascism by student radicals, a trope which had existed since the 1970s. It also was a repeat of a concept developed by those writing for *Spiked* in the 2000s that those who promoted 'no platform' were more dangerous than the BNP, a continuation from similar arguments made in the dying days of the RCP and in *Living Marxism*. For example, in May 2002 (when Mark Collett was still using the Free Speech Society at Leeds University to promote the BNP), Neil Davenport wrote for *Spiked*: 'After a decade of the left demanding state bans on far-right organisations, closures of their shops and sackings of their members – all hallmarks of authoritarianism – the BNP can appear "moderate" and level-headed by comparison.'[148]

The referendum was won by those seeking to abolish the 'no platform' policy, with 75 per cent of the votes cast against the policy, although only 578 votes were cast in total (passing the threshold of 500 votes for the result to be valid).[149] Reynolds described the result as 'a proud moment for the students of UEA, as well as for people who believe in free speech and democracy everywhere', while Dennis Hayes, the founder of Academics for Academic Freedom, reportedly said in *The Guardian*:

> It shows that ordinary students don't need to be told by the NUS, or anyone else, who they should listen to and what they should think. With similar movements in favour of free speech happening in other universities this is an important step forward.[150]

Reynolds and Hayes saw this result at the University of East Anglia as part of a general revolt by students against 'no platform', and while there seemed to be some signs that more student unions were heading in this direction, such as at the University of Sussex (where a motion to overturn the 'no platform' policy was eventually defeated in May 2008),[151] there was no surge of student unions following through at this time.

Spiked Online and free speech absolutism

After the result at UEA, *Spiked* published the new 'pro-free speech policy' of the student union at the university, which replicated many of the tropes that Reynolds used in his campaign and were similar to those espoused on the *Spiked* website.[152] Since the end of the RCP in 1996, those associated with its successor *Living Marxism* and then *Spiked Online*, heavily focused on the campaign for absolute free speech on university campuses.

In 1996, the Revolutionary Communist Party dissolved itself and transformed into a network around the magazine and website, *Living Marxism*. In the final days of the RCP, the Revolutionary Communist Students groups were involved in some of the last actions by the party before dissolution, indicating that the university campus was still an area of great attention for the RCP, even at the end – something which continues be a focus for its successors until the present day.

In January 1996, the Queen Margaret Union at the University of Glasgow rejected an application for affiliation by the Revolutionary Communist Students group over the issue of free speech. According to RCS member Leah Panos, they pushed for a position that 'there should be no exceptions whatsoever in our application of the principle [of free speech]', but the Queen Margaret Union objected to this 'based on the belief that promoting free speech allows a platform for abhorrent ideas such as fascism and sexism to be expressed'.[153] Panos, like many other RCP articles from this time, dressed up free speech absolutism in progressive language, writing:

> One of the most prevalent arguments for censorship is that some people would not be able to cope with hearing dangerous ideas … This is one of the most ridiculous and patronising, not to mention illogical and degrading attitudes towards us, the stupid easily-led mass …
>
> Far from fighting racism and sexism political correctness merely refuses to deal with these important issues preferring to ban the use of offensive terms than actively challenge reactionary opinions in open debate.[154]

For the RCS, the supposed way to fight oppression was to debate the oppressors, rather than asking why those who experienced racism, sexism or homophobia should have to listen to those who expressed these views, or allow them to be promoted on campus.

Stephen Rixon, the President of the Queen Margaret Union, stated that the application for affiliation by the RCS was turned down 'because the RCS's Constitution would theoretically allow them to give a platform to groups such as the BNP'.[155] Another RCS member, Liz Frayne, countered that this was part of the 'ritual raising of the spectre of fascism and the BNP' and that student unions 'use this grown up version of the monster-in-the-cupboard as a justification for sending students to bed early with no rights'.[156] As seen earlier in other discussions of the BNP in *Living Marxism*, the RCP consistently downplayed the threat of fascism in Britain while simultaneously depicting student unions as overly worried about this. Frayne provided a further example of this when she quipped, 'I am not ready to surrender my rights because someone saw a BNP sticker in the toilets a year ago.'[157] As mentioned previously, those writing for *Living Marxism* and *Spiked* also portrayed the discourse around the BNP as a moral panic by left-wing students and less of a threat than the tactic of 'no platforming'.

After the RCP's demise, *Living Marxism* and then *Spiked Online* continued the crusade against any form of 'no platforming' at British universities, and the celebration of absolute freedom of speech on campus. *Living Marxism* folded in

2000 after it lost a 'crushing and expensive libel case which forced the magazine's closure'[158] and many of those involved in the magazine now wrote for the website, *Spiked*. A number of those who edited and wrote for the website still claimed to be on the left in some way, but any pretence of Marxism was shed and there was an enthusiastic embrace of libertarian contrarianism. As demonstrated in this chapter, the people writing for *Spiked* maintained their opposition to 'no platform' throughout the 2000s, and in the 2010s the website launched significant campaigns against what they called 'campus censorship'. This direction has been chiefly pursued by Mick Hume, former editor of *The Next Step, Living Marxism* and *Spiked*, and Tom Slater, the deputy editor at *Spiked*, along with Joanna Williams, Brendan O'Neill and Dennis Hayes amongst others.

In 2014, *Spiked* launched the Down With Campus Censorship campaign, which called on students 'to say no to No Platform, to stuff the Safe Spaces, and to reclaim the university as a space of unfettered debate and the pursuit of knowledge'.[159] The following year, the website launched the Free Speech University Rankings, which attempted to rank universities on their commitment to free speech. These were published annually over the next four years, with the last report being published in February 2018. The rankings used a 'traffic light' system to indicate the alleged level of 'censorship' on campus, with the 2018 report explaining the categories:

> **Red:** has actively censored speech or expression
> **Amber:** has chilled speech or expression through excessive regulation
> **Green:** has not restricted or regulated speech or expression[160]

Actions and policies by both the university administration and student union were considered when devising these rankings, which means that instances of 'no platforming' were considered alongside formal 'no platform' policies, as well as other rules and practices in place to protect students, such as codes of conduct.

The rankings over the four years seemed to reinforce *Spiked*'s narrative that free speech was becoming more and more endangered at British universities. When the rankings started in 2015, Tom Slater wrote that '[c]ensorship on campus has always existed, but it's never felt so free-floating, so unwieldy and indiscriminate'.[161] That year, 41 per cent of universities got an overall ranking of 'red', while 39 per cent received a ranking of 'amber', meaning that 20 per cent achieved a 'green' ranking.[162] By 2018, 54 per cent of universities received a 'red' ranking, alongside 40 per cent being ranked as 'amber' and only 6 per cent achieved a ranking of 'green'.[163] Despite those at the website being generally dismissive of social phenomena as 'moral panics' (something which can be traced back to the days of the RCP), *Spiked*'s discourse around the alleged censorship on campus is an archetype of the 'moral panics' usually railed against. For Slater, student unions 'have become more and more intolerant' and so much so that 'today almost any view can be snuffed out'.[164] Similar to descriptions of the student movement in the 1970s, the 1980s and the 1990s, those at *Spiked* have portrayed the use of 'no platform', codes of conduct and equal opportunities policies as contributing to a crisis in the university system, and themselves as the defenders of free speech against the tsunami of political correctness. When the Free Speech University Rankings were launched in 2015, Slater talked about the notion of freedom of speech at universities in alarmist terms and held up these rankings as a form of 'common sense' resistance:

> The FSUR [Free Speech University Rankings] is a wake-up call. Universities and students' unions must reform, lest they risk completely obliterating their distinct moral obligation to create the atmosphere of tolerance, openness and free debate that is essential to the pursuit of knowledge. Established as an annual survey, the FSUR will continue to keep a check on campus censorship. But reform won't be achieved without the efforts of students and academics, resisting, agitating and insisting that their campuses be censorship-free zones. They must create a culture of freedom on campus that is so strong that university managers or students' union officials will have to censor at their peril.

These rankings have been criticised by many as alarmist and misleading in their analysis. Adam Tickell, the Vice-Chancellor at the University of Sussex, wrote in *The Guardian* that student protests and actions by the student unions were being 'labelled dangerous censorship' and there was '[t]he perception … that we are witnessing a widespread "chilling" of free speech on university campuses', but proposed that a closer examination would show that 'the evidence for this is vanishingly small'.[165] Carl Thompson from the University of Surrey condemned the rankings in a piece in *The Times Higher Education Supplement* as 'misleading, ill-informed and worryingly influential', declaring: 'Spiked is an organisation dedicated to trawling university documents for anything that remotely resembles a free speech infringement but when it came to last year's report it could find no evidence of students preventing anyone speaking on campus'.[166]

The majority of its evidence of censorship on campus, Thompson claimed, 'amounts merely to human resources policies and codes of conduct', with *Spiked* offering 'no evidence that these policies have ever been applied in a fashion that repressed free speech, or that they have generated discontent among staff, students or the wider public'.[167]

Despite the flaws in the rankings and the ideological position of *Spiked* on absolute free speech, the Free Speech University Rankings has certainly been influential in generating this belief in a free speech crisis in higher education. Since first being released in 2015, the mainstream media has reported uncritically on the rankings each year, adding to a concern in recent years that 'no platforming' and safe spaces were inhibiting free speech on campus. The rankings have also been referred to in some academic literature to support an argument that there have been increasing limits to freedom of speech and academic freedom at British universities, without reference to who produced these rankings.[168]

These rankings, as well as a wider coverage of 'no platform' in the media, also led to several leading authors at *Spiked* giving evidence before a parliamentary committee on freedom of speech at universities. As part of a parliamentary inquiry initiated by former Universities Secretary Jo Johnson in late 2017, three authors from *Spiked* gave evidence in November of that year, Tom Slater, Joanna Williams and Dennis Hayes. Dr Williams stated at the beginning of the session that she thought that 'free speech is under threat at universities', while Slater declared, 'I am sad to say that picture over the past three years has been quite bleak and is getting worse.'[169] Although the committee's final report acknowledged that 'Spiked's research methodology has been contentious',[170] the Free Speech University Rankings were still given significant consideration by the committee.

In 2019, Slater announced that there would be no rankings that year, but he celebrated the impact that it had made upon the debate surrounding censorship and free speech at universities. In his piece to signal the end of the Free Speech University Rankings project, Slater said that prior to the first report in 2015, 'many people in politics and the media were blissfully unaware of what was happening to free speech on campus'.[171] This has coincided with an increased media and political interest in the alleged crisis of free speech at universities and concern over 'no platforming', 'trigger warnings' and the establishment of safe spaces on campus.

Transphobia, safe spaces and the current state of 'no platform'

And this brings the narrative to the present day. As this chapter has shown, the tactic of 'no platform' has been consistently used since the student activist heydays of the 1970s and 1980s. Throughout the 1990s and 2000s, certain groups and individuals were 'no platformed', primarily those associated with the British National Party and Hizb ut-Tahrir. Before the events at the Oxford Union in late 2007 when protestors failed to successfully disrupt a debate involving the BNP's Nick Griffin and David Irving, the application of the 'no platform' tactic to prevent Griffin from speaking on campus had been quite effective. In the following two years, the BNP reached their electoral height with Griffin becoming an MEP in June 2009, which gave him a certain electoral legitimacy and there was resistance to efforts to 'no platform' him further.

This came to a head when Griffin was invited to be on the BBC's current affairs panel show, *Question Time*, in October 2009. The BBC justified Griffin's invitation on the grounds that Griffin was an MEP and the BNP were a political party with elected officials at the local government and European level. Labour Justice Secretary Jack Straw broke Labour's policy of not sharing a platform with members of far right groups, which had been established in the late 1970s when there was the threat of the National Front. By most accounts, Griffin struggled with being on television and did not answer questions adequately, which led to a narrative being formed that Griffin's buckling under the pressure of questions from the audience burst the bubble of the BNP as the party's electoral fortunes nosedived over the next few years. However this overlooks the significant campaign mounted after the 2009 European elections to defeat the BNP at the ballot box, involving Hope Not Hate, Unite Against Fascism, trade unions, sections of the Labour Party, left-wing parties and migrant community groups. As Daniel Trilling has written, '[o]nce again, it was grassroots action that confronted the far right'.[172] Despite this, the myth has persisted that it was Griffin's *Question Time* appearance that led to the downfall of the BNP and has been used to justify allowing other far right politicians and individuals on television, such as Nigel Farage (of UKIP and now the Brexit Party) and English Defence League co-founder Tommy Robinson.[173]

While people have argued (and continue to argue) that the far right should be debated instead of 'no platformed', the increasing concern by the media and politicians about 'no platform' is about its extension to figures outside the far right, in particular speakers who are portrayed by their opponents as transphobic. In the last decade, there has been a growing awareness of trans issues in Britain, as well as the rest of the world, and a push to take transphobia as a serious issue, as serious as sexism, racism and homophobia. At the same time, there has been a mounting opposition to trans rights, both from the socially conservative right and from a section of radical feminism (often referred to as trans-exclusionary radical or 'gender critical' feminists). Individual student unions and the National Union of Students have both been at the forefront of pushing back against transphobia and using the tactic of 'no platforming' to combat it on campus.

Writing in the *New Statesman* in 2014, Sarah Ditum wrote an article headlined '"No Platform" Was Once Reserved for Violent Fascists. Now It's Being Used to Silence Debate', in which she argued that by the late 2000s (when the BNP was at its height) 'no platform [had] been more or less abandoned by the anti-fascist movement' as the BNP's electoral success was 'making it difficult to justify refusing them a platform'.[174] As this chapter has shown, this was not the case. But the main thrust of Ditum's piece was that the focus of 'no platforming' students was no longer the far right, but 'individuals who certainly do not trail the organised muscle of a thug army behind them'.[175] Ditum held up radical feminist and author Julie Bindel, who was 'no platformed' by the NUS for alleged transphobic remarks she made in 2004, although Bindel insisted that she didn't say anything 'hateful', but 'question[ed] the essentialist meaning of transgenderism, because, by positing gender as fixed it flies in the face of feminism'.[176] Bindel became a *cause célèbre* for those who were critical of trans rights and opposed the expansion of 'no platform' to those deemed transphobic. Beatrix Campbell defended Bindel in *The Guardian* in 2010 against the students protesting her and proposed that their willingness to be inclusive to trans women was at the expense of solidarity with 'women who feel unsettled by the presence of people who used to be men in women-only spaces and services'.[177] Writing for the *Spiked* website, Ellamay Russell argued that the 'no platforming' of Bindel was a form of 'pre-emptive censorship that is maintaining a babyish climate at British universities'. For Ditum, '[i]ntimidation is at the core of no platform' and saw the tactic as 'a weapon used by the undemocratic against democracy',[178] especially against speakers like Bindel, who were not from the far right.

The NUS and individual student unions argued otherwise. In 2015, the NUS LGBT conference passed a motion that described Bindel as 'a journalist and author who is notorious for transphobic publications and views' and resolved:

1. That the NUS LGBT Officer and members of the NUS LGBT committee shall not share a platform with Julie Bindel.[179]

This was justified by the conference by pointing to Bindel's argument that 'Trans people should be denied medical care', her speaking at events that 'explicitly exclude Trans people', and her argument that 'bisexuality doesn't exist as a sexual identity'.[180] The same conference passed a broader motion arguing that transphobic speakers had 'no place at universities and colleges', which 'should be a place for trans people to thrive where they feel safe and accepted', and that transphobic speech 'should be legally recognised as hate speech'.[181] The motion, 'Hate Has No Place on Campuses', further resolved:

2. To not share platforms with and not to invite onto campuses all transphobic speakers including but not limited to: Germaine Greer, Julie Bindel, Julie Burchill and Milo Yiannapolous [sic].[182]

In October 2014, Bindel was prevented from speaking at SOAS and the University of Sheffield, with the student unions at both universities suggesting that her speaking would violate student union LGBT and 'safe spaces' policies. A statement released by the student union at SOAS said that Bindel had been banned from speaking to the Muslim Students Association:

> based on the fact that Julie Bindel has made numerous and repeated discriminatory comments towards trans people, bisexuals, sex workers, Muslims, and people who identify as Queer, which advocates further prejudice towards, and marginalisation of, these historically discriminated against groups.[183]

The union stated that as some had 'told members of our Executive that they would feel unsafe in SOAS if Julie Bindel was to come and speak here', this would violate the student union's Safe Spaces policy, which had been introduced a few weeks prior.[184] The President of the student union at Sheffield University, Yael Shafitz, simply stated to the student newspaper, *Forge*, that the student union had an LGBT friendly policy that aimed 'to ensure that all activities and events operated by the Union are LGBT friendly and open to all LGBT students', which meant that the debating organisation that had invited Bindel had to be inclusive.[185]

The following year both Bindel and Milo Yiannopoulos, the latter of whom was then a technology writer and leading figure in the 'Gamergate controversy',[186] were invited to speak by the Free Speech and Secular Society at the University of Manchester. The student union executive initially rescinded Bindel's invitation, with Women's Officer Jess Lishak declaring that she 'refuse[d] to allow our campus to be poisoned by this woman's tireless campaign to deny trans people their basic human rights'.[187] The student union allowed Yiannopoulos to speak 'on the provisos that, should the event go ahead, there will be extra security put in place for everyone's safety'.[188] After a number of complaints about allowing Yiannopoulos to speak, while banning Bindel, the student union also disinvited him. A statement by the executive, made two days after the disinvitation of Bindel, said:

> We have been made aware of various comments lambasting rape survivors and trans* people, and as such we are concerned for the safety of our students on the topic of this event. He is a rape apologist and has repeatedly used derogatory and debasing ableist language when describing members of the trans* community.
>
> As such, this undermines the principles of liberation enshrined in the Students' Union, as outlined in the Safe Space policy. We believe these views could incite hatred against both trans* people and women who have experienced sexual violence. As we believe it is probable these views would be aired in this discussion should he be allowed to speak on campus, we have no choice but to ban him.[189]

The same month, Germaine Greer was the subject of a petition to have her invitation to speak at Cardiff University rescinded after she made allegedly transphobic remarks during a talk at the University of Cambridge earlier in the year.[190] The petition, started by the Women's Officer at Cardiff, Rachel Melhuish, pronounced:

> Trans-exclusionary views should have no place in feminism or society. Such attitudes contribute to the high levels of stigma, hatred and violence towards trans people – particularly trans women – both in the UK and across the world.
>
> While debate in a university should be encouraged, hosting a speaker with such problematic and hateful views towards marginalised and vulnerable groups is dangerous. Allowing Greer a platform endorses her views, and by extension, the transmisogyny which she continues to perpetuate.[191]

The petition collected over 3,000 signatures, but Greer's lecture went ahead.[192] Like the 'no platforming' of Bindel, this petition calling for Greer to be disinvited led to major media coverage and further reignited the debate over 'no platform'. Despite claims that 'gender critical' feminists, like Greer and Bindel, were being silenced, Theresa O'Keefe has shown that '[i]n the wake of the Cardiff controversy, Greer was given a number of platforms to exercise her freedom of speech, most notably a prime-time television interview with Kirsty Wark on *BBC Newsnight*'.[193] This, Sally Hines has suggested, is one of the ways in which 'anti-transgender feminism has moved from a marginal sub-cultural position to enter a more mainstream and high profile feminist constituent'.[194] In the aforementioned inquiry into freedom of speech at British universities conducted in 2017–18, the Vice-Chancellor of Cardiff University, Colin Riordan, described the Greer controversy as 'an example of us [the university] valuing these things and protecting academic freedom',[195] as the university administration did not intervene to prevent Greer from speaking in spite of the petition and pressure from some students.

Similar to the extension of 'no platform' to sexists and homophobes in the 1980s, the push for the 'no platforming' of speakers deemed to be transphobic has been part of a wider campaign to fight transphobia and transphobic violence. Just as the feminists in the 1980s argued that sexist speech fed into a broader threat of sexual discrimination, harassment and violence, trans rights activists have argued that transphobic speech is part of 'a system of violence directed against trans people', with Sara Ahmed describing a 'constant stream of anti-trans statements as a "chip, chip, chip" that has violent wearing effects'.[196] While Sarah Ditum and others have attempted to differentiate the 'old' uses of 'no platform' against worthy opponents such as the National Front and 'new' uses of the tactic against radical feminists in order to suggest that trans rights activists are unwilling to debate and instead looking to censor legitimate criticisms of transgenderism, Ahmed has argued that this has meant that trans people have been, for all intents and purposes, requested to debate and justify their existence. As Ahmed wrote in 2016:

> Transphobia and antitrans statements should not be treated as just another viewpoint that we should be free to express at the happy table of diversity. There cannot be a dialogue when some at the table are in effect (or intent on) arguing for the elimination of others at the table. When you have 'dialogue or debate' with those who wish to eliminate you from the conversation (because they do not recognize what is necessary for your survival, or because they don't even think your existence is possible), then 'dialogue and debate' becomes a technique of elimination. A refusal to have some dialogues and some debates is thus a key tactic for survival.[197]

The 'no platforming' of allegedly transphobic speakers has been central to the revitalisation of the debates over 'no platform' and free speech at British universities, with the protests against speakers like Bindel and Greer seen as deviations from the original intent of the policy when it was established back in 1974. An example of this is from Helen Lewis in the *New Statesman* in October 2015:

> Look at the history of no-platforming: it started with organisations like the National Front and the BNP, who trailed thugs and incited violence; then it spread to being used against figures like David Irving, the Holocaust denier – crucially, when he was talking about Holocaust denial. The new no-platforming of feminists means that one duff opinion sees you bundled off the stage, whatever you planned to talk about. Germaine Greer could go to a university to talk about her LP collection and there would be students desperate to ban her.[198]

However as this book has shown, 'no platform' is an ever-changing tactic and was primarily used against fascists and racists, but also extended in the past to protest sexists and homophobes. The use of the tactic against 'gender critical' feminists or anti-trans speakers was part of a gradual shift in how 'no platform' has been implemented by students since the 1970s.

Conclusion

This chapter has outlined how 'no platform' shifted in the 1990s and 2000s. It was used against the BNP after it gained renewed interest in the early 1990s and then in the first decade of the twenty-first century. In particular, the new leader of the BNP, Nick Griffin, was 'no platformed' on several occasions between 2002 and 2007.

The BNP were, however, not the only group to be 'no platformed' during this period. In the 1990s and then again in the 2000s, the Islamic group Hizb ut-Tahrir were banned from many student unions and universities in the 1990s and eventually subject to the NUS' formal 'no platform' policy in 2004. Despite objections from some left-wing and other Muslim groups, Hizb ut-Tahrir were depicted in the mainstream and student press as an objectionable element at British universities, which has led to some arguing that the ban of Hizb ut-Tahrir and other Islamic groups on campus owed much to the general Islamophobia that exists in British society, especially after 9/11.

As the BNP and Hizb ut-Tahrir were 'no platformed' in the 1990s and 2000s, there were increasing calls for the policy of 'no platform' to be abolished and for free speech to be fostered unconditionally (or almost unconditionally within the law). One of the main proponents of this was the Revolutionary Communist Party, which had gone from ultra-left Trotskyism to libertarian contrarianism in the space of ten years. Through their journal *Living Marxism* and its corresponding website, as well as its successor website, *Spiked Online*, the RCP and its post-party descendants virulently pushed a line of absolute free speech, viewing those who promoting 'no platform' as more dangerous than the far right.

This rhetoric had a peculiar effect on student union activities. For example, the Free Speech Society at Leeds University was taken over by two BNP members in 2001, who used the idea of free speech to endorse the politics of the BNP. This led to an exodus from other members of the society and a large anti-fascist campaign at the university, while Nick Griffin was invited to speak to the society. At the University of East Anglia in late 2007, the student union held a referendum on the policy of 'no platform' and after an overwhelming majority voted against the policy, this was celebrated by *Spiked* and others as the start of a student revolt against the tactic.

In the last decade, *Spiked* has become more and more established as a voice of free speech absolutism, with their Free Speech University Rankings used by media commentators, as well as politicians, to publicise the idea that British universities are being sapped of their freedom of speech and under a cloud of censorship by 'snowflake' students.

This notion has been compounded since the early 2010s by the 'no platforming' of alleged transphobic speakers, such as Julie Bindel and Germaine Greer, by some feminist and LGBTQ+ student activists. Similar to the arguments made by feminists in the early 1980s when they pushed for the 'no platforming' of sexists, these student activists have seen the fight against transphobic speech as part of a broader fight against transphobic discrimination, harassment and violence and that such speech contributed to an environment where transphobic violence was considered to be 'minor' problem. Using the notion of the university as a 'safe space', trans rights activists have employed Equal Opportunities and Safe Space policies of student unions in attempts to prevent 'gender critical' speakers from having a platform on campus.

A number of defenders of these 'gender critical' feminists have attempted to contrast the original intention of the 'no platform' as constituted by the NUS in 1974, when it was devised to combat the National Front, with the present, when it is being allegedly used indiscriminately against certain controversial speakers. This dichotomy is false because as this book has shown, 'no platform', as a tactic and a policy, has shifted and changed with the politics of the time, and from the very beginning was altered by individual student unions and student groups to contest different forms of prejudice and oppression. Even in an era like today's, when the far right seems to be in a position of strength across the globe, the merits of using the tactic of 'no platform' continue to be debated.

Notes

1 Roger Eatwell, *Fascism: A History* (London: Pimlico, 2003) p. 343.
2 Ibid.
3 Daniel Trilling, *Bloody Nasty People: The Rise of Britain's Far Right* (London: Verso, 2013) p. 24.
4 James Rhodes, 'White Backlash, "Unfairness" and Justifications of British National party (BNP) Support', *Ethnicities*, 10/1 (2010) p. 85.
5 See: Sean Birchall, *Beating the Fascists: The Untold Story of Anti-Fascist Action* (London: Freedom Press, 2010); Dave Hann, *Physical Resistance: A Hundred Years of Anti-Fascism* (London: Zero Books, 2013) pp. 34–35.
6 Nigel Copsey, *Anti-Fascism in Britain* (Abingdon: Routledge, 2017) pp. 165–166.
7 Ibid., p. 166.
8 Ibid., pp. 167–168.
9 Ibid., p. 174.
10 *Leeds Student*, 22 October, 1993, p. 3.
11 'Campus Watch', *Searchlight* (January 1995) p. 5.
12 Cited in *British Muslims Monthly Survey*, 4/8 (August 1996), http://artsweb.bham.ac.uk/bmms/1996/08August96.html (accessed 17 May, 2019).
13 Miriam & Lionel Kochan, 'Great Britain', *American Jewish Year Book* (1997) p. 272; *The Times Higher Education Supplement*, 16 August, 1996, www.timeshighereducation.com/news/islamic-extremist-threat-to-gays/99566.article (accessed 17 May, 2019).
14 Jennie Bristow, 'Free Speech on Campus', *Living Marxism*, 83 (October 1995) http://web.archive.org/web/19991103220041/http://www.informinc.co.uk/LM/LM83/LM83_Speech.html (accessed 8 March, 2018).
15 Juliet Connor, 'The Problem with "No Platform"', *Living Marxism*, 72 (October 1994) http://web.archive.org/web/20010730211339/www.informinc.co.uk/LM/LM72/LM72_Platform.html (accessed 6 March, 2018).
16 Ibid.
17 Bristow, 'Free Speech on Campus'.
18 Peter Davies, 'Lenin's Crystal Ball', *Marxism Today* (August 1990) pp. 34–35.
19 John Kelly, *Contemporary Trotskyism: Parties, Sects and Social Movements in Britain* (Abingdon: Routledge, 2018) p. 52.

20 Michael Fitzpatrick, 'The Point Is to Change It: A Short Account of the Revolutionary Communist Party', in Evan Smith & Matthew Worley (eds), *Waiting for the Revolution: The British Far Left from 1956* (Manchester: Manchester University Press, 2017) pp. 232–233.
21 Workers Against Racism, *The Roots of Racism* (London: Junius Publications, 1985) pp. 83; 85.
22 Ibid., p. 46.
23 Revolutionary Communist Tendency, *Under a Red Flag: Fascism, Racism and the Labour Movement* (London: RCT pamphlet, 1978) p. 17.
24 Ibid., pp. 47; 82.
25 'Fighting the Bans', *The Next Step* (May 1981) p. 3.
26 Kirk Williams, 'Fight Racism, Not Idiots', *The Next Step* (October 1984) p. 6.
27 Ibid.
28 'Sunderland Poly', *The Next Step*, 19 April, 1985, p. 10.
29 'No Platform?', *The Next Step*, 3 May, 1985, p. 2.
30 Ibid.
31 Ibid.
32 'Saying No to Victoria's Values', *The Next Step*, 6 December, 1985, p. 2.
33 Frank Richards, 'Taking on the Moralists', *The Next Step*, 6 March, 1987, p. 11.
34 Ibid.
35 'The Propaganda War: No Platform?' *The Next Step*, 21 March, 1986, p. 5.
36 'Stonehenge and Free Speech', *The Next Step*, 6 June, 1986, p. 2.
37 Ibid.
38 'The Propaganda War: No Platform', *The Next Step* (December 1986) p. 10.
39 Ibid.
40 'No Platform?' *The Next Step*, 31 October, 1986, p. 10.
41 'What Future for Student Unions?', *The Next Step*, 18 November, 1988, p. 7.
42 'They Can Be Beaten: Tories Get Tough With Students', *The Next Step*, 2 December, 1988, p. 12.
43 See: 'Satanic Flames Ignite British Racism', *The Next Step*, 24 February, 1989, p. 2; Kenan Malik, 'The Culture of Censorship', *The Next Step*, 6 October, 1989, p. 7.
44 Connor, 'The Problem with "No Platform"'.
45 Bristow, 'Free Speech on Campus'.
46 *The Beaver*, 14 March, 1994, p. 4.
47 *Felix*, 13 October, 1995, p. 2.
48 Houriya Ahmed & Hannah Stuart, 'Profile: Hizb ut-Tahrir in the UK', *Current Trends in Islamist Ideology*, 10 (2010) p. 150; Kochan, 'Great Britain', p. 272.
49 *The Beaver*, 8 October, 1996, p. 7.
50 *The Times*, 31 October, 1995, p. 6.
51 *Sunday Telegraph*, 23 January, 1994, p. 7; *The Times*, 31 October, 1995, p. 6.
52 *The Times*, 18 March, 1996, p. 5.
53 Ibid.
54 Ibid.
55 Ibid.
56 *British Muslim Monthly Survey*, 2/10 (October 1994) http://artsweb.bham.ac.uk/bmms/1994/10October94.html (accessed 23 May, 2019).
57 Fahreen Wail, *Radicalism Unveiled* (Farnham: Ashgate, 2013) p. 147.
58 Cited in *British Muslim Monthly Survey* (October 1994).
59 Cited in *The Times Higher Education Supplement*, 4 November, 1994, www.timeshighereducation.com/news/islamic-group-accuses-soas-of-cowardice/154431.article (accessed 23 May, 2019).
60 Nomaan Hanif, 'The Securitisation of Hizb ut Tahrir: A Comparative Case Study' (Royal Holloway, University of London: unpublished Ph.D. thesis, 2014) p. 256; *British Muslim Monthly Survey*, 2/11 (November 1994) http://artsweb.bham.ac.uk/1994/11November94.html (accessed 23 May, 2019).
61 Cited in *British Muslim Monthly Survey* (November 1994).

62 *The New Spirit*, 30 November, 1994, p. 3.
63 Ibid.
64 'The Story So Far …', *SOAS Students' Union*, 20 April, 2017, https://soasunion.org/yourunion/story/ (accessed 23 May, 2019).
65 SWP, 'On Racism and Fascism', *Post Conference Bulletin* (1995) p. 5.
66 SWSS, 'Hizb ut-Tahrir, Islam and the NUS', *Pre-Conference Bulletin*, 3 (1995) p. 7.
67 Ibid.
68 Ibid.
69 Connor, 'The Problem with "No Platform"'; SWSS, 'Hizb ut-Tahrir, Islam and the NUS', p. 7.
70 SWSS, 'Hizb ut-Tahrir, Islam and the NUS', p. 7.
71 Ahmed & Stuart, 'Profile: Hizb ut-Tahrir in the UK', p. 154.
72 Sadek Hamid, *Sufis, Salafis and Islamists: The Contested Ground of British Islamic Activism* (London: I.B. Tauris, 2018) p. 120.
73 Ibid.
74 Ahmed & Stuart, 'Profile: Hizb ut-Tahrir in the UK', p. 154.
75 Katherine E. Brown & Tania Saeed, 'Radicalization and Counter-Radicalization at British Universities: Muslim Encounters and Alternatives', *Ethnic and Racial Studies*, 38/11 (2015) p. 1954.
76 Ian Cram & Helen Fenwick, 'Protecting Free Speech and Academic Freedom in Universities', *Modern Law Review*, 81/5 (2018) p. 835.
77 'Memorandum submitted by the Union of Jewish Students', 23 September, 2004, written evidence submitted to Home Affairs Committee, https://publications.parliament.uk/pa/cm200405/cmselect/cmhaff/165/165we38.htm (accessed 25 May, 2019).
78 For example, see: Karl McDonald, 'These Are the Six Extreme Groups that the NUS Actually "No Platforms"', *iNews*, 3 May, 2018, https://inews.co.uk/news/politics/six-extreme-groups-nus-no-platforms/ (accessed 25 May, 2019).
79 Shaida-Raffat Nabi, 'How is Islamophobia Institutionalised? Racialised Governmentality and the Case of Muslim Students in British Universities' (University of Manchester: unpublished Ph.D. thesis, 2011) p. 116.
80 Runnymede Trust, *Islamophobia: A Challenge for Us All* (London: Runnymede Trust, 1997).
81 Steven Woodbridge, 'Ambivalent Admiration? The Response of Other Extreme-Right Groups to the Rise of the BNP', in Nigel Copsey & Graham Macklin (eds), *The British National Party: Contemporary Perspectives* (Abingdon: Routledge, 2011) p. 105.
82 Nigel Copsey, *Contemporary British Fascism: The British National Party and the Quest for Legitimacy* (London: Routledge, 2004) p. 100.
83 James Rhodes, 'Filling the Void: Burnley and the Everyday Day Politics of the BNP', *Soundings*, 44 (Spring 2010) p. 73.
84 David Renton, 'Examining the Success of the British National Party, 1999–2003', *Race and Class*, 45/2 (2003) p. 80.
85 C. Wood & W.M.L. Findlay, 'British National Party Representations of Muslims in the Month After the London Bombings: Homogeneity, Threat, and the Conspiracy Tradition', *British Journal of Social Psychology*, 47/4 (2008) pp. 707–726.
86 David Renton, '"A Day to Make History"? The 2004 Elections and the British National Party', *Patterns of Prejudice*, 39/1 (2005) p. 27; Copsey, *Contemporary British Fascism*, p. 124.
87 Robert Ford, 'Who Might Vote for the BNP? Survey Evidence on the Electoral Potential of the Extreme Right in Britain', in Roger Eatwell & Matthew J. Goodwin (eds), *The New Extremism in 21st Century Britain* (Abingdon: Routledge, 2010) p. 145.
88 Ibid.
89 Ibid., p. 162.
90 *The Guardian*, 1 May, 2002, www.theguardian.com/politics/2002/may/01/studentpolitics.education (accessed 27 May, 2019).

91 See: 'Workers Against Racism', *Powerbase* (last modified 4 October, 2013) http://powerbase.info/index.php/Workers_Against_Racism (accessed 27 May, 2019).
92 Brendon Craigie, 'This Wasn't Hardcore …', *Living Marxism Comment* (6 October, 1998) http://web.archive.org/web/20000229064746/www.informinc.co.uk/LM/discuss/commentary/10-06-98-HARDCORE.html (accessed 27 May, 2019).
93 *Leeds Student*, 23 February, 2001, p. 11.
94 Patrick Harrington, 'LM and Censorship', 30 January, 2008, http://web.archive.org/web/20120216001144/http://thirdway.eu/2008/01/30/lm-and-censorship/ (accessed 27 May, 2019).
95 *Leeds Student*, 9 February, 2001, p. 3.
96 Ibid.
97 'Fascist Campus Defeat', *Searchlight* (March 2001) p. 12.
98 *Leeds Student*, 23 February, 2001, p. 11.
99 *Leeds Student*, 16 March, 2001, p. 6.
100 Ibid.
101 Ibid.
102 *Leeds Student*, 27 April, 2001, p. 7.
103 Ibid.
104 *Leeds Student*, 1 June, 2001, p. 1.
105 Ibid.
106 Ibid., p. 2.
107 *Leeds Student*, 5 October, 2001, p. 9.
108 *Leeds Student*, 12 October, 2001, p. 9.
109 Ibid.
110 *Leeds Student*, 1 February, 2002, p. 2.
111 *The Guardian*, 1 May, 2002, www.theguardian.com/education/2002/may/01/students.politics (accessed 27 May 2019).
112 *The Guardian*, 28 November, 2002, www.theguardian.com/education/2002/nov/28/highereducation.uk1 (accessed 28 May, 2019).
113 Ibid.
114 Ibid.
115 Ibid.
116 Ibid.
117 Ibid.
118 *The Guardian*, 3 December, 2002, www.theguardian.com/politics/2002/dec/03/uk.highereducation (accessed 28 May, 2019).
119 *The Guardian*, 4 December, 2002, www.theguardian.com/education/2002/dec/04/highereducation.uk4 (accessed 28 May, 2019).
120 Ibid.
121 Ibid.
122 *The Guardian*, 3 December, 2002, www.theguardian.com/uk/2005/feb/03/race.students (accessed 28 May, 2019).
123 Ibid.
124 *The Mitre*, 15 February, 2005, p. 1.
125 Scottish Parliament, *Official Report*, 10 February, 2005, col. 14521–14563.
126 Ibid., p. 10.
127 UCU, *UCU Concern Over BNP Manipulation of Bath University* (press release), www.ucu.org.uk/article/2534/UCU-concern-over-BNP-manipulation-of-Bath-University (accessed 28 May, 2019).
128 Ibid.
129 *Socialist Worker*, 15 May, 2007, https://socialistworker.co.uk/art/11181/Nick+Griffins+Bath+trip+goes+down+the+plug+hole (accessed 28 May, 2019).
130 *The Guardian*, 10 May, 2007, www.theguardian.com/education/2007/may/10/highereducation.race (accessed 28 May, 2019).
131 Ibid.

132 *Socialist Worker*, 15 May, 2007.
133 *The Guardian*, 11 May, 2007, www.theguardian.com/uk/2007/may/11/students.thefarright (accessed 28 May, 2019).
134 Ibid.
135 *Cherwell*, 12 October, 2007, https://cherwell.org/2007/10/12/union-under-fire-over-extremist-invitations/ (accessed 29 May, 2019).
136 *The Guardian*, 26 November, 2007, www.theguardian.com/uk/2007/nov/26/human rights.thefarright (accessed 28 May, 2019).
137 *The Guardian*, 27 November, 2007, www.theguardian.com/uk/2007/nov/27/higher education.studentpoliticseducation (accessed 29 May, 2019).
138 *Socialist Worker*, 15 May, 2007.
139 *Concrete*, 23 October, 2007, p. 3; *Concrete*, 4 December, 2007, p. 3.
140 Joe Conboy, 'Report: Student Nurses Demand Answers', *Socialist Appeal*, 29 May, 2007, www.socialist.net/nursing-students-university-east-anglia-norwich-trainee-compulsory-redundancy-staff.htm (accessed 29 May, 2019).
141 *Concrete*, 23 October, 2007, p. 3.
142 Ibid.
143 Ibid., p. 12.
144 Ibid., p. 12.
145 *Concrete*, 6 November, 2007, p. 4.
146 *Concrete*, 20 November, 2007, p. 3.
147 Ibid.
148 Neil Davenport, 'Doing Fascists a Favour', *Spiked*, 10 May, 2002, www.spiked-online.com/2002/05/10/doing-fascists-a-favour/ (accessed 29 May, 2019).
149 *Concrete*, 4 December, 2007, p. 3.
150 *The Guardian*, 27 November, 2007, www.theguardian.com/education/2007/nov/27/highereducation.uk (accessed 28 May, 2019).
151 *The Socialist*, 14 May, 2008, www.socialistparty.org.uk/articles/4107/14-05-2008/sussex-students-uphold-no-platform (accessed 29 May, 2019).
152 Richard Reynolds, 'Just Say No to "No Platform"', *Spiked*, 26 November, 2007, www.spiked-online.com/2007/11/26/just-say-no-to-no-platform/ (accessed 29 May, 2019).
153 *Glasgow University Guardian*, 17 January, 1996, p. 13.
154 Ibid.
155 *Glasgow University Guardian*, 31 January, 1996, p. 17.
156 Ibid.
157 Ibid.
158 *The Guardian*, 8 July, 2000, www.theguardian.com/uk/2000/jul/08/davidpallister.johnvidal1 (accessed 17 May, 2019).
159 Tom Slater, 'Students, Join Our Fight against Campus Censorship!', *Spiked*, 25 February, 2015, www.spiked-online.com/2015/02/25/students-join-our-fight-against-campus-cen sorship/ (accessed 30 May, 2019).
160 *Free Speech University Rankings: Results Summary* (2018) p. 1, https://media.spiked-on line.com/website/images/2019/02/21153835/FSUR-PACK-2018.pdf (accessed 30 May, 2019).
161 Slater, 'Students, Join Our Fight against Campus Censorship!'
162 Tom Slater, 'Free Speech University Rankings: Exposing the Staggering Scale of Censorship on Campus', *Spiked*, 3 February, 2015, www.spiked-online.com/2015/02/03/free-speech-university-rankings-exposing-the-staggering-scale-of-censorship-on-campus/ (accessed 30 May, 2019).
163 *Free Speech University Rankings: Results Summary* (2018) p. 2.
164 Tom Slater, 'Meet the Students Fighting Campus Censorship', *Spiked*, 27 January, 2016, www.spiked-online.com/2016/01/27/meet-the-students-fighting-campus-cen sorship/ (accessed 29 May, 2019); Slater, 'Students, Join Our Fight against Campus Censorship!'.

165 *The Guardian*, 7 May, 2018, www.theguardian.com/commentisfree/2018/may/07/free-speech-warriors-mistake-student-protest-censorship (accessed 28 May, 2019).
166 *The Times Higher Education Supplement*, 17 February, 2018, www.timeshighereducation.com/blog/free-speech-rankings-misleading-ill-informed-and-worryingly-influential (accessed 31 May, 2019).
167 Ibid.
168 For example, see: Cram & Fenwick, 'Protecting Free Speech and Academic Freedom in Universities', pp. 847–851.
169 Joint Committee on Human Rights, 'Oral Evidence: Freedom of Speech in Universities', HC589, 15 November, 2017, Q2–3, http://data.parliament.uk/writtenevidence/committeeevidence.svc/evidencedocument/human-rights-committee/freedom-of-speech-in-universities/oral/74027.html (accessed 28 May, 2019).
170 Joint Committee on Human Rights, *Freedom of Speech in Universities: Fourth Report of Session 2017–19*, HC589/HL111, pp. 17–18.
171 Tom Slater, 'Free Speech University Rankings', *Spiked*, 24 February, 2019, www.spiked-online.com/free-speech-university-rankings/ (accessed 30 May, 2019).
172 Trilling, *Bloody Nasty People*, p. 179.
173 Lynsey Hanley, 'Airtime for Hitler', *LRB Blog*, 8 August, 2018, www.lrb.co.uk/blog/2018/august/airtime-for-hitler (accessed 1 June, 2019).
174 Sarah Ditum, '"No Platform" Was Once Reserved for Violent Fascists. Now It's Being Used to Silence Debate', *New Statesman*, 18 March, 2014, www.newstatesman.com/sarah-ditum/2014/03/when-did-no-platform-become-about-attacking-individuals-deemed-disagreeable (accessed 1 June, 2019).
175 Ibid.
176 Cited in, ibid.
177 *The Guardian*, 31 January, 2010, www.theguardian.com/commentisfree/2010/jan/31/julie-bindel-transgender-nus (accessed 31 May, 2019).
178 Ditum, '"No Platform" Was Once Reserved for Violent Fascists'.
179 NUS LGBT Conference, *Live Policy 2015–18*, p. 5, https://s3-eu-west-1.amazonaws.com/nusdigital/document/documents/36408/35667a8910ac81d4641fec940877d218/LGBT__Live_policy_201518.pdf (accessed 1 June, 2019).
180 Ibid.
181 Ibid., p. 37.
182 Ibid.
183 *The SOAS Spirit*, 13 November, 2014, p. 6.
184 Ibid.
185 *Forge*, 26 October, 2014, http://forgetoday.com/press/su-bans-bindel (accessed 1 June, 2019).
186 For an explanation of Gamergate, see: Michael Salter, 'From Geek Masculinity to Gamergate: The Technological Rationality of Online Abuse', *Crime Media Culture*, 14/2 (2018) pp. 247–264.
187 *The Mancunion*, 6 October, 2015, https://mancunion.com/2015/10/06/transphobe-julie-bindel-banned-from-free-speech-debate/ (accessed 1 June, 2019).
188 Ibid.
189 Manchester University Students' Union, 'Updated Statement from the Students' Union', 7 October, 2015, https://manchesterstudentsunion.com/articles/updated-statement-from-the-students-union-05-10-2015 (accessed 2 June, 2019).
190 Sally Hines, 'The Feminist Frontier: On Trans and Feminism', *Journal of Gender Studies*, 2017, p. 8, DOI:10.1080/09589236.2017.1411791.
191 Cited in *The Guardian*, 23 October, 2015, www.theguardian.com/education/2015/oct/23/petition-urges-cardiff-university-to-cancel-germain-greer-lecture (accessed 2 June, 2019).
192 Theresa O'Keefe, 'Open Space: Making Feminist Sense of No-Platforming', *Feminist Review*, 113 (2016) p. 85.
193 Ibid., p. 87.

194 Hines, 'The Feminist Frontier', p. 8.
195 Joint Committee on Human Rights, 'Oral Evidence: Freedom of Speech in Universities', HC589, 15 November, 2017, Q12.
196 Sara Ahmed, 'An Affinity of Hammers', *Transgender Studies Quarterly*, 3/1–2 (May 2016) p. 28; Sara Ahmed, 'You Are Oppressing Us!', *Feminist Killjoys*, 15 February, 2015, https://feministkilljoys.com/2015/02/15/you-are-oppressing-us/amp/ (accessed 2 June, 2019).
197 Ahmed, 'An Affinity of Hammers', p. 31.
198 Helen Lewis, 'What the Row Over Banning Germaine Greer Is Really About', *New Statesman*, 27 October, 2017, www.newstatesman.com/politics/feminism/2015/10/what-row-over-banning-germaine-greer-really-about (accessed 3 June, 2019).

8

WHY 'NO PLATFORM' MATTERS

'No platform' continues to be a controversial tactic. With the ascendancy of the far right in Britain, as well as in other parts of the world, the legitimacy and effectiveness of 'no platform' has been contested over the last few years. After inches of newspaper columns, pages of online opinion pieces and millions of social media posts over the last decade, the Conservative government decided to hold an inquiry into the issue, initiated by Jo Johnson and then overseen by his successor as Universities Minister, Sam Gyimah. In October 2017, Johnson launched the Office for Students (OfS) as a new higher education regulatory body, which included in its mission a duty to 'ensure' free speech, with promises of fines for universities that failed to 'protect' it.[1] The inquiry that Johnson launched was part of the initial actions of the OfS.

After more than 100 written submissions and over 35 people presenting oral testimony to the inquiry, run by the Joint Committee on Human Rights, the final report found that while there had been some incursions on 'lawful free speech', the Joint Committee asserted that it 'did not find the wholesale censorship of debate which media coverage has suggested'.[2] The report did, however, call for greater intervention by the Charity Commission against student unions that 'inhibit lawful free speech' and recommended that '[e]ffective action should be taken against protestors' who went 'beyond the law' in attempts to disrupt or shut down events.[3] It was suggested that the OfS take over from the Charity Commission in regulating student unions and publish an annual report on the topic of free speech at universities.[4]

Beyond these findings, the Joint Committee issued a new guidance document for universities and student unions on ensuring free speech, which primarily outlined the numerous pieces of legislation that needed to be taken in consideration when holding speaking events on campus.[5] While taking into account recent legislative changes, this guidance had not greatly differed from the library note provided by the House of Lords in 2015 on the same topic.[6] However, the rhetoric has become more pointed and established the pretext for proposed intervention by the OfS:

> Protest is itself a legitimate expression of freedom of speech. However, protest must not shut down debate. Protesters who attempt to prevent viewpoints being heard infringe upon the rights of others. Student Unions, Universities and law enforcement must hold such people to account – and ensure that sufficient resources are in place to prevent protesters from blocking debate.[7]

As mentioned in Chapter 6, section 43 of the Education (No. 2) Act 1986 was supposed to perform this task. It remains to be seen how the OfS will hold protestors to account if they are deemed to be infringing others' freedom of speech. In many ways, this inquiry echoes the concerns and frustrations by the right about students and the supposed lack of free speech at British universities voiced over the last 50 years, highlighted throughout this book.

This book was written as an outline of the transformation of the 'no platform' tactic and its use by the student movement in Britain, tracing its origins from the anti-fascism of the 1930s and exploring how it has been utilised in the more than 40 years since it was adopted as policy by the National Union of Students. It is meant as an interventionist history to inform those wishing to understand the contemporary debates about 'no platform' and the current moral panic over free speech at British universities – a 'concern' which has spread across the English-speaking world. With this, there are four themes contained within the book that need reflecting upon.

Fascism, as well as racism, sexism, homophobia and transphobia, need to be constantly challenged

Writing about the history of British fascism, Mike Cronin wrote in the mid-1990s, 'Fascism did not die in 1945.'[8] It is evident that the fortunes of British fascism have ebbed and flowed since the British Fascisti of the 1920s, but there have been times when it has threatened to make political in-roads, such as for the British Union of Fascists in the 1930s, the National Front in the 1970s and the British National Party in the 2000s. Exploiting populist views about immigration, national identity, imperial decline and the European Economic Community (or the European Union), as well as broader concerns about political and economic instability, 'law and order' issues or 'cultural decadence', fascism has sought and still seeks to provide a radical reactionary alternative to the status quo.

Although there are numerous factors which have impeded these fascist groups from achieving significant political influence, the role that anti-fascists have played in halting the growth of these groups cannot be overlooked. This can be seen in the mass opposition to the BUF in the 1930s, the work of the 43 Group against the Union Movement in the late 1940s, the political and cultural intervention of

Rock Against Racism and the Anti-Nazi League, the militant anti-fascism of Anti-Fascist Action in the late 1980s and early 1990s and the organised grassroots anti-fascism of Unite Against Fascism and Hope Not Hate in the 2000s. As Nigel Copsey has written, 'anti-fascism's historical importance is the part it has played in the failure of British fascism'.[9]

Central to militant and left-wing anti-fascism has been the notion of the denial of a public platform for fascists to organise, recruit or spruik their message. This can involve physically occupying spaces to prevent fascist activities, blocking pathways on the streets or access to buildings through demonstrations and pickets, heckling and the disruption of public addresses, or bureaucratic measures to deny fascists access to public platforms, such as town halls or lecture theatres. For militant anti-fascists, a victorious fascist movement means violence and death for those specifically targeted by fascists, as well as the denial of a voice for everyone else. Thus fascism needs to be denied a platform in its embryonic stages. This was the basis for the original implementation of the NUS' 'no platform' in the 1970s and a principle maintained to this day.

Inspired by the anti-fascism of the 1930s, the architects of the 'no platform' policy in the 1970s saw the fight against racism and fascism at universities as part of a wider campaign to combat the National Front and other fascists. While universities and colleges have been portrayed by some as discrete venues where the 'marketplace of ideas' reigns supreme, those who pushed for the tactic of 'no platform' argued that fascism and racism could not be allowed to encroach upon this space and that students deserved an environment free from prejudice and violence. As this book has shown, fascists and explicit racists have continually sought to promote their views at universities and in reaction to this, students and other anti-fascists and anti-racists have invoked the policy of 'no platform' in attempts to prevent these fascists from appearing on campus.

Aaron Winter and Aurelien Mondon have proposed that although the far right has electorally made some significant advances since the 1990s, many of the far right's ideas have become increasingly accepted in the political mainstream.[10] Far right talking points around issues of 'race', immigration and multiculturalism, as well as women's rights, homosexuality and trans people, have been amplified by social media, then by the mainstream media and certain politicians. In an era of far right ascendancy and when racist, sexist, homophobic and transphobic violence is a prevalent threat to many, vigilance against the far right is necessary.

It is not just fascism that needs to be challenged, but other forms of discrimination and harassment, such as racism, sexism, homophobia and transphobia. Some have argued that the 'no platform' tactic needs to take into account these other forms of oppression and that the tactic should be extended those who promote these views. This book has outlined the history of these debates and how the principle of 'no platform' has been widened at different points to combat various forms of prejudice.

But it is also important to remember that 'no platform' is not the only tactic for fighting these prejudices. In his book *The New Authoritarians*, David Renton has suggested that combating the far right requires a multitude of approaches, particularly as the space has opened up between the traditional conservative right and fascism, allowing a 'populist' far right to emerge.[11] As organised fascists are only part of a broader far right and as far right ideas are increasingly part of the political mainstream, the militant anti-fascist tactics of yesteryear are not the only ones to be utilised, and fighting the various forms of oppression, such as racism, sexism, homophobia and transphobia, requires a broader approach. But at the heart of this intersectional activism is maintaining the principle that prejudice needs to be challenged – in the electoral sphere, in the streets, online, in the workplace, in our communities, in activist circles, and in our educational institutions.

The far right and those who invite them onto campus have a symbiotic relationship

This book has shown that more than places for potential recruitment, speaking engagements at universities offer fascists and racists the opportunity to portray themselves as legitimate parts of the political discourse. When the Union Movement was in the wilderness in the 1950s and sought to capitalise on popular anti-immigration sentiment against Commonwealth migrants to Britain, Oswald Mosley appeared at several universities, including both Oxford and Cambridge, attempting to promote his opinions as part of the discussion about immigration, 'race relations' and Britain's relationship with apartheid South Africa. In the 2000s, Nick Griffin's efforts to revamp the BNP and present it as a 'respectable' right-wing political party was reinforced by the various speaking engagements that he was invited to at British universities, such as Oxford, Cambridge and St Andrews. When he was able to speak, Griffin exploited these opportunities to cast the BNP as within the acceptable bounds of debate and that his views needed to be listened to. In more recent times, co-founder of the English Defence League, Tommy Robinson, has used invitations to speak at the Oxford Union and other university appearances (including by video in the United States) to help rebrand himself, in the words of Nesrine Malik, 'from convicted street thug to a principled crusader' of free speech.[12] Hsiao-Hung Pai quoted Robinson as saying:

> When we were talking about these issues five years ago, we were shunned and called racists. Now, in the last twelve to eighteen months, they, the politicians and media, are all talking about the same issues. My speech at the Oxford Union was very well received. These ideas become more mainstream. People are listening to us now.[13]

On the other side of the equation, those who invite fascists, racists or other controversial speakers onto campus often have different motives; they are, for the most part, less concerned with legitimising fascism than with indulging in controversialism and fetishising the performativity of debating. When Mosley was invited to speak or debate in the late 1950s and early 1960s, a number of the student groups that invited him claimed that he brought a lively, yet provocative, aspect to the proceedings and praised his oratory skills. Similar was said about

Enoch Powell when he was invited to speak on campuses during the late 1960s, around the time of his 'Rivers of Blood' speech, and then again in the mid-1980s.

Even when their public speaking has not been praised, some on the far right have been invited because their incendiary position on the issues of 'race', immigration and multiculturalism. For example, Nick Griffin was supposedly invited to speak at various universities because his political party seemingly represented a distinct segment of public opinion, even if Griffin himself was not a gifted public speaker. An argument has been made that to develop an informed opinion about certain topics, we need to listen to the extremes and include all voices. This argument has been routinely made by those organising university debates that include the far right. However, by allowing these extreme opinions from the right to be heard, even if rejected by the majority of those listening, it is still giving the appearance that those extreme views can be a legitimate part of the debate.

Student groups have also invited controversial speakers to antagonise the rest of the student movement and attempt to provoke those who have advocated for a policy of 'no platform'. From the late 1970s to the mid-1980s, the Federation of Conservative Students did this on several occasions, such as the invitation of Sir Keith Joseph to LSE in 1978 or the invitation of hard right Conservative MP John Carlisle to several universities in 1986. The FCS used these invitations to upset the student left and as part of their explicit campaign against 'no platform', using each student protest as an alleged example of the denial of free speech for Tories. This antagonistic display of free speech absolutism was not just used by the FCS; several university-based Conservative Associations also partook in inviting right wing MPs, such as Leon Brittan, John Carlisle, Harvey Proctor and Enoch Powell, to speak in the mid-1980s. At the height of Thatcherism and amidst victories over the trade union movement, Conservative students saw the university and the student union as one of the fortresses of the left in Britain. Inviting hard right politicians to speak was used as a symbol of defiance against the supposed hegemony of the student left.

After the FCS was abolished in 1986, its successor organisation, the Conservative Collegiate Forum, still pushed for an end to 'no platform' and stronger laws to protect free speech on campus. The influence of the CCF can be seen in the decision of the Liverpool University Conservative Association, under the then leadership of CCF member Joe Baldwin, to invite two South African diplomats as a test case for the Education (No. 2) Act 1986, which was supposed to uphold freedom of speech on university grounds. After the university administration barred the diplomats from speaking, due to public order concerns, the Conservative Association took the university to court, resulting in a High Court decision that put limits on universities' abilities to abrogate their duties under the 1986 Act under the guise of public order.

In the twenty-first century, free speech societies (or similar) at various universities have invited controversial speakers as an act of rebellion against the continued NUS policy of 'no platform'. In 2001, the Free Speech Society was taken over by members of the BNP and invitations were made to Nick Griffin. In 2015, the Free Speech and Secular Society at the University of Manchester invited both Julie Bindel and Milo Yiannopoulos in defiance of the NUS motion of 'no platforming' Bindel and after Yiannopoulos had been identified as a key player in the Gamergate controversy. At the University of Kent, the Liberty Union had invited both disgraced columnist Katie Hopkins and YouTuber and one-time UKIP MEP candidate Carl Benjamin (better known as 'Sargon of Akkad') in the same academic year.[14] At a time when the moral panic about the alleged lack of free speech on campus has once again come to the fore, these invitations can be viewed as part of a wider challenge to the policy of 'no platform' held by the NUS and individual student unions, supported by *Spiked Online* and other free speech warriors.

The tactic of 'no platforming' has been shifting since its inception

In this current moral panic about the censorious nature of students and the attacks of the 'woke' upon free speech, there has been a juxtaposition by many of the use of 'no platform' being strictly applied to fascists only in the 1970s and the broad use of the tactic nowadays. Jim Butcher, writing for *Spiked*, is an example of this argument when he wrote:

> The National Union of Students' No Platform policy dates back to 1974. Its targets back then were Britain's then sizeable far-right groups: the NUS wanted to keep such outfits off campus. But campus politics has changed a great deal in the intervening decades. Today, a far wider range of controversial speakers falls foul of SU policies. No Platform was wrong in the past, even when it was only aimed at the far right, but it is even worse now – it has become all-encompassing.[15]

The narrative seems to be that the 'snowflake' generation have corrupted the anti-fascist origins of 'no platform' and applied it too widely.

But this book has shown that students have argued for 'no platform' to be extended to other forms of prejudice since the 1970s, and that this has been continually contested within the student unions and the larger student movement from the early days of the NUS policy in the mid-1970s. At its inception, there were disagreements over whether it applied to hard right Conservatives, such as the Monday Club or anti-abortionists such as the Society for the Protection of the Unborn Child. After a resolution was passed at the United Nations in 1975 declaring that Zionism was a form of racism, some student unions attempted to apply the 'no platform' policy to Zionist and pro-Israel student groups, but this was heavily resisted and led to the NUS declaring in April 1978 that Zionist student groups could not be 'no platformed' (amidst a wider discussion about the existence of the 'no platform' policy).

In the first half of the 1980s, some students pushed for the 'no platform' policy undertaken by individual student unions to be extended to include sexists, homophobes and anti-abortionists. These should be seen as part of broader campaigns against sexism and homophobia in British society, as well as against harassment of and violence against women and gay people at universities. Those in favour of the 'no platform' policy to be widened argued that sexist and homophobic speech created an environment that allowed harassment and violence to occur and that to make the campus safe for everyone, proponents of explicit sexism (including anti-abortionists) and homophobia needed to be excluded.

At the same time, there was significant protest against hard right politicians speaking at universities, particularly in the mid-1980s in the wake of the Miners' Strike, the 1985 riots and the growth of the Anti-Apartheid Movement in Britain. While the NUS discouraged the formal use of the 'no platform' policy against politicians like Enoch Powell or John Carlisle, individual student unions and sections of the student population did, on occasions, use the principle of 'no platform' to suggest that these politicians be denied the opportunity to speak on campus. But at other times, the student union leadership defended the right of these politicians to speak and protests against them came from other students, particularly the Trotskyist left and anarchists. Protest actions against these politicians varied widely, from requesting that the university administrations refuse to allow them to publicly speak, to picketing venues, and to physically disrupting speeches. Students involved in these protests did not always frame their actions as 'no platforming' and sometimes it is difficult to clearly describe those protest actions as instances of 'no platform'. Students have long protested the appearance of politicians at British universities, using a variety of protest methods, but in the 1980s, critics of these student protests were more inclined to refer to them as 'no platforming' and portray them all as examples of the denial of free speech by student radicals.

In the 1990s, a concern about Islamic fundamentalist groups, in particular Hizb ut-Tahrir, which was attempting to recruit at British universities, led to student unions implementing bans on these groups, but the NUS was unable to do so at the national level. However, by the mid-2000s when the threat of religious terrorism seemed to be heightened, the NUS was able to apply the 'no platform' policy to Hizb ut-Tahrir and some other smaller Islamic fundamentalist groups. During both periods there were fears raised, from other Muslim student groups and the left, about how the use of 'no platform' against these groups played into the wider prevalence of Islamophobia in Britain, especially after the post-9/11 'War on Terror' began in 2001, but there was less uproar about the policy being applied to Muslims than about its application to the far right amongst those who looked unfavourably at 'no platform'.

The far and populist right is still the focus of student efforts to 'no platform' those such as hard right Tory MP Jacob Rees Mogg at the University of Bristol in 2018, Alice Weidel from Germany's far right group AfD and Marion Maréchal-Le Pen from Front National at the Oxford in 2019, and Katie Hopkins, also at Oxford in the same year. However, the application of the policy by some student groups to speakers such as gay rights activist Peter Tatchell and Hope not Hate's Nick Lowles (for alleged Islamophobia) and to radical feminists such as Germaine Greer and Julie Bindel, for alleged transphobia, has brought renewed criticism of 'no platforming'.

Part of this criticism has been that the tactic of 'no platforming' has strayed too far from its original intention and that this is often seen as part of a generational shift, from the student radicals of the 1970s to the 'snowflakes' of today.

As this book has shown, 'no platform' has shifted as a tactic and as student union policy since its inception in the mid-1970s. Its application over the decades has revealed tensions within the student movement over how it should be used and who should be targeted. These debates at the grassroots level demonstrate how 'no platform' can be used as a democratic expression of the student body, but also wielded as a bureaucratic instrument by student unions, at the local and national level. Like all forms of activism, it is not a perfect process and rather than being operated arbitrarily, it should be used as the result of discussion amongst the student base. But despite being used in controversial circumstances on some occasions, it continues to an effectual tactic for student protest after more than four decades.

Free speech does not exist in a vacuum

It has been a constant refrain over the years since the implementation of the 'no platform' policy that absolute free speech does not exist, is not practical and is not entirely desirable. A guide on freedom of speech at universities produced by the Joint Committee on Human Rights after the parliamentary inquiry in 2017–18 identified nine different Acts that needed to be taken into consideration when inviting external speakers, including the Equality Act 2010, Public Order Act 1986, Counter-Terrorism and Security Act 2015, Terrorism Act 2000 and the Terrorism Act 2006.[16] While section 43 of the Education (No. 2) Act 1986 calls for universities and colleges to ensure free speech, universities, student unions and those invited to speak cannot ignore the legal framework surrounding them.

Some have proposed that all speech within the bounds of the law should be allowed on campus, but students have countered that the freedom of speech cannot supersede all other freedoms, including the freedom from prejudice, harassment and violence. In defence of their 'no platform' policy, the National Union of Students distils this argument succinctly:

> NUS supports freedom of speech, thought and expression. But NUS opposes those who attempt to utilise this 'freedom' in order to remove the freedoms of others. Affording racists and fascists a platform helps them in their search for credibility to promote their messages of hate, which in turn can lead to violence against those that they target.[17]

As seen throughout this book, those in favour of 'no platform' have questioned why ethnic minorities, women and LGBTQ+ people should have to endure speakers airing racist, sexist, homophobic or transphobic messages in public, particularly at their place of higher education, which should be a safe environment for them to learn. The notion that the university should not be a safe space and that students need to be confronted with offensive ideas is one of privilege, envisioning that students had never faced such ideas before reaching university. Many students would have already encountered racism, sexism, homophobia and transphobia before arriving at university; they don't need to be exposed to it as part of their higher education experience.

'No platforming' can be seen as part of the resistance by students to the status quo and the insistence that they need to engage with prejudicial and hateful ideas in order to have a proper university education. The moral panic over freedom of speech at universities is also an element in a much wider culture war over the future of the university, with students leading the charge to challenge the racial, patriarchal and class privileges upon which the British higher education system rests. Starting with the 'Rhodes Must Fall' campaign at the University of Cape Town in South Africa and spreading to universities across the Global North, the push to decolonise the university has gained pace in the last few years. In Britain, the post-imperial (but not post-colonial) metropole, the push to decolonise is particularly important as British universities were, and remain, 'a key site through which colonialism – and colonial knowledge in particular – is produced, consecrated, institutionalised and naturalised'.[18] Even today, as Katy Sian has asserted, '[r]acism at British universities is endemic'.[19]

Several recent studies have reiterated this point, with Kalwant Bhopal recently writing that '[c]urrent scholarship on race in UK higher education consistently highlights the pervasiveness of institutional racism, which persists despite the presence of equality and diversity policies and the 2010 Equalities Act'.[20] Furthermore, despite strong criticisms of its methodologies and findings, a 2019 report by the Equality and Human Rights Commission found that '[r]acial harassment is a common experience for a wide range of students and staff at universities across England, Scotland and Wales'.[21]

Not to mention sexism, homophobia and transphobia. A NUS report from 2018 described the university as 'a highly sexualised higher education environment, where a spectrum of behaviours and responses enable sexism, harassment and other forms of discrimination to embed themselves within this culture'.[22] A Stonewall/YouGov report into LGBTQ+ students in the same year stated:

> LGBT students still face discrimination, exclusion and barriers at university because of being LGBT. Many LGBT students report being excluded by other students and have been subjected to derogatory remarks and behaviour from other students and even staff. A number of trans students have experienced a physical attack by someone at university.[23]

As students attempt to transform the higher education system and challenge the existing state of affairs at universities, students and scholars who have traditionally benefited from the white, patriarchal and capitalist university establishment have felt threatened, with their freedom of speech supposedly jeopardised. Echoing the 'free speech squad' proposed by the Freedom Under Law Group in 1973 after the protests against Hans Eysenck and Samuel P. Huntington (see Chapter 3), US-based British historian Niall Ferguson wrote a column in *The Sunday Times* calling for a similar organisation to NATO 'to protect western intellectuals from a growing threat to academic freedom'.[24] Deploring the protests against several high profile right-wing academics (and former academics), such as Roger Scruton and Jordan Peterson, Ferguson declared forcefully:

> The present danger to free thought and speech is not Red Army tanks pouring through the Fulda Gap in Germany; it is the red army of mediocrities waging war on dissent within academia and the media. It is time to confront these people with the one thing that will deter them, as it once deterred the Soviets: massive retaliation.[25]

Hyperbole aside, Ferguson's reaction to protests against the 'pale, male and stale' composition of the current university system is less about defending free speech and more about defending the system as it stands. As Dawn Foster has recently argued, free speech does not mean freedom from criticism and what irks Ferguson and his peers is that their worldview is being challenged, by campaigns such as 'Rhodes Must Fall' and #MeToo. Foster explains:

> For years, privileged men have been able to frame themselves as agents provocateurs ... Their fury is not that they have been silenced – they have not – but that their victims have argued back, and they have been forced to bear responsibility for their words.[26]

As demonstrated throughout this book, the far right and their fellow travellers have attempted to use the notion of celebrating free speech as a cloak for the dissemination of their prejudiced, discriminatory and often hateful ideas. Going back to the 1930s, the British Union of Fascists proclaimed that they were the only ones who could protect the democratic right to free speech from the communists. In the 1970s and 1980s, the National Front campaigned that the Public Order Act 1986 and Race Relations Act 1976 hindered their free speech, arguing that this was a conspiracy by the establishment to deny the NF their freedom of speech.[27] Under Nick Griffin, the BNP continued this tradition and portrayed themselves as the 'party of free speech, unlike the mainstream parties, in defiance of political correctness'.[28] And nowadays, far right figures, such as Tommy Robinson, have wrapped themselves in the banner of free speech. As Will Davies wrote in *The Guardian*, '[t]he concept of free speech has become a political totem, particularly on the right'.[29]

And free speech at universities has been at the centre of this culture war. Many overlook that the British government's counter-terrorism programme, Prevent, probably has a more chilling effect on freedom of speech in higher education than the student union policies of 'no platform' and 'safe spaces'.[30] A recent report by a number of academics on counter-terrorism policy in Britain stated

> Prevent has had a profoundly negative impact on freedom of speech and academic freedom at universities, noting that the University College Union had also raised this in 2015, 'highlighting racism and discrimination, civil liberties and the undermining of academic freedom as a result of Prevent's deployment in universities.[31]

Andrew W. Neal has written that university actors have claimed that Prevent has had a particular 'chilling effect … among minority groups such as Muslim students and Islamic societies'.[32] Instead, a moral panic has grown over the last half decade with claims that censorious students are shutting down free speech and putting the traditional purpose of the university, the interrogation of ideas, at risk. Shortly after being temporarily fired from his role with the government's Building Better, Building Beautiful Commission, Roger Scruton suggested that in the face of contemporary student activism, one way forward was 'to get rid of universities altogether'.[33] This echoes what conservative *Times* columnist Bernard Levin wrote in the late 1980s after the University of Liverpool banned the Liverpool University Conservative Association from inviting two South African diplomats to speak:

> If we open the gates to the barbarians – even only by a crack no wider than a meeting cancelled 'in face of a potential for disorder' – we shall never shut them again. Parliament passed legislation which laid upon universities the duty to ensure that free speech within their walls would be truly free.[34]

Section 43 of the Education (No. 2) Act 1986 was introduced to save the principle of free speech at British universities in the face of overzealous student radicals, but the subsequent discourse has claimed that this was not enough. While various Universities Ministers have looked to inquiries, guidelines and the Office for Students to 'protect' free speech, the hard right, such as Ferguson and Scruton, contemplate more nuclear options. Despite this intense culture war and heightened moral panic, it doesn't look like 'no platform' is going away either.

This book has sought to explore the history of the tactic of 'no platform' and how the policy has developed at British universities since the 1970s. To understand the contemporary debates about its use, as well as the moral panic that surrounds it, it is important to outline its history and trace how it was developed, especially if the modern discourse focuses on how 'no platform' has deviated from its original intention. This narrative of a tactical break overlooks the fact that 'no platform' is still primarily applied to speakers from the far right and in an age when the populist far right has made political inroads (and the fascist extremes are involved in provocative street marches and acts of political violence), 'no platform' remains an important tactic for anti-fascists and anti-racists to use. As Gavan Titley has written, 'no platforming':

> makes clear a refusal to accept that the claim of free speech magically legitimates turning the humanity of some into a subject of political theatre, or that the rehearsal of practiced and patterned repertoires of racializing discourse constitutes opinions requiring dialogic engagement.[35]

While the university is place of intellectual inquiry, it cannot be a place where racism and fascism, as well as sexism, homophobia and transphobia are deemed suitable ideas to be expressed. The university is a place of teaching, learning, research and intellectual engagement, and everybody that partakes in this needs to do so in a safe and prejudice-free environment. The kind of absolute free speech that would allow these ideas to be aired threatens this. 'No platform' is part of the cache of tactics that students at British universities have used to try and ensure this safe environment, connected to broader struggles against racism and fascism in British society. We must acknowledge its long (and sometimes complicated) history and the role that it plays in current political struggles – because the threats that 'no platform' helps to confront still remain.

Notes

1 Department of Education, 'Jo Johnson Calls for Free Speech to be Protected on Campus', 19 October, 2017, www.gov.uk/government/news/jo-johnson-calls-for-free-speech-to-be-protected-on-campus (accessed 3 June, 2019); *The Guardian*, 26 December, 2017, www.theguardian.com/education/2017/dec/26/jo-johnson-universities-no-platforming-freedom-of-speech (accessed 3 June, 2019).
2 Joint Committee on Human Rights, *Freedom of Speech in Universities: Fourth Report of Session 2017–19*, HC589/HL111, p. 44.
3 Ibid., p. 47.
4 Ibid.
5 Joint Committee on Human Rights, *Free Speech: Guidance for Universities and Students Organising Events*, Annex to HC 589/HL Paper 111, 27 March, 2018.
6 House of Lords, *Freedom of Speech in Higher Education Institutions: Library Note*, LLN2015/045, 2015.
7 Ibid., p. 1.
8 Mike Cronin, 'Introduction: "Tomorrow We Live" – The Failure of British Fascism?', in Mike Cronin (ed.), *The Failure of British Fascism: The Far Right and the Fight for Political Recognition* (Houndmills: Macmillan, 1996) p. 8.
9 Nigel Copsey, *Anti-Fascism in Britain* (Abingdon: Routledge, 2017) p. xvi.
10 Aaron Winter & Aurelien Mondon, 'Understanding the Mainstreaming of the Far Right', *Open Democracy*, 26 August, 2018, www.opendemocracy.net/en/can-europe-make-it/understanding-mainstreaming-of-far-right/ (accessed 22 July, 2019).
11 David Renton, *The New Authoritarians: Convergences on the Right* (London: Pluto Press, 2019) pp. 227–237.
12 Nesrine Malik, *We Need New Stories: Challenging the Toxic Myths behind Our Age of Discontent* (London: Weidenfeld & Nicolson, 2019) p. 116.
13 Cited in, Hsiao-Hung Pai, *Angry White People: Coming Face-to-Face with the British Far Right* (London: Zed Books, 2016) pp. 353–354.
14 *Kent Online*, 21 March, 2019, www.kentonline.co.uk/canterbury/news/university-society-suspended-for-alleged-racism-201229/ (accessed 23 July, 2019).
15 Jim Butcher, 'How No Platform Conquered the Academy', *Spiked*, 5 February, 2018, www.spiked-online.com/2018/02/05/how-no-platform-conquered-the-academy/ (accessed 24 July, 2018).
16 Joint Committee on Human Rights, *Free Speech: Guidance for Universities and Students Organising Events*, pp. 2–6.
17 NUS, *Freedom from Harm, Freedom of Speech*, n.d., https://nusdigital.s3-eu-west-1.amazonaws.com/document/documents/14291/59f16f01802bb0a1228652fc7de986bb/Implementing%20No%20Platform%20policies.pdf (accessed 23 July, 2019).

18 Gurminder K. Bhambra, Dalia Gebrial & Kerem Nişancıoğlu, 'Introduction: Decolonising the University?', in Gurminder K. Bhambra, Dalia Gebrial & Kerem Nişancıoğlu (eds), *Decolonising the University* (London: Pluto Press, 2018) p. 5.
19 Katy P. Sian, *Navigating Institutional Racism in British Universities* (Houndmills: Palgrave Macmillan, 2019) p. 2.
20 Kalwant Bhopal, 'Race Matters: Addressing Competing Inequalities in Higher Education', in Hugo Dale-Rivas (ed.), *The White Elephant in the Room: Ideas for Reducing Racial Inequalities in Higher Education* (Oxford: Higher Education Policy Institute, 2019) p. 11.
21 Equality and Human Rights Commission, *Tackling Racial Harassment: Universities Challenged* (London: EHRC, 2019) p. 6.
22 NUS, *Power in the Academy: Staff Sexual Misconduct in UK Higher Education* (London: NUS, 2018) p. 5.
23 Chaka L. Bachmann & Becca Gooch, *LGBT in Britain: University Report* (London: Stonewall/YouGov, 2018) p. 6.
24 *The Sunday Times*, 14 April, 2019, www.thetimes.co.uk/article/join-my-nato-or-watch-critical-thinking-die-sl5sdqv5v (accessed 23 July, 2019).
25 Ibid.
26 *The Guardian*, 16 April, 2019, www.theguardian.com/commentisfree/2019/apr/15/niall-ferguson-free-speech-power (accessed 24 July, 2019).
27 For example, see: 'We Want Free Speech', *Bulldog*, 5 (February 1978) p. 2; 'Fight for Free Speech', *New Dawn*, 2 (1986) p. 2.
28 Peter John, Helen Margetts, David Rowland & Stuart Weir, *The BNP: The Roots of Its Appeal* (University of Essex: Democratic Audit, Human Rights Centre, 2006) p. 11.
29 *The Guardian*, 26 July, 2018, www.theguardian.com/news/2018/jul/26/the-free-speech-panic-censorship-how-the-right-concocted-a-crisis (accessed 24 July, 2019).
30 *The Guardian*, 1 July, 2019, www.theguardian.com/commentisfree/2019/jul/01/prevent-stopping-free-speech-campus-demonising-muslims (accessed 24 July, 2019).
31 Ruth Blakeley, B. Hayes, N. Kapoor, A. Kundnani, N. Massoumi, D. Miller, T. Mills, R. Sabir, K. Sian & W. Tufail, *Leaving the War on Terror: A Progressive Alternative to Counter-Terrorist Policy* (Amsterdam: Transnational Institute, 2019) pp. 36–37.
32 Andrew W. Neal, 'University Free Speech as a Space of Exception in Prevent?', in Ian Cram (ed.), *Extremism, Free Speech and Counter-Terrorism Law and Policy* (Abingdon: Routledge, 2019) p. 83.
33 'Sir Roger Scruton: "Get Rid of Universities Altogether"', *Human Events*, 13 May, 2019, https://humanevents.com/2019/05/13/roger-scruton-get-rid-of-universities-altogether/ (accessed 24 July, 2019).
34 *The Times*, 8 December, 1988, p. 16.
35 Gavan Titley, *Is Free Speech Racist?* (Cambridge: Polity Press, 2020).

INDEX